KIRSZNER & MANDELL
THE CONCISE WADSWORTH HANDBOOK

THIRD EDITION

Laurie G. Kirszner
University of the Sciences in Philadelphia

Stephen R. Mandell
Drexel University

CENGAGE Learning™

Australia • Brazil • Japan • Korea • Mexico • Singapore • Spain • United Kingdom • United States

WADSWORTH
CENGAGE Learning™

The Concise Wadsworth Handbook, Third Edition
Laurie G. Kirszner
Stephen R. Mandell

Senior Publisher: Lyn Uhl

Acquiring Sponsoring Editor: Kate Derrick

Development Editor: Karen Mauk

Assistant Editor: Kelli Strieby

Editorial Assistant: Laura Ross

Media Editor: Cara Douglass-Graff

Marketing Manager: Christina Shea

Marketing Coordinator: Ryan Ahern

Senior Marketing Communications Manager: Stacey Purviance

Senior Content Project Manager: Lianne Ames

Senior Art Director: Cate Barr

Print Buyer: Susan Spencer

Permissions Editor: Margaret Chamberlain-Gaston

Production Service: Nesbitt Graphics, Inc.

Text Designer: Nesbitt Graphics, Inc.

Photo Manager: John Hill

Cover Designer: Bruce Bond

Compositor: Nesbitt Graphics, Inc.

For product information and technology assistance, contact us at **Cengage Learning Customer & Sales Support, 1-800-354-9706**

For permission to use material from this text or product, submit all requests online at **www.cengage.com/permissions.**
Further permissions questions can be emailed to **permissionrequest@cengage.com.**

Library of Congress Control Number: 2009941909

ISBN-13: 978-0-495-89804-7

ISBN-10: 0-495-89804-X

Wadsworth
20 Channel Center Street
Boston, MA 02210
USA

Cengage Learning is a leading provider of customized learning solutions with office locations around the globe, including Singapore, the United Kingdom, Australia, Mexico, Brazil and Japan. Locate your local office at **international.cengage.com/region**

Cengage Learning products are represented in Canada by Nelson Education, Ltd.

For your course and learning solutions, visit **www.cengage.com.**

Purchase any of our products at your local college store or at our preferred online store **www.ichapters.com.**

Printed in Canada
1 2 3 4 5 6 7 13 12 11 10 09

How to Use This Book

As writers, you already know that to express your ideas clearly, you need to understand the basic principles of grammar, mechanics, and style. And, as writers in the digital age, you also know that you need to use a variety of electronic tools to write and design documents and to navigate the Internet and find information in the library. We wrote *The Concise Wadsworth Handbook* with these needs in mind. The result is a book that you can depend on to give you useful, no-nonsense, practical advice about writing.

Despite its compact size, *The Concise Wadsworth Handbook* is a complete reference for the college writer. Not only does it explain and illustrate the writing process, but it also offers guidance on grammar, style, punctuation, and mechanics and includes extensive sections on research and MLA and APA documentation styles. In addition, a unique section—Part 2, "Developing Strategies for Academic Success"— includes chapters on reading for college, writing essay exams, writing for the workplace, designing effective documents, and writing in a digital environment.

We have worked hard to make *The Concise Wadsworth Handbook* inviting, useful, clear, and—most of all—easy to use. To achieve these goals, we incorporated distinctive design features—icons, close-up boxes, checklists, and marginal cross-references and navigational aids—throughout the text to help you locate information quickly. Familiarizing yourself with the following page, which explains these design features, will help you get the most out of this book.

Throughout *The Concise Wadsworth Handbook* we have made every effort to address the challenges that real writers face in the twenty-first century and to provide you with clear explanations and sound advice. The result is a book that you can rely on—and one that you will use with ease and, perhaps, even with pleasure.

Laurie Kirszner
Steve Mandell
January 2010

The Concise Wadsworth Handbook: Design Features

♦ **New collaborative writing icons** appear alongside features and exercises that emphasize peer review and collaborative work.

♦ **Grammar checker boxes** illustrate the advantages and limitations of using a grammar checker.

♦ **Numerous checklists** summarize key information that you can quickly access as needed.

♦ **Close-up boxes** provide an in-depth look at some of the more perplexing writing-related issues you will encounter.

♦ **Chapter 47, "MLA Documentation Style," and Chapter 48, "APA Documentation Style,"** include the most up-to-date documentation and format guidelines from the Modern Language Association and the American Psychological Association, respectively.

♦ **Documentation directories** make it easy for you to locate models for various kinds of sources, including those found in online databases such as *Academic Search Premier* and *LexisNexis*. In addition, color-coded and annotated diagrams of sample works-cited entries clearly illustrate the elements of proper documentation.

♦ **Marginal cross-references** throughout the book allow you to go directly to other sections that treat topics in more detail.

♦ **Marginal ESL cross-references** throughout the book direct you to sections of Part 8, "Bilingual and ESL Writers," where concepts are presented as they apply specifically to second-language writers.

♦ **ESL tips** are woven throughout the text to explain concepts in relation to the unique experiences of bilingual students.

♦ **Numerous exercises** throughout the text allow you to practice at each stage of the writing, revising, and editing processes. Answers are provided in the back of the book for items marked with a ▶.

♦ **An extensive writing-centered treatment of grammar, punctuation, and mechanics,** including hand-edited examples, explains and illustrates specific strategies for improving your writing.

Acknowledgments

We would like to thank the following reviewers for their advice, which helped us develop the third edition:

Joshua Dickinson, *Jefferson Community College*

Eve Dunbar, *Vassar College*

Tahmineh Entessar, *Webster University*

Matthew Goldstein, *Laney College*

Dianne Gregory, *Cape Cod Community College*

Patti Kurtz, *Minot State University*

Leslie LaChance, *University of Tennessee, Martin*

Janet Landman, *Boston University*
Kelly Magee, *Western Washington University*
Chris Walsh, *Boston University*
Paul Wise, *University of Toledo*

At Wadsworth, we are grateful to Lyn Uhl, Senior Publisher, and Kate Derrick, Acquiring Sponsoring Editor, for keeping the project moving along, and to Lianne Ames, Senior Content Project Manager, for her careful attention to detail. Our biggest thanks go to Karen Mauk, our wonderful Development Editor; as always, it has been a pleasure to work with her.

The staff of Nesbitt Graphics did its usual stellar job, led by our incredibly capable Project Manager and copyeditor Susan McIntyre. Carie Keller's adaptation of Melissa Olson's inviting design is the icing on the cake.

We would also like to thank our families—Mark, Adam, and Rebecca Kirszner and Demi, David, and Sarah Mandell—for being there when we needed them. And, finally, we each thank the person on the other side of the ampersand for making our collaboration work one more time.

Teaching and Learning Resources

Wadsworth's InSite for Writing and Research™
ISBN-10: 1413009204 | **ISBN-13:** 9781413009200 (2-semester Instant Access Card)

This online writing and research tool includes electronic peer review, an originality checker powered by **Turnitin®**, an assignment library, help with common grammar and writing errors, and access to **InfoTrac® College Edition.** Portfolio management gives instructors the ability to grade papers, run originality reports, and offer feedback in an easy-to-use online course management system. Using **InSite's** peer review feature, students can easily review and respond to their classmates' work. Other features include fully integrated discussion boards, streamlined assignment creation, and more. To learn more, visit us online at www.cengage.com/insite.

Enhanced InSite for The Concise Wadsworth Handbook, *3rd Edition*
ISBN-10: 0538487216 | **ISBN-13:** 9780538487214

With **Enhanced InSite** for Kirszner & Mandell, *The Concise Wadsworth Handbook,* 3rd edition, instructors and students gain access to the proven, class-tested capabilities of InSite—such as peer reviewing, electronic grading, and originality checking powered by **Turnitin®**—plus resources designed to help students become more successful and confident writers, including access to **Personal Tutor,** an interactive eBook handbook with integrated text-specific workbook, tutorials, and more. Other features include fully integrated discussion boards, streamlined assignment creation, and access to **InfoTrac® College Edition.** To learn more, visit us online at www.cengage.com/insite.

InfoTrac® College Edition with InfoMarks™
ISBN-10: 0534558534 | **ISBN-13:** 9780534558536

InfoTrac® College Edition, an online research and learning center, offers over 20 million full-text articles from nearly 6,000 scholarly and popular periodicals. The articles cover a broad spectrum of disciplines and topics—ideal for every type of researcher.

Instructor's Edition for Kirszner/Mandell's The Concise Wadsworth Handbook, *3rd Edition*
ISBN-10: 0495906689 | **ISBN-13:** 9780495906681

Companion Web Site for **The Concise Wadsworth Handbook,**
3rd Edition

ISBN-10: 0538741813 | **ISBN-13:** 9780538741811

This complimentary-access **Companion Web Site** contains an extensive library of interactive exercises and animations that cover grammar, diction, mechanics, punctuation, and research and writing concepts. It also includes a complete library of student papers and a section on avoiding plagiarism.

Turnitin®

ISBN-10: 1413030181 | **ISBN-13:** 9781413030181

This proven, online plagiarism-prevention software promotes fairness in the classroom by helping students learn to correctly cite sources and allowing instructors to check for originality before reading and grading papers. Visit www.cengage.com/turnitin to view a demonstration.

Personal Tutor

ISBN-10: 0840035543 | **ISBN-13:** 9780840035547

Access to **Personal Tutor's** private tutoring resources provides students with additional assistance and review as they write their papers. With this valuable resource, students will gain access to multiple sessions to be used as either tutoring services or paper submissions—whichever they need most.

Merriam-Webster's Collegiate® Dictionary, 11th Edition (Casebound)

ISBN-10: 0877798095 | **ISBN-13:** 9780877798095

Available only when packaged with a Wadsworth text, the new 11th Edition of America's best-selling hardcover dictionary merges print, CD-ROM, and Internet-based formats to deliver unprecedented accessibility and flexibility at one affordable price.

Merriam-Webster's Collegiate® Dictionary, 11th Edition (Paperbound)

ISBN-10: 087779930X | **ISBN-13:** 9780877799306

Available only when packaged with a Wadsworth text, this high-quality, economical language reference covers the core vocabulary of everyday life with more than 70,000 definitions.

Dictionary/Thesaurus (Paperbound)

ISBN-10: 0877798516 | **ISBN-13:** 9780877798514

Available only when packaged with a Wadsworth text, this dictionary and thesaurus are two essential language references in one handy volume. Included are nearly 60,000 alphabetical dictionary entries integrated with more than 13,000 thesaurus entries including extensive synonym lists, as well as abundant example phrases that provide clear and concise word guidance.

Ten Habits of
Successful Students

Successful students have *learned* to be successful: they have developed specific strategies for success, and they apply those strategies to their education. If you take the time, you can learn the habits of successful students and apply them to your own college education—and, later on, to your career.

1 Learn to Manage Your Time Effectively

College makes many demands on your time. It is hard, especially at first, to balance studying, coursework, family life, friendships, and a job. But if you don't take control of your schedule, it will take control of you; if you don't learn to manage your time, you will always be struggling to catch up.

Fortunately, there are two tools that can help you manage your time: a **personal organizer** and a **monthly calendar.** Carry your organizer with you at all times, and post your calendar in a prominent place (perhaps above your desk or on your refrigerator). Remember to record *in both places* school-related deadlines, appointments, and reminders (every due date, study group meeting, conference appointment, and exam) and outside responsibilities, such as work hours and medical appointments. (Be sure to record tasks and dates as soon as you learn of them.)

You can also use your organizer to help you plan a study schedule, as illustrated in Figure 1 on page 2. You do this by blocking out times to study or to complete assignment-related tasks—such as a library database search for a research paper—in addition to appointments and deadlines. (It is a good idea to make these entries in pencil so you can adjust your schedule as new responsibilities arise.)

Remember: your college years can be a very stressful time, but although some degree of stress is inevitable, it can be kept in check. If you are organized, you will be better able to handle the pressures of a college workload.

2 Put Studying First

To be a successful student, you need to understand that studying is something you do *regularly,* not right before an exam. You also need to know that studying does not mean just memorizing facts; it also means reading, rereading, and discussing ideas until you understand them.

To make studying a regular part of your day, set up a study space that includes everything you need (supplies, good light, a comfortable chair) and does not include anything you do not need (clutter, distractions). Then, set up a tentative study schedule. Try to designate at least two hours each day to complete assignments due right away, to work on those due later on,

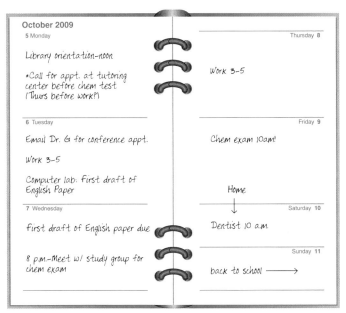

FIGURE 1 Sample organizer pages for one week.

and to reread class notes. When you have exams and papers, you can adjust your schedule accordingly.

Successful students often form **study groups,** and you should use this strategy whenever you can—particularly in a course you find challenging. A study group of four or five students who meet regularly (not just the night before an exam) can make studying more focused and effective as well as less stressful. By discussing concepts with your classmates, you can try out your ideas and get feedback, clarify complex concepts, and formulate questions for your instructor.

CHECKLIST

WORKING IN A STUDY GROUP

To get the most out of your study group, you need to set some ground rules:

- ❏ Meet regularly.
- ❏ Decide in advance who will be responsible for particular tasks.
- ❏ Set deadlines.
- ❏ Listen when someone else is speaking.
- ❏ Don't reject other people's ideas and suggestions without considering them very carefully.
- ❏ Have one person take notes to keep a record of the group's activities.
- ❏ Take stock of the group's problems and progress at regular intervals.
- ❏ Be mindful of other students' learning styles and special needs.

3   Be Sure You Understand School and Course Requirements

To succeed in school, you need to know what is expected of you; if you are not sure, ask.

When you first arrived at school, you probably received a variety of orientation materials—a student handbook, library handouts, and so on—that set forth the rules and policies of your school. (These materials may also be available online.) Read these documents carefully (if you have not already done so). If you do not understand something, ask your peer counselor or your adviser for clarification.

You also need to know the specific requirements of each course you take. A course **syllabus** tells you when assignments are due and when exams are scheduled. In addition, it may explain the instructor's policies about attendance and lateness, assignments and deadlines, plagiarism, and classroom etiquette. A syllabus may also explain penalties for late assignments or missed quizzes, explain how assignments are graded, tell how much each assignment is worth, or note additional requirements, such as fieldwork or group projects. Requirements vary significantly from course to course, so read each syllabus (as well as any supplementary handouts) carefully, and keep track of updates that may appear on your class's Web page.

ESL TIP

If you did not attend high school in the United States, some of your instructors' class policies and procedures may seem strange to you. To learn more about the way US college classes are run, read the syllabus for each of your courses and talk to your instructors about your concerns. You may also find it helpful to talk to older students with cultural backgrounds similar to your own.

4   Be an Active Learner in the Classroom

Education is not about sitting passively in class and waiting for information and ideas to be given to you. It is up to you to be an active participant in your own education.

First, take as many small classes as you can. Small classes enable you to interact with other students and with your instructor. If a large course has recitation sections, be sure to attend them regularly, even if they are not required. Also, be sure to take classes that require writing. Good writing skills are essential to your success as a student (and as a college graduate entering the workforce), and you will need all the practice you can get.

Take responsibility for your education by attending class regularly and arriving on time. Listen attentively, and take careful, complete notes. (Try to review these notes later with other students to make sure you have not missed anything important.) Do your homework on time, and keep up

See
Ch. 9 with the reading. When you read an assignment, use <u>active reading</u> strategies, interacting with the text (for example, underlining the text and making marginal annotations) instead of just looking at what is on the page. If you have time, read beyond the assignment, looking on the Internet and in books, magazines, and newspapers for related information.

Finally, participate in class discussions: ask and answer questions, volunteer opinions, and give helpful feedback to other students. By participating in this way, you learn to consider other points of view, to test your ideas, and to respect the ideas of others.

> **ESL TIP**
>
> Especially in small classes, US instructors usually expect students to participate in class discussion. If you feel nervous about speaking up in class, you might start by expressing your support of a classmate's opinion.

5   Be an Active Learner Outside the Classroom

Taking an active role in your education is also important outside the classroom. Do not be afraid to approach your instructors; take advantage of their office hours, and keep in touch with them by email. Get to know your major adviser well, and be sure he or she knows who you are and where your academic interests lie. Make appointments, ask questions, and explore possible solutions to problems: this is how you learn.

In addition, become part of your school community. Read your school newspaper, check your college Web site regularly, and participate in activities. This involvement can help you develop new interests and friendships as well as enhance your education.

Finally, participate in the life of your community outside your school. Try to arrange an **internship,** a job that enables you to gain practical experience. (Many businesses, nonprofit organizations, and government agencies offer internships—paid or unpaid—to qualified students.) Take **service-learning** courses, if they are offered at your school, or volunteer at a local school or social agency. As successful students know, education is more than just attending classes.

6   Take Advantage of College Services

Colleges and universities offer students a wide variety of support services. For example, if you are struggling with a particular course, you can go to the tutoring service offered by your school's academic support center or by an individual department. If you need help with writing or revising a paper, you can make an appointment with the writing center, where tutors will give you advice. If you are having trouble deciding on what courses to take or what to major in, you can see your academic adviser. If you are having trouble adjusting to college life, a peer counselor or (if you live in a dorm) your resident adviser may be able to help you. Finally, if you have a personal or family problem you would rather not discuss with another student, you can make an appointment at your school's counseling center, where you can get advice from professionals who understand student problems.

ESL TIP

Many ESL students find using their school's writing center very helpful. Most writing centers provide assistance with assignments for any course, and they often assist with writing job application letters and résumés. Many writing centers have tutors who specialize in working with ESL students.

Many other services are available—for example, at your school's computer center, job placement service, and financial aid office. Your academic adviser or instructors can tell you where to find the help you need, but it is up to you to make the appointment.

7   Use the Library

Because so much material is available on the Internet, you may think your college library is outdated or even obsolete. But learning to use the **library** is an important part of your education. See 42a–c

The library can provide a quiet place to study—something you may need if you have a large family or noisy roommates. The library also provides access to materials that cannot be found online—rare books, special collections, audiovisual materials—as well as electronic databases that contain material you will not find on the free Internet.

Finally, the library is the place where you have access to the expert advice of your school's reference librarians. These professionals can answer questions, guide your research, and point you to sources that you might never have found on your own.

8   Use Technology

Technological competence is essential to success in college. For this reason, it makes sense to develop good word-processing skills and to become comfortable with the **Internet.** You should already know how to send and receive email from your university account as well as how to attach files to See Ch. 43

your email. Beyond these basics, you should learn how to manage the files you download, how to evaluate Web sites, and how to use the electronic resources of your library. You might also find it helpful to know how to scan documents (containing images as well as text) and how to paste these files into your documents.

If you do not have these skills, you need to locate campus services that will help you get them. Workshops and online tutorials may be available through your school library or campus computing services, and individual assistance on software and hardware use is available in computer labs.

Part of being technologically savvy in college involves being aware of the online services your campus has to offer. For example, many campuses rely on customizable information-management systems called **portals.** Not unlike commercial services, such as Yahoo! or America Online, a portal requires you to log in with a user ID and password to access services such as locating and contacting your academic adviser and viewing your class schedule and grades.

See
12d1 Finally, you need to know not only how to use technology to enhance a project—for example, how to use *PowerPoint* for an oral presentation or *Excel* to make a <u>table</u>—but also *when* to use technology (and when not to).

9   Make Contacts

One of the most important things you can do for yourself is to make academic and professional contacts that you can use during college and after you graduate.

Your first contacts are your classmates. Be sure you have the names, phone numbers, and email addresses of at least two students in each of your classes. These contacts will be useful to you if you miss class, if you need help understanding your notes, or if you want to start a study group.

You should also build relationships with students with whom you participate in college activities, such as the college newspaper or the tutoring center. These people are likely to share your goals and interests, and so you may want to get feedback from them as you choose a major, consider further education, and make career choices.

Finally, develop relationships with your instructors, particularly those in your major area of study. One of the things cited most often in studies of successful students is the importance of **mentors,** experienced individuals whose advice you trust. Long after you leave college, you will find these contacts useful.

10   Be a Lifelong Learner

Your education should not stop when you graduate from college. To be a successful student, you need to see yourself as a lifelong learner.

Get in the habit of reading newspapers; know what is happening in the world outside school. Talk to people outside the college community so that you don't forget there are issues that have nothing to do with courses and grades. Never miss an opportunity to learn: try to get in the habit of attending plays and concerts sponsored by your school or community and lectures offered at your local library or bookstore.

And think about the life you will lead after college. Think about who you want to be and what you have to do to get there. This is what successful students do.

CLOSE-UP

TEN HABITS TO AVOID

1. **Procrastination**   No matter how tempting it is to postpone studying for a test, writing a paper, making a writing lab appointment, or setting up a meeting with your adviser, you should not procrastinate. Being able to manage time is a skill that almost all good students have. Remember, if you put off your work until the last minute, your responsibilities will eventually overwhelm you.

2. **Lateness**   To avoid penalties that will hurt your grades, you should hand in assignments on time. You should also make sure that you take an exam on the day it is given. (Some instructors give a more difficult make-up exam to those who miss a scheduled test.) Finally, be sure to complete all your semester's coursework on time; request an Incomplete grade only in an emergency.

3. **Cuts**   Even if an instructor allows a certain number of unexcused absences, you should not miss class unless you absolutely have to. If you do miss a class, contact a classmate to find out what you missed. Don't email your instructor and ask, "Did I miss anything?" (The answer to this question is, "Of course you did.") If you will miss a number of classes because of a personal emergency, let your instructors know immediately. Most instructors will try to accommodate you if you keep them informed.

4. **Poor Communication**   Regular communication with your course instructors (as well as with lab assistants and recitation instructors) is vital to your success in college. Good communication will ensure that you understand what is expected of you and know how to achieve it.

5. **Focus on Grades**   Focusing on your grades instead of on your education is a poor strategy for academic success. Instead of asking your instructors (or even yourself), "What do I have to do to get an A?" ask, "How can I improve my understanding of the material?"

6. **Poor Health Habits**   Eat healthy, regular meals; don't smoke; exercise when you can; avoid drugs and alcohol.

7. **Poor Sleep Habits**   Resist the temptation to study (or party) all night. Try to go to sleep and wake up at about the same time each day rather than staying up late and sleeping until noon on the weekends.

(continued)

TEN HABITS TO AVOID (*continued*)

8. **Inappropriate Behavior**   Show proper decorum in the classroom and in instructor conferences. Be polite and respectful, listen when others speak, and don't interrupt. In class, remove your hat, raise your hand when you want to speak, and watch your language.

9. **Negative Attitudes**   Try not to see one poor grade or negative instructor comment as the beginning of a trend that spells failure. Listen to criticism, learn from your mistakes, and take steps to improve.

10. **Overscheduling**   Be realistic when you plan your schedule. Don't sign up for more courses than you can handle or agree to take on more projects than you can reasonably hope to complete. In addition, don't work so many hours at your job that you have no time to study. Take breaks when you need to; schedule some downtime, and use it.

PART 1

Writing Essays

Writing Essays

Understanding Purpose and Audience

Everyone who sets out to write confronts a series of choices. In the writing you do in school, on the job, and in your personal life, your understanding of **purpose** and **audience** is essential, influencing the choices you make about content, emphasis, organization, style, and tone.

1a Determining Your Purpose

In simple terms, your **purpose** for writing is what you want to accomplish. For instance, your purpose may be to *reflect*—to express private feelings—as in the introspective or meditative writing that appears in personal blogs, journals, diaries, and memoirs. Or your purpose may be to *inform*—to convey factual information as accurately and as logically as possible—as in the informational or expository writing that appears in reports, news articles, encyclopedias, and textbooks. At other times, your purpose may be to *persuade*—to convince your readers—as in advertising, proposals, editorials, and some business communications. Finally, your purpose may be to *evaluate*—to make a judgment about something—as in a recommendation report or a comparative analysis.

1 Writing to Reflect

In diaries and journals, writers explore ideas and feelings to make sense of their experiences; in autobiographical memoirs and in personal blog posts, they communicate their emotions and reactions to others.

> At the age of five, six, well past the time when most other children no longer easily notice the difference between sounds uttered at home and words spoken in public, I had a different experience. I lived in a world magically compounded of sounds. I remained a child longer than most; I lingered too long, poised at the edge of language—often frightened by the sounds of *los gringos*, delighted by the sounds of Spanish at home. I shared with my family a language that was startlingly different from that used in the great city around us. (Richard Rodriguez, *Aria: A Memoir of a Bilingual Childhood*)

2 Writing to Inform

In newspaper articles, writers report information, communicating factual details to readers; in reference books, instruction manuals, and textbooks, as well as on Web sites sponsored by nonprofit organizations and government agencies, writers provide definitions and explain concepts or processes, trying to help readers see relationships and understand ideas.

Most tarantulas live in the tropics, but several species occur in the temperate zone and a few are common in the southern U.S. Some varieties are large and have powerful fangs with which they can inflict a deep wound. These formidable-looking spiders do not, however, attack man; you can hold one in your hand, if you are gentle, without being bitten. Their bite is dangerous only to insects and small mammals such as mice; for man it is no worse than a hornet's sting. (Alexander Petrunkevitch, "The Spider and the Wasp")

3 Writing to Persuade

In proposals and editorials, as well as in advertising and on political Web sites and blogs, writers try to convince readers to accept their position on various issues.

Nuclear Energy

Nuclear power is unsafe, uneconomical, and unnecessary. We need ways to fight global warming and power our homes that are fast, safe, and affordable—and nuclear power is not the answer. In fact, it is a truly dangerous distraction from real solutions—after all, terrorists aren't targeting windmills and solar panels. For more information on nuclear power you can read our reports and fact sheets as well as use our nuclear plant locator to see if a reactor is in your backyard. Get informed and join our fight for clean, safe and effective solutions to climate change. (Greenpeace Web site)

4 Writing to Evaluate

In reviews of books, films, or performances and in reports, critiques, and program evaluations, writers assess the validity, accuracy, and quality of information, ideas, techniques, products, procedures, or services, perhaps assessing the relative merits of two or more things.

★☆☆☆☆ **Drivel,** February 28, 2008

By **Augustine J. Fredrich "Reader"** (Little Rock, AR, United States)—See all my reviews

Pure unadulterated drivel. Grisham should be ashamed of himself. This book reads like something produced by a neophyte for a writer's workshop. Not only is the story one-dimensional, the characters are, without exception, stereotypes, and the plot is one only a conspiracy theorist with a liberal bent could love. Every action of every character is so predictable (and the writing so sophomoric) that one wonders what lowest-common-denominator reader Grisham had in mind when he sent this dog of a manuscript to the publisher. If, as some say, fiction is "chewing gum for the mind," this is a single Chiclet! I won't be reading any more of his "legal thrillers." (Amazon.com customer review of John Grisham's *The Appeal*)

Although writers do write to reflect, to inform, to persuade, and to evaluate, these purposes are certainly not mutually exclusive, and writers may have other purposes as well. And, of course, in any piece of writing a writer may have a primary aim and one or more secondary purposes; in fact, a writer may even have different purposes in different sections—or different drafts—of a single document.

CHECKLIST

DETERMINING YOUR PURPOSE

Is your purpose:

❑ to express emotions?	❑ to satirize?
❑ to inform?	❑ to speculate?
❑ to persuade?	❑ to warn?
❑ to explain?	❑ to reassure?
❑ to amuse or entertain?	❑ to take a stand?
❑ to evaluate?	❑ to identify problems?
❑ to discover?	❑ to suggest solutions?
❑ to analyze?	❑ to identify causes?
❑ to debunk?	❑ to predict effects?
❑ to draw comparisons?	❑ to reflect?
❑ to make an analogy?	❑ to interpret?
❑ to define?	❑ to instruct?
❑ to criticize?	❑ to inspire?
❑ to motivate?	

EXERCISE 1.1

The primary purpose of the following article from the *New York Times* is to present information. Suppose you were using the information in an orientation booklet aimed at students entering your school, and your purpose was to persuade students of the importance of maintaining a good credit rating. How would you change the original article to help you achieve this purpose? Would you reorder any details? Would you add or delete anything?

What Makes a Credit Score Rise or Fall?

By Jennifer Bayot

Your financial decisions can affect your credit score in surprising ways. Two credit-scoring simulators can help consumers understand the potential impact.

The Fair Isaac Corporation, which puts out the industry-standard FICO scores, offers the myFICO simulator. A consumer with a score of 707 (considered good) and three credit cards would be likely to add or lose points from his score by making various financial moves. Following are some examples:

▪ By making timely payments on all his accounts over the next month or by paying off a third of the balance on his cards, he could add as many as 20 points.

▪ By failing to make this month's payments on his loans, he could lose 75 to 125 points.

- By using all of the credit available on his three credit cards, he could lose 20 to 70 points.
- By getting a fourth card, depending on the status of his other debts, he could add or lose up to 10 points.
- By consolidating his credit card debt into a new card, also depending on other debts, he could add or lose 15 points.

The other simulator, the What-If, comes from CreditXpert, which designs credit management tools and puts out its own, similar credit score. A consumer with a score of 727 points (also considered good) would be likely to have her score change in the following ways:

- Every time she simply applied for a loan, whether a credit card, home mortgage or auto loan, she would lose five points. (An active appetite for credit, credit experts note, is considered a bad sign. For one thing, taking on new loans may make borrowers less likely to repay their current debts.)
- By getting a mortgage, she would lose two points.
- By getting an auto loan or a new credit card (assuming that she already has several cards) she would lose three points.
- If her new credit card had a credit limit of $20,000 or more, she would lose four points, instead of three. (For every $10,000 added to the limit, the score drops a point.)
- By simultaneously getting a new mortgage, auto loan and credit card, she would lose seven or eight points.

1b   Identifying Your Audience

When you are in the early stages of a writing project, staring at a blank computer screen (or a blank sheet of paper), it is easy to forget that what you write will have an audience. But except for diaries and private journals, you always write for an **audience,** a particular reader or group of readers. In this sense, writing is a public rather than a private activity.

1   Writing for an Audience

At different times, in different roles, you address a variety of audiences:

- **In your personal life,** you may write notes, emails, or texts to friends and family.
- **As a citizen,** consumer, or member of a community, civic, political, or religious group, you may respond to pressing social, economic, or political issues by writing emails or letters to a newspaper, a public official, or a representative of a special interest group.
- **As an employee,** you may write memos and reports to your superiors, to staff members you supervise, or to coworkers; you may also be called on to address customers or critics, board members or stockholders, funding agencies or the general public.

♦ **As a student,** you write reflective statements and response papers as well as essays, reports, exams, and research papers for your instructors. You may also participate in <u>peer review,</u> writing evaluations of classmates' essays and writing responses to their comments about your own work. See
4c2

As you write, you shape your writing in terms of what you believe your audience needs and expects. Your assessment of your readers' interests, educational level, <u>biases,</u> and expectations determines not only the information you include but also what you emphasize and how you arrange your material. See
6c

2 The College Writer's Audience

Writing for Your Instructor   As a student, you usually write for an audience of one: the instructor who assigns the paper. Instructors want to know what you know and whether you can express what you know clearly and accurately. They assign written work to encourage you to use <u>critical thinking</u> skills, so the way you organize and express your ideas can be as important as the ideas themselves. See
Ch. 6

As a group, instructors have certain expectations. Because they are trained as careful readers and critics, your instructors expect accurate information, standard grammar and correct spelling, logically presented ideas, and a reasonable degree of stylistic fluency. They also expect you to define your terms and to support your generalizations with specifics. Finally, every instructor also expects you to draw your own conclusions and to provide full and accurate <u>documentation</u> for ideas that are not your own. See
Chs.
47–48

If you are writing in an instructor's academic field, you can omit long overviews and basic definitions. Remember, however, that outside their areas of expertise, most instructors are simply general readers. If you think you may know more about a subject than your instructor does, be sure to provide background and to supply the definitions, examples, and analogies that will make your ideas clear.

Writing for Other Students   Before you submit a paper to an instructor, you may have an opportunity to participate in **peer review,** sharing your work with your fellow students and responding in writing to their work. In both these cases, you need to see your classmates as an audience whose needs you must take into account.

♦ **Writing Drafts** If you know that other students will read a draft of your paper, you need to consider how they might react to your ideas. For example, are they likely to agree with you? To be shocked or offended by your paper's language or content? To be confused, or even mystified, by any of your references? Even if your readers are your own age, you cannot assume that they share your cultural frame of reference. It is therefore very important that you maintain an appropriate tone and use moderate language in your paper and that you explain any historical, geographical, or cultural references that might be unfamiliar to your audience.

♦ **Writing Comments** When you respond in writing to other students' papers, you need to take into account how this audience will react to your comments. Here too, your tone is important: you want to be as encouraging (and as polite) as possible. In addition, keep in mind that your purpose is not to show how clever you are but to offer constructive comments that can help your classmate write a stronger essay.

CHECKLIST

AUDIENCE CONCERNS FOR PEER-REVIEW PARTICIPANTS

To get the most out of a peer-review session, keep the following guidelines in mind:

❑ **Know your audience.** To be sure you understand what the student writer needs and expects from your comments, read the paper several times before you begin writing your response.

❑ **Focus on the big picture.** Don't get bogged down on minor problems with punctuation or mechanics or become distracted by a paper's proofreading errors.

❑ **Look for a positive feature.** Try to zero in on what you think is the paper's greatest strength.

❑ **Be positive throughout.** Try to avoid words like *weak, poor,* and *bad*; instead, try using a compliment before delivering the "bad news": "Paragraph 2 is very well developed; can you add this kind of support in paragraph 4?"

❑ **Show respect.** It is perfectly acceptable to tell a student that something is confusing or inaccurate, but don't go on the attack.

❑ **Be specific.** Avoid generalizations like "needs more examples" or "could be more interesting"; instead, try to offer helpful, focused suggestions: "You could add an example after the second sentence in paragraph 2"; "Explaining how this process operates would make your discussion more interesting."

❑ **Don't give orders.** Ask questions, and make suggestions.

❑ **Include a few words of encouragement.** Try to emphasize the paper's strong points.

EXERCISE 1.2

Look again at the article in Exercise 1.1 on pages 13–14. This time, try to decide what audience or audiences it seems to be aimed at. Then, consider what (if anything) might have to be changed to address the needs of each of the following audiences:

▪ College students
▪ Middle-school students
▪ The elderly
▪ People with limited English skills
▪ People who do not live in the US

Planning an Essay

CHAPTER 2

2a   Understanding the Writing Process

Writing enables you to discover ideas, make connections, and see from new perspectives. In this sense, writing is a demanding, creative process of thinking and learning—about yourself, about others, and about your world. In another sense, writing is a tool that empowers you: it enables you to participate in the ongoing dialogue that shapes your world. Writing is also a complex process of decision making—of selecting, deleting, and rearranging material.

CLOSE-UP

THE WRITING PROCESS

The writing process includes the following stages:

Planning: Consider your purpose and audience; choose your topic; discover ideas to write about.

Shaping: Decide how to organize your material.

Drafting: Write your first draft.

Revising: "Re-see" what you have written; write additional drafts.

Editing: Check grammar, spelling, punctuation, and mechanics.

Proofreading: Read every word, checking for any remaining errors.

The neatly defined stages listed above communicate neither the complexity nor the flexibility of the writing process. In practice, this process is neither a linear series of steps nor an isolated activity. In fact, a significant part of the writing process can take place online in full view of an audience. Writing is also often interactive: the writing process can be interrupted (and enriched) by emailing, blogging, chat room discussions, or surfing the Internet.

Actually, the stages of the writing process overlap: as you look for ideas, you begin to shape your material; as you shape your material, you begin to write; as you write a draft, you reorganize your ideas; as you revise, you continue to discover new material. Moreover, these stages may be repeated again and again throughout the writing process.

During your college years and in the years that follow, you will develop your own version of the writing process and use it whenever you write, adapting it to the audience, purpose, and writing situation at hand.

2b   Computers and the Writing Process

See
Ch. 11
Computers have changed the way we write and communicate in both academic and <u>workplace</u> settings. In addition to using word-processing applications for typical writing tasks, writers may rely on programs such as *PowerPoint*® for giving presentations, *Publisher*® for creating customized résumés or brochures, and Web-page authoring software such as *Dreamweaver*® or *HomeSite*® for creating Internet-accessible documents that include images, movies, and a wide range of visual effects.

With the prominent role of the Internet in professional, academic, and personal communication, it is increasingly likely that the feedback you receive on your writing will be electronic. For example, if your instructor uses course management software such as *WebCT*™ or *Blackboard*™, you may receive an email from your instructor about a draft that you have submitted to a digital drop box. Or, you may use discussion boards for attaching or sharing your documents with other students. Chat room and Net meeting software also allow you to discuss ideas collaboratively and to offer and receive feedback on drafts.

Although the tools you use may be course- or workplace-specific, you will still have to develop an efficient writing process. **Chapter 13** provides more comprehensive information on the options available to you as you write in a digital environment.

2c   Analyzing Your Assignment

Planning your essay—thinking about what you want to say and how you want to say it—begins well before you actually start recording your thoughts in any organized way. This planning is as important a part of the writing
See
Ch. 1
process as the writing itself. During this planning stage, you determine your <u>purpose</u> for writing, identify your <u>audience,</u> and decide on an appropriate tone. Then, you go on to focus on your assignment, choose and narrow your topic, and gather ideas.

Before you begin writing, be sure you understand the exact requirements of your **assignment,** and keep those guidelines in mind as you write and revise. Don't assume anything; ask questions, and be sure you understand the answers.

See
4c2

See
Ch. 47

CHECKLIST

ANALYZING YOUR ASSIGNMENT

To help you understand your assignment, answer the following questions:

❑ Has your instructor assigned a specific topic, or can you choose your own?
❑ What is the word or page limit?
❑ How much time do you have to complete your assignment?
❑ Will you get feedback from your instructor? Will you have an opportunity to participate in peer review?
❑ Does your assignment require research?
❑ What format (for example, MLA) are you supposed to follow? Do you know what its conventions are?
❑ If your assignment has been given to you in writing, have you read it carefully and highlighted key words?

Rebecca James, a first-year composition student, was given the following assignment.

The free online encyclopedia *Wikipedia* has become a common starting point for researchers seeking information on a topic. Because anyone can alter articles in this database, the reliability of *Wikipedia* as a valid source of information has been criticized by members of the academic community. In an essay of about 3–5 pages, evaluate the benefits and drawbacks of using *Wikipedia* in college research. To support your assessment, focus on a *Wikipedia* entry related to one of your courses.

The class was given three weeks to complete the assignment. Students were expected to do some research and to have the instructor and other students read and comment on at least one draft.

2d Choosing and Narrowing a Topic

Sometimes your instructor will allow you to choose your own topic; more often, however, you will be given a general assignment, which you will have to narrow to a **topic** that suits your purpose, audience, and page limit.

CHOOSING AND NARROWING A TOPIC		
Course	**Assignment**	**Topic**
American History	Analyze the effects of a social program on one segment of American society	How did the GI Bill of Rights affect American servicewomen?

(continued)

CHOOSING AND NARROWING A TOPIC (*continued*)		
Course	**Assignment**	**Topic**
Psychology	Write a three- to five-page paper assessing one method of treating depression.	Animal-assisted therapy for severely depressed patients
Composition	Write an essay about a problem you have encountered since coming to college.	Overcoming my computer illiteracy

Note: If your instructor permits you to do so, you can work with other students to narrow your topic.

Rebecca had no trouble thinking of ways she used *Wikipedia* to find general information, but she knew that the site was controversial in the academic community because several of her instructors discouraged her from using it as a research source. In her paper, she knew she would have to find a balance between the usefulness of *Wikipedia* on the one hand and its possible lack of reliability on the other.

Because her assignment was so specific, Rebecca was easily able to restate it in the form of a topic.

Topic: *Wikipedia* and College Research

EXERCISE 2.1

College campuses across the US are working to achieve sustainability, making an effort to be more sensitive to environmental concerns and to become more "green."

With this exercise, you will begin the process of writing a three- to five-page essay in which you consider how your school is working toward this goal, what more it needs to do in the future, and how your suggestions for improvement will benefit your school.

Begin by looking up the word *sustainability* on the Internet. Think about this issue as it applies to your school, and (with your instructor's permission), talk to your friends and classmates about it. When you think you understand what is being done (and what is not being done) to make your campus more "green," list five specific environmental issues you could write about. Then, choose one of these areas of concern as the topic for your paper, and write a few sentences explaining why you selected this topic.

Your purpose in this essay will be to make recommendations for changes that could be adopted at your school. Your audience will be your composition instructor, members of your **peer review** group, and, possibly, a wider campus audience—for example, readers of your campus newspaper.

2e Finding Something to Say

Once you have a topic, you can begin to collect ideas for your paper, using one (or several) of the strategies that will be discussed in the following pages.

> **ESL TIP**
>
> Don't use all your time making sure you are writing grammatically correct sentences. Remember, the purpose of writing is to communicate ideas. If you want to write an interesting, well-developed essay, you will need to devote plenty of time to the activities described in this section.

1 Reading and Observing

As you read textbooks, magazines, and newspapers and browse the Internet, be on the lookout for ideas that relate to your topic, and make a point of talking informally with friends or family about it.

Films, television programs, interviews, telephone calls, letters, emails, and questionnaires can also provide material. But be sure your instructor permits such research—and remember to <u>document</u> ideas that are not your own.

See Chs. 47–48

2 Keeping a Journal

Many professional writers keep print or electronic **journals** (sometimes in the form of blogs), writing in them regularly whether or not they have a specific project in mind. Journals, unlike diaries, do more than simply record personal experiences and reactions. In a journal, you explore ideas, ask questions, and draw conclusions. You might, for example, analyze your position on a political issue, try to solve an ethical problem, or trace the evolution of your ideas about an academic assignment. One of Rebecca's journal entries appears below.

Journal Entry

I use *Wikipedia* all the time, whenever something comes up that I want to know more about. Once my roommate and I were talking about graffiti art and I started wondering how and where it began. I went to *Wikipedia* and found a long article about graffiti's origins and development as an art form. Some of my instructors say not to use *Wikipedia* as a research source, so I try to avoid going to the site for paper assignments. Still, it can be really helpful when I'm trying to find basic information. There are a lot of business and financial terms that come up in my accounting class, and I can usually find simple explanations on *Wikipedia* of things I don't understand.

3 Freewriting

When you **freewrite,** you write nonstop about anything that comes to mind, moving as quickly as you can. Give yourself a set period of time—say, five minutes—and don't stop to worry about punctuation, spelling, or grammar, or about where your freewriting takes you. This strategy encourages your mind to make free associations; thus, it helps you to discover ideas you probably aren't even aware you have. When your time is up, look over what you have written and underline, circle, bracket, star, boldface, or otherwise highlight the most promising ideas. You can then use one or more of these ideas as the center of a focused freewriting exercise.

When you do **focused freewriting,** you zero in on your topic. Here, too, you write without stopping to reconsider or reread, so you have no time to be self-conscious about style or form, to worry about the relevance of your ideas, or to count how many words you have (and panic about how many more you think you need). At its best, focused freewriting can suggest new details, a new approach to your topic, or even a more interesting topic.

Excerpts from Rebecca's freewriting and focused freewriting exercises appear below.

Freewriting (Excerpt)

I'm just going to list a bunch of things from my class notes that I've recently looked up in *Wikipedia*: shareholder, stakeholder, strategic management, core competency, certified public accountant, certified management accountant, profit and loss. Not really sure which entry to pick for this assignment. Term from accounting? Business class? All the entries have strengths and weaknesses. I guess that's the point: some *Wikipedia* articles are better than others. Maybe I'll choose an article that's sort of in the middle—one that provides some good basic info but could also be improved in some ways.

Focused Freewriting (Excerpt)

I think I'm going to use the "Certified Management Accountant" article as my focus for this paper. It explains this accounting term pretty clearly and concisely, which is good. However, it does have some problems, which are called out at the top of the article: poor writing, lack of cited sources, and not enough internal links. This article seems to represent a good balance of *Wikipedia*'s benefits and drawbacks. I hope I can think of enough things to say about the article in my paper. I could start off with some background info on *Wikipedia* and then lead into the CMA example. That way, I can use the CMA article to support my points about *Wikipedia* in general.

4 Brainstorming

One of the most useful ways to collect ideas is by brainstorming (either on your own or in a group). This strategy enables you to recall bits of information and to see connections among them.

When you **brainstorm,** you list all the points you can think of that seem pertinent to your topic, recording ideas—comments, questions, single words, symbols, or diagrams—as quickly as you can, without pausing to consider their relevance or trying to understand their significance.

An excerpt from Rebecca's brainstorming notes appears below.

Brainstorming Notes (Excerpt)

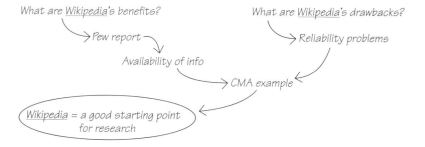

Topic: <u>Wikipedia</u> and College Research

What are <u>Wikipedia</u>'s benefits?

Pew report

Availability of info

CMA example

<u>Wikipedia</u> = a good starting point for research

What are <u>Wikipedia</u>'s drawbacks?

Reliability problems

CLOSE-UP

COLLABORATIVE BRAINSTORMING

In addition to brainstorming on your own, you can also try **collaborative brainstorming,** working with other students to think of ideas to write about. If you and your classmates are working with similar but not identical topics—which is often the case—you will have the basic knowledge to help one another and you can share your ideas without concern that you will all wind up focusing on the same few points.

Typically, collaborative brainstorming is an informal process. It can take place in person (in class or outside of class), on the phone, or in a chat room or class discussion board. Some instructors lead class brainstorming sessions, writing suggestions on the board or on a laptop. Others arrange small-group brainstorming discussions in class.

Whatever the format, the exchange of ideas is likely to produce a lot of material that is not useful (and some that is irrelevant), but it will very likely also produce some ideas you will want to explore further. (Be sure you get your instructor's permission before you brainstorm with other students.)

5 Clustering

Clustering—sometimes called *webbing* or *mapping*—is similar to brainstorming. However, clustering encourages you to explore your topic in a more systematic (and more visual) manner.

Begin your cluster diagram by writing your topic in the center of a sheet of paper. Then, surround your topic with related ideas as they occur to you, moving outward from the general topic in the center and writing down increasingly specific ideas and details as you move toward the edges of the page. Following the path of one idea at a time, draw lines to create a diagram (often lopsided rather than symmetrical) that arranges ideas on spokes or branches radiating out from the center (your topic).

Rebecca's cluster diagram appears below.

Cluster Diagram

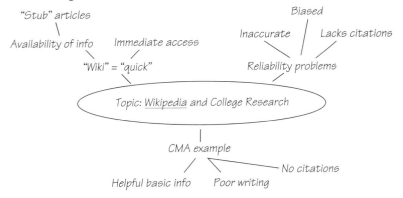

6 Asking Journalistic Questions

Journalistic questions offer an orderly, systematic way of finding material to write about. Journalists ask the questions *Who? What? Why? Where? When?* and *How?* to ensure that they have explored all angles of a story, and you can use these questions to make sure you have considered all aspects of your topic.

Rebecca's list of journalistic questions appears below.

Journalistic Questions

- <u>Who</u> uses *Wikipedia,* and for what purposes?
- <u>What</u> is a wiki? <u>What</u> are *Wikipedia*'s benefits? <u>What</u> are its drawbacks?
- <u>When</u> was *Wikipedia* created? <u>When</u> did it become so popular among college students?
- <u>Where</u> do people go for more information after reading a *Wikipedia* article?
- <u>Why</u> are people drawn to *Wikipedia*? <u>Why</u> do some instructors discourage students from using it as a research source?
- <u>How</u> can *Wikipedia* be used responsibly? <u>How</u> can *Wikipedia* be improved?

ESL TIP

Using your native language for planning activities has both advantages and disadvantages. On the one hand, if you do not have the pressure of trying to think in English, you may be able to come up with better ideas. Also, using your native language may help you record your ideas more quickly and keep you from losing your train of thought. On the other hand, using your native language while planning may make it more difficult for you to move from the planning stages of your writing to drafting. After all, you will eventually have to write your paper in English.

---

7 Asking In-Depth Questions

If you have time, you can search for ideas to write about by asking a series of more focused questions about your topic. These **in-depth questions** can give you a great deal of information, and they can also suggest ways for you to eventually shape your ideas into paragraphs and essays.

IN-DEPTH QUESTIONS	
What happened? When did it happen? Where did it happen?	Questions suggest **narration** (an account of your first day of school; a summary of Emily Dickinson's life)
What does it look like? What does it sound like, smell like, taste like, or feel like?	Questions suggest **description** (of the Louvre; of the electron microscope; of a Web site)
What are some typical cases or examples of it?	Question suggests **exemplification** (three infant day-care settings; four popular fad diets)

(*continued*)

IN-DEPTH QUESTIONS (*continued*)	
How did it happen? What makes it work? How is it made?	Questions suggest **process** (how to apply for financial aid; how a bill becomes a law)
Why did it happen? What caused it? What does it cause? What are its effects?	Questions suggest **cause and effect** (the events leading to the Korean War; the results of global warming; the impact of a new math curriculum on slow learners)
How is it like other things? How is it different from other things?	Questions suggest **comparison and contrast** (of the popular music of the 1980s and 1990s; of two paintings)
What are its parts or types? Can they be separated or grouped? Do they fall into a logical order? Can they be categorized?	Questions suggest **division and classification** (components of the catalytic converter; kinds of occupational therapy; kinds of dietary supplements)
What is it? How does it resemble other members of its class? How does it differ from other members of its class?	Questions suggest **definition** (What is Marxism? What is photosynthesis? What is a MOO?)

An excerpt from Rebecca's list of in-depth questions appears below.

In-Depth Questions (Excerpt)

> <u>What are the elements of a helpful *Wikipedia* article?</u> Comprehensive abstracts, internal links, external links, coverage of current and obscure topics.
>
> <u>What are the elements of an unreliable *Wikipedia* article?</u> Factual inaccuracy, bias, vandalism, lack of citations.

EXERCISE 2.2

List all the sources you encounter in one day (specific people, books, magazines, Web sites, and so on) that could provide you with useful information for the essay you are writing. Exchange lists with a classmate, and add two sources to his or her list.

EXERCISE 2.3

Make a cluster diagram and brainstorming notes for the topic you selected in Exercise 2.1. If you have trouble thinking of material to write about, try freewriting. Then, write a journal entry assessing your progress and evaluating the different strategies for finding something to say. Which strategy worked best for you? Why?

EXERCISE 2.4

Using the two strategies described on pages 24–26 to supplement the work you did in Exercises 2.2 and 2.3, continue generating material for a short essay on your topic from Exercise 2.1.

EXERCISE 2.5

Consider what kinds of visual images might enhance your essay-in-progress. For example, would a photograph of people and places on your campus be helpful? List several possibilities, and write a few sentences explaining what each visual might add to your essay.

EXERCISE 2.6

Go to *Google Image Search* and find a visual to use in your essay. Using the visual as a focus, brainstorm to find additional ideas to write about.

Using a Thesis to Shape Your Material

C H A P T E R 3

After you have gathered material for your essay and begun to see the direction your ideas are taking, you start to sift through these ideas and choose those you can use in your essay. As you do this, you begin to **shape** your material into a thesis-and-support essay.

3a Understanding Thesis and Support

Your **thesis** is the main idea of your essay, the central point your essay supports. The concept of **thesis and support**—stating the thesis and then supplying information that explains and develops it—is central to much of the writing you will do in college.

As the following diagram illustrates, the essays you will write will consist of an <u>introductory paragraph</u>, which opens your essay and states your thesis; a number of **body paragraphs**, which provide the support for your thesis statement; and a <u>concluding paragraph</u>, which reviews your essay's major points and gives it a sense of closure, perhaps restating your thesis.

See 5e2–3

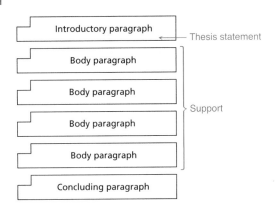

3b Developing a Thesis

1 Stating Your Thesis

An effective **thesis statement** has four characteristics:

1. **An effective thesis statement clearly communicates your essay's main idea.** It tells readers what your essay's topic is and suggests what you will say about it. Thus, your thesis statement reflects your essay's purpose.

2. **An effective thesis statement is more than a general subject, a statement of fact, or an announcement of your intent.**

STATING YOUR THESIS		
Subject	**Statement of Fact**	**Announcement**
The Military Draft	The United States currently has no military draft.	In this essay, I will reconsider our country's need for a draft.

Thesis statement Although an all-volunteer force has replaced the draft, a draft may eventually be necessary if the US is to remain secure.

3. **An effective thesis statement is carefully worded.** Because it communicates your paper's main idea, your thesis statement should be clearly and accurately worded. Your thesis statement—usually expressed in a single concise sentence—should be direct and straightforward. It should not include abstract language, overly complex terminology, or unnecessary details that might confuse or mislead readers.

Be particularly careful to avoid vague, wordy phrases—*centers on, deals with, involves, revolves around, has a lot to do with, is primarily concerned with,* and so on.

The real problem in our schools $\overset{is}{\wedge}$ ~~does~~ not ~~revolve around~~ the absence of nationwide goals and standards; the problem is ~~primarily concerned with~~ the absence of resources.

Finally, an effective thesis statement should not include phrases such as "Personally," "I believe," "I hope to demonstrate," and "It seems to me," which weaken your credibility by suggesting that your conclusions are tentative or are based solely on opinion rather than on reading, observation, and experience.

4. **An effective thesis statement suggests your essay's direction, emphasis, and scope.** Your thesis statement should not make promises that your essay will not fulfill. It should suggest where you will place your emphasis and indicate in what order your major points will be discussed, as the following thesis statement does.

Effective Thesis Statement

Widely ridiculed as escape reading, romance novels are important as a proving ground for many never-before-published writers and, more significantly, as a showcase for strong heroines.

This thesis statement is effective because it tells readers that the essay to follow will focus on two major roles of the romance novel: providing markets for new writers and (more important) presenting strong female characters. It also suggests that the essay will briefly treat the role of the romance novel as escapist fiction. As the following diagram shows, this effective thesis statement also indicates the order in which the various ideas will be discussed.

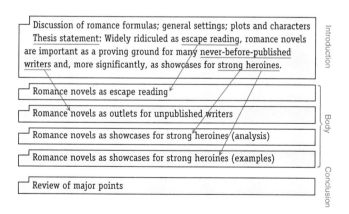

Rebecca James came up with the following thesis statement for her essay about *Wikipedia* and college research.

Thesis Statement: I have found *Wikipedia* to be a valuable tool for locating reliable research sources.

2 | Revising Your Thesis Statement

At this point, your thesis statement is only **tentative.** As you write and re-write, you will think of new ideas and see new connections. As a result, you may change your essay's direction, emphasis, and scope, and if you do so, you must reword your thesis statement to reflect these modifications.

When Rebecca revised her essay, her thesis statement changed. Compare her tentative thesis on page 29 with her revised thesis statement in her paper's final draft on page 54.

CLOSE-UP

USING A THESIS STATEMENT TO SHAPE YOUR ESSAY

The wording of your thesis statement often suggests not only a possible order and emphasis for your essay's ideas, but also a specific pattern of development—*narration, description, exemplification, process, cause and effect, comparison and contrast, division and classification,* or *definition.* (These familiar **patterns of development** may also shape individual paragraphs of your essay.)

See 5d

Thesis Statement	Pattern of Development
As the months went by and I grew more and more involved with the developmentally delayed children at the Learning Center, I came to see how important it is to treat every child as an individual.	Narration
Looking around the room where I spent my childhood, I realized that every object I saw told me I was now an adult.	Description
The risk-taking behavior that has characterized recent years can be illustrated by the increasing interest and involvement in such high-risk sports as mountain biking, ice climbing, sky diving, and bungee jumping.	Exemplification
Armed forces basic training programs take recruits through a series of tasks designed to build camaraderie as well as skills and confidence.	Process
The gap in computer literacy between rich and poor has had many significant social and economic consequences.	Cause and Effect

Thesis Statement	Pattern of Development
Although people who live in cities and people who live in small towns have some similarities, their views on issues like crime, waste disposal, farm subsidies, and educational vouchers tend to be very different.	Comparison and Contrast
The section of the proposal that recommends establishing satellite health centers is quite promising; unfortunately, however, the sections that call for the creation of alternative educational programs, job training, and low-income housing are seriously flawed.	Division and Classification
Many people once assumed that rape was an act perpetrated by a stranger, but today's definition is much broader.	Definition

EXERCISE 3.1

Working in a group of three or four students, analyze each of the following items and explain why none of them qualifies as an effective thesis statement.

▶ 1. In this essay, I will examine the environmental effects of residential and commercial development on the coastal regions of the United States.

▶ 2. Residential and commercial development in the coastal regions of the United States

▶ 3. How to avoid coastal overdevelopment

▶ 4. Coastal Development: Pro and Con

▶ 5. Residential and commercial development of America's coastal regions benefits some people, but it has a number of disadvantages.

6. The environmentalists' position on coastal development

7. More and more coastal regions in the United States are being overdeveloped.

8. Residential and commercial development guidelines need to be developed for coastal regions of the United States.

9. Coastal development is causing beach erosion.

10. At one time I enjoyed walking on the beach, but commercial and residential development ruined the experience for me.

EXERCISE 3.2

Review all the notes you have accumulated so far, and use them to help you develop a thesis for an essay on the topic you chose in Chapter 2, Exercise 1.

3c   Constructing an Informal Outline

Once you have a tentative thesis statement, you may want to construct an informal outline to guide you as you write. An **informal outline** is an organizational plan that arranges your essay's main points and major supporting ideas in an orderly way.

Rebecca's informal outline appears below.

Informal Outline

Thesis statement: I have found *Wikipedia* to be a valuable tool for locating reliable research sources.

Definition of wiki and explanation of *Wikipedia*

- Fast and easy
- Range of topics

Wikipedia's benefits

- Internal links
- External links
- Comprehensive abstracts
- Current and popular culture topics
- "Stub" articles to be expanded

Wikipedia's growth potential

- Current quality control
- Future enhancements?

Wikipedia's drawbacks

- Not accurate
- Bias
- Vandalism
- Lack of citations

CMA example: benefits

- Clear, concise
- Internal links
- External links

CMA example: drawbacks

- Writing style
- No citations
- Needs more internal links

FORMAL OUTLINES

Sometimes—particularly when you are writing a long or complex essay—you will need to construct a **formal outline,** which indicates both the exact order and the relative importance of all the ideas you will explore. (For information on how to construct a formal outline and for an example of a complete **sentence outline, see 4c4.** For an example of an excerpt from another sentence outline, **see 41j1.** For an example of a formal **topic outline, see 41h.**)

At this stage of the writing process, Rebecca decided that her informal outline was all she needed to guide her as she wrote a first draft. (Later on, she might decide to construct a formal topic or sentence outline to check her paper's organization.)

Although you may be used to constructing outlines for your written work by hand, a number of software applications and formatting features can help in this process, including the outlining feature in some desktop publishing and word-processing programs (such as *Microsoft Word*). Another useful tool for outlining (particularly for oral presentations) is *Microsoft PowerPoint,* presentation software that enables you to format information on individual slides with major headings, subheadings, and bulleted lists.

EXERCISE 3.3

Find an editorial on your paper's topic in a newspaper or on the Internet. Then, prepare an informal outline of the editorial that includes all the writer's main points and major supporting ideas.

EXERCISE 3.4

Prepare an informal outline for the paper you have been developing in Chapters 2 and 3.

Drafting and Revising CHAPTER 4

4a Writing a Rough Draft

Once you are able to see a clear order for your ideas, you are ready to write a **rough draft** of your paper.

A rough draft usually includes false starts, irrelevant information, and unrelated details. At this stage, though, the absence of focus and order is not a problem. You write your rough draft simply to get your ideas down so that you can react to them. You should expect to add or delete words, to reword sentences, to rethink ideas, and to reorder paragraphs. You should also expect to discover some new ideas—or even to take an unexpected detour.

When you write your rough draft, concentrate on the body of your essay and don't waste time mapping out an introduction and conclusion. (These paragraphs are likely to change substantially in subsequent drafts.) For now, focus on drafting the support paragraphs of your essay.

ESL TIP

Using your native language occasionally as you draft your paper may keep you from losing your train of thought. However, writing most or all of your draft in your native language and then translating it into English is generally not a good idea. This process will take a long time, and the translation into English may sound awkward.

CHECKLIST

DRAFTING STRATEGIES

The following suggestions should help you write and revise:

☐ **Prepare your work area.** Once you begin to write, you should not have to stop because you need better lighting, important notes, or anything else.

☐ **Fight writer's block.** An inability to start (or continue) writing, writer's block is usually caused by fear that you will not write well or that you have nothing to say. If you really don't feel ready to write, take a short break. If you decide that you really don't have enough ideas to get you started, use one of the strategies for finding something to say.

See 2e

☐ **Get your ideas down on paper as quickly as you can.** Don't worry about sentence structure, about spelling and punctuation, or about finding exactly the right word—just write. Writing quickly helps you uncover new ideas and new connections between ideas. You may find that following an informal outline enables you to move smoothly from one point to the next, but if you find this structure too confining, go ahead and write without consulting your outline.

See 3c

☐ **Write notes to yourself.** As you type your drafts, get into the habit of including bracketed, boldfaced notes to yourself. These comments, suggestions, and questions can help you later, when you revise.

☐ **Take regular breaks as you write.** Try writing one section of your essay at a time. When you have completed a section—for example, one paragraph—take a break. Your mind will continue to focus on your assignment while you do other things. When you return to your essay, writing will be easier.

☐ **Leave yourself enough time to revise.** All writing benefits from revision, so be sure you have time to reconsider your work and to write as many drafts as you need.

CLOSE-UP

MANAGING FILES

As you revise, it is important to manage your files carefully, following these guidelines:

♦ First, be sure to save your drafts. Using the Save option in your word processor's file menu saves only your most recent draft. If you prefer to save every draft you write (so you can return to an earlier draft to locate a different version of a sentence or to reconsider a section you have deleted), use the Save As option instead.

♦ Also, be sure to label your files. To help you keep track of different versions of your paper, label every file in your folder by content and date (for example, **First Draft, Nov. 5**).

♦ Finally, be very careful not to delete material that you may need later; instead, move this material to the end of your document so that you can assess its usefulness later on and retrieve it if necessary.

Using her informal outline to guide her, Rebecca wrote the following rough draft. Notice that she included boldfaced and bracketed notes to remind herself to add or check information later.

Rough Draft

Wikipedia and College Research

When given an assignment, students often turn first to *Wikipedia,* the popular free online encyclopedia that currently includes 10,000,000 articles. I have found *Wikipedia* to be a valuable tool for locating reliable research sources. **[Add more here]**

A wiki is an open-source Web site that allows users to edit or alter its content. Derived from a Hawaiian word meaning "quick," the term *wiki* conveys the swiftness and ease with which users can access information on such sites. **[Do I need to document this? Definition from *Britannica.com*]** *Wikipedia* is the most popular wiki. It includes a range of topics, such as . . . . **[Include a couple of examples here]** *Wikipedia*'s editing tools make it easy for users to add new or edit existing entries.

Wikipedia's slogan is "Making Life Easier." The site offers numerous benefits to its users. One benefit to *Wikipedia* over traditional print encyclopedias is its "wikilinks," or internal links to other content within *Wikipedia.* **[Use Pew report data on *Google* searches and wikilinks]** *Wikipedia* articles also often include external links to other sources as well as comprehensive abstracts. *Wikipedia* articles are constantly being updated and provide unmatched coverage of popular culture topics and

36

current events. **[Make sure this is correct]** Finally, the site includes "stub" articles, which provide basic information that may be expanded by users.

Wikipedia claims that its articles "are continually edited and improved over time, and in general, this results in an upward trend of quality and a growing consensus over a fair and balanced representation of information." **["About" page—need full citation]** *Wikipedia* ranks its articles using the criteria of accuracy, neutrality, completeness, and style, letting users know which articles are among the site's best. In fact, some of *Wikipedia*'s best articles are comparable to those found in professionally edited online encyclopedias, such as *Encyclopaedia Britannica Online.* **[Check on this to make sure]** Although there's no professional editorial board to oversee the development of content within *Wikipedia,* users may be nominated into an editor role that allows them to manage the process by which content is added and updated. Users may also use the "Talk" page to discuss an article's content and make suggestions for improvement.

Wikipedia's popularity has also stimulated emergent technologies. Other companies are now trying to capitalize on *Wikipedia*'s success by enhancing users' experience of the site. Two examples include the online service *Pediaphon,* which converts *Wikipedia* articles into MP3 audio files, and the search-tool software *Powerset,* which allows users to more easily navigate *Wikipedia* articles.

Wikipedia concedes that "not everything in *Wikipedia* is accurate, comprehensive, or unbiased." **["Researching with *Wikipedia*" page—need full citation]** Because anyone can create or edit *Wikipedia* articles, they can be factually inaccurate, biased, and even vandalized. Many *Wikipedia* articles also lack citations to the sources that support their claims, revealing a lack of reliability. **[Need more here]**

Personally, I have benefited from using *Wikipedia* in learning more for my accounting class. For example, the *Wikipedia* article "Certified Management Accountant" describes the CMA's role in relation to other types of accounting positions. The article contains several internal links to related *Wikipedia* articles as well as a list of external links to additional resources. **[Give examples?]** In comparison, *Encyclopaedia Britannica Online* doesn't contain an article on CMAs.

Although the *Wikipedia* article on CMAs provides helpful, general information on this accounting term, it is limited in terms of reliability, scope, and style. **[Explain more here. Add a visual?]** The limitations of the CMA article indicate that *Wikipedia* should be used as a gateway to more reliable and comprehensive research sources.

Wikipedia articles should be used as a starting point for research and as a link to more in-depth sources. *Wikipedia* users should understand the current shortcomings of this popular online tool. **[Add more!]**

EXERCISE 4.1

Write a rough draft of the essay you began planning in Chapter 2.

4b Moving from Rough Draft to Final Draft

As you revise successive drafts of your essay, you should narrow your focus from larger elements, such as overall structure and content, to increasingly smaller elements, such as sentence structure and word choice.

1 Revising Your Drafts

After you finish your rough draft, set it aside for a day or two if you can. When you return to it, focus on only a few areas at a time. As you review this first draft, begin by evaluating your essay's thesis-and-support structure and general organization. Once you feel satisfied that your thesis statement says what you want it to say and that your essay's content supports this thesis and is logically arranged, you can turn your attention to other matters. For example, you can make sure that you have included all the <u>transitional words and phrases</u> that readers will need to follow your discussion. See 5b2

As you review your drafts, you may want to consult the questions in the "Revising Your Essay" checklist on pages 48–49. If you have the opportunity for <u>peer review</u> or a <u>conference</u> with your instructor, consider your readers' comments carefully. See 4c2, 4c3

Because it can be more difficult to read text on the computer screen than on hard copy, you should print out every draft. This will enable you to make revisions by hand on printed pages and then return to the computer to type these changes into your document. (As you type your draft, you may want to leave extra space between lines. This will make any errors or inconsistencies more obvious and at the same time give you plenty of room to write questions, add new material, or edit sentences.)

If you write your revisions by hand on hard copy, you may find it helpful to develop a system of symbols. For instance, you can circle individual words or box groups of words (or even entire paragraphs) that you want to relocate, using an arrow to indicate the new location. You can also use matching numbers or letters to indicate how you want to rearrange ideas. When you want to add words, use a caret like *this*.

An excerpt from Rebecca's draft, with her handwritten revisions, appears below.

Draft with Handwritten Revisions (Excerpt)

The article contains several internal links to related *Wikipedia*
(including the article "Certified Public Accountant")
articles as well as a list of external links to additional
(such as the Web site for the Institute of Management Accountants)
resources. In comparison, *Encyclopaedia Britannica Online* doesn't

contain an article on CMAs.

2 Adding Visuals

As you write and revise, you should consider whether one or more **visuals** might strengthen your paper by providing support for the points you are making. Sometimes you may want to use a visual that appears in one of your sources; at other times, you may be able to create a visual (for example, a photograph or a chart) yourself; at still other times, you may need to search *Google Images* or another image database to find an appropriate visual.

Once you have decided to add a particular visual to your paper, the next step is to determine where to insert it. (In general, you should place the visual in the part of the essay where it will have the greatest impact in terms of conveying information or persuading your audience.) Then, you need to format the visual. (Within *Microsoft Word,* you can double-click on an image to call up a picture-editing menu that allows you to alter the size, color, and position of the image within your essay—and even enables you to wrap text around the image.) Next, you should make sure that the visual stands out in your paper: surround it with white space, add ruled lines, or enclose it in a box.

Once the visual has been inserted where you want it, you need to integrate it into your paper. You can include a sentence that introduces the visual (**The following table illustrates the similarities between the two Web sites**), or you can refer to it in your text (**Figure 1 shows an excerpt from a Wikipedia entry**) to give it some context and explain why you are using it. You should also identify the visual by labeling it (**Fig. 1.** *Wikipedia* **home page**). In addition, if the visual is not one you have created yourself, you must **document** it. In most academic disciplines, this means including full source information directly below the image and sometimes in the list of references as well. (To see how Rebecca integrated a visual into her paper, **see 4e.**)

See
Chs.
47–48

ADDING VISUALS TO YOUR PAPER

To add a visual to your paper, follow these steps:

- ☐ Find an appropriate visual.
- ☐ Place the image in a suitable location.
- ☐ Format the image, and make sure it is clearly set off from the written text.
- ☐ Introduce the visual with a sentence (or refer to it in the text).
- ☐ Label the visual.
- ☐ Document the visual (if necessary).

EXERCISE 4.2

Look carefully at the visual you chose in Exercise 2.6. In one sentence, state the main idea that this visual communicates to its audience. Then, list the individual images and details in the visual that support this main idea. Does this visual help to support or clarify a point you are trying to make in your essay? If it does not, look for one that does. Then, decide where to place the visual in your essay.

4c Using Specific Revision Strategies

Everyone revises differently, and every writing task calls for a slightly different process of revision. Five strategies in particular can help you revise at any stage of the writing process.

1 Using Word-Processing Tools

Your word-processing program includes a variety of tools designed to make the revision process easier. For example, *Microsoft Word*'s **Track Changes** feature allows you to make changes to a draft electronically and to see the original version of the draft and the changes simultaneously. Changes appear in color as underlined or crossed out text, and writers have the option of viewing the changes on the screen or in print. This feature also allows you to accept or reject all changes or just specific changes.

Another useful revision tool is the **Compare** feature. Whereas Track Changes allows you to keep track of changes to a single document, Compare allows you to analyze the changes in two completely separate versions of a document, usually an original and its most recent update. Changes appear in color as highlighted text.

Rebecca used Track Changes as she revised her rough draft. An excerpt from her draft, along with her changes, appears on the following page.

Draft with Track Changes (Excerpt)

> A wiki is an open-source Web site that allows users to edit ~~or alter~~and add to its content. Derived from a Hawaiian word meaning "quick," the term *wiki* conveys the swiftness and ease with which users can access information on such sites~~.~~ as well as contribute content ("Wiki"). With its slogan "Making Life Easier," *Wikipedia* ~~is~~has positioned itself as the most popular wiki. ~~It includes a range~~, providing ever-increasing coverage of topics~~;~~ ~~such as....~~ ranging from contemporary rock bands to obscure scientific and technical concepts. In accordance with the site's policies, users can edit existing articles and add new articles using *Wikipedia*'s editing tools ~~also make it easy for users to add new~~, which do not require specialized programming knowledge or ~~edit existing entries~~expertise.

2 Participating in Peer Review

Peer review—a collaborative revision strategy that enables you to get feedback from your classmates—is another useful activity. With peer review, instead of trying to imagine an audience for your paper, you address a real audience, exchanging drafts with classmates and commenting on their drafts. Such collaborative work can be formal or informal, conducted in person or electronically. For example, you and your classmates may email drafts back and forth, using *Word*'s Comment tool to offer suggestions for revision (see p. 41), or your instructor may conduct the class as a workshop, assigning students to work in groups to critique other students' essays. Students can also comment on classmates' drafts posted on a course discussion board or listserv.

CLOSE-UP

ELECTRONIC PEER REVIEW

Some software is particularly useful for peer-review groups. For example, *Word*'s **Comment** tool allows several readers to insert comments at any point or to highlight a particular portion of the text they would like to comment on and then insert annotations. With this tool, a single paper can receive comments from multiple readers. Comments are identified by the initials of the reviewer and by a color assigned to the reviewer.

Other online programs also facilitate the peer-review process. For example, *InSite* is a Web-based application that allows students to respond to each other's drafts using a set of peer-review questions.

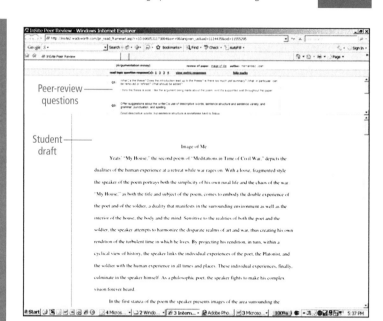

Peer-review questions

Student draft

An excerpt from Rebecca's rough draft with peer reviewers' comments appears below.

Draft with Peer Reviewers' Comments (Excerpt)

Personally, I have benefited from using *Wikipedia* in learning more for my accounting class. For example, the *Wikipedia* article "Certified Management Accountant" describes the CMA's role in relation to other types of accounting positions. The article contains several internal links to related *Wikipedia* articles (including the article "Certified Public Accountant") as well as a list of external links to additional resources (such as the Web site for the Institute of Management Accountants). In comparison, *Encyclopaedia Britannica Online* doesn't contain an article on CMAs.

Comment [KL1]: It's also helpful for other classes outside my major.

Comment [KL2]: Why is this imp.? Maybe explain more??

Comment [BR3]: Yes! This is one of my fav features of *Wikipedia*. ☺

Comment [CB4]: But sometimes these links don't lead to the best sources either . . .

CHECKLIST

QUESTIONS FOR PEER REVIEW

The following questions can help guide you through the peer-review process:

❏ What is the essay about? Does the topic fulfill the requirements of the assignment?

❏ What is the essay's main idea? Is the thesis clearly worded? If not, how can the wording be improved?

❏ Is the essay arranged logically? Do the body paragraphs appear in an appropriate order?

❏ What ideas support the thesis? Does each body paragraph develop one of these ideas?

❏ Is any necessary information missing? Identify any areas that seem to need further development. Is any information irrelevant? If so, suggest possible deletions.

❏ Can you think of any ideas or examples from your own reading, experience, or observations that would strengthen the writer's essay?

❏ Can you follow the writer's ideas? If not, would clearer connections between sentences or paragraphs be helpful? Where are such connections needed?

❏ Is the introductory paragraph interesting to you? Would another opening strategy be more effective?

❏ Does the conclusion leave you with a sense of closure? Would another concluding strategy be more effective?

❏ Is anything unclear or confusing?

❏ What is the essay's greatest strength?

❏ What is the essay's greatest weakness?

For information on audience concerns for peer-review participants, **see 1b.**

3 Using Instructors' Comments

Instructors' comments—in correction symbols, in marginal comments, or in conferences—can also help you revise.

Correction Symbols   Your instructor may indicate concerns about style, grammar, mechanics, or punctuation by using the correction symbols listed on the inside back cover of this book. Instead of correcting a problem, the instructor will simply identify it and supply the number of the section in this handbook that deals with the error. After reading the appropriate pages, you should be able to make the necessary corrections on your own. For example, the symbol and number noted within the following sentence referred a student to **19e2,** the section in this handbook that discusses sexist language.

Instructor's Comment: Equal access to jobs is a desirable goal for all
Sxt—see 19e2
(mankind.)

After reading the appropriate section in the handbook, the student made the
following change.

Revised: Equal access to jobs is a desirable goal for everyone.

Marginal Comments   Instructors frequently write marginal comments on
your essays to suggest changes in content or structure. Such comments may
ask you to add supporting information or to arrange paragraphs differently
within the essay, or they may recommend stylistic changes, such as more
varied sentences. Marginal comments may also question your logic, suggest
a more explicit thesis statement, ask for clearer transitions, or propose a new
direction for a discussion. In some cases, you can consider these comments
to be suggestions rather than corrections. You may decide to incorporate
these ideas into a revised draft of your essay, or you may not. In all instances,
however, you should take your instructor's comments seriously.

An excerpt from Rebecca's rough draft, along with her instructor's comments, follows. (Note that her instructor used *Microsoft Word*'s Comment
tool to insert comments.)

Draft with Instructor's Comments (Excerpt)

Personally, I have benefited from using
Wikipedia in learning more for my accounting class.
For example, the *Wikipedia* article "Certified
Management Accountant" describes the CMA's role
in relation to other types of accounting positions.
The article contains several internal links to related
Wikipedia articles (including the article "Certified
Public Accountant") as well as a list of external links
to additional resources (such as the Web site for the
Institute of Management Accountants). In comparison,
Encyclopaedia Britannica Online doesn't contain an
article on CMAs.

Comment [JB5]: Revise to eliminate use of "person-ally" and the first person ("*I*") in this paper. Use this ¶ to talk about *Wikipedia*'s benefits to college students, using the CMA article as an example.

Comment [JB6]: In your final draft, edit out all contrac-tions. (Contractions are too informal for most college writing.) See 32b1.

Conferences   Many instructors require or encourage one-on-one conferences, and you should certainly schedule a conference if you can. During
a conference, you can respond to your instructor's questions and ask for
clarification of marginal comments. If a certain section of your paper presents
a problem, use your conference time to focus on it, perhaps asking for help in
sharpening your thesis or choosing more accurate words.

GETTING THE MOST OUT OF A CONFERENCE

To make your conference time as productive as possible, follow these guidelines:

- ❑ **Make an appointment.** If you are unable to keep your appointment, be sure to call or email your instructor to reschedule.
- ❑ **Review your work carefully.** Before the conference, reread your notes and drafts, and go over all your instructor's comments and suggestions. Make all the changes you can on your draft.
- ❑ **Bring a list of questions.** Preparing a list in advance will enable you to get the most out of the conference in the allotted time.
- ❑ **Bring your paper-in-progress.** If you have several drafts, you may want to bring them all, but be sure you bring any draft on which your instructor has commented.
- ❑ **Take notes.** As you discuss your paper, write down any suggestions that you think will be helpful so you won't forget them when you revise.
- ❑ **Participate actively.** A successful conference is not a monologue; it should be an open exchange of ideas.

CLOSE-UP

WRITING CENTER CONFERENCES

If you are unable to meet with your instructor—and, in fact, even if you are—it is a good idea to make an appointment with a tutor in your school's writing center. A writing tutor (who may be either a professional or a student) is likely to know a good deal about what your instructor expects and is trained to help you produce an effective essay.

What a writing tutor can do is help you find ideas to write about and develop a thesis statement, identify parts of your essay that need more support (and help you decide what kind of support to include), and coach you as you revise your essay. What a tutor will *not* do is write your paper for you or act as a proofreader.

When you meet in conference with a writing tutor, follow the guidelines in the checklist above. In addition, be sure to bring a copy of your assignment.

Conferences can also take place online—most commonly, through email. If you send emails to your instructor, to your writing center tutor, or to members of your peer-review group, include a specific subject line that clearly identifies the message as coming from a student writer (for example, "question about assignment" or "comments on my paper"). This is especially important if your email address does not include your name. When you attach a document to an email and send it for comments, mention the attachment in your subject line (for example, "first draft—see attachment")—and be sure your name appears on the attachment itself, not just on the email.

COLLABORATION AND THE REVISION PROCESS

In a sense, the feedback you get from your instructor (or from a writing center tutor)—in conference, by email, or in the form of written comments on a draft—opens a dialogue that initiates a process of collaboration. Like the comments you get from your classmates during peer review, these comments present ideas for you to react to, questions for you to answer, and answers to questions you may have. As you react to these comments, you engage in a collaboration that can help you revise your work.

4 Using a Formal Outline

Outlining can be helpful early in the revision process, when you are reworking the larger structural elements of your essay, or later on, when you are checking the logic of a completed draft. A formal outline reveals at once whether points are irrelevant or poorly placed—or, worse, missing. It also reveals the hierarchy of your ideas—which points are dominant and which are subordinate.

THE CONVENTIONS OF OUTLINING

Formal outlines conform to specific conventions of structure, content, and style. If you follow the conventions of outlining carefully, your formal outline can help you make sure that your paper presents all relevant ideas in an effective order, with appropriate emphasis.

Structure

◆ Outline format should be followed strictly.

    I. First major point of your paper
      A. First subpoint
      B. Next subpoint
         1. First supporting example
         2. Next supporting example
            a. First specific detail
            b. Next specific detail
    II. Second major point

◆ Headings should not overlap.
◆ No heading should have a single subheading. (A category cannot be subdivided into one part.)
◆ Each entry should be preceded by an appropriate letter or number, followed by a period.
◆ The first word of each entry should be capitalized.

(continued)

THE CONVENTIONS OF OUTLINING (*continued*)

Content

- ◆ The outline should include the paper's thesis statement.
- ◆ The outline should cover only the body of the essay, not the introductory or concluding paragraphs.
- ◆ Headings should be concise and specific.
- ◆ Headings should be descriptive, clearly related to the topic to which they refer.

Style

- ◆ Headings of the same rank should be grammatically parallel.
- ◆ A **sentence outline** should use complete sentences, with all sentences in the same tense.
- ◆ In a sentence outline, each entry should end with a period.
- ◆ A **topic outline** should use words or short phrases, with all headings of the same rank using the same parts of speech.
- ◆ In a topic outline, entries should not end with periods.

As part of her revision process, Rebecca made the following sentence outline of her rough draft (shown on pages 35–37) to help her check her paper's organization.

Sentence Outline

Thesis statement: I have found *Wikipedia* to be a valuable tool in locating more reliable research sources.

I. A wiki is an open-source Web site that allows users to edit or alter its content.

    A. *Wikipedia* is the most popular wiki.

    B. *Wikipedia* includes a range of topics.

II. *Wikipedia* offers numerous benefits to its users.

    A. Many *Wikipedia* articles contain internal links.

    B. Many *Wikipedia* articles contain external links.

    C. Many *Wikipedia* articles contain comprehensive abstracts.

    D. Many *Wikipedia* articles cover current and popular culture topics.

    E. Site includes "stub" articles.

III. *Wikipedia* is making efforts to improve the quality of its content.

    A. *Wikipedia* ranks its articles using the criteria of accuracy, neutrality, completeness, and style.

    B. Users may serve as editors of the site's content.

    C. Users may use the "Talk" page to make suggestions for improvement.

IV. *Wikipedia's* popularity has stimulated emergent technologies.

    A. The online service *Pediaphon* converts *Wikipedia* articles into MP3 audio files.

    B. The search-tool software *Powerset* allows users to more easily navigate *Wikipedia* articles.

V. *Wikipedia* also has several drawbacks.

    A. *Wikipedia* articles may be factually inaccurate.

    B. *Wikipedia* articles may be biased.

    C. *Wikipedia* articles may be vandalized.

    D. Many *Wikipedia* articles lack citations.

VI. The *Wikipedia* article "Certified Management Accountant" offers certain benefits.

    A. It gives a clear, concise description of the CMA's role.

    B. It provides internal and external links to additional resources.

VII. *Wikipedia's* "Certified Management Accountant" article is limited in the information it offers.

    A. It is unreliable.

    B. It is limited in scope.

    C. It is poorly written.

This outline revealed some problems in Rebecca's draft. For example, she saw that point IV was irrelevant to her discussion, and she realized that she needed to develop the sections in which she discussed the benefits and drawbacks of the specific *Wikipedia* entry that she selected for this assignment. Thus, the outline helped her to revise her rough draft.

CLOSE-UP

FORMATTING AN OUTLINE

If you use your computer's word-processing program to construct a formal outline, the Bullets and Numbering feature and the Auto Format feature will help you to format it properly. Usually found in the Format menu, Bullets and Numbering allows you to select the format type of your outline, including styles that use roman numerals, letters, and/or numbers. Once you have selected your outline style, Auto Format will arrange what you type in the selected format and allow you to customize the formatting further.

EXERCISE 4.3

Outline the most recent draft of your paper, and use this outline to help you check the arrangement of your essay's ideas. Make any structural revisions you think are necessary. (Try not to worry at this point about stylistic issues, such as sentence variety and word choice.)

5 Using Checklists

The revision checklist that follows is keyed to sections of this text. Moving from global to specific concerns, it parallels the actual revision process. As your understanding of the writing process increases and you become better able to assess the strengths and weaknesses of your writing, you may want to add items to (or delete items from) this checklist. You can also use your instructors' comments to tailor the checklist to your own needs.

CHECKLIST

REVISING YOUR ESSAY

The whole essay

- ❑ Do you understand your essay's purpose? (**See 1a.**)
- ❑ Have you taken your audience's needs into account? (**See 1b.**)
- ❑ Are thesis and support logically related, with each body paragraph supporting your thesis statement? (**See 3a.**)
- ❑ Is your thesis statement clearly and specifically worded? (**See 3b1.**)
- ❑ Have you discussed everything promised in your thesis statement? (**See 3b1.**)
- ❑ Have you presented your ideas in a logical sequence? Can you think of a different arrangement that might be more appropriate for your purpose? (**See 3c.**)

Paragraphs

- ❑ Does each body paragraph have just one main idea? (**See 5a.**)
- ❑ Are topic sentences clearly worded and logically related to your thesis? (**See 5a1.**)
- ❑ Does each body paragraph have a clear organizing principle? (**See 5b1.**)
- ❑ Are the relationships between sentences within your paragraphs clear? (**See 5b2–4.**)
- ❑ Are your body paragraphs developed fully enough to support your points? (**See 5c.**)
- ❑ Does your introductory paragraph arouse reader interest and prepare readers for what is to come? (**See 5e2.**)
- ❑ Are your paragraphs arranged according to familiar patterns of development? (**See 5d.**)
- ❑ Have you provided transitional paragraphs where necessary? (**See 5e1.**)
- ❑ Does your concluding paragraph sum up your main points? (**See 5e3.**)

Sentences

- ❑ Have you used correct sentence structure? (**See Chs. 24 and 25.**)
- ❑ Have you avoided potentially confusing shifts in tense, voice, mood, person, or number? (**See 28a1–4.**)
- ❑ Are your sentences constructed logically? (**See 28b–d.**)
- ❑ Have you placed modifiers clearly and logically? (**See Ch. 27.**)

❑ Are your sentences varied? (**See Ch. 15.**)

❑ Have you combined sentences where ideas are closely related? (**See 15b.**)

❑ Have you used emphatic word order? (**See 16a.**)

❑ Have you used sentence structure to signal the relative importance of clauses in a sentence and their logical relationship to one another? (**See 16b.**)

❑ Have you strengthened your sentences with repetition, balance, and parallelism? (**See 16c–d, 18a.**)

❑ Have you eliminated nonessential words and unnecessary repetition? (**See 17a–b.**)

❑ Have you avoided overloading your sentences with too many words, phrases, and clauses? (**See 17c.**)

Words

❑ Is your level of diction appropriate for your audience and your purpose? (**See 19a.**)

❑ Have you selected words that accurately reflect your intentions? (**See 19b1.**)

❑ Have you chosen words that are specific, concrete, and unambiguous? (**See 19b3–4.**)

❑ Have you enriched your writing with figures of speech? (**See 19c.**)

❑ Have you eliminated jargon, neologisms, pretentious diction, clichés, and offensive language from your writing? (**See 19d–e.**)

EXERCISE 4.4

Review the most recent draft of your paper, this time focusing on paragraphing, topic sentences, and transitions and on the way you structure your sentences and select your words. (Use the appropriate items in the checklist above as a guide.)

EXERCISE 4.5

Using the revision checklist above as a model, create a ten-item customized checklist—one that reflects the specific concerns that you need to consider when you revise an essay. Then, use this checklist to help you in your revision.

CLOSE-UP

CHOOSING A TITLE

When you are ready to decide on a title for your essay, keep these criteria in mind:

♦ A title should be descriptive, giving an accurate sense of your essay's focus. Whenever possible, use a key word or phrase that is central to your paper.

(continued)

CHOOSING A TITLE (*continued*)

♦ A title can echo the wording of your assignment, reminding you (and your instructor) that you have not lost sight of it.

♦ Ideally, a title should arouse interest, perhaps by using a provocative question or a quotation or by taking a controversial position.

Assignment: Write about a problem faced on college campuses today.

Topic: Free speech on campus

Possible titles:

Free Speech: A Problem for Today's Colleges (echoes wording of assignment and includes key words of essay)

How Free Should Free Speech on Campus Be? (provocative question)

The Right to "Shout 'Fire' in a Crowded Theater" (quotation)

Hate Speech: A Dangerous Abuse of Free Speech on Campus (controversial position)

4d Editing and Proofreading

Once you have revised your drafts to your satisfaction, two final tasks remain: **editing** and **proofreading.**

1 Editing

When you **edit,** you concentrate on grammar and spelling, punctuation and mechanics. Although you have dealt with these issues as you revised previous drafts of your paper, editing is now your primary focus. As you proceed, read each sentence carefully, consulting the items on the editing checklist below. Keep your preliminary notes and drafts and your reference books (such as this handbook and a dictionary) nearby as you work. Some reference works (such as *Dictionary.com* and *Merriam-Webster Online*) are also available online.

CHECKLIST

EDITING YOUR ESSAY

Grammar

❏ Do subjects and verbs agree? (**See 26a.**)

❏ Do pronouns and antecedents agree? (**See 26b.**)

❏ Are verb forms correct? (**See 22a.**)

❏ Are tense, mood, and voice of verbs logical and appropriate? (**See 22b–d.**)

❏ Have you used the appropriate case for each pronoun? (**See 21a–b.**)

❏ Are pronoun references clear and unambiguous? (**See 21c.**)

❏ Are adjectives and adverbs used correctly? (**See Ch. 23.**)

Punctuation

❑ Is end punctuation used correctly? (**See Ch. 29.**)

❑ Are commas used correctly? (**See Ch. 30.**)

❑ Are semicolons used correctly? (**See Ch. 31.**)

❑ Are apostrophes used correctly? (**See Ch. 32.**)

❑ Are quotation marks used where they are required? (**See Ch. 33.**)

❑ Are quotation marks used correctly with other punctuation marks? (**See 33e.**)

❑ Are other punctuation marks—colons, dashes, parentheses, brackets, slashes, and ellipses—used correctly? (**See Ch. 34.**)

Spelling

❑ Are all words spelled correctly? (**See Ch. 35.**)

Mechanics

❑ Is capitalization consistent with standard English usage? (**See Ch. 36.**)

❑ Are italics used correctly? (**See Ch. 37.**)

❑ Are hyphens used where required and placed correctly within and between words? (**See Ch. 38.**)

❑ Are abbreviations used where convention calls for their use? (**See Ch. 39.**)

❑ Are numerals and spelled-out numbers used appropriately? (**See Ch. 40.**)

2 Proofreading

After you have completed your editing, print out a final draft and **proofread,** rereading every word carefully to make sure neither you nor your computer missed any typos or other errors.

> **CLOSE-UP**
>
> **PROOFREADING STRATEGIES**
>
> To help you proofread more effectively, try using these strategies:
> - Read your paper aloud.
> - Have a friend read your paper aloud to you.
> - Read silently word by word, using your finger or a sheet of paper to help you keep your place.
> - Read your paper's sentences in reverse order, beginning with the last sentence.

Use the Search or Find command to look for usage errors you commonly make—for instance, confusing *it's* with *its, lay* with *lie, effect* with *affect, their* with *there,* or *too* with *to.* You can also uncover <u>sexist language</u> by searching for words like *he, his, him,* or *man.*

See 19e2

Keep in mind that neatness does not equal correctness. The clean text that your computer produces can mask flaws that might otherwise be apparent; for this reason, it is up to you to make sure spelling errors and typos do not slip by. When you have finished proofreading, check to make sure the final typed copy of your paper conforms to your instructor's format requirements.

CLOSE-UP

USING SPELL CHECKERS AND GRAMMAR CHECKERS

Although spell checkers and grammar checkers can make the process of editing and proofreading your papers easier, they have limitations. For this reason, neither a spell checker nor a grammar checker is a substitute for careful editing and proofreading.

♦ **Spell Checkers** A spell checker simply identifies strings of letters it does not recognize; it does *not* distinguish between homophones or spot every typographical error. For example, it does not recognize *there* in "They forgot there books" as incorrect, nor does it identify a typo that produces a correctly spelled word, such as *word* for *work* or *thing* for *think*. Moreover, a spell checker may not recognize every technical term, proper noun, or foreign word you may use.

♦ **Grammar Checkers** Grammar checkers scan documents for certain features (the number of words in a sentence, for example); however, they are not able to read a document to see if it makes sense. As a result, grammar checkers are not always accurate. For example, they may identify a long sentence as a run-on when it is, in fact, grammatically correct, and they generally advise against using passive voice—even in contexts where it is appropriate. Moreover, grammar checkers do not always supply answers; often, they ask questions—for example, whether *which* should be *that* or whether *which* should be preceded by a comma—that you must answer. In short, grammar checkers can guide your editing and proofreading, but you must be the one who decides when a sentence is (or is not) correct.

EXERCISE 4.6

Using the checklist on pages 50–51 as a guide, edit your essay. Then, proofread it carefully, give it an appropriate title, and print out your final draft.

EXERCISE 4.7

Review your responses to Exercises 2.1 and 2.2 in Chapter 2. Then, write a paragraph explaining how your personal writing process has changed since you wrote those responses.

4e Preparing a Final Draft

The annotated essay that follows is the final draft of Rebecca James's essay, which you first saw on pages 35–37. It incorporates the suggestions that her peer reviewers and her instructor made on her rough draft.

This final draft is very different from the rough draft of the essay. As she revised, Rebecca provided more examples to illustrate her points. She also moved from a focus on her own experiences using *Wikipedia* to a broader view of the issue, and she revised her thesis statement accordingly. In addition, she added specific information from sources to support her points, including parenthetical documentation and a works-cited list that conform to <u>MLA</u> documentation style. Finally, she added a <u>visual</u> (accompanied by a caption) to illustrate the specific shortcomings of the *Wikipedia* article she selected for the assignment.

See Ch. 47

See 4b2

James 1

Rebecca James

Professor Burks

English 101

14 November 2008

Wikipedia: Friend or Foe?

Introduction

When given a research assignment, students often turn first to *Wikipedia,* the popular free online encyclopedia. With 10,000,000 articles and counting, *Wikipedia* is a valuable source for anyone seeking general information on a topic. For college-level research, however, *Wikipedia* is most valuable when it serves not as an end in itself but as a gateway to reliable research sources.

Thesis statement

Background on wikis and *Wikipedia*

A wiki is an open-source Web site that allows users to edit and add to its content. Derived from a Hawaiian word meaning "quick," the term *wiki* conveys the swiftness and ease with which users can access information on such sites as well as contribute content ("Wiki"). With its slogan "Making Life Easier," *Wikipedia* has positioned itself as the most popular wiki, providing ever-increasing coverage of topics ranging from contemporary rock bands to obscure scientific and technical concepts. In accordance with the site's policies, users can edit existing articles and add new articles using *Wikipedia*'s editing tools, which do not require specialized programming knowledge or expertise.

Benefits of *Wikipedia*

Wikipedia offers several benefits to researchers seeking information on a topic. Longer *Wikipedia* articles often include comprehensive abstracts that summarize their content. Articles also often include hyperlinks to other *Wikipedia* articles. In fact, *Wikipedia*'s internal links, or "wikilinks," are so prevalent that they significantly increase *Wikipedia*'s Web presence. According to a 2007 report by the

James 2

Pew Internet & American Life Project, Internet users conducting a *Google* search most frequently click first on the *Wikipedia* link, which usually appears at the top of *Google*'s list of search results (Rainie and Tancer 3). This suggests that many Internet users are satisfied with what they find on *Wikipedia*. In addition, many *Wikipedia* articles contain external links to other print and online sources, including reliable, peer-reviewed sources. Finally, because its online format allows users to update its content at any time from any location, *Wikipedia* offers up-to-the-minute coverage of political and cultural events as well as information on popular culture topics that receive little or no attention from other sources. Even when the available information on a particular topic is sparse, *Wikipedia* allows users to create "stub" articles, which provide basic information that users can expand over time. In this way, *Wikipedia* offers an online forum for a developing bank of information on a range of topics.

Another benefit of *Wikipedia* is that it has the potential to become an even more comprehensive database of information. As *Wikipedia*'s "About" page claims, the site's articles "are continually edited and improved over time, and in general, this results in an upward trend of quality and a growing consensus over a fair and balanced representation of information." Using the criteria of accuracy, neutrality, completeness, and style, *Wikipedia* classifies its best articles as "featured" and its second-best articles as "good." In addition, *Wikipedia*'s policies state that the information in its articles must be verifiable and must be based on documented, preexisting research. Although no professional editorial board oversees the development of content within *Wikipedia*,

Benefits of
Wikipedia

James 3

users may be nominated into an editor role that allows
them to manage the process by which content is added and
updated. Users may also use the "Talk" page to discuss an
article's content and make suggestions for improvement.
With these control measures in place, some *Wikipedia* articles
are comparable to articles in professionally edited online
encyclopedias, such as *Encyclopaedia Britannica Online*.

Despite its numerous benefits and its growth potential,
Wikipedia falls short as an authoritative research source.
As the site's "Researching with *Wikipedia*" page concedes,
"not everything in *Wikipedia* is accurate, comprehensive,
or unbiased." Because anyone can create or edit *Wikipedia*
articles, they can be factually inaccurate, biased, and even
vandalized. Many *Wikipedia* articles, especially those that
are underdeveloped, do not supply citations to the sources
that support their claims. This absence of source information
should lead users to question the articles' reliability. It is true
that many underdeveloped *Wikipedia* articles include labels
to identify their particular shortcomings—for example, poor
grammar or missing documentation. Still, users cannot always
determine the legitimacy of information contained in the
Wikipedia articles they consult.

For college students, *Wikipedia* can provide useful
general information and links to helpful resources. For
example, accounting students will find that the *Wikipedia*
article "Certified Management Accountant" describes the
CMA's role in relation to other types of accounting positions.
In particular, this article can help students in introductory
accounting classes to assess the basic differences in focus and
responsibilities between a CMA and a CPA, or Certified Public
Accountant. The article contains several internal links to

Drawbacks
of *Wikipedia*

Strengths of
"CMA" *Wikipedia*
entry

James 4

related *Wikipedia* articles (including the article "Certified
Public Accountant") as well as a list of external links to
additional resources (such as the Web site for the Institute
of Management Accountants) In comparison, *Encyclopaedia
Britannica Online* does not contain an article on CMAs.

Although the *Wikipedia* article on CMAs provides helpful
general information on this accounting term, it is limited in
terms of reliability, scope, and style. The top of the article
displays three warning labels that identify the article's
shortcomings. As fig. 1 illustrates, the article's problems
include poor writing and a lack of cited sources. In addition,
the article would benefit from more internal links to related
Wikipedia articles. The specific limitations of the CMA article
reinforce the sense that *Wikipedia* best serves as a gateway to
more reliable and comprehensive research sources.

Weakness of
"CMA" *Wikipedia*
entry

Fig. 1. "Certified Management Accountant"; *Wikipedia*;
Wikimedia Foundation, 2009; Web; 7 Nov. 2008.

As with any encyclopedia article, *Wikipedia* articles
should be used as a starting point for research and as a link to
more in-depth sources. Moreover, *Wikipedia* articles can include
more factual errors, bias, and inconsistencies than professionally
edited encyclopedia articles. Although future enhancements
to the site may make it more reliable, *Wikipedia* users should
understand the current shortcomings of this popular online tool.

Conclusion

James 5

Works Cited

"About." *Wikipedia*. Wikimedia Foundation, 2008. Web. 28 Oct.
2008.

Rainie, Lee, and Bill Tancer. "Online Activities & Pursuits:
Wikipedia Users." Data memo. 24 Apr. 2007. Web. 1 Nov.
2008.

"Researching with *Wikipedia*." *Wikipedia*. Wikimedia Foundation,
2008. Web. 28 Oct. 2008.

"Wiki." *Encyclopaedia Britannica Online*. Encyclopaedia
Britannica, 2008. Web. 27 Oct. 2008.

4f   Creating a Writing Portfolio

A **writing portfolio,** a collection of coursework in print or electronic form, offers a unique opportunity for you to present your intellectual track record, showing where you've been and how you've developed as a writer. Increasingly, colleges have been using portfolios as a way to assess individual students' performance—and sometimes to see if the student body as a whole is meeting university standards.

The purpose of a writing portfolio is to demonstrate a writer's improvement and achievements. Portfolios allow writers to collect a body of writing in one place and to organize and present it in an effective, attractive format, giving the instructor a view of a student's writing that focuses more on the complete body of work than on individual assignments. While compiling individual items (sometimes called **artifacts**) to include in their portfolios, students reflect on their work and measure their progress; as they do so, they may improve their ability to evaluate their own work.

1   Assembling Your Portfolio

The first step in collecting artifacts for your portfolio is making sure you understand your instructor's requirements.

Many academic disciplines are moving toward electronic portfolios because, when posted on the Internet, they are immediately accessible to peers and instructors (as well as to prospective employers). However, not all material lends itself to an electronic format. You may need to supplement your electronic portfolio with print documents if they cannot be easily scanned.

CHECKLIST

SUGGESTED CONTENT FOR PORTFOLIOS

The following material might be included in a portfolio:

- ❑ **Table of contents or home page with internal hyperlinks** to artifacts in the portfolio
- ❑ <u>Reflective statement</u> in the form of a cover memo, letter, or essay, with internal hyperlinks to portfolio content
- ❑ **Writing assignments** that provide context for portfolio content
- ❑ **Planning material,** such as journal or blog entries and brainstorming notes
- ❑ **Shaping material,** such as thesis statements and outlines
- ❑ **Rough drafts with revisions** made by hand or with Track Changes
- ❑ **Scanned rough drafts with comments** made by peer reviewers, instructors, and writing center tutors
- ❑ **Photocopies of source material**
- ❑ **Final drafts**
- ❑ **External hyperlinks** to online source material and other Web sites that support the portfolio
- ❑ **Visuals** that enhance your documents
- ❑ **Audio and video clips of oral presentations**
- ❑ *PowerPoint* **slides**
- ❑ **Collaborative work,** with your own contributions clearly marked
- ❑ **A print or electronic résumé,** if the portfolio will be submitted to a prospective employer

See 4f2

EXERCISE 4.8

List the specific items you might include in a portfolio for one of your classes. Then, discuss your proposed portfolio content with a group of two or three other students, and consider whether you could add any of your classmates' suggested items to your list.

2 | Writing a Reflective Statement

Instructors usually require students to introduce their portfolios with a **reflective statement**—a memo, letter, or essay in which students honestly assess their writing improvement and achievements over a period of time. Reflective statements allow students to see themselves as writers and to discover both their strengths and the areas in which there is still room for improvement. Keep in mind that a reflective statement is not merely a summary of your completed work; it is an opportunity for you to look closely and analytically at your writing and thus to gain insights about your development as a writer.

CHECKLIST

WRITING A REFLECTIVE STATEMENT

In your reflective statement, try to answer the following questions:

❑ What skills or knowledge does each item in your portfolio demonstrate? How do these skills and knowledge relate to your instructor's goals? How do they relate to your own academic or professional goals?

❑ How are the individual items in your portfolio related? What have you learned about each assignment in the context of your entire portfolio?

❑ How have comments made by peer reviewers and by your instructor helped you revise your work?

❑ How, specifically, has your writing changed throughout the course? What skills will you continue to work on?

❑ Which items in your portfolio best represent your development as a writer? Now that you have some distance from these pieces, do you have new insights about your writing that you didn't have before?

Following is an excerpt from her portfolio's reflective statement, in which Rebecca James discusses her paper about *Wikipedia*.

Excerpt from Reflective Statement

What has always scared me even more than staring at a blank computer screen is working hard on an essay only to have it returned covered in red ink. The step-by-step *Wikipedia* essay assignment helped me to confront my fear of revision and realize that revision—including outside feedback—is essential to writing.

Comments I received in peer review showed me that feedback could be constructive. I was relieved to see my classmates' comments were tactful and not too critical of my paper's flaws. I think the electronic format was easier for me than face-to-face discussions would have been because I tend to get discouraged and start apologizing when I hear negative comments.

EXERCISE 4.9

Write a few paragraphs of a reflective statement in which you discuss what you learned as you wrote your research paper.

C H A P T E R 5

A **paragraph** is a group of related sentences. It may be complete in itself or part of a longer piece of writing.

5a   Writing Unified Paragraphs

A paragraph is **unified** when it develops a single main idea. The **topic sentence** states the main idea of the paragraph, and the other sentences in the paragraph support that idea.

1   Using Topic Sentences

A topic sentence usually comes at the beginning of a paragraph. Occasionally, a topic sentence may occur at the end of a paragraph, particularly if a writer wants to present an unexpected conclusion.

Topic Sentence at the Beginning   A topic sentence at the beginning of a paragraph tells readers what to expect and helps them to understand your paragraph's main idea immediately.

> I was a listening child, careful to hear the very different sounds of Spanish and English. Wide-eyed with hearing, I'd listen to sounds more than words. First, there were English (*gringo*) sounds. So many words were still unknown that when the butcher or the lady at the drugstore said something to me, exotic polysyllabic sounds would bloom in the midst of their sentences. Often the speech of people in public seemed to me very loud, booming with confidence. The man behind the counter would literally ask, "What can I do for you?" But by being so firm and so clear, the sound of his voice said that he was a *gringo;* he belonged in public society. (Richard Rodriguez, *Aria: A Memoir of a Bilingual Childhood*)

Topic Sentence at the End   A topic sentence at the end of a paragraph is useful if you are presenting an unusual or hard-to-accept idea. If you present facts and examples before you state your conclusion, you are more likely to convince readers that your conclusion is reasonable.

> These sprays, dusts and aerosols are now applied almost universally to farms, gardens, forests, and homes—nonselective chemicals that have the power to kill every insect, the "good" and the "bad," to still the song of birds and the leaping of fish in the streams, to coat the leaves with a deadly film, and to linger on in soil—all this though the intended target may be only a few weeds or insects. Can anyone believe it is possible to lay down such a barrage of poisons on the surface without making it unfit for life? They should not be called "insecticides," but "biocides." (Rachel Carson, "The Obligation to Endure," *Silent Spring*)

2 Testing for Unity

Each sentence in a paragraph should support the main idea that is stated in the topic sentence. The following paragraph is not unified because it includes sentences that do not support the main idea.

Paragraph Lacking Unity

One of the first problems I had as a college student was learning to use a computer. All students were required to buy a computer before school started. Throughout the first semester, we took a special course to teach us to use a computer. My laptop has a large memory and can do word processing and spreadsheets. It has a large screen and a DVD drive. My parents were happy that I had a computer, but they were concerned about the price. Tuition was high, and when they added in the price of the computer, it was almost out of reach. To offset expenses, I got a part-time job in the school library.

Sentences do not support main idea

When he revised, the writer deleted the sentences about his parents' financial situation and the computer's characteristics and added details related to his main idea (expressed in his topic sentence).

Revised Paragraph

One of the first problems I had as a college student was learning to use a computer. All first-year students were required to buy a computer before school started. Throughout the first semester, we took a special course to teach us to use the computer. In theory this system sounded fine, but in my case it was a disaster. In the first place, I had never owned a computer before. The closest I had ever come to having my own computer was the computer I shared with my sister. In the second place, I could not type well. And to make matters worse, many of the people in my computer orientation course already knew everything there was to know about operating a computer. By the end of the first week, I was convinced that I would never be able to keep up with them.

Sentences now support main idea

EXERCISE 5.1

The following paragraph is unified by one main idea, but that idea is not explicitly stated. Identify the main idea, write a topic sentence that expresses it, and decide where in the paragraph to place it.

"Lite" can mean that a product has fewer calories, or less fat, or less sodium, or it can simply mean that the product has a "light" color, texture, or taste. It may also mean none of these. Food can be advertised as 86 percent fat free when it is actually 50 percent fat because the term "fat free" is based on weight, and fat is extremely light. Another misleading term is "no cholesterol," which is found on some products that never had any cholesterol in the first place. Peanut butter, for example, contains no cholesterol—a fact that manufacturers have recently made an issue—but it is very high in fat and so would not be a very good food for most dieters. Sodium labeling presents still another problem. The terms "sodium free," "very low sodium," "low sodium," "reduced sodium," and "no salt added" have very specific meanings, frequently not explained on the packages on which they appear.

5b Writing Coherent Paragraphs

A paragraph is **coherent** when all its sentences clearly relate to one another. You can create coherence by arranging details according to an organizing principle, by using transitional words and phrases, by using parallel structure, and by repeating key words and phrases.

1 Arranging Details

Even if its sentences are all about the same subject, a paragraph lacks coherence if the sentences are not arranged according to a general organizing principle—that is, if they are not arranged *spatially, chronologically,* or *logically.*

♦ **Spatial order** establishes the perspective from which readers will view details. For example, an object or scene can be viewed from top to bottom or from near to far. Spatial order is central to **descriptive paragraphs**. See 5d2
♦ **Chronological order** presents events in sequence, using transitional words and phrases that establish the time order of events—*at first, yesterday, later, in 1930,* and so on. Chronological order is central to **narrative paragraphs** and **process paragraphs**. See 5d1, 4
♦ **Logical order** presents details or ideas in terms of their logical relationship to one another. Transitional words and phrases such as *first, second,* and *finally* establish these relationships and lead readers through the paragraphs. For example, a paragraph may move from *general to specific* or from *least important to most important.* Logical order is central to **exemplification paragraphs** and **comparison-and-contrast paragraphs**. See 5d3, 6

2 Using Transitional Words and Phrases

Transitional words and phrases clarify the relationships between sentences by identifying the spatial, chronological, and logical organizing principles discussed above. The following paragraph, which has no transitional words and phrases, illustrates just how important these words and phrases are.

Paragraph without Transitional Words and Phrases

Napoleon certainly made a change for the worse by leaving his small kingdom of Elba. He went back to Paris, and he abdicated for a second time. He fled to Rochefort in hope of escaping to America. He gave himself up to the English captain of the ship *Bellerophon*. He suggested that the Prince Regent grant him asylum, and he was refused. All he saw of England was the Devon coast and Plymouth Sound as he passed on to the remote island of St. Helena. He died on May 5, 1821, at the age of fifty-two.

In the narrative paragraph above, the topic sentence clearly states the main idea of the paragraph, and the rest of the sentences support this idea. Because of the absence of transitional words and phrases, however, readers cannot tell exactly how one event in the paragraph relates to another in time. Notice how much easier it is to read this passage once transitional words and phrases (such as *after, finally, once again,* and *in the end*) have been added.

Paragraph with Transitional Words and Phrases

Napoleon certainly made a change for the worse by leaving his small kingdom of Elba. After Waterloo, he went back to Paris, and he abdicated for a second time. A hundred days after his return from Elba, he fled to Rochefort in hope of escaping to America. Finally, he gave himself up to the English captain of the ship *Bellerophon*. Once again, he suggested that the Prince Regent grant him asylum, and once again, he was refused. In the end, all he saw of England was the Devon coast and Plymouth Sound as he passed on to the remote island of St. Helena. After six years of exile, he died on May 5, 1821, at the age of fifty-two. (Norman Mackenzie, *The Escape from Elba*)

FREQUENTLY USED TRANSITIONAL WORDS AND PHRASES

To Signal Sequence or Addition

again	in addition
also	moreover
besides	one . . . another
first . . . second . . . third	too
furthermore	

To Signal Time

afterward	later
as soon as	meanwhile
at first	next
at the same time	now
before	soon
earlier	subsequently
finally	then
in the meantime	until

To Signal Comparison

also	likewise
by the same token	similarly
in comparison	

To Signal Contrast

although	nevertheless
but	nonetheless
despite	on the contrary
even though	on the one hand . . . on the
however	other hand
in contrast	still
instead	whereas
meanwhile	yet

To Introduce Examples

for example	specifically
for instance	thus
namely	

To Signal Narrowing of Focus

after all	in particular
indeed	specifically
in fact	that is
in other words	

To Introduce Conclusions or Summaries

as a result	in summary
consequently	therefore
in conclusion	thus
in other words	to conclude

To Signal Concession

admittedly	naturally
certainly	of course
granted	

To Introduce Causes or Effects

accordingly	since
as a result	so
because	then
consequently	therefore
hence	

3 Using Parallel Structure

<u>Parallelism</u>—the use of matching words, phrases, clauses, or sentence structures to emphasize similar ideas—can increase coherence in a paragraph. Note in the following paragraph how parallel constructions beginning with "He was . . ." link Thomas Jefferson's accomplishments.

See 16c, 18a

Thomas Jefferson was born in 1743 and died at Monticello, Virginia, on July 4, 1826. During his eighty-four years, he accomplished a number of things. Although best known for his draft of the Declaration of Independence, Jefferson was a man of many talents who had a wide intellectual range. He was a patriot who was one of the revolutionary founders of the United States. He was a reformer who, when he was governor of Virginia, drafted the Statute for Religious Freedom. He was an innovator who drafted an ordinance for governing the West and devised the first decimal monetary system. He was a president who abolished internal taxes, reduced the national debt, and made the Louisiana Purchase. And, finally, he was an architect who designed Monticello and the University of Virginia. (student writer)

4   Repeating Key Words and Phrases

Repeating **key words and phrases**—those essential to meaning—throughout a paragraph connects the sentences to one another and to the paragraph's main idea. The following paragraph repeats the key word *mercury* to help readers focus on the subject.

Mercury poisoning is a problem that has long been recognized. "Mad as a hatter" refers to the condition prevalent among nineteenth-century workers who were exposed to mercury during the manufacturing of felt hats. Workers in many other industries, such as mining, chemicals, and dentistry, were similarly affected. In the 1950s and 1960s, there were cases of mercury poisoning in Minamata, Japan. Research showed that there were high levels of mercury pollution in streams and lakes surrounding the village. In the United States, this problem came to light in 1969, when a New Mexico family got sick from eating food tainted with mercury. Since then, pesticides containing mercury have been withdrawn from the market, and chemical wastes can no longer be dumped into the ocean. (student writer)

5   Achieving Coherence between Paragraphs

See 5e1 The same methods you use to establish coherence within paragraphs may also be used to link paragraphs in an essay. (You can also use a **transitional paragraph** as a bridge between two paragraphs.) The following group of related paragraphs shows how the strategies discussed in **5b1–4** create coherence from paragraph to paragraph.

A language may borrow a word directly or indirectly. A direct borrowing means that the borrowed item is a native word in the language it is borrowed from. *Festa* was borrowed directly from French and can be traced back to Latin *festa*. On the other hand, the word *algebra* was borrowed from Spanish, which in turn borrowed it from Arabic. Thus *algebra* was indirectly borrowed from Arabic, with Spanish as an intermediary.

Some languages are heavy borrowers. Albanian has borrowed so heavily that few native words are retained. On the other hand, most Native American languages have borrowed little from their neighbors.

English has borrowed extensively. Of the 20,000 or so words in common use, about three-fifths are borrowed. Of the 500 most frequently used words, however, only two-sevenths are borrowed, and because these "common" words are used over and over again in sentences, the actual frequency of appearance of native words is about 80 percent. Morphemes such as *and, be, have, it, of, the, to, will, you, on, that,* and *is* are all native to English. (Victoria Fromkin and Robert Rodman, *An Introduction to Language*)

These paragraphs are arranged according to a logical organizing principle, moving from the general concept of borrowing words to a specific language (English). In addition, each topic sentence repeats a variation of the word group *A language may borrow.* Throughout the three paragraphs, some form of this word group (as well as *word* and the names of various languages) appears in almost every sentence.

EXERCISE 5.2

A. Read the following paragraph, and determine how the author achieves coherence. Underline parallel elements, repeated words, and transitional words and phrases that link sentences.

> Some years ago the old elevated railway in Philadelphia was torn down and replaced by the subway system. This ancient El with its barnlike stations containing nut-vending machines and scattered food scraps had, for generations, been the favorite feeding ground of flocks of pigeons, generally one flock to a station along the route of the El. Hundreds of pigeons were dependent upon the system. They flapped in and out of its stanchions and steel work or gathered in watchful little audiences about the feet of anyone who rattled the peanut-vending machines. They even watched people who jingled change in their hands, and prospected for food under the feet of the crowds who gathered between trains. Probably very few among the waiting people who tossed a crumb to an eager pigeon realized that this El was like a food-bearing river, and that the life which haunted its banks was dependent upon the running of the trains with their human freight. (Loren Eiseley, *The Night Country*)

B. Revise the following student paragraph to make it more coherent.

> The theory of continental drift was first put forward by Alfred Wegener in 1912. The continents fit together like a gigantic jigsaw puzzle. The opposing Atlantic coasts, especially South America and Africa, seem to have been attached. He believed that at one time, probably 225 million years ago, there was one supercontinent. This

continent broke into parts that drifted into their present positions. The theory stirred controversy during the 1920s and eventually was ridiculed by the scientific community. In 1954, the theory was revived. The theory of continental drift is accepted as a reasonable geological explanation of the continental system. (student writer)

5c   Writing Well-Developed Paragraphs

A paragraph is **well developed** when it includes all the supporting information—examples, statistics, expert opinion, and so on—that readers need to understand and accept its main idea.

Keep in mind that length alone does not determine whether a paragraph is well developed. To determine the amount and kind of support you need, consider your audience, your purpose, and your paragraph's main idea.

1   Testing for Adequate Development

At first glance, the following paragraph may seem adequately developed.

Underdeveloped Paragraph

> From Thanksgiving until Christmas, children and their parents are bombarded by ads for violent toys and games. Toy manufacturers persist in thinking that only toys that appeal to children's aggressiveness will sell. Despite claims that they (unlike action toys) have educational value, video games have escalated the level of violence. The real question is why parents continue to buy these violent toys and games for their children. (student writer)

Although the paragraph above may seem to be adequately developed, it does not include enough support to convince readers that children and parents are "bombarded by ads for violent toys and games." For example, what kinds of toys appeal to a child's aggressive tendencies? What particular video games does the writer object to?

2   Revising Underdeveloped Paragraphs

You can strengthen underdeveloped paragraphs like the preceding one by adding specific examples that illustrate the points made in the paragraph.

Revised Paragraph (Examples Added)

> From Thanksgiving until Christmas, children and their parents are bombarded by ads for violent toys and games. Toy manufacturers persist in thinking that only toys that appeal to children's aggressiveness will
>
Examples   sell. One television commercial praises the merits of a commando team

that attacks and captures a miniature enemy base. Toy soldiers wear realistic uniforms and carry automatic rifles, pistols, knives, grenades, and ammunition. Another commercial shows laughing children shooting one another with plastic rocket launchers and tanklike vehicles. Despite claims that they (unlike action toys) have educational value, video games have escalated the level of violence. The most popular video games involve children in strikingly realistic combat simulations. One game lets children search out and destroy enemy fighters on the ground and in the air. Other   Examples best-selling games graphically simulate hand-to-hand combat on city streets and feature dismembered bodies and the sound of breaking bones. The real question is why parents continue to buy these violent toys and games for their children.

EXERCISE 5.3

Write a paragraph for two of the following topic sentences. Be sure to include all the examples and other support necessary to develop the paragraphs adequately. Assume that you are writing your paragraphs for the students in your composition class.

1. First-year students can take specific steps to make sure that they are successful in college.
2. Setting up a first apartment can be quite a challenge.
3. Whenever I get depressed, I think of _____, and I feel better.
4. The person I admire most is _____.
5. If I won the lottery, I would do three things.

5d   Patterns of Paragraph Development

Patterns of paragraph development—*narration, exemplification,* and so on—reflect the way a writer arranges material to express ideas most effectively.

1   Narration

A **narrative** paragraph tells a story by presenting events in chronological (time) order. Most narratives move in a logical, orderly sequence from beginning to end, from first event to last. Clear transitional words and phrases (*later, after that*) and time markers (*in 1990, two years earlier, the next day*) establish the chronological sequence.

My academic career almost ended as soon as it began when, three   Topic weeks after I arrived at college, I decided to pledge a fraternity. By   sentence midterms, I was wearing a pledge cap and saying "Yes, sir" to every   establishes fraternity brother I met. When classes were over, I ran errands for the   subject of fraternity members, and after dinner I socialized and worked on projects   narrative with the other people in my pledge class. In between these activities,   Sequence of events

I tried to study. Somehow I managed to write papers, take tests, and attend lectures. By the end of the semester, though, my grades had slipped, and I was exhausted. It was then that I began to ask myself some important questions. I realized that I wanted to be popular, but not at the expense of my grades and my future career. At the beginning of my second semester, I dropped out of the fraternity and got a job in the biology lab. Looking back, I realize that it was then that I actually began to grow up. (student writer)

2 Description

A **descriptive** paragraph communicates how something looks, sounds, smells, tastes, or feels. The most natural arrangement of details in a description reflects the way you actually look at a person, scene, or object: near to far, top to bottom, side to side, or front to back. This arrangement of details is made clear by transitions that identify precise spatial relationships: *next to, near, beside, under, above,* and so on.

Sometimes a descriptive paragraph (such as the one below) does not have an explicitly stated topic sentence. Instead, it is unified by a **dominant impression**—the effect created by all the details in the description.

No topic sentence

Details create dominant impression

When you are inside the jungle, away from the river, the trees vault out of sight. It is hard to remember to look up the long trunks and see the fans, strips, fronds, and sprays of glossy leaves. Inside the jungle you are more likely to notice the snarl of climbers and creepers round the trees' boles, the flowering bromeliads and epiphytes in every bough's crook, and the fantastic silk-cotton tree trunks thirty or forty feet across, trunks buttressed in flanges of wood whose curves can make three high walls of a room—a shady, loamy-aired room where you would gladly live, or die. Butterflies, iridescent blue, striped, or clear-winged, thread the jungle paths at eye level. And at your feet is a swath of ants bearing triangular bits of green leaf. The ants with their leaves look like a wide fleet of sailing dinghies—but they don't quit. In either direction they wobble over the jungle floor as far as the eye can see. I followed them off the path as far as I dared, and never saw an end to ants or to those luffing chips of green they bore. (Annie Dillard, "In the Jungle")

3 Exemplification

An **exemplification** paragraph supports a topic sentence with a series of specific examples (or, sometimes, with a single extended example). These examples can be drawn from personal observation or experience or from research.

Topic sentence identifies paragraph's main idea

Illiterates cannot travel freely. When they attempt to do so, they encounter risks that few of us can dream of. They cannot read traffic signs and, while they often learn to recognize and to decipher symbols, they cannot manage street names which they haven't seen before. The same is true for bus and subway stops. While ingenuity can sometimes help a man or woman to discern directions from familiar landmarks, buildings, cemeteries, churches, and *Series of* the like, most illiterates are virtually immobilized. They seldom wander past *examples* the streets and neighborhoods they know. Geographical paralysis becomes a bitter metaphor for their entire existence. They are immobilized in almost every sense we can imagine. They can't move up. They can't move out. They cannot see beyond. Illiterates may take an oral test for drivers' permits in most sections of America. It is a questionable concession. Where will they go? How will they get there? How will they get home? Could it be that some of us might like it better if they stayed where they belong? (Jonathan Kozol, *Illiterate America*)

4 Process

Process paragraphs describe how something works, presenting a series of steps in strict chronological order. The topic sentence identifies the process, and the rest of the paragraph presents the steps involved. Transitional words such as *first, then, next, after this,* and *finally* link steps in the process.

Members of the court have disclosed, however, the general way the con- *Topic* ference is conducted. It begins at ten a.m. and usually runs on until late after- *sentence* noon. At the start each justice, when he enters the room, shakes hands with *identifies* all others there (thirty-six handshakes altogether). The custom, dating back *process* generations, is evidently designed to begin the meeting at a friendly level, no matter how heated the intellectual differences may be. The conference takes *Steps in* up, first, the applications for review—a few appeals, many more petitions for *process* certiorari. Those on the Appellate Docket, the regular paid cases, are considered first, then the pauper's applications on the Miscellaneous Docket. (If any of these are granted, they are then transferred to the Appellate Docket.) After this the justices consider, and vote on, all the cases argued during the preceding Monday through Thursday. These are tentative votes, which may be and quite often are changed as the opinion is written and the problem thought through more deeply. There may be further discussion at later conferences before the opinion is handed down. (Anthony Lewis, *Gideon's Trumpet*)

CLOSE-UP

INSTRUCTIONS

When a process paragraph presents **instructions** to enable readers to actually perform the process, it is written in the present tense and in the imperative mood— "*Remove* the cover . . . and *check* the valve."

---

5 Cause and Effect

A **cause-and-effect** paragraph explores causes or predicts or describes results; sometimes a single cause-and-effect paragraph does both. Clear transitional words and phrases such as *one cause, another cause, a more important result, because,* and *as a result* convey the cause-and-effect relationship.

Some paragraphs examine causes.

The main reason that a young baby sucks his thumb seems to be that he hasn't had enough sucking at the breast or bottle to satisfy his sucking needs. Dr. David Levy pointed out that babies who are fed every 3 hours don't suck their thumbs as much as babies fed every 4 hours, and that babies who have cut down on nursing time from 20 minutes to 10 minutes . . . are more likely
to suck their thumbs than babies who still have to work for 20 minutes. Dr. Levy fed a litter of puppies with a medicine dropper so that they had no chance to suck during their feedings. They acted just the same as babies who don't get enough chance to suck at feeding time. They sucked their own and each other's paws and skin so hard that the fur came off. (Benjamin Spock, *Baby and Child Care*)

Other paragraphs focus on effects.

On December 8, 1941, the day after the Japanese attack on Pearl Harbor in Hawaii, my grandfather barricaded himself with his family—my grandmother, my teenage mother, her two sisters and two brothers—inside of his home in La'ie, a sugar plantation village on Oahu's North Shore. This was my maternal grandfather, a man most villagers called by his last name, Kubota. It could mean either "Wayside Field" or else "Broken Dreams," depending on which ideograms he used. Kubota ran La'ie's general store, and the previous
night, after a long day of bad news on the radio, some locals had come by, pounded on the front door, and made threats. One was said to have brandished a machete. They were angry and shocked, as the whole nation was in the aftermath of the surprise attack. Kubota was one of the few Japanese Americans in the village and president of the local Japanese language school. He had become a target for their rage and suspicion. A wise man, he locked all his doors and windows and did not open his store the next day, but stayed closed and waited for news from some official. (Garrett Hongo, "Kubota")

6   Comparison and Contrast

Comparison-and-contrast paragraphs examine the similarities and differences between two subjects. **Comparison** focuses on similarities; **contrast** emphasizes differences.

Comparison-and-contrast paragraphs can be organized in one of two ways: **point-by-point** or **subject-by-subject.**

Point-by-point comparisons discuss two subjects together, alternating points about one subject with comparable points about the other.

There are two Americas. One is the America of Lincoln and Adlai Stevenson; the other is the America of Teddy Roosevelt and the modern superpatriots. One is generous and humane, the other narrowly egotistical; one is self-critical, the other self-righteous; one is sensible, the other romantic; one
is good-humored, the other solemn; one is inquiring, the other pontificating; one is moderate, the other filled with passionate intensity; one is judicious and the other arrogant in the use of great power. (J. William Fulbright, *The Arrogance of Power*)

Subject-by-subject comparisons treat one subject completely and then move on to the other subject. In the following paragraph, the writer shifts from one subject to the other with the transitional word *however*.

> First, it is important to note that men and women regard conversation quite differently. For women it is a passion, a sport, an activity even more important to life than eating because it doesn't involve weight gain. The first sign of closeness among women is when they find themselves engaging in endless, secretless rounds of conversation with one another. And as soon as a woman begins to relax and feel comfortable in a relationship with a man, she tries to have that type of conversation with him as well. However, the first sign that a man is feeling close to a woman is when he admits that he'd rather she please quiet down so he can hear the TV. A man who feels truly intimate with a woman often reserves for her and her alone the precious gift of one-word answers. Everyone knows that the surest way to spot a successful long-term relationship is to look around a restaurant for the table where no one is talking. Ah . . . now that's real love. (Merrill Markoe, "Men, Women, and Conversation")

Topic sentence establishes comparison

First subject discussed

Second subject discussed

7 Division and Classification

Division paragraphs take a single item and break it into its components.

> The blood can be divided into four distinct components: plasma, red cells, white cells, and platelets. Plasma is 90 percent water and holds a great number of substances in suspension. It contains proteins, sugars, fat, and inorganic salts. Plasma also contains urea and other by-products from the breaking down of proteins, hormones, enzymes, and dissolved gases. In addition, plasma contains the red blood cells that give it color, the white cells, and the platelets. The red cells are most numerous; they get oxygen from the lungs and release it in the tissues. The less numerous white cells are part of the body's defense against invading organisms. The platelets, which occur in almost the same number as white cells, are responsible for clotting. (student writer)

Topic sentence identifies components

Components discussed

Classification paragraphs take many separate items and group them into categories according to the qualities or characteristics they share.

> Charles Babbage, an English mathematician, reflecting in 1830 on what he saw as the decline of science at the time, distinguished among three major kinds of scientific fraud. He called the first "forging," by which he meant complete fabrication—the recording of observations that were never made. The second category he called "trimming"; this consists of manipulating the data to make them look better, or, as Babbage wrote, "in clipping off little bits here and there from those observations which differ most in excess from the mean and in sticking them on to those which are too small." His third category was data selection, which he called "cooking"—the choosing of those data that fitted the researcher's hypothesis and the discarding of those that did not. To this day, the serious discussion of scientific fraud has not improved on Babbage's typology. (Morton Hunt, *New York Times Magazine*)

Topic sentence establishes categories

Categories discussed

8 Definition

Definition paragraphs develop formal definitions by using other patterns—
for instance, defining *happiness* by telling a story (narration) or defining a
diesel engine by telling how it works (process).

The following definition paragraph is developed by means of exemplification: it begins with a formal definition of *gadget* and then presents an
example.

Topic
sentence
gives formal
definition

Definition
expanded
with
examples

> A gadget is a small device that is nearly always novel in design or con-
> cept and it often has no proper name. For example, the semaphore which
> signals the arrival of the mail in our rural mailbox certainly has no proper
> name. It is a contrivance consisting of a piece of shingle. Call it what you
> like, it saves us frequent frustrating trips to the mailbox in winter when
> you have to dress up and wade through snow to get there. That's a gadget!
> (*Smithsonian*)

EXERCISE 5.4

A. Read each of the following paragraphs, and then answer these questions:
In general terms, how could each paragraph be developed further? What
pattern of development might be used in each case?

B. Choose one paragraph, and rewrite it to develop it further.

▶ 1. Many new words and expressions have entered the English language
in the last ten years or so. Some of them come from the world of computers. Others come from popular music. Still others have politics as
their source. There are even some expressions that have their origins in
films or television shows.

2. Making a good spaghetti sauce is not a particularly challenging task.
First, assemble the basic ingredients: garlic, onion, mushrooms, green
pepper, and ground beef. Sauté these ingredients in a large saucepan.
Then, add canned tomatoes, tomato paste, and water, and stir. At this
point, you are ready to add the spices: oregano, parsley, basil, and salt
and pepper. Don't forget a bay leaf! Simmer for about two hours, and
serve over spaghetti.

3. High school and college are not at all alike. Courses are a lot easier in
high school, and the course load is lighter. In college, teachers expect
more from students; they expect higher quality work, and they assign
more of it. Assignments tend to be more difficult and more comprehensive, and deadlines are usually shorter. Finally, college students
tend to be more focused on a particular course of study—even a particular career—than high school students are.

5e Writing Special Kinds of Paragraphs

So far, this chapter has focused on **body paragraphs,** the paragraphs that carry the weight of your essay's discussion. Other kinds of paragraphs—*transitional paragraphs, introductory paragraphs,* and *concluding paragraphs*—have special functions in an essay.

1 Transitional Paragraphs

A **transitional paragraph** connects one section of an essay to another. At their simplest, transitional paragraphs can be single sentences that move readers from one point to the next.

What is true for ants is also true for people.

More often, writers use transitional paragraphs to summarize what they have already said before they move on to a new point. The following transitional paragraph uses a series of questions to sum up some of the ideas the writer has been discussing. In the next part of his essay, he goes on to answer these questions.

> Can we bleed off the mass of humanity to other worlds? Right now the number of human beings on Earth is increasing by 80 million per year, and each year that number goes up by 1 and a fraction percent. Can we really suppose that we can send 80 million people per year to the Moon, Mars, and elsewhere, and engineer those worlds to support those people? And even so, nearly remain in the same place ourselves? (Isaac Asimov, "The Case against Man")

2 Introductory Paragraphs

An **introductory paragraph** prepares readers for the essay to follow. It typically introduces the subject, narrows it, and then states the essay's thesis.

> Christine was just a girl in one of my classes. I never knew much about her except that she was strange. She didn't talk much. Her hair was dyed black and purple, and she wore heavy black boots and a black turtleneck sweater, even in the summer. She was attractive—in spite of the ring she wore through her left eyebrow—but she never seemed to care what the rest of us thought about her. Like the rest of my classmates, I didn't really want to get close to her. It was only when we were assigned to do our chemistry project together that I began to understand why Christine dressed the way she did. (student writer)

To arouse their audience's interest, writers may vary this direct approach by using one of the following introductory strategies.

Quotation or Series of Quotations

When Mary Cassatt's father was told of her decision to become a painter, he said: "I would rather see you dead." When Edgar Degas saw a show of Cassatt's etchings, his response was: "I am not willing to admit that a woman can draw that well." When she returned to Philadelphia after twenty-eight years abroad, having achieved renown as an Impressionist painter and the esteem of Degas, Huysmans, Pissarro, and Berthe Morisot, the *Philadelphia Ledger* reported: "Mary Cassatt, sister of Mr. Cassatt, president of the Pennsylvania Railroad, returned from Europe yesterday. She has been studying painting in France and owns the smallest Pekingese dog in the world." (Mary Gordon, "Mary Cassatt")

Question or Series of Questions

Of all the disputes agitating the American campus, the one that seems to me especially significant is that over "the canon." What should be taught in the humanities and social sciences, especially in introductory courses? What is the place of the classics? How shall we respond to those professors who attack "Eurocentrism" and advocate "multiculturalism"? This is not the sort of tedious quarrel that now and then flutters through the academy; it involves matters of public urgency. I propose to see this dispute, at first, through a narrow, even sectarian lens, with the hope that you will come to accept my reasons for doing so. (Irving Howe, "The Value of the Canon")

Definition

Moles are collections of cells that can appear on any part of the body. With occasional exceptions, moles are absent at birth. They first appear in the early years of life, between ages two and six. Frequently, moles appear at puberty. New moles, however, can continue to appear throughout life. During pregnancy, new moles may appear and old ones darken. There are three major designations of moles, each with its own unique distinguishing characteristics. (student writer)

Controversial Statement

Many Americans would probably be surprised to learn that Head Start has not been an unqualified success. Founded in 1965, the Head Start program provides early childhood education, social services, and medical check-ups to poor children across the US. In recent years, it has also focused on the children of migrant workers and on children who are homeless. For the most part, Americans view Head Start not just as a success but also as a model for other social programs. What many people do not know, however, is that although Head Start is a short-term success for many children, the ambitious long-term goals of the program have not been met. For this reason, it may be time to consider making significant changes in the way Head Start is run. (student writer)

INTRODUCTORY PARAGRAPHS

An introductory paragraph should make readers want to read further. For this reason, avoid opening statements that simply announce your subject ("In my paper, I will talk about Lady Macbeth") or that undercut your credibility ("I don't know much about alternative energy sources, but I would like to present my opinion about the subject").

3 Concluding Paragraphs

A **concluding paragraph** typically begins with specifics—reviewing the essay's main points, for example—and then moves to more general statements. Whenever possible, it should end with a sentence that readers will remember.

> As an Arab-American, I feel I have the best of two worlds. I'm proud to be part of the melting pot, proud to contribute to the tremendous diversity of cultures, customs and traditions that makes this country unique. But Arab-bashing—public acceptance of hatred and bigotry—is something no American can be proud of. (Ellen Mansoor Collier, "I Am Not a Terrorist")

Writers may also use one of the following concluding strategies to end their essays.

STRATEGIES FOR EFFECTIVE CONCLUSIONS

Prediction

Looking ahead, [we see that] prospects may not be quite as dismal as they seem. As a matter of fact, we are not doing so badly. It is something of a miracle that creatures who evolved as nomads in an intimate, small-band, wide-open-spaces context manage to get along at all as villagers or surrounded by strangers in cubicle apartments. Considering that our genius as a species is adaptability, we may yet learn to live closer and closer to one another, if not in utter peace, then far more peacefully than we do today. (John Pheiffer, "Seeking Peace, Making War")

Warning

The Internet is the twenty-first century's talking drum, the very kind of grass-roots communication tool that has been such a powerful source of education and culture for our people since slavery. But this talking drum we have not yet learned to play. Unless we master the new information technology to build and deepen the forms of social connection that a tragic history has eroded, African-Americans will face a form of cybersegregation in the next century as devastating to our aspirations as Jim Crow segregation was to those of our ancestors. But this time, the fault will be our own. (Henry Louis Gates Jr., "One Internet, Two Nations")

(*continued*)

STRATEGIES FOR EFFECTIVE CONCLUSIONS (*continued*)

Recommendation for Action

Computers have revolutionized learning in ways that we have barely begun to appreciate. We have experienced enough, however, to recognize the need to change our thinking about our purposes, methods, and outcome of higher education. Rather than resisting or postponing change, we need to anticipate and learn from it. We must harness the technology and use it to educate our students more effectively than we have been doing. Otherwise, we will surrender our authority to those who can. (Peshe Kuriloff, "If John Dewey Were Alive Today, He'd Be a Webhead")

Quotation

When we let freedom ring, when we let it ring from every village and every hamlet, from every state and every city, we will be able to speed up that day when all of God's children, black men and white men, Jews and Gentiles, Protestants and Catholics, will be able to join hands and sing in the words of the old Negro spiritual, "Free at last! Free at last! Thank God almighty, we are free at last!" (Martin Luther King Jr., "I Have a Dream")

CLOSE-UP

CONCLUDING PARAGRAPHS

Because a dull conclusion can weaken an essay, try to make your conclusion as interesting as you can. Your conclusion is your essay's last word, so don't waste time repeating your introduction in different words or apologizing or undercutting your credibility ("I may not be an expert" or "At least, this is my opinion"). And remember, your conclusion should not introduce new points or go off in new directions.

Thinking Critically   CHAPTER 6

See
Ch. 7 As you read and write essays, you should carefully consider the ideas they present. This is especially true in <u>argumentative essays</u>—those that take a stand in a debatable thesis.

Although some writers try their best to be fair, others attempt to manipulate readers by using emotionally charged language, by unfairly emphasizing certain facts over others, and by using flawed logic. For this reason, it is particularly important that you **think critically** when you read and write. Specifically, you need to distinguish fact from opinion, evaluate supporting evidence, detect bias, evaluate visuals, and understand the basic principles of inductive and deductive reasoning.

6a Distinguishing Fact from Opinion

A **fact** is a verifiable statement that something is true or that something occurred. An **opinion** is a personal judgment or belief that can never be substantiated beyond any doubt and is, therefore, debatable.

Fact: Measles is a potentially deadly disease.

Opinion: All children should be vaccinated against measles.

An opinion may be **supported** or **unsupported.**

Unsupported Opinion: All children in Pennsylvania should be vaccinated against measles.

Supported Opinion: Despite the fact that an effective measles vaccine is widely available, several unvaccinated Pennsylvania children have died of measles each year since 1992. States that have instituted vaccination programs have had no deaths in the same time period. For this reason, all children in Pennsylvania should be vaccinated against measles.

As the examples above show, supported opinion is more convincing than unsupported opinion. Remember, however, that support can only make an opinion more convincing; it cannot turn an opinion into a fact.

Opinions can be supported with **examples, statistics,** or **expert opinion.**

Examples

The American Civil Liberties Union is an organization that has been unfairly characterized as left wing. It is true that it has opposed prayer in the public schools, defended conscientious objectors, and challenged police methods of conducting questioning and searches of suspects. However, it has also backed the antiabortion group Operation Rescue in a police brutality suit and presented a legal brief in support of a Republican politician accused of violating an ethics law.

Statistics

A recent National Institute of Mental Health study concludes that mentally ill people account for more than 30 percent of the homeless population (Young 27). Because so many homeless people have psychiatric disabilities, the federal government should seriously consider expanding the state mental hospital system.

Expert Opinion

Clearly no young soldier ever really escapes the emotional consequences of war. As William Manchester, noted historian and World War II combat veteran, observes in his essay "Okinawa: The Bloodiest Battle of All," "the invisible wounds remain" (72).

See
Chs.
47–48 *Note:* Remember that all words and ideas that you borrow from a source must be <u>documented</u>.

EXERCISE 6.1

Some of the following statements are facts; others are opinions. Identify each fact with the letter *F* and each opinion with the letter *O*. Then, consider what kind of information, if any, could support each opinion.

▶ 1. The incidence of violent crime fell in the first six months of this year.
▶ 2. Tougher gun laws and more police officers led to a decrease in crime early in the year.
▶ 3. The television rating system uses a system similar to the familiar movie rating codes to let parents know how appropriate a certain show might be for their children.
▶ 4. The television rating system would be better if it gave specifics about the violence, sexual content, and language in rated television programs.
▶ 5. Affirmative action laws and policies have helped women and minority group members advance in the workplace.
6. Affirmative action policies have outlived their usefulness.
7. Women who work are better off today than they were twenty years ago.
8. The wage gap between men and women in similar jobs is smaller now than it was twenty years ago.
9. The Charles River and Boston Harbor are less polluted than they were ten years ago.
10. We do not need to worry about environmental legislation anymore because we have made great advances in cleaning up our environment.

6b Evaluating Supporting Evidence

See
7b1 The examples, statistics, or expert opinion that a writer uses to support a statement is called **evidence.** The more reliable the <u>supporting evidence</u>, the more willing readers will be to accept a statement.

All evidence, however—no matter what kind—must be *accurate, sufficient, representative,* and *relevant.*

♦ Evidence is likely to be **accurate** if it comes from a reliable source. Such a source quotes *exactly* and does not present remarks out of context. It also supports points with examples, statistics, and expert testimony from other trustworthy sources.
♦ Evidence is likely to be **sufficient** if a writer presents an adequate amount of information. It is not enough, for instance, for a writer to cite just one example in an attempt to demonstrate that most poor women do not receive adequate prenatal care. Similarly, the opinion of a single expert, no matter how reputable, is not enough to support this position.

♦ Evidence is likely to be **representative** if it reflects a fair range of sources and viewpoints. Writers should not just choose evidence that supports their position and ignore evidence that docs not. In other words, they should not permit their biases to govern their choice of evidence. For example, a writer who is making the point that the United States Congress should pass a bill to grant limited amnesty to undocumented immigrants should not include only evidence from sources that agree with this position. The writer should also address the arguments against this position and point out their weaknesses and inaccuracies.

♦ Evidence is likely to be **relevant** if it applies to the case being discussed. For example, a writer cannot support the position that airport security in Europe has discouraged terrorist activity by citing examples from the United States.

EXERCISE 6.2

Read the following student paragraph, and evaluate its supporting evidence.

The United States is becoming more and more violent every day. I was talking to my friend Gayle, and she mentioned that a guy her roommate knows was attacked at dusk and had his skull crushed by the barrel of a gun. Later she heard that he was in the hospital with a blood clot in his brain. Two friends of mine were walking home from a party when they were attacked by armed men right outside the A-Plus Mini Market. These two examples make it very clear to me how violent our nation is becoming. My English professor, who is in his fifties, remembers a few similar violent incidents occurring when he was growing up, and he was even mugged in London last year. He believes that if more London police carried guns, the city would be safer. Two of the twenty-five people in our class have been the victims of violent crime, and I feel lucky that I am not one of them.

6c   Detecting Bias

Bias is the tendency to base conclusions on preconceived ideas or on emotions rather than on evidence. As a critical reader, you should be aware that bias may sometimes lead writers to see what they want to see and therefore to select only that evidence that is consistent with their own points of view.

CLOSE-UP

DETECTING BIAS

When you read, look for the following kinds of bias:

♦ **The Writer's Stated Beliefs** If a writer declares herself to be a strong opponent of childhood vaccinations, this statement should alert you to the possibility that the writer may not present a balanced view of the subject.

(*continued*)

DETECTING BIAS (*continued*)

♦ **Sexist or Racist Statements** A writer who assumes all engineers are male or all nurses are female reflects a clear bias. A researcher who assumes certain racial or ethnic groups are intellectually superior to others is also likely to present a biased view.
♦ **Slanted Language** Some writers use **slanted language**—language that contains value judgments—to influence readers' reactions. For example, a newspaper article that states "The politician gave an impassioned speech" gives one impression; the statement "The politician delivered a diatribe" gives another.
♦ **Biased Tone** The tone of a piece of writing indicates a writer's attitude toward readers or toward his or her subject. For example, an angry tone might suggest that the writer is overstating his or her case, while a dismissive tone might suggest that the writer is ignoring opposing points of view.
♦ **Biased Choice of Evidence** Frequently, the examples or statistics cited in a piece of writing reveal the writer's bias. For example, a writer may include only examples that support a point and leave out examples that may contradict it.
♦ **Biased Choice of Experts** A writer should cite experts who represent a fair range of opinion. If, for instance, a writer assessing the president's policy on stem-cell research includes only statements by experts who vehemently oppose this procedure, he or she is presenting a biased case.

EXERCISE 6.3

Read the following essay about home schooling, a movement supported by parents who have abandoned traditional schools in favor of teaching their children at home. After evaluating the quality of the writer's supporting evidence, identify her biases, and decide if these biases undercut her argument in any way.

Questioning the Motives of Home-Schooling Parents

America's most famous home-schooling parents at the moment are Andrea Yates and JoAnn McGuckin. Yates allegedly drowned her five children in a Houston suburb. McGuckin was arrested and charged with child neglect in Idaho. Her six kids barricaded themselves in the family's hovel when child-care workers came to remove them.

The intention here is not to smear the parents who instruct 1.5 million mostly normal children at home. But a social phenomenon that isolates children from the outside world deserves closer inspection.

The home-schooling movement runs an active propaganda machine. It portrays its followers in the most flattering terms—as bulwarks against the moral decay found in public, and presumably private, schools. Although now associated with conservative groups, modern home-schooling got its start among left-wing dropouts in the '60s.

Home-schooled students do tend to score above average on standardized tests. The most likely reason, however, is that most of the parents are themselves upper income and well educated. Students from those backgrounds also do well in traditional schools.

Advocates of home-schooling have become a vocal lobbying force in Washington, D.C. Children taught at home may be socially isolated, but the parents have loads of interaction. Membership in the anti-public-education brigade provides much comradeship.

The mouthpiece for the movement, the Home School Legal Defense Association (*www.hslda.org*), posts articles on its Web site with headlines like, "The Clinging Tentacles of Public Education." Trashing the motivations of professional teachers provides much sport.

Perhaps the time has come to question the motives of some home-schooling parents. Are the parents protecting their children from a cesspool of bad values in the outside world? Or are the parents just people who can't get along with others? Are they "taking charge" of their children's education? Or are they taking their children captive?

Yates and McGuckin are, of course, extreme cases and probably demented. But a movement that insists on parents' rights to do as they wish with their children gives cover for the unstable, for narcissists and for child-abusers.

In West Akron, Ohio, reporters would interview Thomas Lavery on how he successfully schooled his five children in their home. The kids all had top grades and fine manners. They recalled how their father loved to strut before the media.

Eventually, however, the police came for Lavery and charged him with nine counts of child endangerment. According to his children, Lavery smashed a daughter over the head with a soda can after she did poorly in a basketball game. Any child who wet a bed would spend the night alone, locked in the garage.

A child who spilled milk had to drop on his or her knees and lick it up from the floor. And in an especially creepy attempt to establish himself as master, Lavery would order his children to damn the name of God.

The best way to maintain the sanctity of a family madhouse is to keep the inmates inside. Allowing children to move about in the world could jeopardize the deal.

In some cases, it might also prevent tragedy. Suppose one of Andrea Yates' children had gone to a school and told a teacher of the mother's spiraling mental state. The teacher could have called a child-welfare officer and five little lives might have been saved.

Putting the horror stories aside, there's something sad about home-schooled children. During the New Hampshire presidential primary race, I attended an event directed at high-school and college students. The students were a lively bunch, circulating around the giant room, debating and arguing. Except for my table.

About four young people and a middle-aged woman were just sitting there. The teenagers were clearly intelligent and well behaved. I tried to chat, but they seemed wary of talking with strangers. The woman proudly informed me that they were her children and home-schooled.

The Home School Legal Defense Association condemns government interference in any parent's vision of how a child might be educated. The group's chairman, Michael Farris, says things like, "We just want to say to the government: We are doing a good job, so leave us alone."

Could that be where JoAnn McGuckin found her twisted sense of grievance? "Those are my kids," she said as Idaho removed her children from their filthy home. "The state needs to mind its own business." (Froma Harrop, *Seattle Times*)

See
Ch. 7

6d Understanding Inductive Reasoning

Argumentative essays rely primarily on **logic**—the study of the principles of clear reasoning. Logical reasoning enables you to construct arguments that reach conclusions in a systematic and persuasive way. Before you can evaluate (or write) arguments, you need to understand the basic principles of inductive and deductive reasoning.

See
6e

1 Moving from Specific to General

Inductive reasoning moves from specific facts, observations, or experiences to a general conclusion. Writers use inductive reasoning when they address a skeptical audience that requires a great deal of evidence before it will accept a conclusion. You can see how inductive reasoning operates by studying the following list of specific statements that focus on the relationship between SAT scores and admissions at one particular liberal arts college.

♦ The SAT is an admission requirement for all applicants.
♦ High school grades and rank in class are also examined.
♦ Nonacademic factors, such as sports, activities, and interests, are taken into account as well.
♦ Special attention is given to the applications of athletes, minorities, and children of alumni.
♦ Fewer than 52 percent of applicants for a recent class with SAT verbal scores between 600 and 700 were accepted.
♦ Fewer than 39 percent of applicants with similar math scores were accepted.
♦ Approximately 18 percent of applications with SAT verbal scores between 450 and 520 and about 19 percent of applicants with similar SAT math scores were admitted.

After reading the statements above, you can use inductive reasoning to reach the general conclusion that although they are important, SAT scores are not the single factor that determines whether or not a student is admitted to this college.

2 Making Inferences

No matter how much evidence you present, an inductive conclusion is never certain, only probable. The best you can do is present a convincing case to readers. You arrive at an inductive conclusion by making an **inference,** a statement about the unknown based on the known. In order to bridge the gap that exists between your specific observations and your general conclusion, you have to make an **inductive leap,** which enables you to make a reasonable inference from the available information. If you have presented enough specific evidence, this gap will be relatively small and your readers will readily accept your conclusion. If the gap is too big, your readers will accuse you of making a <u>hasty generalization</u> and will not accept your conclusion. Even with the most effective support, however, absolute certainty is not possible with inductive reasoning.

See 6f

6e Understanding Deductive Reasoning

1 Moving from General to Specific

Deductive reasoning moves from a generalization believed to be true or self-evident to a more specific conclusion. Writers use deductive reasoning when they address an audience that is more likely to be influenced by logic than by evidence. The process of deduction has traditionally been illustrated with a **syllogism,** a three-part set of statements or propositions that includes a **major premise,** a **minor premise,** and a **conclusion.**

Major Premise: All books from that store are new.

Minor Premise: These books are from that store.

Conclusion: Therefore, these books are new.

The **major premise** of a syllogism makes a general statement that the writer believes to be true. The **minor premise** presents a specific example of the belief that is stated in the major premise. If the reasoning is sound, the **conclusion** should follow from the two premises. (Note that the conclusion introduces no terms that have not already appeared in the major and minor premises.) The advantage of a deductive argument is that if readers accept the premises, they must grant the conclusion.

When you write an <u>argumentative essay,</u> you can use a syllogism during the planning stage (to test the validity of your points), or you can use it as a revision strategy (to test your logic). In either case, the syllogism enables you to express your deductive argument in its most basic form and to see whether it makes sense.

See Ch. 7

2 Constructing Sound Syllogisms

A syllogism is **valid** (or logical) when its conclusion follows from its premises. A syllogism is **true** when it makes accurate claims—that is, when the information it contains is consistent with the facts. To be **sound,** a syllogism must be both valid and true. However, a syllogism may be valid without being true or true without being valid. The following syllogism, for example, is valid but not true.

Major Premise: All politicians are male.

Minor Premise: Nancy Pelosi is a politician.

Conclusion: Therefore, Nancy Pelosi is male.

As odd as it may seem, this syllogism is valid. In the major premise, the phrase *all politicians* establishes that the entire class *politicians* is male. After Nancy Pelosi is identified as a politician, the conclusion that she is male automatically follows—but, of course, she is not. Because the major premise of this syllogism is not true, no conclusion based on it can be true. Even though the logic of the syllogism is correct, its conclusion is not. Therefore, the syllogism is not sound.

3 Recognizing Enthymemes

An **enthymeme** is a syllogism in which one of the premises—often the major premise—is unstated. Enthymemes often occur as sentences containing words that signal conclusions—*therefore, consequently, for this reason, for, so, since,* or *because.*

> Melissa is on the Dean's List; therefore, she is a good student.

The preceding sentence contains the minor premise and the conclusion of a syllogism. The reader must fill in the missing major premise in order to complete the syllogism and see whether or not the reasoning is logical.

Major Premise: All those on the Dean's List are good students.

Minor Premise: Melissa is on the Dean's List.

Conclusion: Therefore, Melissa is a good student.

Bumper stickers often take the form of enthymemes, stating just a conclusion ("Eating meat is murder") and leaving readers to supply both the major and minor premises. Careful readers, however, are not so easily fooled. They supply the missing premise (or premises), and then determine if the resulting syllogism is sound.

6f Recognizing Logical Fallacies

Fallacies are flawed arguments. A writer who inadvertently uses logical fallacies is not thinking clearly or logically; a writer who intentionally uses them is dishonest and is trying to mislead readers. It is important that you learn to recognize fallacies so that you can challenge them when you read and avoid them when you write.

CLOSE-UP

LOGICAL FALLACIES

♦ **Hasty Generalization** Drawing a conclusion based on too little evidence
The person I voted for is not doing a good job in Congress. Therefore, voting is a waste of time. (One disappointing experience does not warrant the statement that you will never vote again.)

♦ **Sweeping Generalization** Making a generalization that cannot be supported no matter how much evidence is supplied

Everyone should exercise. (Some people, for example those with severe heart conditions, might not benefit from exercise.)

♦ **Equivocation** Shifting the meaning of a key word or phrase during an argument

It is not in the public interest for the public to lose interest in politics. (Although clever, the shift in the meaning of the term *public interest* clouds the issue.)

♦ **Non Sequitur (Does Not Follow)** Arriving at a conclusion that does not logically follow from what comes before

Kim Williams is a good lawyer, so she will make a good senator. (Kim Williams may be a good lawyer, but it does not necessarily follow that she will make a good senator.)

♦ **Either/Or Fallacy** Treating a complex issue as if it has only two sides

Either we institute universal health care, or the health of all Americans will decline. (Good health does not necessarily depend on universal health care.)

♦ **Post Hoc** Establishing an unjustified link between cause and effect

The United States sold wheat to Russia. This must be what caused the price of wheat to rise. (Other factors, unrelated to the sale, could have caused the price to rise.)

♦ **Begging the Question (Circular Reasoning)** Stating a debatable premise as if it were true

Stem-cell research should be banned because nothing good can come from something so inherently evil. (Where is the evidence that stem-cell research is "inherently evil"?)

♦ **False Analogy** Assuming that because things are similar in some ways, they are similar in other ways

When forced to live in crowded conditions, people act like rats. They turn on each other and act violently. (Both people and rats might dislike living in crowded conditions, but unlike rats, most people do not necessarily resort to violence in this situation.)

♦ **Red Herring** Changing the subject to distract readers from the issue

Our company may charge high prices, but we give a lot to charity each year. (What does charging high prices have to do with giving to charity?)

♦ **Argument to Ignorance** Saying that something is true because it cannot be proved false, or vice versa

How can you tell me to send my child to a school where there is a child who has AIDS? After all, doctors can't say for sure that my child won't catch AIDS, can they? (Just because a doctor cannot prove the speaker's claim to be false, it does not follow that the claim is true.)

♦ **Bandwagon** Trying to establish that something is true because everyone believes it is true

(continued)

LOGICAL FALLACIES (*continued*)

Since most people believe in global warming, it must be a genuine threat.
(Where is the evidence to support this claim?)

♦ **Argument to the Person** (*Ad Hominem*) Attacking the person and not the issue

Of course my opponent supports drilling for oil in the Arctic wildlife preserve. He worked for an oil company before he was elected to Congress.
(By attacking his opponent, the speaker attempts to sidestep the issue.)

♦ **Argument to the People** Appealing to people's prejudices or emotions

Why should gay couples get the same benefits that married couples get?
(By appealing to prejudice, the speaker attempts to distract the audience from the issue.)

ESL TIP

In many cultures, people present arguments in order to persuade others to believe something. However, the rules for constructing such arguments are different in different cultures. In US academic settings, writers are discouraged from using the types of arguments listed in the Close-up box on pages 86–88 because they are not considered fair.

EXERCISE 6.4

Working in a group of three students, identify the logical fallacies in the following statements. In each case, name the fallacy, and then rewrite the statement to correct the problem. Finally, select one person in each group to present the results to the class.

▶ 1. Membership in the Coalition Against Pornography has more than quadrupled since the 1990s. Convenience stores in many parts of the country have limited their selection of pornography and, in many cases, taken pornography off the shelves. In 1995, the defense appropriations bill included a ban on the sale of pornography on military installations. The American public clearly believes that pornography has a harmful effect on its audience.

▶ 2. With people like Larry Flynt and Hugh Hefner arguing that pornography is harmless, you know that pornography is causing its readers to live immoral lifestyles.

▶ 3. The Republican Party and conservative thinkers are all for the free market when the issue is the environment, but they will be the first ones to call for a limit to what can be shown on movies, television, and the Internet.

▶ 4. Television is out of control. There is more foul language, sex, and sexual innuendo on television than there has ever been before. The effects of this obscene and pornographic material have been documented in studies that suggest that serial killers and other criminals are very likely to be regular consumers of pornographic materials.

▶ 5. We know that television causes children to be more violent. So what can we use to control television? The V-chip, television ratings, and more governmental control of television content will help us reduce violence.

6. Study after study has been completed, and none of the researchers has presented incontrovertible evidence that rap music causes an increase in violent behavior among its listeners.

7. A boy in Idaho set fire to his family's home after watching a television stunt show. From this incident, we can conclude that television has a negative influence on children's behavior.

8. We want our children to grow up in safe neighborhoods. We would like to see less violence in the schools and on the playgrounds. We would like to be less fearful when we have to go out at night. If we stop polluting our culture with violent images from television and popular music, we can reclaim our communities and our children.

9. Ted Bundy and Richard Ramirez, two serial killers, both viewed pornography regularly. Pornography caused them to kill women.

10. Some people believe that violence on television affects children and want the government to find ways to limit violence. Others believe that children are unaffected by the violence they see on television. I do not think violence on television causes children to become violent.

Writing Argumentative Essays

CHAPTER 7

For most students, the true test of their critical thinking skills comes when they write an **argumentative essay,** an essay that takes a stand on an issue and uses logic and evidence to convince readers. When you write an argument, you follow the same process you use when you write any essay. See Chs. 2–4 However, because the purpose of an argument is to change the way readers think or to move them to action, you need to use some additional strategies to present your ideas to your audience.

1 Choosing a Topic

As with any type of essay, choosing the right topic for your argumentative essay is important. You should choose a topic that interests and challenges you, one in which you have an emotional and intellectual stake. It stands to reason that the more you care about a topic, the more enthusiastically you will pursue it. You should also choose a topic that you know something about. The more you know about your topic, the easier it will be to gather the information you need to write your argumentative essay. Even though you care about your topic, you should be willing to consider other people's viewpoints—even those that contradict your own beliefs. If the situation warrants—for example, if the evidence goes against your position—you should be willing to change your position. If you find that you cannot be open-minded, you should consider choosing another topic. Remember, in order to be persuasive, you will have to demonstrate to readers that your position is fair and that you have considered both the strengths and the weaknesses of opposing arguments.

You should also consider other factors when choosing a topic. Your topic should be narrow enough so that you can write about it within your page limit. If your topic is too broad, you will not be able to treat it in enough detail. In addition, your topic should be interesting to your readers. Keep in mind that some topics—such as "The Need for Gun Control" or "The Fairness of the Death Penalty"—have been discussed and written about so often that you may not be able to say anything new or interesting about them. Instead of relying on an overused topic, choose one that enables you to contribute something to the debate.

2 Taking a Stand

See
3b After you have chosen a topic, your next step is to **take a stand**—to state your position in the form of a <u>thesis statement</u>. Properly worded, this thesis statement lays the foundation for the rest of your argument.

Next, you should make sure that your thesis is **debatable**—that it presents an idea with which some people will disagree. A **factual statement**—a verifiable assertion about which reasonable people *do not* disagree—is not suitable as a thesis for an argumentative essay.

> **Fact:** First-year students are not required to purchase a meal plan from the university.

> **Thesis Statement:** First-year students should not be required to purchase a meal plan from the university.

One way to make sure that your thesis statement actually is debatable is to formulate an **antithesis**, a statement that takes the opposite position.

If you can state an antithesis, you can be certain that your thesis statement actually is debatable.

> **Thesis Statement:** Term limits would improve government by bringing people with fresh ideas into office every few years.

> **Antithesis:** Term limits would harm government because elected officials would always be inexperienced.

3 Defining Your Terms

You should always define the key terms you use in your argument; after all, the soundness of an entire argument may hinge on the definition of a word that may mean one thing to one person and another thing to someone else. For example, in the United States, *democratic* elections involve the selection of government officials by popular vote; in other countries, the same term may be used to describe elections in which only one candidate is running or in which all candidates represent the same party. For this reason, if your argument hinges on a key term like *democratic,* you should make sure that your readers know exactly what you mean by it.

CLOSE-UP

DEFINING YOUR TERMS

Be careful to use precise terms in your thesis statement. Avoid vague and judgmental words, such as *wrong, bad, good, right*, and *immoral*.

Vague: Censorship of the Internet would be wrong.

Clearer: Censorship of the Internet would unfairly limit free speech.

---

4 Considering Your Audience

See 1b

As you plan your essay, keep a specific audience in mind. Are your readers unbiased observers or people deeply concerned about the issue you plan to discuss? Can they be cast in a specific role—concerned parents, victims of discrimination, irate consumers—or are they so diverse that they cannot be categorized? If you cannot be certain who your readers are, direct your arguments to a general audience.

Always assume a **skeptical audience**—one that will question your assumptions. Skeptical readers will need a good deal of reassurance that you understand their concerns and that you concede some of their points. Even if your readers are sympathetic to your position, you cannot assume that they will accept your ideas without question. They will still need to see that your argument is logical and that your evidence is solid. (If readers are hostile to your position, you may never be able to convince them that your conclusion is valid. The best you can hope for is that these readers will acknowledge the strengths of your argument even if they reject your conclusion.)

5 Refuting Opposing Arguments

As you develop your argument, you should also **refute**—that is, disprove—opposing arguments by showing that they are untrue, unfair, illogical, unimportant, or irrelevant. (If an opponent's position is so strong that it cannot be refuted, concede the point, and then identify its limitations.) In the following paragraph, a student refutes the argument that Sea World should keep whales in captivity.

> Of course, some will say that Sea World wants to capture only a few whales, as George Will points out in his commentary in *Newsweek*. Unfortunately, Will downplays the fact that Sea World wants to capture a hundred whales, not just "a few." And, after releasing ninety of these whales, Sea World intends to keep ten for "further work." At hearings in Seattle last week, several noted marine biologists went on record as condemning Sea World's research program.

Note: When you acknowledge an opposing view, be careful not to distort or oversimplify it. This tactic, known as creating a **straw man,** can seriously undermine your credibility.

7b Using Evidence Effectively

1 Supporting Your Argument

See 6b

See Chs. 47–48

Most arguments are built on **assertions**—statements that you make about your topic—backed by evidence—supporting information in the form of examples, statistics, or expert opinion. (Keep in mind that all information—words and ideas—that you get from a source requires documentation.)

Only assertions that are **self-evident** ("All human beings are mortal"), **true by definition** ($2 + 2 = 4$), or **factual** ("The Atlantic Ocean separates England and the United States") need no proof. All other kinds of assertions require support.

Note: Remember that you can never prove a thesis conclusively—if you could, there would be no argument. The best you can do is to provide enough evidence to establish a high probability that your thesis is reasonable or valid.

2 Establishing Credibility

Clear reasoning, compelling evidence, and strong refutations go a long way toward making an argument solid. But these elements in themselves are not sufficient to create a convincing argument. In order to convince readers, you have to satisfy them that you are someone they should listen to—in other words, that you have **credibility.**

Establishing Common Ground　When you write an argument, it is tempting to go on the attack, emphasizing the differences between your position and those of your opponents. Writers of effective arguments, however, know they can gain a greater advantage by establishing common ground between their opponents and themselves.

One way to establish common ground is to use the techniques of **Rogerian argument,** based on the work of the psychologist Carl Rogers. According to Rogers, you should think of the members of your audience as colleagues with whom you must collaborate to find solutions to problems. Instead of verbally assaulting them, you should emphasize points of agreement. In this way, rather than taking a confrontational stance, you establish common ground and work toward a resolution of the problem you are discussing.

Demonstrating Knowledge　Including relevant personal experiences in your argumentative essay can show readers that you know a lot about your subject; demonstrating this kind of knowledge gives you authority. For example, describing what you observed at a National Rifle Association convention can give you authority in an essay arguing for (or against) gun control.

You can also demonstrate knowledge by showing that you have done research into a subject. By referring to important sources of information and by providing accurate <u>documentation</u> for your information, you show readers that you have done the necessary background reading.

See Chs. 47–48

Maintaining a Reasonable Tone　Your tone is almost as important as the information you present. Talk *to* your readers, not *at* them. If you lecture your readers or appear to talk down to them, you will alienate them. Remember that readers are more likely to respond to a writer who seems sensible than to one who is strident or insulting. For this reason, you should use moderate language, qualify your statements, and avoid words and phrases such as *never, all,* and *in every case,* which can make your claims seem exaggerated and unrealistic.

Presenting Yourself as Someone Worth Listening To　Present your argument in positive terms, and don't apologize for your views. For example, do not rely on phrases—such as "In my opinion" and "It seems to me"—that undercut your credibility. Be consistent, and be careful not to contradict yourself. Finally, limit your use of the first person ("I"), and avoid slang and colloquialisms.

3　Being Fair

Argument promotes one point of view, so it is seldom objective. However, college writing requires that you stay within the bounds of fairness and

See
6c avoid <u>bias</u>. To be sure that the support for your argument is not misleading or distorted, you should take the following steps.

Avoid Distorting Evidence   Distortion is misrepresentation. Writers sometimes intentionally misrepresent their opponents' views by exaggerating them and then attacking this extreme position, but you should avoid this unfair tactic in your college writing.

Avoid Quoting Out of Context   Be careful not to take someone's words out of their original setting and use them in another. When you select certain statements and ignore others, you can change the meaning of what someone has said or suggested.

Avoid Slanting   Slanting occurs when you select only information that supports your case and ignore information that does not. Slanting also occurs when you use **inflammatory language**—language calculated to arouse strong emotions—to create bias.

Avoid Using Unfair Appeals   Traditionally, writers of arguments try to influence readers by appealing to their sense of reason. Problems arise when See
6f writers attempt to influence readers unfairly. For example, writers can use <u>fallacies</u> to fool readers into thinking that a conclusion is logical when it is not. Writers can also employ inappropriate emotional appeals—to prejudice or fear, for example—to influence readers. These unfair appeals are unacceptable in college writing.

7c   Organizing an Argumentative Essay

In its simplest form, an argument consists of a thesis statement and sup-See
6d–e porting evidence. However, argumentative essays frequently use <u>inductive</u> and <u>deductive reasoning</u> and other specialized strategies to win audience approval and overcome potential opposition.

CLOSE-UP

ELEMENTS OF AN ARGUMENTATIVE ESSAY

Introduction

See
5e2   The <u>introduction</u> of your argumentative essay acquaints readers with your subject. Here you can show how your subject concerns your audience, establish common ground with your readers, and perhaps explain how your subject has been misunderstood.

Thesis Statement

See
3b   Your <u>thesis statement</u> can appear anywhere in your argumentative essay. Most often, you present your thesis in your introduction. However, if you are presenting a highly controversial argument—one to which you believe your readers might react negatively—you may postpone stating your thesis until later in your essay.

Background

In this section, you can briefly present a narrative of past events, an overview of others' opinions on the issue, definitions of key terms, or a review of basic facts.

Arguments in Support of Your Thesis

Here you present your assertions and the evidence to support them. Begin with your weakest argument and work up to your strongest. If all your arguments are equally strong, begin with those with which your readers are already familiar and therefore likely to accept.

Refutation of Opposing Arguments

In an argumentative essay, you should summarize and **refute**—disprove or call into question—the major arguments against your thesis. If the opposing arguments are relatively weak, refute them after you have made your case. However, if the opposing arguments are strong, concede their strengths and then discuss their limitations before you present your own arguments.

Conclusion

Often, the <u>conclusion</u> restates the major arguments in support of your thesis. Your conclusion can also summarize key points, restate your thesis, remind readers of the weaknesses of opposing arguments, or underscore the logic of your position. Many writers like to end their arguments with a strong last line, such as a quotation or a statement that sums up your argument.

See 5e3

7d   Writing and Revising an Argumentative Essay

The following student essay includes many of the elements discussed in this chapter. The student, Samantha Masterton, was asked to write an argumentative essay on a topic of her choice, drawing her supporting evidence from her own knowledge and experience as well as from other sources.

Samantha Masterton

Professor Egler

English 102

14 April 2009

The Returning Student: Older Is Definitely Better

After graduating from high school, young people must decide what they want to do with the rest of their lives. Many graduates (often without much thought) decide to continue their education uninterrupted, and they go on to college. This group of teenagers makes up what many see as typical first-year college students. Recently, however, this stereotype has been challenged by an influx of older students, including myself, into American colleges and universities. Not only do these students make a valuable contribution to the schools they attend, but they also offer an alternative to young people who go to college simply because they do not know what else to do. A few years off between high school and college can give many students the life experience they need to appreciate the value of higher education and to gain more from it.

The college experience of an eighteen-year-old is quite different from that of an older "nontraditional" student. The typical high school graduate is often concerned with things other than studying—for example, going to parties, dating, and testing personal limits. However, older students—those who are twenty-five years of age or older—are serious about the idea of returning to college. Although many high school students do not think twice about whether or not to attend college, older students have much more to consider when they think about returning to college. For example, they must decide how much time they can spend getting their degree

Introduction (margin label)

Thesis statement (margin label)

Background (margin label)

Masterton 2

and consider the impact attending college will have on their family and their finances.

In the United States, the makeup of college students is changing. According to the 2002 US Department of Education report *Nontraditional Undergraduates,* the percentage of students who could be classified as "nontraditional" has increased over the last decade (7). So, despite the challenges that older students face when they return to school, more and more are choosing to make the effort.

Background (continued)

Most older students return to school with clear goals. The *Nontraditional Undergraduates* report shows that more than one-third of nontraditional students decided to attend college because it was required by their job, and 87 percent enrolled in order to gain skills (10). Getting a college degree is often a requirement for professional advancement, and older students are therefore more likely to take college seriously. In general, older students enroll in college with a definite course of study in mind. For older students, college is an extension of work rather than a place to discover what they want to be when they graduate. A study by psychologists R. Eric Landrum, Je T'aime Hood, and Jerry M. McAdams concluded, "Nontraditional students seemed to be more appreciative of their opportunities, as indicated by their higher enjoyment of school and appreciation of professors' efforts in the classroom" (744).

Argument in support of thesis

Older students also understand the actual benefits of doing well in school and successfully completing a degree program. Older students I have known rarely cut lectures or put off studying. This is because older students are often balancing the demands of home and work, and they know how important it is to do well. The difficulties of juggling

Argument in support of thesis

school, family, and work force older students to be disciplined
and focused—especially concerning their schoolwork. This
pays off: older students tend to spend more hours per week
studying and tend to have a higher GPA than younger
students do (Landrum, Hood, and McAdams 742-43).

Argument in
support of
thesis

My observations of older students have convinced me that
many students would benefit from delaying entry into college.
Eighteen-year-olds are often immature and inexperienced.
They cannot be expected to have formulated definite goals
or developed firm ideas about themselves or about the world
in which they live. In contrast, older students have generally
had a variety of real-life experiences. Most have worked for
several years, many have started families. Their years in the
"real world" have helped them become more focused and more
responsible than they were when they graduated from high
school. As a result, they are better prepared for college than
they would have been when they were young.

Refutation
of opposing
argument

Of course, postponing college for a few years is not for
everyone. Certainly some teenagers have a definite sense of
purpose and these individuals would benefit from an early
college experience. Charles Woodward, a law librarian, went to
college directly after high school, and for him the experience
was positive. "I was serious about learning, and I loved my
subject," he said. "I felt fortunate that I knew what I wanted
from college and from life." Many younger students, however,
are not like Woodward; they graduate from high school
without any clear sense of purpose. For this reason, it makes
sense for them to postpone college until they are mature
enough to benefit from the experience.

Refutation
of opposing
argument

Granted, some older students have difficulties when
they return to college. Because these students have been

Masterton 4

out of school so long, they may have problems studying and adapting to academic life. As I have seen, though, these problems disappear after a period of adjustment. Of course, it is true that many older students find it difficult to balance the needs of their family with college and to deal with the financial burden of tuition. However, this challenge is becoming easier with the growing number of online courses, the availability of distance education, and the introduction of governmental programs, such as educational tax credits (Agbo 164-65).

All things considered, higher education is often wasted on the young, who are either too immature or too unfocused to take advantage of it. Taking a few years off between high school and college would give these students the time they need to make the most of a college education. The increasing number of older students returning to college seems to indicate that many students are taking this path. According to a US Department of Education report, *Digest of Education Statistics, 2007,* 31.3 percent of students enrolled in American colleges in 2005 were twenty-five years of age or older (273). Older students such as these have taken time off to serve in the military, to gain valuable work experience, or to raise a family. In short, they have taken the time to mature. By the time they get to college, these students have defined their goals and made a firm commitment to achieve them.

Conclusion

Concluding statement

Masterton 5

Works Cited

Agbo, S. "The United States: Heterogeneity of the Student
    Body and the Meaning of 'Nontraditional' in U.S. Higher
    Education." *Higher Education and Lifelong Learners:
    International Perspectives on Change*. Ed. Hans G.
    Schuetze and Maria Slowey. London: Routledge, 2000.
    149-69. Print.

Landrum, R. Eric, Je T'aime Hood, and Jerry M. McAdams.
    "Satisfaction with College by Traditional and
    Nontraditional College Students." *Psychological
    Reports* 89.3 (2001): 740-46. Print.

United States. Dept. of Educ. Office of Educ. Research and
    Improvement. Natl. Center for Educ. Statistics. *Digest of
    Education Statistics, 2007*. By Thomas D. Snyder, Sally A.
    Dillow, and Charlene M. Hoffman. 2008. *National Center
    for Education Statistics*. Web. 5 Apr. 2009.

---. ---. ---. ---. *Nontraditional Undergraduates*. By Susan Choy.
    2002. *National Center for Education Statistics*. Web. 7 Apr.
    2009.

Woodward, Charles B. Personal interview. 21 Mar. 2009.

Works-cited
list begins
new page

Four sets of
unspaced
hyphens
indicate that
*United States,
Dept. of Educ.,
Office of Educ.
Research and
Improvement,*
and *Natl.
Center for Educ.
Statistics* are
repeated from
previous entry

CHECKLIST

WRITING ARGUMENTATIVE ESSAYS

☐ Is your topic debatable?

☐ Does your essay have an argumentative thesis?

☐ Have you adequately defined the terms you use in your argument?

☐ Have you considered the opinions, attitudes, and values of your audience?

☐ Have you summarized and refuted opposing arguments?

☐ Have you supported your points with evidence?

☐ Have you documented all information that is not your own?

☐ Have you established your credibility?

☐ Have you been fair?

☐ Have you constructed your arguments logically?

☐ Have you avoided logical fallacies?

☐ Have you provided your readers with enough background information?

☐ Have you presented your points clearly and organized them logically?

☐ Have you written an interesting introduction and a strong conclusion?

CLOSE-UP

USING TRANSITIONS IN ARGUMENTATIVE ESSAYS

Argumentative essays should include transitional words and phrases to indicate which paragraphs are arguments in support of the thesis, which are refutations of arguments that oppose the thesis, and which are conclusions.

Arguments in Support of Thesis

accordingly	given
because	generally
for example	in general
for instance	since

Refutations

although	in all fairness
admittedly	naturally
certainly	nonetheless
despite	of course
granted	

Conclusions

all things considered	in summary
as a result	therefore
in conclusion	thus

Writing Essays about Literature

CHAPTER 8

Learning to read, respond to, and write about literature are important skills that can serve you while you are a college student as well as later in your life beyond the classroom.

8a Reading Literature

See
Ch. 9

When you read a literary work you plan to write about, you use the same critical thinking skills and <u>active reading</u> strategies you apply to other works you read: you preview the work and highlight it to identify key ideas and cues to meaning; then, you annotate it carefully.

As you read and take notes, focus on the special concerns of **literary analysis,** considering elements like a short story's plot, a poem's rhyme or meter, or a play's staging. Look for *patterns,* related groups of words, images, or ideas that run through a work. Look for *anomalies,* unusual forms, unique uses of language, unexpected actions by characters, or original treatments of topics. Finally, look for *connections,* links with other literary works, with historical events, or with biographical or cultural information.

8b Writing about Literature

See
2e4

See
3a–c

When you have finished your reading and annotating, you decide on a topic, and then you <u>brainstorm</u> to find ideas to write about; after that, you decide on a <u>thesis</u> and use it to help you organize your material. As you arrange related material into categories, you will begin to see a structure for your paper. At this point, you are ready to start drafting your essay.

When you write about literature, your goal is to make a point and support it with appropriate references to the work under discussion or to related works or secondary sources. As you write, you observe the conventions of literary criticism, which has its own specialized vocabulary and formats. You also respond to certain discipline-specific assignments. For instance, you may be asked to **analyze** a work, to take it apart and consider one or more of its elements—perhaps the plot or characters in a story or the use of language in a poem. Or, you may be asked to **interpret** a work, to explore its possible meanings. Finally, you may be called on to **evaluate** a work, to assess its strengths and weaknesses.

More specifically, you may be asked to trace the critical or popular reception to a work, to compare two works by a single writer (or by two different writers), or to consider the relationship between a work of literature and a literary movement or historical period. You may be asked to analyze a character's motives or the relationship between two characters or to comment on a story's setting or tone. Whatever the case, understanding exactly what you are expected to do will make your writing task easier.

CHECKLIST

CONVENTIONS OF WRITING ABOUT LITERATURE

When you write about a literary work, keep the following conventions in mind:

❏ Use present-tense verbs when discussing works of literature (**The character of Mrs. Mallard's husband is not developed**).

❏ Use past-tense verbs only when discussing historical events (**Owen's poem conveys the destructiveness of World War I, which at the time the poem was written was considered to be . . .**); when presenting historical or biographical data (**Her first novel, published in 1811 when Austen was thirty-six, . . .**); or when identifying events that occurred prior to the time of the story's main action (**Miss Emily is a recluse; since her father died she has lived alone except for a servant**).

❏ Support all points with specific, concrete examples from the work you are discussing, *briefly* summarizing key events, quoting dialogue or description, describing characters or setting, or paraphrasing ideas.

❏ Combine paraphrase, summary, and quotation with your own interpretations, weaving quotations smoothly into your paper (**see 44d1**).

❏ Be careful to acknowledge all the sources you use, including the literary work or works under discussion. Introduce the words or ideas of others with a reference to the source, and follow borrowed material with appropriate parenthetical documentation (**see 47a1**). Be sure you have quoted accurately and enclosed the words of others in quotation marks.

❏ Include a works-cited list (**see 47a2**) in accordance with MLA documentation style.

❏ When citing a part of a short story or novel, supply the page number (**168**). For a poem, give the line numbers (**2-4**) if they are included in the text; in your first reference, include the word *line* or *lines* (**lines 2-4**). For a classic verse play, include act, scene, and line numbers (**1.4.29-31**). For other plays, supply act and/or scene numbers. (When quoting more than four lines of prose or more than three lines of poetry, follow the guidelines outlined in **33b.**)

❏ Avoid subjective expressions such as *I feel, I believe, it seems to me,* and *in my opinion.* They weaken your paper by suggesting that its ideas are "only" your opinion and have no validity in themselves.

❏ Avoid unnecessary plot summary. Your goal is to draw a conclusion about one or more works and to support that conclusion with pertinent details. If a plot development supports a point you wish to make, a *brief* summary is acceptable, but plot summary is no substitute for analysis.

(continued)

> **CONVENTIONS OF WRITING ABOUT LITERATURE** (*continued*)
>
> ❑ Use literary terms accurately. For example, be careful not to confuse *narrator* or *speaker* with *writer*. Feelings or opinions expressed by a narrator or character do not necessarily represent those of the writer. You should not say, **In the poem's last stanza, Frost expresses his indecision** when you mean the poem's *speaker* (not the poet) is indecisive. For a glossary of literary terms, go to http://cengage.com/english/kirsznermandell ▶ *The Concise Wadsworth Handbook* ▶ Chapter 8 ▶ Glossary.
>
> ❑ Underline titles of books and plays (**see 37a**); enclose titles of short stories and poems in quotation marks (**see 33c**). Book-length poems are treated as long works, and their titles should be underlined.

8c Sample Essay about Literature (without Sources)

Daniel Johanssen, a student in an introductory literature course, wrote an essay about Delmore Schwartz's 1959 poem "The True-Blue American," which appears on page 105. Daniel's essay, which begins on page 106, includes annotations that highlight some conventions of writing about poetry.

THE TRUE-BLUE AMERICAN

Jeremiah Dickson was a true-blue American,

For he was a little boy who understood America, for he felt that he must

Think about *everything*; because that's *all* there is to think about,

Knowing immediately the intimacy of truth and comedy,

Knowing intuitively how a sense of humor was a necessity   5

For one and for all who live in America. Thus, natively, and

Naturally when on an April Sunday in an ice cream parlor Jeremiah

Was requested to choose between a chocolate sundae and a banana split

He answered unhesitatingly, having no need to think of it

Being a true-blue American, determined to continue as he began: 10

Rejecting the either-or of Kierkegaard,[1] and many another European;

Refusing to accept alternatives, refusing to believe the choice of between;

Rejecting selection; denying dilemma; electing absolute affirmation: knowing

    in his breast   15

        The infinite and the gold

        Of the endless frontier, the deathless West.

"Both: I will have them both!" declared this true-blue American

In Cambridge, Massachusetts, on an April Sunday, instructed

    By the great department stores, by the Five-and-Ten,   20

Taught by Christmas, by the circus, by the vulgarity and grandeur of Niagara Falls and the Grand Canyon,

Tutored by the grandeur, vulgarity, and infinite appetite gratified and Shining in the darkness, of the light

On Saturdays at the double bills of the moon pictures,   25

The consummation of the advertisements of the imagination of the light

Which is as it was—the infinite belief in infinite hope—of Columbus, Barnum, Edison, and Jeremiah Dickson.

---

[1]Søren Kierkegaard (1813–1855)—Danish philosopher who greatly influenced twentieth-century existentialism. *Either-Or* (1841) is one of his best-known works.

Johanssen 1

Daniel Johanssen

Professor Stang

English 1001

8 April 2009

Irony in "The True-Blue American"

The poem "The True-Blue American," by Delmore

Schwartz, is not as simple and direct as its title suggests.

In fact, the title is extremely ironic. At first, the poem

seems patriotic, but actually the flag-waving strengthens

the speaker's criticism. The poem may seem to

support and celebrate America, but it is actually a bitter

critique of the negative aspects of American culture.

According to the speaker, the primary problem with

America is that its citizens falsely believe themselves to

be authorities on everything. The following lines

introduce the theme of the "know-it-all" American: "For

he was a little boy who understood America, for he felt

that he must / Think about *everything*; because that's

all there is to think about" (lines 2-3). This theme is

developed later in a series of parallel phrases that seem to

celebrate the value of immediate intuitive knowledge and

a refusal to accept or to believe anything other than what

is American (4-6).

Americans are ambitious and determined, but these

qualities are not seen in the poem as virtues. According to

the speaker, Americans reject sophisticated "European"

concepts like doubt and choices and alternatives and

instead insist on "absolute affirmation" (13)—simple

solutions to complex problems. This unwillingness to

compromise translates into stubbornness and materialistic

greed. This tendency is illustrated by the boy's asking for

Marginal notes:

Title of poem is in quotation marks

Thesis statement

Slash separates lines of poetry (space before and after slash)

Parenthetical documentation indicates line numbers (the word *line* or *lines* is included only in the first reference to the poem)

Johanssen 2

both a chocolate sundae *and* a banana split at the ice cream parlor—not "either-or" (11). Americans are characterized as pioneers who want it all, who will stop at nothing to achieve "The infinite and the gold / Of the endless frontier, the deathless West" (16-17). For the speaker, the pioneers who seek this "endless frontier" are not noble or self-sacrificing; they are like greedy little boys at an ice cream parlor.

According to the speaker, the greed and materialism of America began as grandeur but ultimately became mere vulgarity. Similarly, the "true-blue American" is not born a vulgar parody of grandeur; he learns from his true-blue fellow Americans, who in turn were taught by experts:

> By the great department stores, by the
> Five-and-Ten,
> Taught by Christmas, by the circus, by the
> vulgarity and grandeur of Niagara Falls and
> the Grand Canyon,
> Tutored by the grandeur, vulgarity, and infinite
> appetite gratified. . . . (20-22)

Among the "tutors" the speaker lists are such American institutions as department stores and national monuments. Within these institutions, grandeur and vulgarity coexist; in a sense, they are one and the same.

The speaker's negativity climaxes in the phrase "Shining in the darkness, of the light" (23). This paradoxical statement suggests that negative truths are hidden beneath America's glamorous surface. All the grand and illustrious things of which Americans are so proud are personified by Jeremiah Dickson, the spoiled brat in the ice cream parlor.

More than 3 lines of poetry are set off from text and introduced by a colon. Quotation is indented 1" from left margin; no quotation marks are used.

Documentation is placed one space after final punctuation.

Johanssen 3

Conclusion   Like America, Jeremiah has unlimited potential. He
has native intuition, curiosity, courage, and a pioneer
spirit. Unfortunately, however, both America and Jeremiah
Dickson are limited by their willingness to be led by others,
by their greed and impatience, and by their preference for
quick, easy, unambiguous answers rather than careful
philosophical analysis. Regardless of his—and America's—
potential, Jeremiah Dickson is doomed to be hypnotized
and seduced by glittering superficialities, light without
substance, and to settle for the "double bills of the moon
pictures" (24) rather than the enduring truths of a
philosopher such as Kierkegaard.

Johanssen 4

Work Cited

Schwartz, Delmore. "The True-Blue American." *Literature:*
    Reading, Reacting, Writing. Ed. Laurie G. Kirszner and
    Stephen R. Mandell. 6th ed. Boston: Wadsworth, 2007.
    1044-45. Print.

8d   Excerpts from Sample Essay about Literature (with Sources)

See 47a Tim Westmoreland, a student in an introductory literature course, wrote an analysis of John Updike's short story "A&P." Excerpts from this paper, which uses **MLA documentation style,** follow.

Note: For an example of a complete source-based paper that uses MLA documentation, **see 47c.**

Westmoreland 1

Tim Westmoreland

Professor Adkins

Literature 2101

25 February 2009

"A&P": A Class Act

John Updike's "A&P," like many of his other works, is a "profoundly American" story about social inequality and an attempt to bridge the gap between social classes (Steiner). The story is told by an eighteen-year-old boy who is working as a checkout clerk in an A&P in a small New England town five miles from the beach. The narrative is delivered in a slangy, colloquial voice that tells of a brief but powerful encounter with a "beautiful but inaccessible girl" from another social and economic level (Wells 128). Sammy, the narrator, is working his cash register on a slow Thursday afternoon when, as he says, "In walks these three girls in nothing but bathing suits" (Updike, "A&P" 259). Lengel, the store's manager—a Sunday school teacher and "self-appointed moral policeman"—confronts the girls, telling them that they should be decently dressed (Wells 131). It is a moment of embarrassment and insight for all parties concerned, and in an apparently impulsive act, Sammy quits his job. Although the plot is simple, what is at the heart of the story is complex: a noble gesture that serves as a futile attempt to cross social and economic boundaries.

Through Sammy's eyes, we see the class conflict that defines the story. The privileged young girls in bathing suits are very different from the few customers who are shopping in the store. Sammy refers to the customers as "sheep" (Updike, "A&P" 261) and describes one of them as

Introduction (combines paraphrase, summary, and quotation)

Title included in parenthetical citation because paper cites two sources by Updike

Thesis statement

Westmoreland 2

"a witch about fifty with rouge on her cheekbones and no eyebrows" (259). Other customers are characterized in equally negative terms—for example, "houseslaves in pin curlers" (261) and "an old party in baggy gray pants" (262). Unlike the other customers, the leader of the three girls is described as a "queen":

> She came down a little hard on her heels, as
> if she didn't walk in her bare feet that much,
> putting down her heels and then letting
> the weight move along to her toes as if she
> was testing the floor with every step, putting
> a little deliberate extra action into it. (260)

It seems clear that Sammy realizes that Queenie and her friends come from farther away than just the beach. They have come to test the floors of a store patronized by the less well-off and do it openly, in defiance of social rules. In a sense, they are "slumming."

Long prose quotation (more than four lines) is set off from text and introduction by a colon. Quotation is indented 1" from left margin; no quotation marks are used.

Westmoreland 6

Works Cited

Oates, Joyce Carol. "John Updike's American Comedies." *Joyce Carol Oates on John Updike*. U of San Francisco, 5 Apr. 1998. Web. 15 Jan. 2009.

Steiner, George. "Supreme Fiction: America Is in the Details." *The New Yorker*. Condé Nast, 11 Mar. 1996. Web. 20 Feb. 2009.

Updike, John. "A&P." *Literature: Reading, Reacting, Writing*. Ed. Laurie G. Kirszner and Stephen R. Mandell. 7th ed. Boston: Wadsworth, 2010. 259-64. Print.

---. Interview by Donald Murray. *The Heinle Original Film Series in Literature*. Dir. Bruce Schwartz. Thomson, 2004. DVD.

---. "Still Afraid of Being Caught." *New York Times*. New York Times, 8 Oct. 1995. Web. 16 Feb. 2009.

Wells, Walter. "John Updike's 'A&P': A Return Visit to Araby." *Studies in Short Fiction* 30.2 (1993): 127-33. *Magazine Index Plus*. Web. 15 Feb. 2009.

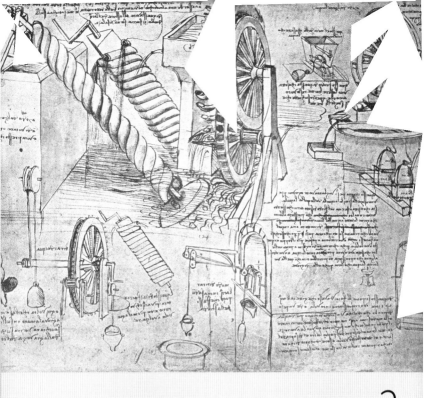

PART 2

Developing Strategies
for Academic Success

Developing Strategies for Academic Success

Reading to Write

Central to developing effective reading skills is learning the techniques of **active reading.** Being an active reader means being actively involved in the text: reading with pen in hand, physically marking the text in order to identify parallels, question ambiguities, distinguish important points from not-so-important ones, and connect causes with effects and generalizations with specific examples. The understanding you gain from active reading prepares you to think (and write) critically about a text.

ESL TIP

When you read a text for the first time, don't worry about understanding every word. Instead, just try to get a general idea of what the text is about and how it is organized. Later on, you can use a dictionary to look up any unfamiliar words.

9a Previewing a Text

Before you actually begin reading a text, you should **preview** it—that is, skim it to get a sense of the writer's subject and emphasis.

When you preview an **article** (in print or online), scan the introductory and concluding paragraphs for summaries of the writer's main points. (Journal articles in the sciences and social sciences often begin with summaries called **abstracts.**) Thesis statements, topic sentences, repeated key terms, transitional words and phrases, and transitional paragraphs can also help you to identify the points a writer is making. In addition, look for the **visual cues**—such as <u>headings</u>—that writers use to emphasize ideas.

See 12b

When you preview a **book,** start by looking at its table of contents; then, turn to its index. A quick glance at the index will reveal the amount of coverage the book gives to subjects that may be important to you. As you leaf through the chapters, look at pictures, graphs, or tables and the captions that appear with them.

9b Highlighting a Text

When you have finished previewing a work, photocopy relevant sections of articles and books, and print out useful material from online sources. Then, **highlight** the pages, using symbols and underlining to help you identify the writer's key points and their relationships to one another.

> **CHECKLIST**
>
> **USING HIGHLIGHTING SYMBOLS**
> - ❑ Underline to indicate information you should read again.
> - ❑ Box or circle key words or important phrases.
> - ❑ Put question marks next to confusing passages, unclear points, or words you need to look up.
> - ❑ Draw lines or arrows to show connections between ideas.
> - ❑ Number points that are discussed in sequence.
> - ❑ Draw a vertical line in the margin to set off an important section.
> - ❑ Star especially important ideas.

9c   Annotating a Text

After you have read through a text once, read it again—this time, more critically. At this stage, you should **annotate** the pages, recording your responses to what you read. This process of recording notes in the margins or between the lines will help you understand the writer's ideas and your own reactions to those ideas.

> **ESL TIP**
>
> You may find it useful to use your native language when you annotate a text.

Some of your annotations may be relatively straightforward. For example, you may define new words, identify unfamiliar references, or jot down brief summaries. Other annotations may be more personal: you may identify a parallel between your own experience and one described in the reading selection, or you may record your opinion of the writer's position.

See Ch. 6

As you start to **think critically** about a text, your annotations may identify points that confirm (or dispute) your own ideas, question the appropriateness or accuracy of the writer's support, uncover the writer's biases, or even question (or challenge) the writer's conclusion.

The following passage illustrates a student's highlighting and annotations of a passage from Michael Pollan's book *The Omnivore's Dilemma*.

> <u>In the early years of the nineteenth century, Americans began drinking more than they ever had before</u> or since, embarking on a collective bender that confronted the young republic with its <u>first major public health crisis</u>—the obesity epidemic of its day. <u>Corn whiskey, suddenly superabundant and cheap</u>, became the drink of choice, and in 1820 the typical American was putting away half a pint of the stuff every day. That comes to more than five gallons of spirits a year for every man, woman, and child in America. The figure today is less than one.

People drank 5x as much as they do today

As the historian W. J. Rorabaugh tells the story in *The Alcoholic Republic,* <u>we drank the hard stuff at breakfast, lunch, and dinner, before work and after and very often during.</u> <u>Employers were expected to supply spirits over the course of the workday</u>; in fact, the modern coffee break began as a late-morning whiskey break called "the elevenses." (Just to pronounce it makes you sound tipsy.) Except for a brief respite Sunday morning in church, Americans simply did not gather—whether for a barn raising or quilting bee, corn husking or political rally—without passing the whiskey jug. Visitors from Europe—hardly models of sobriety themselves—marveled at the free flow of American spirits. "Come on then, if you love (toping)," the journalist William Cobbett   ?
wrote his fellow Englishmen in a dispatch from America. "For here you may drink yourself blind at the price of sixpence."

[The results] of all this toping were entirely predictable: <u>a rising tide</u>   *
<u>of public drunkenness, violence, and family abandonment, and a spike in alcohol-related diseases.</u> Several of the Founding Fathers—   *Did the*
including George Washington, Thomas Jefferson, and John Adams—   *gov't take*
denounced the excesses of "the Alcoholic Republic," inaugurating an   *action?*
American quarrel over drinking that would culminate a century later in Prohibition.

But the outcome of our national drinking binge is not nearly as rele-   *why?*
vant to our own situation as its (underlying cause.) Which, put simply, was this: <u>American farmers were producing far too much corn.</u> This was   *
particularly true in the newly settled regions west of the Appalachians, where fertile, virgin soils yielded one bumper crop after another. A mountain of surplus corn piled up in the Ohio River Valley. <u>Much as</u>   *Examples*
<u>today, the astounding productivity of American farmers proved to be</u>   *from con-*
<u>their own worst enemy, as well as a threat to public health.</u> For when   *temporary*
yields rise, the market is flooded with grain, and its price collapses.   *US farming?*
What happens next? The excess biomass works like a vacuum in reverse: <u>Sooner or later, clever marketers will figure out a way to induce the</u>   *This is*
<u>human omnivore to consume the surfeit of cheap calories.</u>   *his point*

EXERCISE 9.1

Find an article that interests you in a newspaper or magazine (or online). Read it carefully, highlighting it as you read. When you have finished, annotate the article.

CHECKLIST

READING TEXTS

As you read a text, keep the following questions in mind:

❑ Does the writer provide any information about his or her background? If so, how does this information affect your reading of the text?

❑ Are there parallels between the writer's experiences and your own?

(continued)

READING TEXTS (*continued*)

❏ What is the writer's purpose? How can you tell?

❏ What audience is the text aimed at? How can you tell?

❏ What is the most important idea? What support does the writer provide for that idea?

❏ What information can you learn from the introduction and conclusion?

❏ What information can you learn from the thesis statement and topic sentences?

❏ What key words are repeated? What does this repetition tell you about the writer's purpose and emphasis?

❏ How would you characterize the writer's tone?

❏ Where do you agree with the writer? Where do you disagree?

❏ What, if anything, is not clear to you?

Writing Essay Exams CHAPTER 10

To write an essay examination, or even a paragraph-length answer, you must do more than memorize facts; you must see the relationships among them. In other words, you must **think critically** about your subject.

See Ch. 6

10a Planning an Essay Exam Answer

Because you are under time pressure during an exam, you may be tempted to skip the planning and revision stages of the writing process. But if you write in a frenzy and hand in your exam without a second glance, you are likely to produce a disorganized or even incoherent answer. With careful planning and editing, you can write an answer that demonstrates your understanding of the material.

1 Review Your Material

Be sure you know beforehand the scope and format of the exam. How much of your text and class notes will be covered—the entire semester's work or only the material presented since the last exam? Will you have to answer every question, or will you be able to choose among alternatives? Will the exam be composed entirely of fill-in, multiple-choice, or true/false questions, or will it call for sentence-, paragraph-, or essay-length answers? Will the exam test your ability to recall specific facts, or will it require you to demonstrate your understanding of the course material by drawing conclusions?

All exams challenge you to recall and express in writing what you already know—what you have read, what you have heard in class, what you have reviewed in your notes. Before you take any exam, then, you must study: reread your text and class notes, highlight key points, and perhaps outline particularly important sections of your notes.

Different kinds of exams, however, require different strategies. When you prepare for a short-answer exam, you may memorize facts without analyzing their relationship to one another or their relationship to a body of knowledge as a whole: the definition of pointillism, the date of Queen Victoria's death, or the formula for a quadratic equation, for example. When you prepare for an essay exam, however, you must do more than remember bits of information; you must also make connections among ideas.

When you are sure you know what to expect, see if you can anticipate the essay questions your instructor might ask. Try out likely questions on classmates in a **study group,** and see whether you can do some collaborative brainstorming to outline answers to possible questions. (If you have time, you might even practice answering one or two in writing.)

CHECKLIST

WORKING IN A STUDY GROUP

Working collaboratively in a **study group** requires some degree of organization. To get the most out of your study group, you need to set some ground rules:

❑ Meet regularly.

❑ Decide in advance who will be responsible for particular tasks.

❑ Set deadlines.

❑ Listen when someone else is speaking.

❑ Don't reject other people's ideas and suggestions without considering them very carefully.

❑ Take stock of the group's problems and progress at regular intervals.

❑ Be mindful of other students' learning styles and special needs.

---

2 Consider Your Audience and Purpose

The <u>audience</u> for an exam is the instructor who prepared it. As you read the questions, think about what your instructor has emphasized in class. Keep in mind that your <u>purpose</u> is to demonstrate that you understand the material, not to make clever remarks or introduce irrelevant information. Also, try to use the vocabulary of the particular academic discipline and to follow any discipline-specific stylistic conventions your instructor has discussed.

See Ch. 1

3 Read through the Entire Exam

Before you begin to write, read the questions carefully to determine your priorities and your strategy. First, be sure that your copy of the test is complete and that you understand exactly what each question requires. If you need clarification, ask your instructor or proctor for help. Then, plan carefully, deciding how much time you should devote to answering each question. Often, the point value of each question or the number of questions on the exam indicates how much time you should spend on each answer. If an essay question is worth fifty out of one hundred points, for example, you will probably have to spend at least half (and perhaps more) of your time planning, writing, and proofreading your answer.

Next, decide where to start. Responding first to questions whose answers you are sure of is usually a good strategy. This tactic ensures that you will not become bogged down in a question that baffles you, left with too little time to write a strong answer to a question that you understand well. Moreover, starting with the questions that you are sure of can help build your confidence.

4 Read Each Question Carefully

To write an effective answer, you need to understand the question. As you read any essay question, you may find it helpful to underline key words and important terms.

Sociology: Distinguish among Social Darwinism, instinct theory, and sociobiology, giving examples of each.

Music: Explain how Milton Babbitt used the computer to expand Schoenberg's twelve-tone method.

Philosophy: Define existentialism and identify three influential existentialist works, explaining why they are important.

Look carefully at the wording of each question. If the question calls for a comparison and contrast of two styles of management, an analysis of one style, no matter how comprehensive, will not be acceptable. If the question asks for causes and effects, a discussion of causes alone will not do.

CLOSE-UP

KEY WORDS IN EXAM QUESTIONS

Pay careful attention to the words used in exam questions:

◆ analyze	◆ describe	◆ interpret
◆ clarify	◆ discuss	◆ justify
◆ classify	◆ evaluate	◆ relate
◆ compare	◆ explain	◆ summarize
◆ contrast	◆ identify	◆ support
◆ define	◆ illustrate	◆ trace

The wording of a question suggests what you should emphasize. For instance, an American history instructor would expect very different answers to the following two exam questions:

♦ Give a detailed explanation of the major <u>causes</u> of the Great Depression, noting briefly some of the effects of the economic collapse on the United States.

♦ Give a detailed summary of the <u>effects</u> of the Great Depression on the United States, briefly discussing the major causes of the economic collapse.

Although the two questions above look alike, the first calls for an essay that stresses *causes*, whereas the second calls for one that stresses *effects*.

5 Brainstorm to Find Ideas

Once you think you understand the question, you need to <u>**find something**</u> See 2e
<u>**to say.**</u> Begin by **brainstorming,** quickly listing all the relevant ideas you can remember. Then, identify the most important points on your list, and delete the others. A quick review of the exam question and your supporting ideas should lead you toward a workable thesis for your essay answer.

10b Shaping an Essay Exam Answer

Like an essay, an effective exam answer has a <u>**thesis-and-support**</u> structure. See 3a–b

1 Stating a Thesis

Often, you can answer the exam question in the form of a **thesis statement.** For example, the American history exam question "Give a detailed summary of the effects of the Great Depression on the United States, briefly discussing the major causes of the economic collapse" suggests the following thesis statement:

Effective Thesis Statement: The Great Depression, caused by the American government's economic policies, had major political, economic, and social effects on the United States.

This effective thesis statement addresses all aspects of the question but highlights only relevant concerns.

The following thesis statements are not effective:

Vague Thesis Statement: The Great Depression, caused largely by profligate spending patterns, had a number of very important results.

Incomplete Thesis Statement: The Great Depression caused major upheaval in the United States.

Irrelevant Thesis Statement: The Great Depression, caused largely by America's poor response to the 1929 stock market crash, had more important consequences than World War II did.

2 Constructing an Informal Outline

Because time is limited, you should plan your answer before you write it.
See 3c Therefore, once you have decided on a suitable thesis, you should make an <u>informal outline</u> that lists your major points. Once you have completed your outline, check it against the exam question to make certain it covers everything the question calls for—and *only* what the question calls for.

10c   Writing and Revising an Essay Exam Answer

Referring to your outline, you can now begin to draft your answer. Don't bother crafting an elaborate or unusual **introduction;** your time is precious, and so is your reader's. A simple statement of your thesis that summarizes your answer is your best introductory strategy: this approach is efficient, and it reminds you to address the question directly.

To develop the **body** of the essay, follow your outline point by point, using clear topic sentences and transitions to indicate your progression and See 18a to help your instructor see that you are answering the question in full. Such signals, along with <u>parallel</u> sentence structure and repeated key words, make your answer easy to follow.

The most effective **conclusion** for an essay examination is a clear, simple restatement of the thesis or a summary of the essay's main points.

Although essay answers should be complete and detailed, they should not contain irrelevant material. Every unnecessary fact or opinion increases your chance of error, so don't repeat yourself or volunteer unrequested information, and don't express your own feelings or opinions unless such information is specifically asked for. In addition, be sure to support all your general statements with specific examples.

Finally, be sure to leave enough time to revise what you have written. If you suddenly remember something you want to add, you can insert a few additional words with a caret (∧). Neatly insert a longer addition at the end of your answer, box it, and label it so your instructor will know where it belongs.

ESL TIP

Because of time pressure, it is difficult to write in-class essay exam answers that are as polished as your out-of-class writing. You should do your best to convey your ideas as clearly as you can, but keep in mind that instructors are usually more concerned with your content than with your writing style. Therefore, instead of wasting time searching for the "perfect" words or phrases, use words and grammatical constructions that are familiar to you. You can use any remaining time to check your grammar and mechanics. Finally, don't waste time recopying your work unless what you have written is illegible.

In the one-hour essay exam answer that appears below, notice how the student restates the question in her thesis statement and keeps the question in focus by repeating key words like *cause, effect, result, response,* and *impact.*

Effective Essay Exam Answer

Question: Give a detailed summary of the effects of the Great Depression on the United States, briefly discussing the major causes of the economic collapse.

The Great Depression, caused by the American government's economic policies, had major political, economic, and social effects on the United States.

Introduction— thesis statement rephrases exam question

The Depression was precipitated by the stock market crash of October 1929, but its actual causes were more subtle: they lay in the US government's economic policies. First, personal income was not well distributed. Although production rose during the 1920s, the farmers and other workers got too little of the profits; instead, a disproportionate amount of income went to the richest 5 percent of the population. The tax policies at this time made inequalities in income even worse. A good deal of income also went into development of new manufacturing plants. This expansion stimulated the economy but encouraged the production of more goods than consumers could purchase. Finally, during the economic boom of the 1920s, the government did not attempt to limit speculation or impose regulations on the securities market; it also did little to help build up farmers' buying power. Even after the crash began, the government made mistakes: instead of trying to address the country's deflationary economy, the government focused on keeping the budget balanced and making sure the United States adhered to the gold standard.

Policies leading to Depression (¶ 2 summarizes causes)

The Depression, devastating to millions of individuals, had a tremendous impact on the nation as a whole. Its political, economic, and social consequences were great.

Transition from causes to effects

Between October 1929 and Roosevelt's inauguration on March 4, 1933, the economic situation grew worse. Businesses were going bankrupt, banks were failing, and stock prices were falling. Farm prices fell drastically, and hungry farmers were forced to burn their

Early effects (¶s 4–8 summarize important results in chronological order)

corn to heat their homes. There was massive unemployment, with millions of workers jobless and humiliated, losing skills and self-respect. President Hoover's Reconstruction Finance Corporation made loans available to banks, railroads, and businesses, but Hoover thought state and local funds (not the federal government) should finance public works programs and relief. Confidence in the president declined as the country's economic situation worsened.

Additional effects: Roosevelt's emergency measures

One result of the Depression was the election of Franklin Delano Roosevelt. By the time of his inauguration, most American banks had closed, thirteen million workers were unemployed, and millions of farmers were threatened by foreclosure. Roosevelt's response was immediate: two days after he took office, he closed all the remaining banks and took steps to support the stronger ones with loans and to prevent the weaker ones from reopening. During the first hundred days of his administration, he kept Congress in special session. Under his leadership, Congress enacted emergency measures designed to provide "Relief, Recovery, and Reform."

Additional effects: Roosevelt's reform measures

In response to the problems caused by the Depression, Roosevelt set up agencies to reform some of the conditions that had helped to cause the Depression in the first place. The Tennessee Valley Authority, created in May 1933, was one of these. Its purposes were to control floods by building new dams and improving old ones and to provide cheap, plentiful electricity. The TVA improved the standard of living of area farmers and drove down the price of power all over the country. The Agricultural Adjustment Administration, created the same month as the TVA, provided for taxes on basic commodities, with the tax revenues used to subsidize farmers to produce less. This reform measure caused prices to rise.

Additional effects: NIRA, other laws, and so on

Another response to the problems of the Depression was the National Industrial Recovery Act. This act established the National Recovery Administration, an agency that set minimum wages and maximum hours for workers and set limits on production and prices. Other laws passed by Congress between 1935 and 1940 strengthened federal regulation of power, interstate commerce, and air traffic. Roosevelt also changed the federal tax structure to redistribute American income.

One of the most important results of the Depression was the Social Security Act of 1935, which established unemployment insurance and provided financial aid for the blind and disabled and for dependent children and their mothers. The Works Progress Administration (WPA) gave jobs to over two million workers, who built public buildings, roads, streets, bridges, and sewers. The WPA also employed artists, musicians, actors, and writers. The Public Works Administration (PWA) cleared slums and created public housing. In the National Labor Relations Act (1935), workers received a guarantee of government protection for their unions against unfair labor practices by management.

Additional effects: Social Security, WPA, and so on

As a result of the economic collapse known as the Great Depression, Americans saw their government take responsibility for providing immediate relief, for helping the economy recover, and for taking steps to ensure that the situation would not be repeated. The economic, political, and social impact of the laws passed during the 1930s is still with us, helping to keep our government and our economy stable.

Conclusion—restatement of thesis

Notice that in her answer the student does not include any irrelevant material: she does not, for example, describe the conditions of people's lives in detail, blame anyone in particular, discuss the president's friends and enemies, or consider parallel events in other countries. She covers only what the question asks for. Notice, too, how topic sentences (**"One result of the Depression . . ."**; **"In response to the problems caused by the Depression . . ."**; **"One of the most important results of the Depression . . ."**) keep the primary purpose of the discussion in focus and guide her instructor through the essay.

Writing for the Workplace
CHAPTER 11

Work is often a part of the college experience, with many students having part-time jobs, internships, community-service positions, or cooperative education experiences. The skills that you develop in these activities are frequently transferable to the employment that you will have after you graduate.

11a Writing Letters of Application

The **letter of application** summarizes your qualifications for a specific position.

Begin your letter of application by identifying the job you are applying for and stating where you heard about it—in a newspaper, in a professional journal, on a Web site, or from your school's job placement service, for example. Be sure to include the date of the advertisement and the exact title of the position. End your introduction with a statement that expresses your ability to do the job.

In the body of your letter, supply the information that will convince your reader of your qualifications—for example, relevant courses you have taken and pertinent job experience. Be sure to address any specific points mentioned in the advertisement. Above all, emphasize your strengths, and explain how they relate to the specific job for which you are applying.

Conclude by saying that you have enclosed your résumé and that you are available for an interview, noting any dates on which you will not be available. (Be sure to include your phone number and your email address.)

Note: After you have been interviewed, be sure to send a follow-up letter or email to the person (or persons) who interviewed you. First, thank your interviewer for taking the time to see you. Then, briefly summarize your qualifications and mention your interest in the position. Because many applicants do not write follow-up letters, such letters can have a very positive effect on those who receive them.

Sample Letter of Application

246 Hillside Drive
Urbana, IL 61801
Kr237@metropolis.105.com

Heading

March 20, 2009

Mr. Maurice Snyder, Personnel Director
Guilford, Fox, and Morris
22 Hamilton Street
Urbana, IL 61822

Inside
address

Dear Mr. Snyder:

Salutation
(followed
by a colon)

My college advisor, Dr. Raymond Walsh, has told me that you are interested in hiring a summer accounting intern. I believe that my academic background and my work experience qualify me for this position.

I am presently a junior accounting major at the University of Illinois. During the past year, I have taken courses in taxation, trusts, and business law. I am also proficient in *PeachTree Complete* and *QuickBooks Pro*. Last spring, I gained practical accounting experience by working in our department's tax clinic.

Body

←— Double-spaced

After I graduate, I hope to get a master's degree in taxation and then return to the Urbana area. I believe that my experience in taxation as well as my familiarity with the local business community would enable me to contribute to your firm.

←— Single-spaced

I have enclosed a résumé for your review. I will be available for an interview any time after midterm examinations, which end March 25. I look forward to hearing from you.

Sincerely yours,

Complimentary
close

Sandra Kraft

Written
signature

Sandra Kraft

Typed
signature

Enc: Résumé

Additional
data

EXERCISE 11.1

Look through the employment advertisements in your local newspaper or in the files of your college placement service. Choose one job, and write a letter of application in which you summarize your achievements and discuss your qualifications for the position.

11b Designing Print Résumés

A **résumé** lists relevant information about your education, your job experience, your goals, and your personal interests.

There is no single correct format for a résumé. You will most likely arrange your résumé in **chronological order** (see page 129), listing your education and work experience in sequence (beginning with the most recent), but in some situations you may want to use **emphatic order,** beginning with the material that will be of most interest to an employer (for example, important skills). Whatever a résumé's arrangement, it should be brief—one page is usually sufficient for an undergraduate—easy to read, clear and emphatic, logically organized, and free of errors.

CLOSE-UP

RÉSUMÉ STYLE

Use strong action verbs to describe your duties, responsibilities, and accomplishments:

accomplished	achieved	supervised
communicated	collaborated	instructed
completed	implemented	proposed
performed	organized	trained

 Note: Use past tense for past positions and present tense for current positions.

Sample Résumé: Chronological Order

KAREN L. OLSON

SCHOOL	HOME
3812 Hamilton St. Apt. 18	110 Ascot Ct.
Philadelphia, PA 19104	Harmony, PA 16037
215-382-0831	412-452-2944
olsont@dunm.ocs.drexel.edu	

EDUCATION

DREXEL UNIVERSITY, Philadelphia, PA 19104
Bachelor of Science in Graphic Design
Anticipated Graduation: June 2010
Cumulative Grade Point Average: 3.2 on a 4.0 scale

COMPUTER SKILLS AND COURSEWORK

HARDWARE

Familiar with both Macintosh and PC systems

SOFTWARE

Adobe Illustrator, Photoshop, and *Type Align; QuarkXPress 8; CorelDRAW; Adobe InDesign CS4*

COURSES

Corporate Identity, Environmental Graphics, Typography, Photography, Painting and Print-making, Sculpture, Computer Imaging, Art History

EMPLOYMENT EXPERIENCE

THE TRIANGLE, Drexel University, Philadelphia, PA 19104
January 2007–present
Graphics Editor. Design all display advertisements submitted to Drexel's student newspaper.

UNISYS CORPORATION, Blue Bell, PA 19124
June–September 2007, Cooperative Education
Graphic Designer. Designed interior pages as well as covers for target marketing brochures. Created various logos and spot art designed for use on interoffice memos and departmental publications.

CHARMING SHOPPES, INC., Bensalem, PA 19020
June–December 2006, Cooperative Education
Graphic Designer/Fashion Illustrator. Created graphics for future placement on garments. Did some textile designing. Drew flat illustrations of garments to scale in computer. Prepared presentation boards.

DESIGN AND IMAGING STUDIO, Drexel University, Philadelphia, PA 19104
October 2006–June 2007
Monitor. Supervised computer activity in studio. Answered telephone. Assisted other graphic design students in using computer programs.

ACTIVITIES AND AWARDS

The Triangle, Graphics Editor: 2006–present
Kappa Omicron Nu Honor Society, vice president: 2007–present
Dean's List: spring 2006, fall and winter 2007
Graphics Group, vice president: 2006–present

REFERENCES AND PORTFOLIO

Available upon request.

11c Designing Electronic Résumés

The majority of résumés are still submitted on paper (usually as email attachments), but electronic résumés—both scannable and Web-based—are gaining in popularity.

1 Scannable Résumés

Many employers request scannable résumés that they can store in a database for future reference. If you have to prepare such a résumé, keep in mind that scanners will not pick up columns, bullets, or italics and that shaded or colored paper will make your résumé difficult to scan.

Whereas in a print résumé you use specific action verbs (**edited**) to describe your accomplishments, in a scannable résumé you also use key nouns (**editor**) that can be entered into a company database. These words will help employers find your résumé when they carry out a keyword search for applicants with certain skills. To facilitate a keyword search, applicants often include a Skills section on their résumé. For example, if you wanted to emphasize your computer skills, you would include keywords such as *WordPerfect, FileMaker Pro,* and *PowerPoint*.

Sample Résumé: Scannable

Constantine G. Doukakis
2000 Clover Lane
Fort Worth, TX 76107

Phone: (817) 735-9120
Email: Douk@aol.com

Employment Objective: Entry-level position in an organization that will enable me to use my academic knowledge and the skills that I learned in my work experience.

Education:

University of Texas at Arlington, Bachelor of Science in Civil Engineering, June 2009. Major: Structural Engineering. Graduated Magna Cum Laude. Overall GPA: 3.754 on a 4.0 base.

Scholastic Honors and Awards:

Member of Phi Eta Sigma First-Year Academic Honor Society, Chi Epsilon Civil Engineering Academic Society, Tau Beta Pi Engineering Academic Society, Golden Key National Honor Society.

Jack Woolf Memorial Scholarship for Outstanding Academic Performance.

Cooperative Employment Experience:

Johnson County Electric Cooperative, Clebume, TX, Jan. 2009 to June 2009. Junior Engineer in Plant Dept. of Maintenance and Construction Division. Inspected and supervised in-plant construction. Devised solutions to construction problems. Estimated costs of materials for small construction projects. Presented historical data relating to the function of the department.

Dallas-Fort Worth International Airport, Tarrant County, TX, Dec. 2007 to June 2008. Assistant Engineer. Supervised and inspected airfield paving, drainage, and utility projects as well as terminal building renovations. Performed on-site and laboratory soil tests. Prepared concrete samples for load testing.

Dallas-Fort Worth International Airport, Tarrant County, TX, Jan. 2007 to June 2007. Draftsperson in Design Office. Prepared contract drawings and updated base plans as well as designed and estimated costs for small construction projects.

Skills:

Organizational and leadership skills. Written and oral communication skills, C++, IBM, Macintosh, DOS, Windows Vista, Mac OS X Snow Leopard, Word, Excel, FileMakerPro, PowerPoint, WordPerfect, and Internet client software. Computer model development. Technical editor.

2 Web-Based Résumés

See
Ch. 13 It is becoming common to have a PDF version of your résumé posted on a personal **Web site.** Usually, a Web-based résumé is an alternative to a print résumé that you have mailed or a scannable version that you have submitted to a database or as an email attachment. Figure 11.1 shows a Web-based version of a student's résumé.

FIGURE 11.1 Sample student Web-based résumé.

EXERCISE 11.2

Prepare two versions of your résumé—one print and the other scannable—that you could include with the letter of application you wrote for Exercise 11.1. How are these two résumés alike? How are they different?

11d Writing Memos

Memos communicate information within an organization. Begin your memo with a purpose statement, followed by a background section. In the body of your memo, support your main point. If your memo is short, use bulleted or numbered lists to emphasize information. If it is more than two or three paragraphs, use headings to designate individual sections. End your memo by stating your conclusions and recommendations.

Sample Memo

TO: Ina Ellen, Senior Counselor   Opening
FROM: Kim Williams, Student Tutor Supervisor   component
SUBJECT: Construction of a Tutoring Center
DATE: November 10, 2009

This memo proposes the establishment of a tutoring center in   Purpose
the Office of Student Affairs.   statement

BACKGROUND
Under the present system, tutors must work with students at a
number of facilities scattered across the university campus. As
a result, tutors waste a lot of time running from one facility to
another and are often late for appointments.

NEW FACILITY   Body
I propose that we establish a tutoring facility adjacent to the
Office of Student Affairs. The two empty classrooms next to the
office, presently used for storage of office furniture, would be
ideal for this use. We could furnish these offices with the desks
and file cabinets already stored in these rooms.

BENEFITS
The benefits of this facility would be the centralizing of the tutoring services and the proximity of the facility to the Office of
Student Affairs. The tutoring facility could also use the secre-
tarial services of the Office of Student Affairs.

RECOMMENDATIONS   Conclusion
To implement this project we would need to do the following:
1. Clean up and paint rooms 331 and 333
2. Use folding partitions to divide each room into five single-
   desk offices
3. Use stored office equipment to furnish the center

I am certain these changes would do much to improve the tutoring service. I look forward to discussing this matter with you
in more detail.

11e Writing Emails

In many workplaces, virtually all internal (and some external) communications are transmitted as email. Although personal email tends to be quite informal, business email should observe the conventions of standard written communication.

CHECKLIST

WRITING EMAILS

The following guidelines can help you communicate effectively in an electronic environment:

❏ Write in complete sentences. Avoid the slang, imprecise diction, and abbreviations that are commonplace in personal email.

❏ Use an appropriate tone. Address readers with respect, just as you would in a standard business letter.

❏ Include a subject line that clearly identifies your content. If your subject line is vague, your email may be deleted without being read.

❏ Make your message as short as possible. Because most emails are read on the screen, long discussions are difficult to follow.

❏ Use short paragraphs, and leave an extra space between paragraphs.

❏ Use lists and internal headings to make your message easier to read and understand. (Keep in mind, however, that your recipient may not be able to view certain formatting elements, such as boldface, italics, and indentation.)

❏ Take the time to edit your email, and delete excess words and phrases.

❏ Proofread carefully before sending your email. Look for errors in grammar, spelling, and punctuation.

❏ Make sure that your list of recipients is accurate and that you do not send your email to unintended recipients.

❏ Do not send your email until you are absolutely certain your message says exactly what you want it to say.

❏ Do not forward an email unless you have the permission of the sender.

❏ Watch what you write. Always remember that email written at work is the property of the employer, who has the legal right to access it, even without your permission.

Designing Effective Documents

Document design refers to the principles that help you determine how to design a piece of written work so that it communicates your ideas clearly and effectively. Although formatting conventions—for example, how tables and charts are constructed and how information is arranged on a title page—may differ from discipline to discipline, all well-designed documents share the same general characteristics: an effective format, clear headings, useful lists, and helpful visuals.

12a Creating an Effective Visual Format

An effective document contains visual cues that help readers find, read, and interpret information on a page. For example, wide margins can give a page a balanced, uncluttered appearance; white space can break up a long discussion; and a distinctive type size and typeface can make a word or phrase stand out on a page.

1. Margins

Margins frame a page and keep it from looking overcrowded. Because long lines of text can overwhelm readers and make a document difficult to read, a page should have margins of at least one inch all around. If the material you are writing about is highly technical or unusually difficult, use wider margins (one and a half inches).

Except for documents such as flyers and brochures, where you might want to isolate blocks of text for emphasis, you should justify (uniformly align, except for paragraph indentations) the left-hand margin. You can either leave a ragged edge on the right, or you can justify your text so all the words are aligned evenly along the right margin. (A ragged edge is usually preferable because it is less formal than fully justified text.)

2. White Space

White space is the area of a page that is intentionally left blank. Used effectively, white space can isolate material and thereby focus a reader's attention on it. You can use white space around a block of text—a paragraph or a section, for example—or around visuals such as charts, graphs, and photographs. White space can eliminate clutter, break a discussion into manageable components, and help readers process information more easily.

BORDERS, HORIZONTAL RULES, AND SHADING

Most word-processing programs enable you to create borders, horizontal rules, and shaded areas of text. Border and shading options are usually found under the Format menu (or in the Formatting Palette) of your word-processing program. With these features, you can select line style, thickness, and color and adjust white space, boxed text, and the degree of shading. Keep in mind that these features should be used only when appropriate, so check with your instructor.

3 Color

Color (when used in moderation) can help to emphasize and clarify information while making it visually appealing. In addition to using color to emphasize information, you can use it to distinguish certain types of information—for example, titles can be one color and subheadings can be another, complementary color. You can also use color to differentiate the segments of a chart or the bars on a graph. Remember, however, that too many colors can confuse readers and detract from your visual emphasis.

4 Typeface and Type Size

Your computer gives you a wide variety of typefaces and type sizes (measured in **points**) from which to choose. **Typefaces** are distinctively designed sets of letters, numbers, and punctuation marks. The typeface you choose should be suitable for your purpose and audience. In your academic writing, avoid fancy or elaborate typefaces—*script* or 𝔬𝔩𝔡 𝔈𝔫𝔤𝔩𝔦𝔰𝔥, for example— that call attention to themselves and distract readers. Instead, select a typeface that is simple and direct—Courier, Times New Roman, or Arial, for example. In nonacademic documents—such as Web pages and flyers— decorative typefaces may be used to emphasize a point or attract a reader's attention.

You also have a wide variety of **type sizes** available to you. For most of your academic papers, you will use 10- or 12-point type (headings will sometimes be larger). Documents such as advertisements, brochures, and Web pages, however, may use a variety of type sizes.

5 Line Spacing

Line spacing refers to the amount of space between the lines of a document. If the lines are too far apart, the text will seem to lack cohesion; if the lines are too close together, the text will appear crowded and be difficult to read. The type of writing you do may determine line spacing: the paragraphs of business letters, memos, and some reports are usually single-spaced and separated by a double space, but the paragraphs of academic papers are usually double-spaced.

12b Using Headings

Used effectively, **headings** act as signals that help readers process information, and they also break up a text, making it inviting and easy to read. Different academic disciplines have different requirements concerning headings. For this reason, you should consult the appropriate style manual before inserting headings in a paper.

1 Number of Headings

The number of headings you use depends on the document. A long, complicated document will need more headings than a shorter, less complicated one. Keep in mind that too few headings may not be of much use, but too many headings will make your document look like an outline.

2 Phrasing

Headings should be brief, informative, and to the point. They can be single words—**Summary** or **Introduction**, for example—or they can be phrases (always stated in <u>parallel</u> terms): **Traditional Family Patterns, Alternate Family Patterns, Modern Family Patterns.** Finally, headings can be questions (**How Do You Choose a Major?**) or statements (**Choose Your Major Carefully**).

See 18a

3 Indentation

Indenting is one way of distinguishing one level of heading from another. The more important a heading is, the closer it is to the left-hand margin: first-level headings are justified left, second-level headings are indented one-half inch, and third-level headings are indented further. Headings and subheadings may also be *centered, placed flush left,* or *run into the text.*

4 Typographical Emphasis

You can emphasize important words in headings by using **boldface,** *italics,* or ALL CAPITAL LETTERS. Used in moderation, these distinctive typefaces make a text easier to read. Used excessively, however, they slow readers down.

5 Consistency

Headings at the same level should have the same typeface, type size, spacing, and color. In addition, if one first-level heading is boldfaced and centered, all other first-level headings must be boldfaced and centered. Using consistent patterns reinforces the connection between content and ideas and makes a document easier to understand.

Note: Never separate a heading from the text that goes with it: if a heading is at the bottom of one page and the text that goes with it is on the next page, move the heading onto the next page so readers can see the heading and the text together.

12c Constructing Lists

By breaking long discussions into a series of key ideas, a list makes information easier to understand. By isolating individual pieces of information this way and by providing visual cues (such as bullets or numbers), a list also directs readers to important information on a page.

CHECKLIST

CONSTRUCTING EFFECTIVE LISTS

When constructing lists, you should follow these guidelines:

❑ **Indent each item**. Each item on a list should be indented so that it stands out from the text around it.

❑ **Set off items with numbers or bullets.** Use **bullets** when items are not organized according to any particular sequence or priority (the members of a club, for example). Use **numbers** when you want to indicate that items are organized according to a sequence (the steps in a process, for example).

❑ **Introduce a list with a complete sentence.** Do not simply drop a list into a document; introduce it with a complete sentence (followed by a colon) that tells readers what to look for in the list.

❑ **Use parallel structure.** Lists are easiest to read when all items are parallel and about the same length.

A decrease in several factors can cause high unemployment:
• consumer spending
• factory orders
• factory output

❑ **Punctuate correctly.** If the items on a list are fragments (as in the example above), begin each item with a lowercase letter, and do not end it with a period. However, if the items on a list are complete sentences (as in the example below), begin each item with a capital letter and end it with a period.

Here are the three steps we must take to reduce our spending:
1. We must cut our workforce by 10 percent.
2. We must use less expensive vendors.
3. We must decrease overtime payments.

❑ **Don't overuse lists.** Too many lists will give readers the impression that you are simply listing points instead of discussing them.

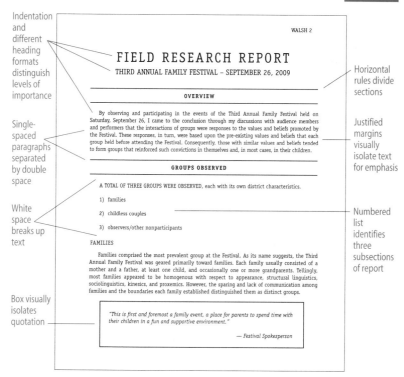

FIGURE 12.1 A well-designed page from a student's report.

Figure 12.1 shows a page from a student's report that incorporates some of the effective design elements discussed in 12a–c. Notice that the use of different typefaces and type sizes contributes to the document's overall readability.

EXERCISE 12.1

Select two different documents—for example, a page from a procedure manual and an invitation, or a report and a flyer. Then, make a list of the design elements each document contains. Finally, evaluate the relative effectiveness of the two documents, given their intended audiences.

12d Using Visuals

Visuals, such as tables, graphs, diagrams, and photographs, can help you convey complex ideas that are difficult to communicate with words and can also help you attract readers' attention.

1 Tables

Tables present data in a condensed, visual format—arranged in rows and columns. Tables may contain numerical data, text, or a combination of the two. When you plan your table, make sure you include only the data that you will need; discard information that is too detailed or difficult to understand. Keep in mind that tables can distract readers, so include only those necessary to support your discussion. (The table in Figure 12.2 reports the student writer's original research and therefore does not require documentation.)

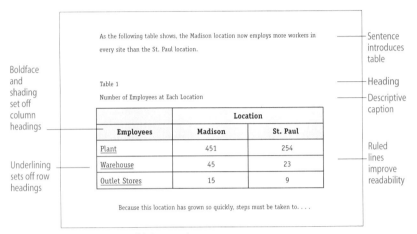

As the following table shows, the Madison location now employs more workers in every site than the St. Paul location. — Sentence introduces table

Boldface and shading set off column headings —

Table 1
Number of Employees at Each Location — Heading / Descriptive caption

Employees	Location	
	Madison	St. Paul
Plant	451	254
Warehouse	45	23
Outlet Stores	15	9

Underlining sets off row headings —

Ruled lines improve readability —

Because this location has grown so quickly, steps must be taken to. . . .

FIGURE 12.2 Table in a student paper.

2 Graphs

Like tables, **graphs** present data in visual form. Whereas tables may present specific numerical data, graphs convey the general pattern or trend that the data suggest. Because graphs tend to be more general (and therefore less accurate) than tables, they are frequently accompanied by tables. Figure 12.3 is an example of a bar graph showing data from a source.

3 Diagrams

A **diagram** calls readers' attention to specific details of a mechanism or object. Diagrams are often used in scientific and technical writing to clarify concepts that are difficult to explain in words. Figure 12.4, which illustrates the sections of an orchestra, serves a similar purpose in a music education paper.

4 Photographs

Photographs enable you to show exactly what something or someone looks like—an animal in its natural habitat, a work of fine art, or an actor in

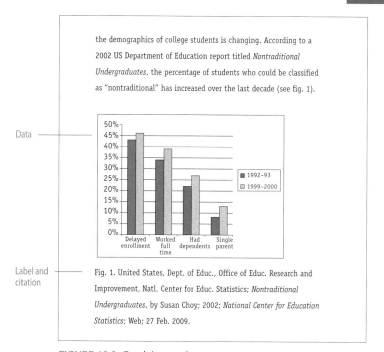

Data

the demographics of college students is changing. According to a 2002 US Department of Education report titled *Nontraditional Undergraduates*, the percentage of students who could be classified as "nontraditional" has increased over the last decade (see fig. 1).

Label and citation

Fig. 1. United States, Dept. of Educ., Office of Educ. Research and Improvement, Natl. Center for Educ. Statistics; *Nontraditional Undergraduates*, by Susan Choy; 2002; *National Center for Education Statistics*; Web; 27 Feb. 2009.

FIGURE 12.3 Graph in a student paper.

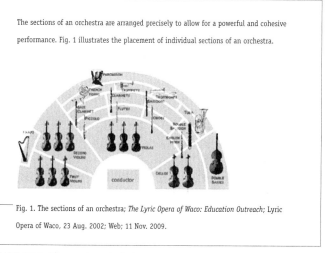

The sections of an orchestra are arranged precisely to allow for a powerful and cohesive performance. Fig. 1 illustrates the placement of individual sections of an orchestra.

Label, descriptive caption, and citation

Fig. 1. The sections of an orchestra; *The Lyric Opera of Waco: Education Outreach*; Lyric Opera of Waco, 23 Aug. 2002; Web; 11 Nov. 2009.

FIGURE 12.4 Diagram in a student paper.

costume, for example. Although it is easy to paste photographs directly into a text, you should do so only when they support or enhance your points. The photograph of a wooded trail in Figure 12.5 illustrates the student writer's description.

Photo sized and placed appropriately within text with consistent white space above and below

travelers are well advised to be prepared, to always carry water, and to dress for the conditions. Loose fitting, lightweight wicking material covering all exposed skin is necessary in summer, and layers of warm clothing are needed for cold-weather outings. Hats and sunscreen are always a good idea no matter what the temperature, although most of the trails are quite shady with huge oak trees. Fig. 1 shows a shady portion of the trail.

Reference to photo provides context

Label and descriptive caption

Fig. 1. Greenbelt Trail in springtime (author photo).

FIGURE 12.5 Photograph in a student paper.

USING VISUALS

When using visuals in your papers, follow these guidelines:

- ❑ Use a visual only when it contributes something important to the discussion, not for embellishment.
- ❑ Use the visual in the text only if you plan to discuss it in your paper (place the visual in an appendix if you do not).
- ❑ Introduce each visual with a complete sentence.
- ❑ Follow each visual with a discussion of its significance.
- ❑ Leave wide margins around each visual.
- ❑ Place the visual as close as possible to the section of your document in which it is discussed.
- ❑ Label each visual appropriately.
- ❑ Document each visual borrowed from a source.

EXERCISE 12.2

Analyze the chart in Figure 12.6, noting the visual elements that are used to convey the billing costs of material, labor, and equipment on a construction project. Summarize the data in a brief paragraph. Then, list the advantages and disadvantages of presenting the data visually as opposed to verbally.

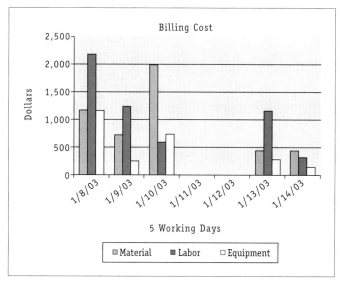

FIGURE 12.6 Billing cost chart.

12e   Using Desktop Publishing

During your college career, you may be required to use your computer for **desktop publishing**—using graphics as well as words to produce documents. For example, you may produce a brochure, flyer, or newsletter for a student organization to which you belong or as a service-learning project for a course you are taking. (Figures 12.7 and 12.8 on page 144 show a student brochure.) Brochures and flyers are frequently aimed at consumers of a product or service or at members of an organization. These documents may be informative, persuasive, or both.

Most word-processing programs, such as *Microsoft Word*, contain templates that can help you design your flyer, newsletter, or brochure. With these templates, you can select layout, color scheme, and typeface as well as document dimensions and paper size.

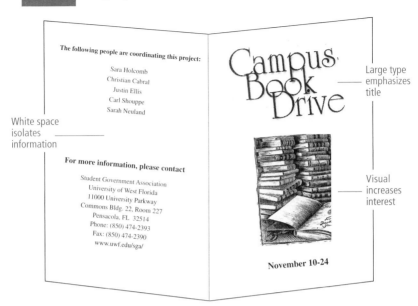

FIGURE 12.7 Front and back cover of brochure.

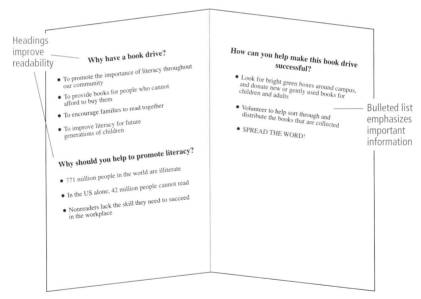

FIGURE 12.8 Inside pages of brochure.

EXERCISE 12.3

Create a promotional document for an organization on your campus. Before you begin the document-design process, interview someone affiliated with the organization to determine the type of information you will need, the format in which the information should be delivered, and the image the organization wishes to project to the campus community.

Because of the nature of the Internet, online communication is different from print communication. In order to write effectively for an online audience, you should be aware of the demands of writing in a digital environment.

13a Considering Audience and Purpose

The most obvious difference between electronic communication and print communication is the nature of the **audience.** Audiences for print documents read a discussion from beginning to end and form their own ideas about it. Audiences for electronic documents, however, can respond quite differently. Readers can post responses in chat rooms and directly communicate with the writer (sometimes in real time) as well as with one another.

The **purpose** of electronic communication may also be quite different from that of print communication. Unlike print documents, which appear as carefully crafted finished products in newspapers and magazines, electronic documents are frequently written in immediate response to other people's arguments or ideas. In fact, by including links to a writer's email address or to a blog or chat room, many online documents encourage readers to respond. For this reason, in addition to trying to inform or persuade, the purpose of electronic documents may also be to support, refute, react, clarify, or correct.

Internet documents also tend to be shorter and more to the point than articles written for magazines and newspapers. Typically, people come to the Internet for information, and they want to access that information as quickly as possible. For this reason, they tend to reject long, discursive articles and to turn instead to articles that are direct and easy to read. Because most people read Internet articles on the screen, they do not have the patience or the inclination to read articles that are more than a page or two in length. (However, some long articles—for example, journal articles that students use for their research—appear in print and electronic versions and are intended to be printed out.)

13b Creating Electronic Documents

Because of the dynamic environment of Internet communication, electronic documents tend to be relatively informal. Much like a conversation, these documents frequently begin by making a single point, which is then

5. Re: Cure? What cure?

by Booga

at Tue 21 Dec 1:25pm

score of 2
intriguing

in reply to comment 1

If we actually had a cure for autism nobody would be asking us not to administer it.

Not necessarily.

[...reply just to this I comment on the story... I next new]

20. Autism as a Communication Disorder

by Catch22

at Tue 21 Dec 3:07pm

score of 3
compelling

in reply to comment 1

I for one doubt that there will ever be a "cure" to autism at least in my lifetime. Autism is a spectrum disorder with an extraordinarily broad number of manifestations. It requires speculation, but I suspect that autism is an umbrella term for a broad category of manifestations that may result from different causes. We dont know what causes autism, but rather only that it appears to have a genetic basis.

FIGURE 13.1 *Plastic.com* blog postings.

expanded over time through comments and discussions (see Figure 13.1). In order to follow a discussion, a reader often has to scroll through several pages of online postings. In this sense, these electronic documents are more like works in progress than finished products.

Even when electronic documents physically resemble print documents (as they do in online newspaper articles and in blog posts), the way they present information may be different. Print documents are **linear;** that is, readers move in a straight line from the beginning to the end. Also, in order to be effective, a print document must include all the background information, explanations, supporting evidence, and visuals necessary to make its point.

Electronic documents, however, are not usually linear. Because writers of electronic documents (such as the one shown in Figure 13.2) rely on hyperlinks to supplement their discussions, an electronic document will often address just the main points of a discussion. Links then enable readers to go to other sites that include the facts, statistical data, and other articles that supplement the discussion. When readers access these sites, they can take in as much or as little information as they want or need.

EXERCISE 13.1

Find a document that someone has posted on the Web. Identify the elements that make it different from a print document. Then, decide what else the writer could have done to make the document more effective.

13c Writing in a Wired Classroom

Increasingly instructors are using the Internet as well as specific Web-based technology to teach writing. Some of the most popular tools that students can use to create Web-based content in an electronic writing environment are discussed here.

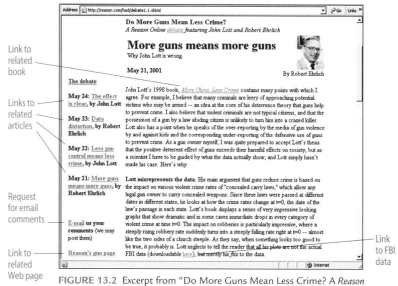

Link to related book

Links to related articles

Request for email comments

Link to related Web page

Link to FBI data

FIGURE 13.2 Excerpt from "Do More Guns Mean Less Crime? A *Reason Online* Debate."

1 Using Email

Email enables you to exchange ideas with classmates, ask questions of your instructors, and communicate with the writing center or other campus services. You can insert email links in Web documents, and you can transfer files as email attachments from one computer to another. In many classes, writing assignments are submitted to instructors as email attachments.

CLOSE-UP

EMAIL ADDRESSES

Avoid using email addresses that are cute or witty or that contain puns or double entendres. Although they may be fine for your friends, these addresses are not appropriate for the classroom or for a résumé or job application letter.

---

2 Using Blogs

A **blog** (short for Weblog) is like an online personal journal (see Figure 13.1). Most blogs offer commentary, news, or personal reactions—usually presented in reverse chronological order, with the most recent entry first. Blogs can function as online diaries, communicating the personal views of the author. As well as being personal, blogs can be used by a business or educational institution to further communication. A **microblogging** service such as **Twitter** allows users to instantly send (and receive) **tweets**—posts of up to 140 characters in length—to a group of people who have signed up to receive them.

Some teachers of writing encourage students to create and maintain blogs that function as online writing journals. Blogs are not limited to text; they can contain photographs, videos, music, audio, and personal artwork as well as links to other blogs or Web sites. Most browsers (as well as course management tools such as *Blackboard* and *Angel*) make it easy to create a blog. Although many blogs are open to everyone, some are password protected.

3 Using Wikis

Unlike a blog, which is created by an individual and does not allow visitors to edit the posted content, a **wiki** (Hawaiian for *fast*) is a Web site that allows users to add, remove, or change content using any Web browser. With wikis, individuals can work together on a project, adding, deleting, and modifying content as the need arises. Although many wiki sites are open to the general public, some are restricted to members of a particular group or organization.

The best-known wiki is *Wikipedia,* the online encyclopedia. Some writing instructors create wikis to encourage students to collaborate on reports, encyclopedia entries, or brochures. The result is a project that is the collective work of all the students who contributed to the project.

4 Using Listservs

Listservs (sometimes called **discussion lists**), electronic mailing lists to which users must subscribe, enable individuals to communicate with groups of people interested in particular topics. (Many schools, and even individual courses, have listservs.) Subscribers to a listserv send emails to a main email address, and these messages are automatically routed to all members of the group.

Listservs can be especially useful in composition classes, permitting students to post comments on reading assignments as well as to discuss other subjects with the entire class.

5 Using Newsgroups

Like listservs, **newsgroups** are discussion groups. Unlike listserv messages, which are sent as email, newsgroup messages are collected on the Usenet system, a global collection of news servers, where anyone who subscribes can access them. In a sense, newsgroups function as gigantic bulletin boards where users post messages that others read and respond to.

Some composition instructors establish newsgroups for their classes. Students access the newsgroup to get messages from their classmates or to download papers and assignments. One advantage of newsgroups is that messages are posted and downloaded only when needed, so they don't take up space in students' email files.

6 Using Synchronous and Asynchronous Communication

Some Internet tools enable you to send and receive messages in real time. In other words, communication is **synchronous:** messages are sent and received as they are typed. With other Internet communication tools, there is a delay between the time a message is sent and the time it is received. These types of messages are **asynchronous.**

With **synchronous communication,** all parties involved in the communication process are present at the same time and can be involved in the conversation. Chat rooms, instant messaging, MOOs, and MUDs are examples of synchronous communication. Course management tools such as *Angel* and *Blackboard* offer discussion boards that allow for the transmission of images as well as shared viewing of whiteboard drawings and specific Internet sites. Synchronous communication tools are often used in distance-learning classes to create a virtual classroom environment.

With **asynchronous communication,** there is a delay between the time a message is sent and the time it is received. Asynchronous exchanges occur with email, newsgroups, listservs, Web forums, and bulletin boards. With asynchronous communication, students can work at their own pace, contributing to a discussion by posting comments or by sending email messages and reading comments posted by their instructors or other students.

CHECKLIST

OBSERVING NETIQUETTE

Netiquette refers to the guidelines that responsible users of the Internet should follow when they write in cyberspace. When you communicate via the Internet, keep the following guidelines in mind:

- ❏ **Don't shout.** All-uppercase letters indicate that a person is SHOUTING.
- ❏ **Watch your tone.** Make sure your message conveys what you actually intend. What might seem humorous or clever to you may seem disrespectful to someone else.
- ❏ **Be careful what you write.** Remember, once you hit Send, it is often too late to call the message back. Be sure to consider carefully what you have written.
- ❏ **Don't flame.** When you flame, you send an insulting electronic message. This tactic is not only immature, it is rude and annoying.
- ❏ **Make sure you use the correct electronic address.** Be certain that your message goes to the right person. Nothing is more embarrassing than sending an email to the wrong address.
- ❏ **Use your computer ethically and responsibly.** Don't use computer labs for personal communications or for entertainment. Not only is this a misuse of the facility but it also ties up equipment that others may be waiting to use.

7 Using Podcasts

A **podcast** is any broadcast—audio or visual—that has been converted to an MP3 or similar format for playback on the Internet. You can access a podcast with a computer or with an MP3 playback device.

Podcasting is becoming increasingly common in composition classrooms. On the most basic level, instructors podcast class lectures that students can access at their leisure. Instructors also use podcasts to present commentary on students' writing, to distribute supplementary material such as audio recordings or speeches, to record student presentations, or to communicate class information or news.

13d Writing Collaboratively Online

Collaborative writing means creating a piece of writing that has more than one author. Every time you post a written passage and get feedback from a classmate or from your instructor, you are engaging in collaborative writing. Digital writing environments present special opportunities for collaboration. For example, if your writing class has an online component, your instructor has most likely set up a virtual space where writing can be posted and commented on. In addition, electronic tools such as email, text messages, and blogs allow for collaboration at every stage of the writing process.

See
4c2

1 Peer Review

Participating in <u>peer review</u> online has a number of advantages. You can easily exchange papers with members of a group or even with the entire class, and you can get feedback on your work from a number of people. If you are working on a group project, you do not have to arrange meetings or travel to campus. In fact, most of your collaborative activities can take place in front of your computer. Finally, because most of your communications are archived, you will usually have a record of your drafts and your correspondence.

Although online writing environments present unique opportunities for collaboration, they also present challenges. Because feedback can come from so many different sources—for example, from blogs, chat rooms, and wikis as well as from editorial suggestions made with *Word*'s Comment tool—it is easy to become overwhelmed by your classmates' comments and suggestions. For this reason, it is extremely important to keep track of the various drafts of your essay and to keep your own ideas separate from the comments you get in response to your essay.

If for some reason you need to compare two drafts of a paper, use the Track Changes "Compare Versions" tool. Everything that was deleted will be shaded, and everything that has been changed will be highlighted. Some document management systems—*Writeboard,* for example—enable you to access every version of a piece of writing that you have saved. This feature enables you to revise and edit a document without losing an earlier version that might possibly be better.

2 Group Projects

See 12e

Sometimes you may be assigned to a group or team to work together on a writing project—for example, a proposal, a **brochure,** or a flyer. When you work online as part of a group, you follow many of the same procedures that you do in any online collaboration. In addition, you follow procedures that are specifically tailored to working as a group. As you set up and organize your group, keep the following advice in mind:

- **Decide how your group will meet.** Will you exchange comments in a chat room or post comments on a discussion board? Some instant message and chat room technologies allow multiuser discussions and enable you to record and save transcripts of discussions for use later.
- **Divide tasks.** Make sure each member of the group knows exactly what his or her role is. For example, one person might be responsible for coordinating the project, another for finding information, another for finding visuals, another for writing, and still another for revising and editing.
- **Determine how you will collaborate.** Will you send drafts to each other as email attachments? Work on a wiki site? Or will you use some other method?
- **Keep a list of email and phone numbers.** Set up an email or listserv group so that you can easily communicate with everyone.
- **Set up files to store communications.** Make sure you keep a file (or files) of all communications sent and received from members of the group.
- **Decide on editing guidelines in advance.** To avoid confusion, agree on a consistent set of responses to writing—for example, what kind of comments you might insert on documents with *Word*'s Comment feature.
- **Set up a realistic schedule.** Be sure to set up a schedule that includes deadlines and due dates, and be sure each person understands his or her responsibilities and is willing (and able) to meet deadlines.
- **Agree on specific dates for checking progress.** Periodically check to make sure you are all on schedule. Don't let a missed deadline take the group by surprise.

EXERCISE 13.2

What electronic tools does your writing instructor use on a regular basis? What other tools do you think could be used to teach writing?

Sentence Style

Sentence Style

A **sentence** is an independent grammatical unit that includes a <u>subject</u> and a <u>predicate</u> and expresses a complete thought.

> The quick brown fox <u>jumped over the lazy dog.</u>

> It <u>came from outer space.</u>

A **simple subject** is a noun or noun substitute (*fox, it*) that tells who or what the sentence is about. A **simple predicate** is a verb or <u>**verb phrase**</u> (*jumped, came*) that tells or asks something about the subject. The **complete subject** of a sentence includes the simple subject plus all its modifiers (*the quick brown fox*). The **complete predicate** includes the verb or verb phrase as well as all the words associated with it—such as modifiers, objects, and complements (*jumped over the lazy dog, came from outer space*).

See 14b1

> **ESL TIP**
>
> In some languages, such as Spanish, the subject of a sentence can sometimes be omitted. In English, however, every sentence must have a subject.

14a Constructing Simple Sentences

A **simple sentence** consists of at least one subject and one predicate. Simple sentences conform to one of five basic patterns.

1 Subject + Intransitive Verb (s + v)

The most basic simple sentence consists of just a subject and a verb or **verb phrase** (the <u>main verb</u> plus all its <u>auxiliary verbs</u>).

See 20c1

> s   v
> The price of gold <u>rose.</u>

> s   v
> Stock prices <u>may fall.</u>

Here the verbs *rose* and *may fall* are **intransitive**—that is, they do not need an object to complete their meaning.

2 Subject + Transitive Verb + Direct Object (s + v + do)

Another kind of simple sentence consists of the subject, a verb, and a direct object.

        s   v   do

Van Gogh <u>created</u> *The Starry Night.*

       s   v   do

Caroline <u>saved</u> Jake.

Here the verbs *created* and *saved* are **transitive**—each requires an object to complete its meaning in the sentence. In each sentence, the **direct object** indicates where the verb's action is directed and who or what is affected by it.

ESL TIP

To determine whether a verb is intransitive or transitive, consult a dictionary. Remember, though, that some verbs, such as *write,* can be intransitive or transitive.

    She <u>wrote</u> all night. (intransitive)

    She <u>wrote</u> a paper about her semester in Spain. (transitive)

---

3   Subject + Transitive Verb + Direct Object +
       Object Complement (s + v + do + oc)

Some simple sentences include an **object complement,** a word or phrase that renames or describes the direct object.

     s   v   do   oc

The class <u>elected</u> Bridget treasurer. (Object complement *treasurer* renames direct object *Bridget.*)

  s   v   do   oc

I <u>found</u> the exam easy. (Object complement *easy* describes direct object *exam.*)

4   Subject + Linking Verb + Subject Complement
       (s + v + sc)

See
20c1 Another kind of simple sentence consists of a subject, a <u>linking verb</u> (a verb that connects a subject to its complement), and the **subject complement** (the word or phrase that describes or renames the subject).

      s   v   sc

The injection <u>was</u> painless.

      s   v   sc

Nancy Pelosi <u>became</u> House Democratic Leader.

Note that the linking verb is like an equal sign, equating the subject with its complement (*Nancy Pelosi = House Democratic Leader*).

5 Subject + Transitive Verb + Indirect Object +
Direct Object (s + v + io + do)

Some simple sentences include an **indirect object,** which indicates to whom
or for whom the verb's action was done.

    s   v   io   do
<u>Cyrano</u> <u>wrote</u> Roxanne a poem. (Cyrano wrote a poem for Roxanne.)

    s   v   io   do
<u>The officer</u> <u>handed</u> Frank a ticket. (The officer handed a ticket to Frank.)

EXERCISE 14.1

In each of the following sentences, underline the subject once and the predicate
twice. Then, label direct objects, indirect objects, subject complements, and
object complements.

                      sc
Example: <u>Isaac Asimov</u> <u>was</u> a science fiction writer.

▶ 1. Isaac Asimov first saw science fiction stories in his parents' Brooklyn
store.
▶ 2. He practiced writing by telling his schoolmates stories.
▶ 3. Asimov published his first story in *Astounding Science Fiction*.
▶ 4. The magazine's editor, John W. Campbell, encouraged Asimov to continue writing.
▶ 5. The young writer researched scientific principles to make his stories more
accurate.
   6. Asimov's "Foundation" series of novels is a "future history."
   7. The World Science Fiction Convention gave the series a Hugo Award.
   8. Sometimes Asimov used "Paul French" as a pseudonym.
   9. *Biochemistry and Human Metabolism* was Asimov's first nonfiction book.
 10. Asimov coined the term *robotics*.

14b Identifying Phrases and Clauses

Individual words may be combined into *phrases* and *clauses*.

1 Identifying Phrases

A **phrase** is a group of related words that lacks a subject or predicate or both
and functions as a single part of speech. It cannot stand alone as a sentence.

♦ A **verb phrase** consists of a main verb and all its auxiliary verbs.

Time <u>is flying</u>.

♦ A **noun phrase** includes a noun or pronoun plus all related modifiers.

I'll climb <u>the highest mountain</u>.

♦ A **prepositional phrase** consists of a preposition, its object, and any modifiers of that object.

They discussed the ethical implications <u>of the animal studies</u>.
He was last seen heading <u>into the orange sunset</u>.

♦ A **verbal phrase** consists of a **verbal** (participle, gerund, or infinitive) and its related objects, modifiers, or complements. A verbal phrase may be a **participial phrase,** a **gerund phrase,** or an **infinitive phrase.**

<u>Encouraged by the voter turnout</u>, the candidate predicted a victory. (participial phrase)

<u>Taking it easy</u> always makes sense. (gerund phrase)

The jury recessed <u>to evaluate the evidence</u>. (infinitive phrase)

♦ An **absolute phrase** usually consists of a noun and a participle, accompanied by modifiers. It modifies an entire independent clause rather than a particular word or phrase.

<u>Their toes tapping</u>, they watched the auditions.

2 Identifying Clauses

A **clause** is a group of related words that includes a subject and a predicate. An **independent** (main) **clause** can stand alone as a sentence, but a **dependent** (subordinate) **clause** cannot. It must always be combined with an independent clause to form a <u>complex sentence.</u>

See 14d

[Lucretia Mott was an abolitionist.] [She was also a pioneer for women's rights.] (two independent clauses)

[Lucretia Mott was an abolitionist] [who was also a pioneer for women's rights.] (independent clause, dependent clause)

[Although Lucretia Mott is widely known for her support of women's rights,] [she was also a prominent abolitionist.] (dependent clause, independent clause)

Dependent clauses may be *adjective, adverb,* or *noun* clauses.

♦ **Adjective clauses,** sometimes called **relative clauses,** modify nouns or pronouns and always follow the nouns or pronouns they modify. They are introduced by relative pronouns—*that, what, whatever, which, who, whose, whom, whoever,* or *whomever*—or by the adverbs *where* or *when*.

The television series *M*A*S*H*, <u>which depicted life in an army hospital in Korea during the Korean War</u>, ran for eleven years. (Adjective clause modifies the noun *M*A*S*H*.)

William Styron's novel *Sophie's Choice* is set in Brooklyn, <u>where the narrator lives in a house painted pink</u>. (Adjective clause modifies the noun *Brooklyn*.)

Note: Some adjective clauses, called **elliptical clauses,** are grammatically incomplete but nevertheless can be easily understood from the context of the sentence. Typically, a part of the subject or predicate (or the entire subject or predicate) is missing: *Although [they were] <u>full</u>, they could not resist dessert.*

♦ **Adverb clauses** modify single words (verbs, adjectives, or adverbs), entire phrases, or independent clauses. They are always introduced by subordinating conjunctions. Adverb clauses provide information to answer the questions *how? where? when? why?* and *to what extent?*

Exhausted <u>after the match was over</u>, Kim decided to take a long nap. (Adverb clause modifies *exhausted*, telling *when* Kim was exhausted.)

Mark will go <u>wherever there's a party</u>. (Adverb clause modifies *will go*, telling *where* Mark will go.)

<u>Because 75 percent of its exports are fish products</u>, Iceland's economy is heavily dependent on the fishing industry. (Adverb clause modifies independent clause, telling *why* the fishing industry is so important.)

♦ **Noun clauses** function as subjects, objects, or complements. A noun clause may be introduced by a relative pronoun or by *whether, when, where, why,* or *how.*

<u>What you see</u> is <u>what you get</u>. (Noun clauses serve as subject and subject complement.)

They finally decided <u>which candidate was most qualified</u>. (Noun clause serves as direct object of verb *decided*.)

EXERCISE 14.2

Which of the following groups of words are independent clauses? Which are dependent clauses? Which are phrases? Label each word group *IC, DC,* or *P.*

Example: Coming through the rye. (P)

▶ 1. Beauty is truth.
▶ 2. When knights were bold.
▶ 3. In a galaxy far away.
▶ 4. He saw stars.
▶ 5. I hear a symphony.

6. Whenever you're near.
7. The clock struck ten.
8. The red planet.
9. Slowly I turned.
10. For the longest time.

14c Building Compound Sentences

A **compound sentence** consists of two or more independent clauses joined with *coordinating conjunctions, transitional words or phrases, correlative conjunctions, semicolons,* or *colons.*

1 Using Coordinating Conjunctions

You can join two independent clauses with a **coordinating conjunction**— *and, or, nor, but, for, so,* or *yet*—preceded by a comma.

> She carried a thin, small cane made from an umbrella, <u>and</u> with this she kept tapping the frozen earth in front of her. (Eudora Welty, "A Worn Path")

> In the fall the war was always there, <u>but</u> we did not go to it any more. (Ernest Hemingway, "In Another Country")

> **ESL TIP**
>
> Some languages, such as Arabic, typically use coordination more than English does. If you think you are overusing compound sentences, try experimenting with complex sentences **(see 15b).**

2 Using Transitional Words and Phrases

You can join two independent clauses with a **transitional word or phrase,** preceded by a semicolon (and followed by a comma).

> Aerobic exercise can help lower blood pressure; <u>however</u>, people with high blood pressure should still limit salt intake.

> The saxophone does not belong to the brass family; <u>in fact</u>, it is a member of the woodwind family.

See 5b2

Note: Commonly used <u>transitional words and phrases</u> include **conjunctive adverbs** like *however, therefore, nevertheless, consequently, finally, still,* and *thus* as well as expressions like *for example, in fact, on the other hand,* and *for instance.*

3 Using Correlative Conjunctions

You can use <u>correlative conjunctions</u> to join two independent clauses into a compound sentence.

See
20g

<u>Either</u> he left his coat in his locker, <u>or</u> he left it on the bus.

4 Using Semicolons

A <u>semicolon</u> can join two closely related independent clauses into a compound sentence.

See
31a

Alaska is the largest state; Rhode Island is the smallest.

Theodore Roosevelt was president after the Spanish-American War; Andrew Johnson was president after the Civil War.

5 Using Colons

A <u>colon</u> can join two independent clauses.

See
34a

He got his orders: he was to leave for France on Sunday.

They thought they knew the outcome: Truman would lose to Dewey.

CLOSE-UP

USING COMPOUND SENTENCES

Joining independent clauses into compound sentences helps to show readers the relationships between the clauses. Compound sentences can indicate the following relationships:

♦ Addition (*and, in addition, not only . . . but also*)
♦ Contrast (*but, however*)
♦ Causal relationships (*so, therefore, consequently*)
♦ Alternatives (*or, either . . . or*)

EXERCISE 14.3

Add appropriate coordinating conjunctions, transitional words or phrases, or correlative conjunctions (as indicated) to combine each pair of sentences into one well-constructed compound sentence that retains the meaning of the original pair. Be sure to use correct punctuation.

, so people

Example: The American population is aging./People seem to be increasingly concerned about what they eat. (coordinating conjunction)

▶ 1. The average American consumes 128 pounds of sugar each year. Most of us eat much more sugar than any other food additive, including salt. (transitional word or phrase)
▶ 2. Many of us are determined to reduce our sugar intake. We have consciously eliminated sweets from our diets. (transitional word or phrase)
▶ 3. Unfortunately, sugar is not found only in sweets. It is also found in many processed foods. (correlative conjunction)
▶ 4. Processed foods like puddings and cake contain sugar. Foods like ketchup and spaghetti sauce do too. (coordinating conjunction)
▶ 5. We are trying to cut down on sugar. We find limiting sugar intake extremely difficult. (coordinating conjunction)
6. Processors may use sugar in foods for taste. They may also use it to help prevent foods from spoiling and to improve the texture and appearance of food. (correlative conjunction)
7. Sugar comes in many different forms. It is easy to overlook on a package label. (coordinating conjunction)
8. Sugar may be called sucrose or fructose. It may also be called corn syrup, corn sugar, brown sugar, honey, or molasses. (coordinating conjunction)
9. No sugar is more nourishing than the others. It really does not matter which is consumed. (transitional word or phrase)
10. Sugars contain empty calories. Whenever possible, they should be avoided. (transitional word or phrase)

(Adapted from *Jane Brody's Nutrition Book*)

14d Building Complex Sentences

A **complex sentence** consists of one **independent clause** and at least one **dependent clause.**

A dependent clause cannot stand alone; it must be combined with an independent clause to form a sentence. In a complex sentence, a **subordinating conjunction** or **relative pronoun** links the independent and dependent clauses and indicates the relationship between them.

dependent clause · · · · · · · · · · · · independent clause
[After the town was evacuated,] [the hurricane began.]

independent clause · · · · · · · · · · · · dependent clause
[Officials watched the storm,] [which threatened to destroy the town.]

Note: Sometimes a dependent clause may be embedded within an independent clause.

dependent clause
Town officials, [who were very concerned,] watched the storm.

FREQUENTLY USED SUBORDINATING CONJUNCTIONS

after	in order that	until
although	now that	when
as	once	whenever
as if	rather than	where
as though	since	whereas
because	so that	wherever
before	that	while
even though	though	
if	unless	

RELATIVE PRONOUNS

that	whatever	who (whose, whom)
what	which	whoever (whomever)

CLOSE-UP

USING COMPLEX SENTENCES

When you join clauses to create complex sentences, you help readers to see the relationships between your ideas. Complex sentences can indicate the following relationships:

♦ Time relationships (*before, after, until, when, since*)
♦ Contrast (*however, although*)
♦ Causal relationships (*therefore, because, so that*)
♦ Conditional relationships (*if, unless*)
♦ Location (*where, wherever*)
♦ Identity (*who, which, that*)

EXERCISE 14.4

Use a subordinating conjunction or relative pronoun to combine each of the following pairs of sentences into one well-constructed complex sentence. Be sure to choose a connecting word that indicates the relationship between the two sentences. You may have to change or reorder words.

Example: *Because some* Some colleges are tightening admissions requirements. *Their* Their pool of students is growing smaller. *, their*

▶ 1. Many high school graduates are currently out of work. They need new skills for new careers.

▶ 2. Talented high school students are usually encouraged to go to college. Some high school graduates are now starting to see that a college education may not guarantee them a job.

▶ 3. A college education can cost a student more than $100,000. Vocational education is becoming an increasingly attractive alternative.

▶ 4. Vocational students complete their work in less than four years. They can enter the job market more quickly.

▶ 5. Nurses' aides, paralegals, travel agents, and computer technicians do not need college degrees. They have little trouble finding work.

   6. Some four-year colleges are experiencing growth. Public community colleges and private trade schools are growing much more rapidly.

   7. The best vocational schools are responsive to the needs of local businesses. They train students for jobs that actually exist.

   8. For instance, a school in Detroit might offer advanced automotive design. A school in New York City might focus on fashion design.

   9. Other schools offer courses in horticulture, respiratory therapy, and computer programming. They are able to place their graduates easily.

   10. Laid-off workers, housewives returning to school, recent high school graduates, and even college graduates are reexamining vocational education. They all hope to find rewarding careers.

CLOSE-UP

COMPOUND-COMPLEX SENTENCES

A **compound-complex sentence** consists of two or more independent clauses and at least one dependent clause.

                              dependent clause
[When small foreign imports began dominating the US automobile
                    independent clause   **independent clause**
industry,] [consumers were very responsive,] but [American auto workers

were dismayed.]

Writing Varied Sentences

CHAPTER 15

Using **varied** sentences can help make your writing livelier and more interesting and can also ensure that you emphasize the most important ideas in your sentences.

15a Combining Choppy Simple Sentences

Strings of short simple sentences can be tedious—and sometimes hard to follow, as this paragraph illustrates.

> John Peter Zenger was a newspaper editor. He waged and won an important battle for freedom of the press in America. He criticized the policies of the British governor. He was charged with criminal libel as a result. Zenger's lawyers were disbarred. Andrew Hamilton defended him. Hamilton convinced the jury that Zenger's criticisms were true. Therefore, the statements were not libelous.

You can revise choppy sentences like these by using *coordination, subordination,* or *embedding* to combine them with adjacent sentences.

1 Using Coordination

Coordination pairs similar elements—words, phrases, or clauses—giving equal weight to each. The following revision links two of the choppy simple sentences in the paragraph above with *and* to create a **compound sentence.**

See 14c

> John Peter Zenger was a newspaper editor. He waged and won an important battle for freedom of the press in America. He criticized the policies of the British governor, and as a result, he was charged with criminal libel. Zenger's lawyers were disbarred. Andrew Hamilton defended him. Hamilton convinced the jury that Zenger's criticisms were true. Therefore, the statements were not libelous.

ESL TIP

Some ESL students rely on simple sentences and coordination in their writing because they are afraid of making sentence structure errors. The result is a monotonous style. To add variety, try using **subordination** and **embedding** (explained in **15a2** and **15a3**) in your sentences.

---

2 Using Subordination

Subordination places the more important idea in the independent clause and the less important idea in the dependent clause. The following revision of the preceding paragraph uses subordination to change two simple sentences into dependent clauses, creating two **complex sentences.**

See 14d

> John Peter Zenger was a newspaper editor who waged and won an important battle for freedom of the press in America. He criticized the policies of the British governor, and as a result, he was charged with criminal libel. When Zenger's lawyers were disbarred, Andrew Hamilton defended him. Hamilton convinced the jury that Zenger's criticisms were true. Therefore, the statements were not libelous.

3 Using Embedding

Embedding is the working of additional words and phrases into a sentence. In the following revision, the sentence *Hamilton convinced the jury . . .* has been reworded to create a phrase (*convincing the jury*) that is embedded into another sentence, where it now modifies the independent clause *Andrew Hamilton defended him.*

> John Peter Zenger was a newspaper editor who waged and won an important battle for freedom of the press in America. He criticized the policies of the British governor, and as a result, he was charged with criminal libel. When Zenger's lawyers were disbarred, Andrew Hamilton defended him, convincing the jury that Zenger's criticisms were true. Therefore, the statements were not libelous.

This final revision of the original string of choppy sentences is interesting and readable because it is now composed of varied and logically linked sentences. The final short simple sentence has been retained for emphasis.

EXERCISE 15.1

Using coordination, subordination, and embedding, revise this string of choppy simple sentences into a more varied and interesting paragraph.

> ▶The first modern miniature golf course was built in New York in 1925. ▶It was an indoor course with 18 holes. ▶Entrepreneurs Drake Delanoy and John Ledbetter built 150 more indoor and outdoor courses. ▶Garnet Carter made miniature golf a worldwide fad. ▶Carter built an elaborate miniature golf course. ▶He later joined with Delanoy and Ledbetter. ▶Together they built more miniature golf courses. They abbreviated playing distances. They highlighted the game's hazards at the expense of skill. This made the game much more popular. By 1930, there were 25,000 miniature golf courses in the United States. Courses grew more elaborate. Hazards grew more bizarre. The craze spread to London and Hong Kong. The expansion of miniature golf grew out of control. Then, interest in the game declined. By 1931, most miniature golf courses were out of business. The game was revived in the early 1950s. Today, there are between eight and ten thousand miniature golf courses. The architecture of miniature golf remains an enduring form of American folk art. (Adapted from *Games*)

15b Breaking Up Strings of Compound Sentences

When you write, try to avoid creating an unbroken series of compound sentences. A string of compound sentences can be extremely monotonous; moreover, if you connect clauses only with coordinating conjunctions, you may find it difficult to indicate exactly how ideas are related and which is most important.

All Compound Sentences: A volcano that is erupting is considered *active,* but one that may erupt is designated *dormant,* and one that has not erupted for a long time is called *extinct.* Most active volcanoes are located in "The Ring of Fire," a belt that circles the Pacific Ocean, and they can be extremely destructive. Italy's Vesuvius erupted in AD 79, and it destroyed the town of Pompeii. In 1883, Krakatoa, located between the Indonesian islands of Java and Sumatra, erupted, and it caused a tidal wave, and more than 36,000 people were killed. Martinique's Mont Pelée erupted in 1902, and its hot gas and ash killed 30,000 people, and this completely wiped out the town of St. Pierre.

Varied Sentences: A volcano that is erupting is considered *active.* (simple sentence) One that may erupt is designated *dormant,* and one that has not erupted for a long time is called *extinct.* (compound sentence) Most active volcanoes are located in "The Ring of Fire," a belt that circles the Pacific Ocean. (simple sentence with modifier) Active volcanoes can be extremely destructive. (simple sentence) Erupting in AD 79, Italy's Vesuvius destroyed the town of Pompeii. (simple sentence with modifier) When Krakatoa, located between the Indonesian islands of Java and Sumatra, erupted in 1883, it caused a tidal wave that killed 36,000 people. (complex sentence with modifier) The eruption of Martinique's Mont Pelée in 1902 produced hot gas and ash that killed 30,000 people, completely wiping out the town of St. Pierre. (complex sentence with modifier)

EXERCISE 15.2

Revise the compound sentences in this passage so the sentence structure is varied. Be sure that the writer's emphasis and the relationships between ideas are clear.

▶Dr. Alice I. Baumgartner and her colleagues at the Institute for Equality in Education at the University of Colorado surveyed two thousand Colorado schoolchildren, and they found some startling results. ▶They asked, "If you woke up tomorrow and discovered that you were a (boy) (girl), how would your life be different?" and the answers were sad and shocking. The researchers assumed they would find that boys and girls would see advantages in being either male or female, but instead they found that both boys and girls had a fundamental contempt for females. Many elementary school boys titled their answers "The Disaster" or "Doomsday," and they described the terrible lives they would lead as girls, but the girls seemed to feel they would be better off as boys, and they expressed feelings that they would be able to do more and have easier lives. (Adapted from *Redbook*)

15c Varying Sentence Openings

Rather than beginning every sentence with the subject (*I* or *It,* for example), add interest and variety by beginning with a modifying *word*, *phrase*, or *clause.*

Beginning with Modifying Words

<u>Proud</u> and <u>relieved</u>, they watched their daughter receive her diploma. (adjectives)

<u>Hungrily</u>, he devoured his lunch. (adverb)

Beginning with Modifying Phrases

<u>For better or worse</u>, credit cards are now widely available to college students. (prepositional phrase)

<u>Located on the west coast of Great Britain</u>, Wales is part of the United Kingdom. (participial phrase)

<u>His interests widening</u>, Picasso designed ballet sets and illustrated books. (absolute phrase)

Beginning with Modifying Clauses

<u>After President Woodrow Wilson was incapacitated by a stroke</u>, his wife unofficially performed many presidential duties. (adverb clause)

GRAMMAR CHECKER

COORDINATING CONJUNCTIONS AND FRAGMENTS

If you begin a sentence with a coordinating conjunction, your grammar checker may identify the word group as a **fragment**. If so, you may need to revise your sentence, following the guidelines in **24b**.

EXERCISE 15.3

Each of these sentences begins with the subject. Revise each so that it has a different opening; then, identify your opening strategy.

Example: N. Scott Momaday, the prominent Native American writer, tells the story of his first fourteen years ~~in The Names.~~ (prepositional phrase)
         In The Names,

▶ 1. Momaday was taken as a very young child to Devil's Tower, the geological formation in Wyoming that is called Tsoai (Bear Tree) in Kiowa, and there he was given the name Tsoai-talee (Bear Tree Boy).

▶ 2. The Kiowa myth of the origin of Tsoai is about a boy who playfully chases his seven sisters up a tree, which rises into the air as the boy is transformed into a bear.

3. The boy-bear becomes increasingly ferocious and claws the bark of the tree, which becomes a great rock with a flat top and deeply scored sides.

4. The sisters climb higher and higher to escape their brother's wrath, and eventually they become the seven stars of the Big Dipper.
5. This story, from which Momaday received one of his names, appears in his works *The Way to Rainy Mountain, House Made of Dawn,* and *The Ancient Child.*

Writing Emphatic Sentences

CHAPTER 16

In speaking, we emphasize certain ideas and deemphasize others with intonation and gesture; in writing, we convey **emphasis**—the relative importance of ideas—through the selection and arrangement of words.

16a Conveying Emphasis through Word Order

Because readers tend to focus on the beginning and end of a sentence, you should place the most important information there.

1 Beginning with Important Ideas

Placing key ideas at the beginning of a sentence stresses their importance. The unedited version of the following sentence places emphasis on the study, not on those who conducted it or on those who participated in it. Editing shifts this focus and puts the emphasis on the researcher, not on the study.

~~In a landmark study of alcoholism,~~ Dr. George Vaillant of
Harvard, *, in a landmark study of alcoholism,* followed two hundred Harvard graduates and four
hundred inner-city, working-class men from the Boston area.

Situations that demand a straightforward presentation—laboratory reports, memos, technical papers, business correspondence, and the like—call for sentences that present vital information first and qualifiers later.

Treating cancer with interferon has been the subject of a good deal of **research.** (emphasizes the treatment, not the research)

Dividends will be paid if the stockholders agree. (emphasizes the dividends, not the stockholders)

CLOSE-UP

USING *THERE IS* AND *THERE ARE*

Using an empty phrase like *there is* or *there are* at the beginning of a sentence generally weakens the sentence.

MIT places
~~There is~~ heavy emphasis on the development of computational skills ~~at MIT.~~

2 Ending with Important Ideas

Placing key elements at the end of a sentence is another way to convey their importance.

Using a Colon or a Dash A colon or a dash can emphasize an important word or phrase by isolating it at the end of a sentence.

Beth had always dreamed of owning one special car: a 1953 Corvette.

The elderly need a good deal of special attention — and they deserve that attention.

CLOSE-UP

PLACING TRANSITIONAL WORDS AND PHRASES

When placed at the end of a sentence, conjunctive adverbs and other transitional words or expressions lose their power to indicate the relationship between ideas. Placed earlier in the sentence, <u>transitional words and phrases</u> can link ideas and add emphasis.

See
5b2

however,
Smokers do have rights; they should not try to impose their habit on

others./ ~~however.~~

Using Climactic Word Order **Climactic word order,** the arrangement of a series of items from the least to the most important, places emphasis on the most important idea at the end of the sentence.

Binge drinking can lead to unwanted pregnancies, car accidents, and even death. (Death is the most serious consequence.)

EXERCISE 16.1

Underline the most important idea in each sentence of the following paragraph. Then, identify the strategy that the writer uses to emphasize each idea. Is the key idea placed at the beginning or the end of a sentence? Does the writer use climactic order?

▶Listening to diatribes by angry callers or ranting about today's news, the talk radio host spreads ideas over the air waves. ▶Every day at the same time, the political talk show host discusses national events and policies, the failures of the opposing view, and the foibles of the individuals who espouse those opposing views. ▶Listening for hours a day, some callers become recognizable contributors to many different talk radio programs. ▶Other listeners are less devoted, tuning in only when they are in the car and never calling to voice their opinions. Political radio hosts usually structure their programs around a specific agenda, espousing the party line and ridiculing the opponent's position. With a style of presentation aimed both at entertainment and information, the host's ideas become caricatures of party positions. Sometimes, in order to keep the information lively and interesting, a host may either state the issues too simply or deliberately mislead the audience. A host can excuse these errors by insisting that the show is harmless: it's for entertainment, not information. Many are concerned about how the political process is affected by this misinformation.

3 Experimenting with Word Order

ESL
49f

In English sentences, the most common <u>word order</u> is subject-verb-object (or subject-verb-complement). By intentionally departing from this expected word order, you can emphasize the word, phrase, or clause that you have relocated.

> More modest and less inventive than Turner's paintings are John Constable's landscapes.

Here the writer calls attention to the modifying phrase *more modest and less inventive than Turner's paintings* by inverting word order, placing the complement and the verb before the subject.

EXERCISE 16.2

Revise the following sentences to make them more emphatic. For each, decide which ideas should be highlighted, and place these key ideas at sentence beginnings or endings. Use climactic order or depart from conventional word order where appropriate.

▶ 1. Police want to upgrade their firepower because criminals are better armed than ever before.
▶ 2. A few years ago, felons used so-called Saturday night specials, small-caliber six-shot revolvers.
3. Now, semiautomatic pistols capable of firing fifteen to twenty rounds, along with paramilitary weapons like the AK-47, have replaced these weapons.
4. Police are adopting such weapons as new fast-firing shotguns and 9mm automatic pistols in order to gain an equal footing with their adversaries.
5. Faster reloading and a hair trigger are two of the numerous advantages that automatic pistols, the weapons of choice among law-enforcement officers, have over the traditional .38-caliber police revolver.

16b Conveying Emphasis through Sentence Structure

As you write, try to construct sentences that emphasize more important ideas and deemphasize less important ones.

1 Using Cumulative Sentences

A **cumulative sentence** begins with an independent clause, followed by additional words, phrases, or clauses that expand or develop it.

> She holds me in strong arms, arms that have chopped cotton, dismembered trees, scattered corn for chickens, cradled infants, shaken the daylights out of half-grown upstart teenagers. (Rebecca Hill, *Blue Rise*)

Because a cumulative sentence presents its main idea first, it tends to be clear and straightforward. (Most English sentences are cumulative.)

2 Using Periodic Sentences

A **periodic sentence** moves from supporting details, expressed in modifying phrases and dependent clauses, to the key idea, which is placed in the independent clause at the end of the sentence.

> Unlike World War II, which ended decisively with the unconditional surrender of Germany and Japan, the war in Vietnam did not end when American troops withdrew.

Note: In some periodic sentences, the modifying phrase or dependent clause comes between subject and predicate: *Columbus, after several discouraging and unsuccessful voyages, finally reached America.*

EXERCISE 16.3

A. Bracket the independent clause(s) in each sentence, and underline each modifying phrase and dependent clause. Label each sentence cumulative or periodic.
B. Relocate the supporting details to make cumulative sentences periodic and periodic sentences cumulative, adding words or rephrasing to make your meaning clear.
C. Be prepared to explain how your revision changes the emphasis of the original sentence.

Example: Feeling isolated, sad, and frightened, [the small child sat alone in the train depot.] (periodic)

Revised: The small child sat alone in the train depot, feeling isolated, sad, and frightened. (cumulative)

▶ 1. However different in their educational opportunities, both Jefferson and Lincoln as young men became known to their contemporaries as "hard students." (Douglas L. Wilson, "What Jefferson and Lincoln Read," *Atlantic Monthly*)
2. The road came into being slowly, league by league, river crossing by river crossing. (Stephen Harrigan, "Highway 1," *Texas Monthly*)
3. Without willing it, I had gone from being ignorant of being ignorant to being aware of being aware. (Maya Angelou, *I Know Why the Caged Bird Sings*)

16c   Conveying Emphasis through Parallelism and Balance

By reinforcing the similarity between grammatical elements, <u>parallelism</u> can help you emphasize information.

> **See 18a**

We seek an individual <u>who is</u> a self-starter, <u>who owns</u> a late-model automobile, and <u>who is</u> willing to work evenings. (classified advertisement)

<u>Do not pass</u> Go; <u>do not collect</u> $200. (instructions)

The Faust legend is central <u>in Benét's *The Devil and Daniel Webster,*</u> <u>in Goethe's *Faust,*</u> and <u>in Marlowe's *Dr. Faustus*.</u> (exam answer)

A **balanced sentence** is neatly divided between two parallel structures— for example, two independent clauses in a compound sentence. The symmetrical structure of a balanced sentence adds emphasis by highlighting similarities or differences between the ideas in the two clauses.

In the 1950s, the electronic miracle was the television; in the 1980s, the electronic miracle was the computer.

Alive, the elephant was worth at least a hundred pounds; dead, he would only be worth the value of his tusks, five pounds, possibly. (George Orwell, "Shooting an Elephant")

16d   Conveying Emphasis through Repetition

<u>Unnecessary repetition</u> makes sentences dull and monotonous as well as wordy.

> **See 17b**

He had a good pitching arm and <u>also</u> could field well and was <u>also</u> a fast runner.

Effective repetition, however, can emphasize key words or ideas.

They decided to begin again: <u>to begin</u> hoping, <u>to begin</u> trying to change, <u>to begin</u> working toward a goal.

During those years when I was just learning to speak, my mother and father addressed me only <u>in Spanish</u>; <u>in Spanish</u> I learned to reply. (Richard Rodriguez, *Aria: A Memoir of a Bilingual Childhood*)

EXERCISE 16.4

Revise the sentences in this paragraph, using parallelism and balance to high-light corresponding elements and using repetition of key words and phrases to add emphasis. You may combine sentences and add, delete, or reorder words.

►Many readers distrust newspapers. ►They also distrust what they read in maga-zines. ►They do not trust what they hear on the radio and what television shows them, either. ►Of these media, newspapers have been the most responsive to audi-ence criticism. ►Some newspapers even have ombudsmen. ►They are supposed to listen to readers' complaints. ►They are also charged with acting on these griev-ances. One complaint that many people have is that newspapers are inaccurate. Newspapers' disregard for people's privacy is another of many readers' criticisms. Reporters are seen as arrogant, and readers feel that journalists can be unfair. They feel that reporters tend to glorify criminals, and they believe there is a ten-dency to place too much emphasis on bizarre or offbeat stories. Finally, readers complain about poor writing and editing. Polls show that despite its efforts to respond to reader criticism, the press continues to face hostility. (Adapted from *Newsweek*)

16e Conveying Emphasis through Active Voice

See
22d
ESL
49a6

The <u>active voice</u> is generally more emphatic than the <u>passive voice</u>.

Passive: The prediction that oil prices will rise is being made by economists.

Active: Economists are predicting that oil prices will rise.

Notice that the passive voice sentence above does not draw readers' atten-tion to who is performing the action. In a passive voice sentence, the subject is the recipient of the action, so the actor fades into the background (*by economists*)—or may even be omitted entirely (*the prediction . . . is being made*). In contrast, active voice places the emphasis where it belongs: on the actor or actors (*Economists*).

Sometimes, of course, you *want* to stress the action rather than the actor; when this is the case, use the passive voice.

Passive: The West was explored by Lewis and Clark. (stresses the exploration of the West, not who explored it)

Active: Lewis and Clark explored the West. (stresses the contribution of the explorers)

Note: Passive voice is also used when the identity of the person perform-ing the action is irrelevant or unknown (*The course was canceled*). For this reason, the passive voice is frequently used in scientific and technical writing: *The beaker was filled with a saline solution.*

GRAMMAR CHECKER

USING PASSIVE VOICE

Your grammar checker will highlight passive voice constructions in your writing and offer revision suggestions. Sometimes, however, the clearest way to express your ideas is by using passive verbs. For example, passive voice may be necessary for clarity or emphasis. In such cases, the grammar checker's suggestion will be awkward—and incorrect.

EXERCISE 16.5

Revise this paragraph to eliminate awkward or excessive use of passive constructions.

► Jack Dempsey, the heavyweight champion between 1919 and 1926, had an interesting but uneven career. ► He was considered one of the greatest boxers of all time. ► Dempsey began fighting as "Kid Blackie," but his career did not take off until 1919, when Jack "Doc" Kearns became his manager. ► Dempsey won the championship when Jess Willard was defeated by him in Toledo, Ohio, in 1919. ► Dempsey immediately became a popular sports figure; President Franklin D. Roosevelt was one of his biggest fans. Influential friends were made by Jack Dempsey. Boxing lessons were given by him to the actor Rudolph Valentino. He made friends with Douglas Fairbanks Sr., Damon Runyon, and J. Paul Getty. Hollywood serials were made by Dempsey, but the title was lost by him to Gene Tunney, and Dempsey failed to regain it the following year. After his boxing career declined, a restaurant was opened by Dempsey, and many major sporting events were attended by him. This exposure kept him in the public eye until he lost his restaurant. Jack Dempsey died in 1983.

Writing Concise Sentences

CHAPTER 17

A sentence is not concise simply because it is short; a **concise** sentence contains only the words necessary to make its point.

17a Eliminating Wordiness

Whenever possible, delete nonessential words—*deadwood, utility words,* and *circumlocution*—from your writing.

1 Eliminating Deadwood

The term **deadwood** refers to unnecessary phrases that take up space and add nothing to meaning.

Many
~~There were many~~ factors ~~that~~ influenced his decision to become a priest.

The two plots are ~~both~~ similar in ~~the way~~ that they trace the characters' increasing rage.

This
~~In this~~ article ~~it~~ discusses lead poisoning.

is
The most tragic character in *Hamlet* ~~would have to be~~ Ophelia.

Deadwood also includes unnecessary statements of opinion, such as *I believe, I feel, it seems to me, as far as I'm concerned,* and *in my opinion.*

2 Eliminating Utility Words

Utility words function as filler; they contribute nothing to the meaning of a sentence. Utility words include nouns with imprecise meanings (*factor, situation, type, aspect,* and so on); adjectives so general that they are almost meaningless (*good, bad, important*); and common adverbs denoting degree (*basically, actually, quite, very, definitely*). Often, you can just delete the utility word; if you cannot, replace it with a more precise word.

Registration
~~The registration situation~~ was disorganized.

an
The scholarship ~~basically~~ offered Fran ~~a good~~ opportunity to study Spanish in Spain.

It was ~~actually~~ a worthwhile book, but I didn't ~~completely~~ finish it.

3 Avoiding Circumlocution

Circumlocution is taking a roundabout way to say something (using ten words when five will do). Instead of complicated constructions, use concise, specific words and phrases that come right to the point.

The *probably*
~~It is not unlikely that the~~ trend will ~~continue.~~

The curriculum was ~~of a~~ unique ~~nature.~~

while
Joe was in the army ~~during the same time that~~ I was in college.

CLOSE-UP

REVISING WORDY PHRASES

A wordy phrase can almost always be replaced by a more concise, more direct term.

Wordy	Concise
at the present time	now
at this point in time	now
for the purpose of	for
due to the fact that	because
on account of	because
until such time as	until
in the event that	if
by means of	by
in the vicinity of	near
have the ability to	can

EXERCISE 17.1

Revise the following paragraph to eliminate deadwood, utility words, and circumlocution. Whenever possible, delete wordy phrases or replace them with more concise expressions.

► For all intents and purposes, the shopping mall is no longer an important factor in the American cultural scene. ► In the '80s, shopping malls became gathering places where teenagers met, walkers came to get in a few miles, and shoppers who were looking for a wide selection and were not concerned about value went to shop. ► There are several factors that have worked to undermine the mall's popularity. ► First, due to the fact that today's shoppers are more likely to be interested in value, many of them have headed to the discount stores. ► Today's shopper is now more likely to shop in discount stores or bulk-buying warehouse stores than in the small, expensive specialty shops in the large shopping malls. Add to this a resurgence of the values of community, and we can see how mall shopping would have to be less attractive than shopping at local stores. Many malls actually have up to 20 percent empty storefronts, and some have had to close down altogether. Others have met the challenge by expanding their roles from shopping centers into community centers. They have added playgrounds for the children and more amusements and restaurants for the adults. They have also appealed to the growing sense of value shopping by giving gift certificates and discounts to shoppers who spend money in their stores. For a while, it seemed as if the huge shopping malls that had become familiar cultural icons were dying out, replaced by catalog and Internet shopping. Now, however, it looks as if some of those icons just might make it and survive by reinventing themselves as more than just places to shop.

17b Eliminating Unnecessary Repetition

Although <u>repetition</u> can make your sentences more emphatic, unnecessary repetition and **redundant** word groups (repeated words or phrases that say the same thing, such as *free gift* and *unanticipated surprise*) can lessen the impact of your writing.

See 16d

You can correct unnecessary repetition by using any of the following strategies.

1 Deleting Redundancy

People's clothing ~~attire~~ can reveal a good deal about their personalities.

The two candidates share several positions ~~in common.~~

GRAMMAR CHECKER

DELETING REDUNDANCY

Your word processor's grammar checker will often highlight redundant expressions and offer suggestions for revision.

---

2 Creating an Appositive

Red Barber ,~~was~~ a sportscaster./ ,He was known for his colorful expressions.

3 Creating a Compound

John F. Kennedy was the youngest man ever elected president./

and

,~~He was~~ the first Catholic to hold this office.

4 Creating a Complex Sentence

, which

Americans value freedom of speech./ ~~Freedom of speech~~ is guaranteed by the First Amendment.

EXERCISE 17.2

Eliminate any unnecessary repetition of words or ideas in this paragraph. Also revise to eliminate deadwood, utility words, and circumlocution.

▶For a wide variety of different reasons, more and more people today are choosing a vegetarian diet. ▶There are three kinds of vegetarians: strict vegetarians eat no animal foods at all; lactovegetarians eat dairy products, but they do not eat meat, fish, poultry, or eggs; and ovolactovegetarians eat eggs and dairy products, but they do not eat meat, fish, or poultry. ▶Famous vegetarians include such well-known people as George Bernard Shaw, Leonardo da Vinci, Ralph Waldo Emerson, Henry David Thoreau, and Mahatma Gandhi. ▶Like these well-known vegetarians, the vegetarians of today have good reasons for becoming vegetarians. For instance, some religions recommend a vegetarian diet. Some of these religions are Buddhism, Brahmanism, and Hinduism. Other people turn to vegetarianism for reasons of health or for reasons of hygiene. These people believe that meat is a source of potentially harmful chemicals, and they believe meat contains infectious organisms. Some people feel meat may cause digestive problems and may lead to other difficulties as well. Other vegetarians adhere to a vegetarian diet because they feel it is ecologically wasteful to kill animals after we feed plants to them. These vegetarians believe we should eat the plants. Finally, there are facts and evidence to suggest that a vegetarian diet may possibly help people live longer lives. A vegetarian diet may do this by reducing the incidence of heart disease and lessening the incidence of some cancers. (Adapted from *Jane Brody's Nutrition Book*).

17c Tightening Rambling Sentences

The combination of nonessential words, unnecessary repetition, and complicated syntax creates **rambling sentences.** Revising rambling sentences frequently requires extensive editing.

1 Eliminating Excessive Coordination

When you string a series of independent clauses together with coordinating conjunctions, you create a rambling, unfocused <u>compound sentence</u> that presents your ideas as if they all have equal weight. To revise such sentences, identify the main idea or ideas, and then subordinate the supporting details.

See 14c

> **Wordy:** Puerto Rico is a large island in the Caribbean, and it is very mountainous, and it has steep slopes, and they fall to gentle plains along the coast.

> **Concise:** A large island in the Caribbean, Puerto Rico is very mountainous, with steep slopes falling to gentle plains along the coast.
> (Puerto Rico's mountainous terrain is the sentence's main idea.)

2 Eliminating Adjective Clauses

A series of <u>adjective clauses</u> is also likely to produce a rambling sentence. To revise, substitute more concise modifying words or phrases for the adjective clauses.

See 14b2

> **Wordy:** *Moby-Dick,* <u>which is a novel about a white whale,</u> was written by Herman Melville, <u>who was friendly with Nathaniel Hawthorne,</u> <u>who urged him to revise the first draft.</u>

> **Concise:** *Moby-Dick,* a novel about a white whale, was written by Herman Melville, who revised the first draft at the urging of his friend Nathaniel Hawthorne.

3 Eliminating Passive Constructions

Excessive use of the <u>passive voice</u> can create rambling sentences. Correct this problem by changing passive to active voice.

See 22d1 ESL 49a6

~~Water rights are being fought for in court by~~ Indian tribes like the Papago in Arizona and the Pyramid Lake Paiute in Nevada. *are fighting in court for water rights.*

4 Eliminating Wordy Prepositional Phrases

See
14b1
When you revise, substitute adjectives or adverbs for wordy <u>prepositional</u> <u>phrases</u>.

            dangerous   *exciting*
The trip was ~~one of danger~~ but also ~~one of excitement~~.

          confidently   *authoritatively*
He spoke ~~in a confident manner~~ and ~~with a lot of authority~~.

5 Eliminating Wordy Noun Constructions

See
14b1
Substitute strong verbs for wordy <u>noun phrases</u>.

         decided
We have ~~made the decision~~ to postpone the meeting until ~~the~~
                                  appear
~~appearance of~~ all the board members.

                                   accumulates
Sometimes ~~there is an accumulation of~~ water on the roof.

EXERCISE 17.3

Revise the rambling sentences in these paragraphs by eliminating excessive coordination; unnecessary use of the passive voice; and overuse of adjective clauses, prepositional phrases, and noun constructions. As you revise, make your sentences more concise by deleting nonessential words and unnecessary repetition.

▶Some colleges that have been in support of fraternities for a number of years are at this time in the process of conducting a reevaluation of the position of those fraternities on campus. ▶In opposition to the fraternities are a fair number of students, faculty members, and administrators who claim fraternities are inherently sexist, which they say makes it impossible for the groups to exist in a coeducational institution, which is supposed to offer equal opportunities for members of both sexes. ▶More and more members of the college community also see fraternities as elitist as well as sexist and favor their abolition. ▶In addition, many point out that fraternities are associated with dangerous practices, such as hazing and alcohol abuse.

However, some students, faculty, and administrators remain wholeheartedly in support of traditional fraternities, which they believe are responsible for helping students make the acquaintance of people and learn the leadership skills that they believe will be of assistance to them in their future lives as adults. Supporters of fraternities believe that students should retain the right to make their own social decisions and that joining a fraternity is one of those decisions, and they also believe fraternities are responsible for providing valuable services. Some of these are tutoring, raising money for charity, and running campus escort services. Therefore, these individuals are not of the opinion that the abolition of traditional fraternities makes sense.

Using Parallelism

CHAPTER 18

Parallelism—the use of matching words, phrases, or clauses to express equivalent ideas—adds unity, balance, and coherence to your writing. Effective parallelism makes sentences easy to follow and emphasizes relationships among equivalent ideas, but <u>faulty parallelism</u> can create awkward sentences that obscure your meaning and confuse readers.

See
18b

18a Using Parallelism Effectively

Parallelism highlights the correspondence between *items in a series, paired items,* and elements in *lists and outlines.*

1 With Items in a Series

<u>Eat</u>, <u>drink</u>, and <u>be</u> merry.

<u>I came</u>; <u>I saw</u>; <u>I conquered</u>.

<u>Baby food consumption</u>, <u>toy production</u>, and <u>school construction</u> are likely to decline as the US population grows older.

Three factors influenced his decision to seek new employment: <u>his desire to relocate</u>, <u>his need for greater responsibility</u>, and <u>his dissatisfaction with his current job</u>.

 For information on punctuating elements in a series, **see 30b** and **31c.**

2 With Paired Items

Because parallelism emphasizes their equivalence, paired ideas (words, phrases, or clauses) should be presented in parallel form.

The thank-you note was <u>short</u> but <u>sweet</u>.

<u>Roosevelt represented the United States</u>, and <u>Churchill represented Great Britain</u>.

The research focused on <u>muscle tissue</u> and <u>nerve cells</u>.

<u>Ask not what your country can do for you</u>; <u>ask what you can do for your country</u>. (John F. Kennedy, inaugural address)

Paired elements linked by **correlative conjunctions** (such as *not only/ but also, both/and, either/or, neither/nor,* and *whether/or*) should always be parallel.

The design team paid close attention not only <u>to color</u> but also <u>to texture</u>.

181

Parallelism also highlights the contrast between paired elements linked by *than* or *as*.

Richard Wright and James Baldwin chose <u>to live in Paris</u> rather than <u>to remain in the United States</u>.

Success is as much <u>a matter of hard work</u> as <u>a matter of luck</u>.

3   In Lists and Outlines

Elements in a list should be presented in parallel form.

The Irish potato famine had four major causes:
1. The establishment of the landlord-tenant system
2. The failure of the potato crop
3. The reluctance of England to offer adequate financial assistance
4. The passage of the Corn Laws

See
4c4 Elements in a **formal outline** should also be parallel.

EXERCISE 18.1

Identify the parallel elements in these sentences by bracketing parallel phrases and clauses.

Example: Manek spent six years in America [going to school] and [working for a computer company].

▶ 1. After he completed his engineering degree, Manek returned to India to visit his large extended family and to find a wife.
▶ 2. Unfamiliar with marriage practices in India and accustomed to the American notion of marriage for love, Manek's American friends disapproved of his plans.
   3. Not only Manek but also his parents wanted an arranged marriage.
   4. He didn't believe that either you married for love or you had a loveless marriage.
   5. His parents' marriage, an arranged one, continues happily; his aunt's marriage, also arranged, has lasted thirty years.

18b   Revising Faulty Parallelism

Faulty parallelism occurs when elements in a sentence that express equivalent ideas are not presented in parallel terms.

Many people in developing countries suffer because the
                                                  sufficient
countries lack sufficient housing, sufficient food, and ‸~~their~~

health-care facilities‸ ~~are also insufficient~~.

To correct faulty parallelism, match nouns with nouns, verbs with verbs, and phrases or clauses with similarly constructed phrases or clauses.

Popular exercises for men and women include yoga, weight *lifting* ~~lifters~~, and jogging.

I look forward to hearing from you and to *having* ~~have~~ an opportunity to tell you more about myself.

CLOSE-UP

REPEATING KEY WORDS

Although the use of similar grammatical structures may sometimes be enough to convey parallelism, sentences are often clearer if certain key words (for example, articles, prepositions, and the *to* in infinitives) are also repeated in each element of a pair or a series. In the following sentence, repeating the preposition *by* makes it clear that *not* applies only to the first phrase.

Computerization has helped industry by not allowing labor costs to
skyrocket, *by* increasing the speed of production, and *by* improving efficiency.

GRAMMAR CHECKER

REVISING FAULTY PARALLELISM

Grammar checkers are not very useful for identifying faulty parallelism. Although your grammar checker may highlight some nonparallel constructions, it may miss others.

EXERCISE 18.2

Identify and correct faulty parallelism in these sentences. Then, underline the parallel elements—words, phrases, and clauses—in your corrected sentences. If a sentence is already correct, mark it with a *C*, and underline the parallel elements.

Example: Alfred Hitchcock's films include <u>North by Northwest</u>, <u>Vertigo</u>, <u>Psycho</u>, ~~and he also directed~~ <u>Notorious</u>, and <u>Saboteur</u>.

▶ 1. The world is divided between those with galoshes on and those who discover continents.

▶ 2. World leaders, members of Congress, and religious groups are all concerned about global warming.

3. A national task force on education recommended improving public education by making the school day longer, higher teachers' salaries, and integrating more technology into the curriculum.

4. The fast food industry has expanded to include many kinds of restaurants: those that serve pizza, fried chicken chains, some offering Mexican-style menus, and hamburger franchises.
5. The consumption of Scotch in the United States is declining because of high prices, tastes are changing, and increased health awareness has led many whiskey drinkers to switch to wine or beer.

Choosing Words   CHAPTER 19

19a   Choosing an Appropriate Level of Diction

Diction, which comes from the Latin word for *say,* refers to the choice and use of words. Different audiences and situations call for different levels of diction.

1 Formal Diction

Formal diction is grammatically correct and uses words familiar to an educated audience. A writer who uses formal diction often maintains emotional distance from the audience by using the impersonal *one* rather than the more personal *I* and *you.* In addition, the tone of the writing—as determined by word choice, sentence structure, and choice of subject—is dignified and objective.

2 Informal Diction

Informal diction is the language that people use in conversation and in informal emails. You should use informal diction in your college writing only to reproduce speech or dialect or to give a paper a conversational tone.

Colloquial Diction   **Colloquial diction** is the language of everyday speech. Contractions—*isn't, I'm*—are typical colloquialisms, as are **clipped forms**—*phone* for *telephone, TV* for *television, dorm* for *dormitory.* Other colloquialisms include placeholders like *kind of* and utility words like *nice* for *acceptable, funny* for *odd,* and *great* for almost anything. Colloquial English also includes expressions like *get across* for *communicate, come up with* for *find,* and *check out* for *investigate.*

Slang   **Slang,** language that calls attention to itself, is used to establish or reinforce identity within a group—urban teenagers, rock musicians, or computer users, for example. One characteristic of slang vocabulary is that it is usually relatively short-lived, coming into existence and fading out much more quickly than other words do. Because slang terms can emerge and disappear so quickly, no dictionary—even a dictionary of slang—can list all or even most of the slang terms currently in use.

Regionalisms   **Regionalisms** are words, expressions, and idiomatic forms that are used in particular geographical areas but may not be understood by a general audience. In eastern Tennessee, for example, a paper bag is a *poke,* and empty soda bottles are *dope bottles.* And New Yorkers stand *on line* for a movie, whereas people in most other parts of the country stand *in line.*

Nonstandard Diction   **Nonstandard diction** refers to words and expressions not generally considered a part of standard English—words like *ain't, nohow, anywheres, nowheres, hisself,* and *theirselves.*

No absolute rules distinguish standard from nonstandard usage. In fact, some linguists reject the idea of nonstandard usage altogether, arguing that this designation relegates both the language and those who use it to second-class status.

Note: Keep in mind that colloquial expressions, slang, regionalisms, and nonstandard diction are almost always inappropriate in your college writing.

> **ESL TIP**
>
> Some of the spoken expressions you learn from other students or from television are not appropriate for use in college writing. When you hear new expressions, pay attention to the contexts in which they are used.

3 College Writing

The level of diction appropriate for college writing depends on your assignment and your audience. A personal-experience essay calls for a somewhat informal style, but a research paper, an exam, or a report requires a more formal level of diction. In general, most college writing falls somewhere between formal and informal English, using a conversational tone but maintaining grammatical correctness and using a specialized vocabulary when the situation requires it. (This is the level of diction that is used in this book.)

> **CLOSE-UP**
>
> **DICTION AND ELECTRONIC COMMUNICATION**
>
> In email, instant messages, and text messages, writers commonly use **emoticons**—typed characters, such as :-) and ;-), that indicate emotions or feelings—and **abbreviations,** such as BTW (by the way) and LOL (laughing out loud). Although these typographical devices are common in informal electronic communication, they are inappropriate in formal electronic or print situations as well as in college writing.

EXERCISE 19.1

After reading the following paragraph, underline the words and phrases that identify it as formal diction. Then, rewrite the paragraph, using the level of diction that you would use in your college writing. Consult a dictionary if necessary.

> In looking at many small points of difference between species, which, as far as our ignorance permits us to judge, seem quite unimportant, we must not forget that climate, food, etc., have no doubt produced some direct effect. It is also necessary to bear in mind that owing to the law of correlation, when one part varies and the variations are accumulated through natural selection, other modifications, often of the most unexpected nature, will ensue. (Charles Darwin, *The Origin of Species*)

19b   Choosing the Right Word

Choosing the right word to use in a particular context is very important. If you use the wrong word—or even *almost* the right one—you run the risk of misrepresenting your ideas.

1   Denotation and Connotation

A word's **denotation** is its basic dictionary meaning, what it stands for without any emotional associations. A word's **connotations** are the emotional, social, and political associations it has in addition to its denotative meaning.

Word	Denotation	Connotation
politician	someone who holds a political office	opportunist; wheeler-dealer

Selecting a word with the appropriate connotation can be challenging. For example, the word *skinny* has negative connotations, whereas *thin* is neutral, and *slender* is positive. And words and expressions like *mentally ill, insane, neurotic, crazy, psychopathic,* and *emotionally disturbed,* although similar in meaning, have different emotional, social, and political connotations that affect the way people respond. If you use terms without considering their connotations, you run the risk of undercutting your credibility, to say nothing of confusing and possibly angering your readers.

CLOSE-UP

USING A THESAURUS

Synonyms are words that have similar meanings, such as *well* and *healthy*. **Antonyms** are words that have opposite meanings, such as *courage* and *cowardice*.

When you consult a **thesaurus**, a list of synonyms and antonyms, remember that no two words have exactly the same meanings. Use synonyms carefully, checking your dictionary to make sure the connotation of the synonym is very close to that of the original word.

EXERCISE 19.2

The following words have negative connotations. For each, list one word with a similar meaning whose connotation is neutral and another whose connotation is favorable.

Example: *Negative* skinny
Neutral thin
Favorable slender

▶ 1. deceive   6. blunder
▶ 2. antiquated   7. weird
▶ 3. pushy   8. politician
▶ 4. pathetic   9. shack
▶ 5. cheap   10. stench

2 Euphemisms

A **euphemism** is a mild or polite term used in place of a blunt or harsh term that describes something unpleasant or embarrassing. College writing is no place for euphemisms. Say what you mean—*pregnant,* not *expecting; died,* not *passed away;* and *strike,* not *work stoppage.*

3 Specific and General Words

Specific words refer to particular persons, items, or events; **general** words denote entire classes or groups. *Queen Elizabeth II,* for example, is more specific than *monarch; jeans* is more specific than *clothing;* and *SUV* is more specific than *vehicle.* You can use general words to describe entire classes of items, but you should use specific words to clarify such generalizations.

CLOSE-UP

USING SPECIFIC WORDS

Take particular care to avoid general words such as *nice, great,* and *terrific* that say nothing and could be used in almost any sentence. These <u>utility words</u> convey only enthusiasm, not precise meanings. Replace them with more specific words.

See
17a2

---

4 Abstract and Concrete Words

Abstract words—*beauty, truth, justice,* and so on—refer to ideas, qualities, or conditions that cannot be perceived by the senses. **Concrete** words name things that readers can see, hear, taste, smell, or touch. As with general and specific words, whether a word is abstract or concrete is relative. The more concrete your words and phrases, the more vivid the image you evoke in the reader.

EXERCISE 19.3

Revise the following paragraph from a job application letter by substituting specific, concrete language for general or abstract words and phrases.

▶I have had several part-time jobs lately. ▶Some of them would qualify me for the position you advertised. ▶In my most recent job, I sold products in a store. My supervisor said I was a good worker who had a number of valuable qualities. I am used to dealing with different types of people in different settings. I feel that my qualifications would make me a good candidate for your job opening.

19c   Using Figures of Speech

Writers often use **figures of speech** (such as *similes* and *metaphors*) to go beyond the literal meanings of words. By doing so, they make their writing more vivid or emphatic.

CLOSE-UP

COMMONLY USED FIGURES OF SPEECH

♦ A **simile** is a comparison between two unlike things on the basis of a shared quality. A simile is introduced by *like* or *as*.

Like travelers with exotic destinations on their minds, the graduates were remarkably forgetful. (Maya Angelou, *I Know Why the Caged Bird Sings*)

♦ A **metaphor** also compares two dissimilar things, but instead of saying that one thing is *like* another, it *equates* them.

Perhaps it is easy for those who have never felt the stings and darts of segregation to say, "Wait." (Martin Luther King Jr., "Letter from Birmingham Jail")

♦ An **analogy** explains an unfamiliar item or concept by comparing it to a more familiar one.

According to Robert Frost, writing free verse is like playing tennis without a net.

♦ **Personification** gives an idea or inanimate object human attributes, feelings, or powers.

Truth strikes us from behind, and in the dark, as well as from before in broad daylight. (Henry David Thoreau, *Journals*)

♦ A **hyperbole** (or overstatement) is an intentional exaggeration for emphasis. For example, Jonathan Swift uses hyperbole in his essay "A Modest Proposal" when he suggests that eating Irish babies would help the English solve their food shortage.

♦ **Understatement** intentionally makes something seem less important than it actually is.

According to Mao Tse-tung, a revolution is not a tea party.

19d Avoiding Inappropriate Language

1 Jargon

Jargon, the specialized or technical vocabulary of a trade, a profession, or an academic discipline, is useful for communicating in the field for which it was developed. Outside that field, however, it is often imprecise and confusing. For example, business executives may want departments to *interface* effectively, and sociologists may identify the need for *perspectivistic thinking* to achieve organizational goals. If they are addressing other professionals in their respective fields, these terms can facilitate communication. If, however, they are addressing a general audience, these terms are confusing and should be avoided.

2 Neologisms

Neologisms are newly coined words that are not part of standard English. New situations call for new words, and frequently such coinages become part of the language—*email, carjack,* and *outsource,* for example. Others, however, are never fully accepted. For example, questionable neologisms are created when the suffix *-wise* is added to existing words—creating nonstandard words like *weatherwise, sportswise, timewise,* and *productwise.*

3 Pretentious Diction

Good writing is clear and direct, not pompous or flowery. Revise to eliminate **pretentious diction,** inappropriately elevated and wordy language.

As I fell ~~into slumber~~ *asleep*, I ~~cogitated~~ *thought* about my day ~~ambling~~ *hiking* through ~~the splendor of~~ the Appalachian Mountains.

CLOSE-UP

USING PRETENTIOUS DICTION

Frequently, pretentious diction is formal diction used in a relatively informal situation. In such a context, it is always out of place. For every pretentious word, there is usually a clear and direct alternative.

Pretentious	Clear	Pretentious	Clear
ascertain	discover	reside	live
commence	start	terminate	end
implement	carry out	utilize	use
minuscule	small	individual	person

---

4 Clichés

Clichés are figures of speech that have been used so often that their power to affect readers has been drained away. At one time, expressions such as "hit the nail on the head" and "pass the buck" might have called up vivid

images in a reader's mind, but because of overuse, they have become clichés—pat, meaningless phrases.

better late than never
the bottom line
face the music
give 110 percent
hard as a rock
a level playing field
water under the bridge
what goes around comes around

Writers sometimes resort to clichés when they run out of ideas. To cap-
ture your readers' attention, you should take the time to think of original
expressions.

> **ESL TIP**
>
> Many ESL students have learned a long list of English idioms. Some of these,
> however, have become clichés. Although becoming familiar with these idioms
> can help you understand them when you encounter them, university instructors
> discourage students from using clichés in their writing, preferring language that is
> more original and more precise.

EXERCISE 19.4

Go through a newspaper or magazine, and list the examples of jargon, neologisms,
pretentious diction, or clichés that you find. Then, substitute more appropriate
words for the ones you identified. Be prepared to discuss your interpretation of
each word and of the word you chose to put in its place.

19e Avoiding Offensive Language

Because the language we use not only expresses our ideas but also shapes
our thinking, you should avoid using words that insult or degrade others.

1 Stereotypes

Racial and Ethnic   When referring to any racial, ethnic, or religious group,
use words with neutral connotations or words that the group uses in *formal*
speech or writing to refer to itself.

Age   Avoid potentially offensive labels relating to age. Many older people
like to call themselves *senior citizens* or *seniors,* and these terms are commonly used by the media and the government.

Class   Do not demean certain jobs because they are low paying or praise
others because they have impressive titles. Similarly, do not use words—

hick, cracker, redneck, and *trailer trash,* for example—that denigrate people based on their social class.

Sexual Orientation   Always use neutral terms (such as *gay* and *lesbian*), but do not mention a person's sexual orientation unless it is relevant to your discussion.

2 Sexist Language

Sexist language entails much more than the use of derogatory words. Assuming that some professions are exclusive to one gender—for instance, that *nurse* denotes only women and that *doctor* denotes only men—is also sexist. So is the use of outdated job titles, such as *postman* for *letter carrier, fireman* for *firefighter,* and *stewardess* for *flight attendant.*

Sexist language also occurs when a writer fails to apply the same terminology to both men and women. For example, refer to two scientists with PhDs not as Dr. Sagan and Mrs. Yallow, but as Dr. Sagan and Dr. Yallow. Refer to two writers as James and Wharton, or Henry James and Edith Wharton, not James and Mrs. Wharton.

In your writing, always use *women*—not *girls, gals,* or *ladies*—when referring to adult females. Use *Ms.* as the form of address when a woman's marital status is unknown or irrelevant (for example, in business correspondence). Finally, avoid using the generic *he* or *him* when your subject could be either male or female. Use the third-person plural (*they*) or the phrase *he or she* (not *he/she*).

Sexist: Before boarding, each passenger should make certain that <u>he</u> has <u>his</u> ticket.

Revised: Before boarding, <u>passengers</u> should make certain that they have <u>their</u> tickets.

Revised: Before boarding, each <u>passenger</u> should make certain that <u>he or she</u> has a ticket.

Note: Remember not to overuse *his or her* or *he or she* constructions, which can make your writing repetitious and wordy.

CLOSE-UP

ELIMINATING SEXIST LANGUAGE

For every sexist usage, there is usually a nonsexist alternative.

Sexist Usage	Possible Revisions
Mankind	People, human beings
Man's accomplishments	Human accomplishments
Man-made	Synthetic
Female engineer/lawyer/accountant, and so on; male model	Engineer/lawyer/accountant, and so on; model
Policeman/woman	Police officer

(continued)

ELIMINATING SEXIST LANGUAGE (*continued*)

Sexist Usage	Possible Revisions
Salesman/woman/girl	Salesperson, sales representative
Businessman/woman	Businessperson, executive
<u>Everyone</u> should complete <u>his</u> application by Tuesday.	<u>Everyone</u> should complete <u>his or her</u> application by Tuesday.
	<u>All students</u> should complete <u>their</u> applications by Tuesday.

Note: When trying to avoid sexist use of *he* and *him* in your writing, be careful not to use the plural pronoun *they* or *their* to refer to a singular antecedent.

Drivers
~~Any driver~~ caught speeding should have their driving privileges suspended.

EXERCISE 19.5

Suggest at least one alternative form for each of the following words or phrases. In each case, comment on the advantages and disadvantages of the alternative you recommend. If you feel that a particular term is not sexist, explain why.

- forefathers
- man-eating shark
- manpower
- workman's compensation
- men at work
- waitress
- first baseman
- congressman
- manhunt
- longshoreman
- committeeman
- (to) man the battle stations

Girl Friday
point man
draftsman
man overboard
fisherman
foreman
manned space program
gentleman's agreement
no man's land
spinster
old maid
old wives' tale

EXERCISE 19.6

Each of the following pairs of terms includes a feminine form that was at one time in wide use; most are still used to some extent. Which do you think are likely to remain in our language for some time, and which do you think will disappear? Explain your reasoning.

heir/heiress
benefactor/benefactress
murderer/murderess
actor/actress
hero/heroine
host/hostess
aviator/aviatrix
executor/executrix

author/authoress
poet/poetess
tailor/seamstress
comedian/comedienne
villain/villainess
prince/princess
widow/widower

PART 4

Understanding Grammar

Understanding Grammar

Using the Parts of Speech

The eight basic **parts of speech**—the building blocks for all English sentences—are nouns, pronouns, verbs, adjectives, adverbs, prepositions, conjunctions, and interjections. How a word is classified depends on its function in a sentence.

20a Using Nouns

ESL
49b

Nouns name people, animals, places, things, ideas, actions, or qualities.

A **common noun** names any one of a class of people, places, or things: *artist, judge, building, event, city*.

A **proper noun,** always capitalized, designates a particular person, place, or thing: *Mary Cassatt, World Trade Center, Crimean War*.

A **count noun** names something that can be counted: five *dogs*, two dozen *grapes*.

A **noncount noun** names a quantity that is not countable: *time, dust, work, gold*. Noncount nouns generally have only a singular form.

A **collective noun** designates a group thought of as a unit: *committee, class, navy, band, family*. Collective nouns are generally singular unless the members of the group are referred to as individuals.

See
26a5

An **abstract noun** designates an intangible idea or quality: *love, hate, justice, anger, fear, prejudice*.

20b Using Pronouns

ESL
49c

Pronouns are words used in place of nouns. The word for which a pronoun stands is called its **antecedent.**

If you use a quotation in your paper, you must document it. (Pronoun *it* refers to antecedent *quotation*.)

A **personal pronoun** stands for a person or thing. Personal pronouns include *I, me, we, us, my, mine, our, ours, you, your, yours, he, she, it, its, him, his, her, hers, they, them, their,* and *theirs*.

The firm made Debbie an offer, and she couldn't refuse it.

An indefinite pronoun does not refer to any particular person or thing, so it does not require an antecedent. Indefinite pronouns include *another, any, each, few, many, some, nothing, one, anyone, everyone, everybody, every-thing, someone, something, either,* and *neither*.

See
26b3

Many are called, but few are chosen.

A **reflexive pronoun** ends with -*self* and refers to a recipient of an action that is the same as the initiator of the action. The reflexive pronouns are *myself, yourself, himself, herself, itself, oneself, themselves, ourselves,* and *yourselves.*

They found <u>themselves</u> in downtown Pittsburgh.

An **intensive pronoun** emphasizes a noun or pronoun that directly precedes it. (Intensive pronouns have the same form as reflexive pronouns.)

Darrow <u>himself</u> was sure his client was innocent.

A **relative pronoun** introduces an adjective clause or a noun clause in a sentence. Relative pronouns include *which, who, whom, that, what, whose, whatever, whoever, whomever,* and *whichever.*

Gandhi was the charismatic man <u>who</u> helped lead India to independence. (introduces adjective clause)
<u>Whatever</u> happens will be a surprise. (introduces noun clause)

An **interrogative pronoun** introduces a question. Interrogative pronouns include *who, which, what, whom, whose, whoever, whatever,* and *whichever.*

<u>Who</u> was that masked man?

A **demonstrative pronoun** points to a particular thing or group of things. *This, that, these,* and *those* are demonstrative pronouns.

<u>This</u> is one of Shakespeare's early plays.

A **reciprocal pronoun** denotes a mutual relationship. The reciprocal pronouns are *each other* and *one another. Each other* indicates a relationship between two individuals; *one another* denotes a relationship among more than two.

Romeo and Juliet declared their love for <u>each other</u>.
Concertgoers jostled <u>one another</u> in the ticket line.

Note: Although different types of pronouns may have the same form, they are distinguished from one another by their function in a sentence.

20c Using Verbs

1 Recognizing Verbs

ESL 49a A <u>verb</u> may express an action or a state of being.

He <u>ran</u> for the train. (physical action)

He <u>worried</u> about being late. (emotional action)

Elizabeth II <u>became</u> queen after the death of her father, George VI. (state of being)

Verbs can be classified into two groups: *main verbs* and *auxiliary verbs.*

Main Verbs   **Main verbs** carry most of the meaning in a sentence. Some main verbs are **action verbs.**

Emily Dickinson <u>wrote</u> poetry.

Other main verbs function as linking verbs. A **linking verb** does not show any physical or emotional action. Its function is to link the sentence's subject to a **subject complement,** a word or phrase that renames or describes the subject.

Carbon disulfide <u>smells</u> bad.

FREQUENTLY USED LINKING VERBS				
appear	believe	look	seem	taste
be	feel	prove	smell	turn
become	grow	remain	sound	

Auxiliary Verbs   Auxiliary verbs (also called **helping verbs**), such as *be* and *have,* combine with main verbs to form **verb phrases.** Auxiliary verbs indicate tense, voice, or mood.

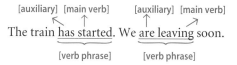

The train <u>has started</u>. We <u>are leaving</u> soon.

Certain auxiliary verbs, known as **modal auxiliaries,** indicate necessity, possibility, willingness, obligation, or ability.

In the future, farmers <u>might</u> cultivate seaweed as a food crop.

Coal mining <u>would</u> be safer if dust were controlled in the mines.

MODAL AUXILIARIES			
can	might	ought [to]	will
could	must	shall	would
may	need [to]	should	

2 Recognizing Verbals

Verbals, such as *known* or *swimming* or *to go,* are verb forms that act as adjectives, adverbs, or nouns. A verbal can never serve as a sentence's main verb unless it is used with one or more auxiliary verbs (<u>has *known*, *should be*</u> <u>*swimming*</u>). Verbals include *participles, infinitives,* and *gerunds.*

Participles   Virtually every verb has a **present participle,** which ends in -*ing*
See
22a2   (*loving, learning, going, writing*), and a **past participle,** which usually ends in -*d* or -*ed* (*agreed, learned*). Some verbs have <u>irregular</u> past participles (*gone, begun, written*). Participles may function in a sentence as adjectives or as nouns.

> Twenty brands of <u>running</u> shoes were displayed at the exhibition. (Present participle *running* serves as adjective modifying noun *shoes.*)
>
> The <u>crowded</u> bus went past those waiting at the corner. (Past participle *crowded* serves as adjective modifying noun *bus.*)
>
> The <u>wounded</u> were given emergency first aid. (Past participle *wounded* serves as a noun, the sentence's subject.)

See   Note: Participles also combine with helping verbs to form the <u>perfect tense</u>
22b2–3   and the <u>progressive tense.</u>

Infinitives   An **infinitive** is made up of *to* and the base form of the verb: <u>*to*</u> *defeat.* (The **base form** is the form of the verb used with *I, you, we,* and *they* in the present tense.) An infinitive may function as an adjective, an adverb, or a noun.

> Ann Arbor was clearly the place <u>to be.</u> (Infinitive serves as adjective modifying noun *place.*)
>
> They say that breaking up is hard <u>to do.</u> (Infinitive serves as adverb modifying adjective *hard.*)
>
> Carla went outside <u>to think.</u> (Infinitive serves as adverb modifying verb *went.*)
>
> <u>To win</u> was everything. (Infinitive serves as noun, the sentence's subject.)

Gerunds   **Gerunds** (which, like present participles, end in -*ing*) always function as nouns.

> <u>Seeing</u> is <u>believing.</u> (Gerund *seeing* serves as sentence's subject; gerund *believing* serves as subject complement.)
>
> He worried about <u>interrupting.</u> (Gerund *interrupting* is object of preposition *about.*)

Andrew loves <u>skiing</u>. (Gerund *skiing* is direct object of verb *loves*.)

Note: When the *-ing* form of a verb is used as a noun, it is a *gerund*; when it is used as an adjective, it is a *present participle*.

20d Using Adjectives

ESL 49d

<u>Adjectives</u> describe, limit, qualify, or in some other way modify nouns or pronouns.

1 Descriptive Adjectives

Descriptive adjectives name a quality of the noun or pronoun they modify.

After the game, they were <u>exhausted</u>.

They ordered a <u>chocolate</u> soda and a <u>butterscotch</u> sundae.

Some descriptive adjectives are formed from common nouns or from verbs (*friend/friendly, agree/agreeable*). Others, called **proper adjectives,** are formed from proper nouns.

A <u>Shakespearean</u> sonnet consists of an octave and a sestet.

Two or more words may be joined (hyphenated before a noun, without a hyphen after a noun) to form a <u>compound adjective</u>: *His parents are very well-read people; most people are not so well read.* See 38b1

2 Determiners

When articles, pronouns, numbers, and the like function as adjectives, limiting or qualifying nouns or pronouns, they are referred to as <u>determiners</u>. ESL 49b2–3

♦ **Articles** (*a, an, the*)

The boy found <u>a</u> four-leaf clover.

♦ **Possessive nouns**

<u>Lesley's</u> mother lives in New Jersey.

♦ **Possessive pronouns** (the personal pronouns *my, your, his, her, its, our, their*)

<u>Their</u> lives depended on <u>my</u> skill.

♦ **Demonstrative pronouns** (*this, these, that, those*)

<u>This</u> song reminds me of <u>that</u> song we heard yesterday.

♦ **Interrogative pronouns** (*what, which, whose*)

Whose book is this?

♦ **Indefinite pronouns** (*another, each, both, many, any, some,* and so on)

Both candidates agreed to return another day.

♦ **Relative pronouns** (*what, whatever, which, whichever, whose, whoever*)

I forgot whatever reasons I had for leaving.

♦ **Numbers** (*one, two, first, second,* and so on)

The first time I played baseball, I got only one hit.

20e Using Adverbs

**ESL
49d1** Adverbs describe the action of verbs or modify adjectives, other adverbs, or complete phrases, clauses, or sentences. They answer the questions "How?" "Why?" "Where?" "When?" "Under what conditions?" and "To what extent?"

He walked rather hesitantly toward the front of the room. (walked *how*?)

Let's meet tomorrow for coffee. (meet *when*?)

Adverbs that modify other adverbs or adjectives limit or qualify the words they modify.

He pitched an almost perfect game.

Interrogative adverbs—*how, when, why,* and *where*—introduce questions.

Why did the compound darken?

**See
5b2** **Conjunctive adverbs** act as transitional words, joining and relating independent clauses. Conjunctive adverbs may appear in various positions in a sentence.

Jason forgot to register for chemistry. However, he managed to sign up during the drop/add period.

Jason forgot to register for chemistry; however, he managed to sign up during the drop/add period.

Jason forgot to register for chemistry. He managed, however, to sign up during the drop/add period.

Jason forgot to register for chemistry. He managed to sign up during the drop/add period, however.

FREQUENTLY USED CONJUNCTIVE ADVERBS

accordingly	furthermore	meanwhile	similarly
also	hence	moreover	still
anyway	however	nevertheless	then
besides	incidentally	next	thereafter
certainly	indeed	nonetheless	therefore
consequently	instead	now	thus
finally	likewise	otherwise	undoubtedly

20f Using Prepositions

A <u>preposition</u> introduces a noun or pronoun (or a phrase or clause functioning in the sentence as a noun), linking it to other words in the sentence. The word or word group the preposition introduces is called its **object**.

ESL 49e

prep   obj   prep   obj
They received a postcard <u>from</u> Bobby telling <u>about</u> his trip.

FREQUENTLY USED PREPOSITIONS

about	beneath	inside	since
above	beside	into	through
across	between	like	throughout
after	beyond	near	to
against	by	of	toward
along	concerning	off	under
among	despite	on	underneath
around	down	onto	until
as	during	out	up
at	except	outside	upon
before	for	over	with
behind	from	past	within
below	in	regarding	without

20g Using Conjunctions

Conjunctions connect words, phrases, clauses, or sentences.

♦ **Coordinating conjunctions** (*and, or, but, nor, for, so, yet*) connect words, phrases, or clauses of equal weight.

The choice was simple: chicken <u>or</u> fish. (*Or* links two nouns.)

The United States is a government "of the people, by the people, <u>and</u> for the people." (*And* links three prepositional phrases.)

Thoreau wrote *Walden* in 1854, <u>and</u> he died in 1862. (*And* links two independent clauses.)

♦ **Correlative conjunctions,** always used in pairs, also link grammatically equivalent items.

<u>Both</u> Hancock <u>and</u> Jefferson signed the Declaration of Independence. (Correlative conjunctions link two nouns.)

<u>Either</u> I will renew my lease, <u>or</u> I will move. (Correlative conjunctions link two independent clauses.)

CORRELATIVE CONJUNCTIONS	
both . . . and	neither . . . nor
either . . . or	not only . . . but also
just as . . . so	whether . . . or

♦ **Subordinating conjunctions** include *since, because, although, if, after, when, while, before, unless,* and so on. A subordinating conjunction introduces a dependent (subordinate) clause, connecting it to an independent (main) clause to form a <u>complex sentence</u>.

See 14d

<u>Although</u> drug use is a serious concern for parents, many parents are afraid to discuss it with their children.

It is best to diagram your garden <u>before</u> you start to plant it.

20h Using Interjections

Interjections are exclamations used to express emotion: *Oh! Ouch! Wow! Alas! Hey!* These words are grammatically independent; that is, they do not have a grammatical function in a sentence.
An interjection may be set off in a sentence by commas.

The message, <u>alas,</u> arrived too late.

For greater emphasis, an interjection can be punctuated as an independent unit, set off with an exclamation point.

<u>Alas!</u> The message arrived too late.

Note: Other kinds of words may also be used in isolation. They include *yes, no, hello, good-bye, please,* and *thank you.* All such words, including interjections, are collectively referred to as **isolates.**

Using Nouns and Pronouns

CHAPTER 21

21a Understanding Case

Case is the form a noun or pronoun takes to indicate its function in a sentence. **Nouns** change form only in the possessive case: the *cat's* eyes, *Molly's* book. **Pronouns,** however, have three cases: *subjective, objective,* and *possessive.*

PRONOUN CASE FORMS						
Subjective						
I	he, she	it	we	you	they	who whoever
Objective						
me	him, her	it	us	you	them	whom whomever
Possessive						
my mine	his, her hers	its	our ours	your yours	their theirs	whose

1 Subjective Case

A pronoun takes the **subjective case** in the following situations.

Subject of a Verb: <u>I</u> bought a new mountain bike.

Subject Complement: It was <u>he</u> who volunteered to drive.

2 Objective Case

A pronoun takes the **objective case** in the following situations.

Direct Object: Our supervisor asked Adam and <u>me</u> to work on the project.

Indirect Object: The plumber's bill gave <u>him</u> quite a shock.

Object of a Preposition: Between <u>us</u>, we own ten shares of stock.

3 Possessive Case

A pronoun takes the **possessive case** when it indicates ownership (*our* car, *your* book). The possessive case is also used before a <u>gerund.</u> See 20c2

Napoleon gave <u>his</u> approval to <u>their</u> ruling Naples. (*His* indicates ownership; *ruling* is a gerund.)

CLOSE-UP

PRONOUN CASE WITH PREPOSITIONS

I is not necessarily more appropriate than *me*. In the following situation, *me* is correct.

> Just between you and me [not *I*], I think we're going to have a quiz. (*Me* is the object of the preposition *between*.)

EXERCISE 21.1

Underline the correct form of the pronoun within the parentheses. Be prepared to explain why you chose each form.

Example: Toni Morrison, Alice Walker, and (<u>she</u>, her) are perhaps the most widely recognized African-American women writing today.

▶ 1. Both Walt Whitman and (he, him) wrote a great deal of poetry about nature.
▶ 2. Our instructor gave Matthew and (me, I) an excellent idea for our project.
    3. The sales clerk objected to (me, my) returning the sweater.
    4. I understand (you, your) being unavailable to work tonight.
    5. The waiter asked Michael and (me, I) to move to another table.

21b Determining Pronoun Case in Special Situations

1 Comparisons with *Than* or *As*

When a comparison ends with a pronoun, the pronoun's function in the sentence determines your choice of pronoun case. If the pronoun functions as a subject, use the subjective case; if it functions as an object, use the objective case. You can determine the function of the pronoun by completing the comparison.

> Darcy likes John more than <u>I</u>. (*more than* <u>I</u> *like John:* I is the subject.)

> Darcy likes John more than <u>me</u>. (*more than she likes* <u>me</u>: me is the object.)

2 *Who* and *Whom*

The case of the pronouns *who* and *whom* depends on their function *within their own clause*. When a pronoun serves as the subject of its clause, use *who* or *whoever*; when it functions as an object, use *whom* or *whomever*.

> The Salvation Army gives food and shelter to <u>whoever</u> is in need. (*Whoever* is the subject of the dependent clause *whoever is in need*.)

> I wonder <u>whom</u> jazz musician Miles Davis influenced. (*Whom* is the object of *influenced* in the dependent clause *whom jazz musician Miles Davis influenced*.)

CLOSE-UP

PRONOUN CASE IN QUESTIONS

To determine whether to use subjective case (*who*) or objective case (*whom*) in a question, use a personal pronoun to answer the question. If the personal pronoun is the subject, use *who*; if the personal pronoun is the object, use *whom*.

Who wrote *The Age of Innocence*? She wrote it. (subject)

Whom do you support for mayor? I support her. (object)

---

3 Appositives

An **appositive** is a noun or noun phrase that identifies or renames an adjacent noun or pronoun. The case of a pronoun in an appositive depends on the function of the word the appositive identifies or renames.

ESL
49c4

We heard two Motown recording artists, Smokey Robinson and him. (*Artists* is the object of the verb *heard*, so the pronoun in the appositive *Smokey Robinson and him* takes the objective case.)

Two recording artists, he and Smokey Robinson, had contracts with Motown Records. (*Artists* is the subject of the sentence, so the pronoun in the appositive *he and Smokey Robinson* takes the subjective case.)

4 *We* and *Us* before a Noun

When a first-person plural pronoun directly precedes a noun, the case of the pronoun depends on the way the noun functions in the sentence.

We women must stick together. (*Women* is the subject of the sentence, so the pronoun *we* must be in the subjective case.)

Teachers make learning easy for us students. (*Students* is the object of the preposition *for*, so the pronoun *us* must be in the objective case.)

EXERCISE 21.2

Using the word in parentheses, combine each pair of sentences into a single sentence. You may change word order and add or delete words.

Example: After he left the band The Police, bass player Sting continued as a solo artist. He once taught middle-school English. (who)

Revised: After he left the band The Police, bass player Sting, who once taught middle-school English, continued as a solo artist.

▶ 1. Herb Ritts has photographed world leaders, leading artistic figures in dance and drama, and a vanishing African tribe. He got his start by taking photographs of Hollywood stars. (who)

▶ 2. Tim Green has written several novels about a fictional football team. He played for the Atlanta Hawks and has a degree in law. (who)

3. Some say Carl Sagan did more to further science education in America than any other person. He wrote many books on science and narrated many popular television shows. (who)

4. Jodie Foster has won two Academy Awards for her acting. She was a child star. (who)

5. Sylvia Plath met the poet Ted Hughes at Cambridge University in England. She later married him. (whom)

21c Revising Pronoun Reference Errors

An **antecedent** is the word or word group to which a pronoun refers. The connection between a pronoun and its antecedent should always be clear. If the <u>pronoun reference</u> is not clear, you will need to revise the sentence.

ESL
49c1

1 Ambiguous Antecedent

Sometimes it is not clear to which antecedent a pronoun—for example, *this, that, which,* or *it*—refers. In such cases, eliminate the ambiguity by substituting a noun for the pronoun.

> When you make a promise to give someone a gift, you should
> *that promise.*
> keep~~ it.~~ (The pronoun *it* can refer either to *promise* or to *gift*.)

2 Remote Antecedent

If a pronoun is far from its antecedent, readers will have difficulty making a connection between them. To eliminate this problem, replace the pronoun with a noun.

> During the mid-1800s, many Czechs began to immigrate to America.
> By 1860, about 23,000 Czechs had left their country; by 1900, 13,000
> *America's*
> Czech immigrants were coming to~~ its~~ shores each year.

3 Nonexistent Antecedent

Sometimes a pronoun—for example, *this*—refers to an antecedent that does not exist. In such cases, add the missing antecedent.

> Some one-celled organisms contain chlorophyll yet are considered
> *paradox*
> animals. This~~ illustrates the difficulty of classifying single-celled
> organisms. (Exactly what does *this* refer to?)

Note: Colloquial expressions such as "*It* says in the paper" and "*They* said on the news," which refer to unidentified antecedents, are not acceptable in college writing. Substitute the appropriate noun for the unclear pronoun: "*The article* in the paper says . . ."; "*In his commentary, George Will* said. . . ."

4 *Who, Which,* and *That*

In general, *who* refers to people or to animals that have names. *Which* and *that* refer to things or to unnamed animals. When referring to an antecedent, be sure to choose the appropriate pronoun (*who, which,* or *that*).

> David Henry Hwang, who wrote the Tony Award-winning play *M. Butterfly,* also wrote *Yellow Face.*

> The spotted owl, which lives in old growth forests, is in danger of extinction.

> Houses that are built today are usually more energy efficient than those built twenty years ago.

Never use *that* to refer to a person.

who
The man ~~that~~ won the hot-dog-eating contest is my neighbor.

Note: Be sure to use *which* in <u>nonrestrictive clauses,</u> which are always set off with commas, and to use *that* in <u>restrictive clauses,</u> which are not set off with commas. See 30d1

EXERCISE 21.3

Analyze the pronoun reference errors in each of the following sentences. After doing so, revise each sentence by substituting an appropriate noun or noun phrase for the underlined pronoun.

Clark
Example: Jefferson asked Lewis to head the expedition, and Lewis selected him as his associate. (*Him* refers to a nonexistent antecedent.)

▶ 1. The purpose of the expedition was to search out a land route to the Pacific and to gather information about the West. The Louisiana Purchase increased the need for <u>it</u>.

▶ 2. The expedition was going to be difficult. <u>They</u> trained the men in Illinois, the starting point.

3. Clark and most of the men who descended the Yellowstone River camped on the bank. <u>It</u> was beautiful and wild.

4. Both Jefferson and Lewis had faith that <u>he</u> would be successful in this transcontinental journey.

5. The expedition was efficient, and only one man was lost. <u>This</u> was extraordinary.

Using Verbs

22a Understanding Verb Forms

Every verb has four **principal parts:** a **base form** (the form of the verb used with *I* in the present tense), a **present participle** (the *-ing* form of the verb), a **past tense form,** and a **past participle.**

Note: The verb *be* is so irregular that it is the one exception to this definition; its base form is *be.*

1 Regular Verbs

A **regular verb** forms both its past tense and its past participle by adding *-d* or *-ed* to the base form of the verb.

PRINCIPAL PARTS OF REGULAR VERBS		
Base Form	**Past Tense Form**	**Past Participle**
smile	smiled	smiled
talk	talked	talked
jump	jumped	jumped

2 Irregular Verbs

Irregular verbs do not follow the pattern discussed above. The chart that follows lists the principal parts of the most frequently used irregular verbs.

FREQUENTLY USED IRREGULAR VERBS		
Base Form	**Past Tense Form**	**Past Participle**
arise	arose	arisen
awake	awoke, awaked	awoken, awaked
be	was/were	been
beat	beat	beaten
begin	began	begun
bend	bent	bent
bet	bet, betted	bet
bite	bit	bitten
blow	blew	blown
break	broke	broken

Base Form	Past Tense Form	Past Participle
bring	brought	brought
build	built	built
burst	burst	burst
buy	bought	bought
catch	caught	caught
choose	chose	chosen
cling	clung	clung
come	came	come
cost	cost	cost
deal	dealt	dealt
dig	dug	dug
dive	dived, dove	dived
do	did	done
drag	dragged	dragged
draw	drew	drawn
drink	drank	drunk
drive	drove	driven
eat	ate	eaten
fall	fell	fallen
fight	fought	fought
find	found	found
fly	flew	flown
forget	forgot	forgotten, forgot
freeze	froze	frozen
get	got	gotten
give	gave	given
go	went	gone
grow	grew	grown
hang (execute)	hanged	hanged
hang (suspend)	hung	hung
have	had	had
hear	heard	heard
keep	kept	kept
know	knew	known
lay	laid	laid
lead	led	led
lend	lent	lent
let	let	let
lie (recline)	lay	lain
lie (tell an untruth)	lied	lied
make	made	made
prove	proved	proved, proven
read	read	read
ride	rode	ridden
ring	rang	rung
rise	rose	risen

(*continued*)

FREQUENTLY USED IRREGULAR VERBS (continued)

Base Form	Past Tense Form	Past Participle
run	ran	run
say	said	said
see	saw	seen
set (place)	set	set
shake	shook	shaken
shrink	shrank, shrunk	shrunk, shrunken
sing	sang	sung
sink	sank	sunk
sit	sat	sat
sneak	sneaked, snuck	sneaked, snuck
speak	spoke	spoken
speed	sped, speeded	sped, speeded
spin	spun	spun
spring	sprang	sprung
stand	stood	stood
steal	stole	stolen
strike	struck	struck, stricken
swear	swore	sworn
swim	swam	swum
swing	swung	swung
take	took	taken
teach	taught	taught
throw	threw	thrown
wake	woke, waked	waked, woken
wear	wore	worn
wring	wrung	wrung
write	wrote	written

GRAMMAR CHECKER

USING CORRECT VERB FORMS

Your grammar checker will highlight incorrect verb forms in your writing and offer revision suggestions.

CLOSE-UP

LIE/LAY AND *SIT/SET*

Lie means "to recline" and does not take an object ("He likes to *lie* on the floor"); *lay* means "to place" or "to put" and does take an object ("He wants to *lay* a rug on the floor").

Base Form	Past Tense Form	Past Participle
lie	lay	lain
lay	laid	laid

Sit means "to assume a seated position" and does not take an object ("She wants to *sit* on the table"); *set* means "to place" or "to put" and usually takes an object ("She wants to *set* a vase on the table").

Base Form	Past Tense Form	Past Participle
sit	sat	sat
set	set	set

EXERCISE 22.1

Complete the sentences in the following paragraph with an appropriate form of the verbs in parentheses.

Example: An air of mystery surrounds many of those who have _____*sung*_____ (sing) and played the blues.

▶The legendary bluesman Robert Johnson supposedly _____ (sell) his soul to the devil in order to become a guitar virtuoso. ▶Myth has it that the young Johnson could barely chord his instrument and annoyed other musicians by trying to sit in at clubs, where he _____ (sneak) onto the bandstand to play every chance he got. He disappeared for a short time, the story goes, and when he returned he was a phenomenal guitarist, having _____ (swear) a Faustian oath to Satan. Johnson's song "Crossroads Blues"—rearranged and recorded by the sixties band Cream as simply "Crossroads"—supposedly recounts this exchange, telling how Johnson _____ (deal) with the devil. Some of his other songs, such as "Hellhound on My Trail," are allegedly about the torment he suffered as he _____ (fight) for his soul.

EXERCISE 22.2

Complete the following sentences with appropriate forms of the verbs in parentheses.

Example: Mary Cassatt _____*laid*_____ down her paintbrush. (lie, lay)

▶ 1. Impressionist artists of the nineteenth century preferred everyday subjects and used to _____ fruit on a table to paint. (sit, set)

▶ 2. They were known for their technique of _____ dabs of paint quickly on canvas, giving an "impression" of a scene, not extensive detail. (lying, laying)

3. Claude Monet's *Women in the Garden* featured one woman in the foreground who _____ on the grass in a garden. (sat, set)

4. In Pierre Auguste Renoir's *Nymphs,* two nude figures talk while _____ on flowers in a garden. (lying, laying)

5. Paul Cézanne liked to _____ in front of his subject as he painted and often completed paintings out of doors rather than in a studio. (sit, set)

22b Understanding Tense

ESL
49a2
Tense is the form a verb takes to indicate when an action occurred or when a condition existed.

ENGLISH VERB TENSES

Simple Tenses

Present (I *finish*, she or he *finishes*)
Past (I *finished*)
Future (I *will finish*)

Perfect Tenses

Present perfect (I *have finished*, she or he *has finished*)
Past perfect (I *had finished*)
Future perfect (I *will have finished*)

Progressive Tenses

Present progressive (I *am finishing*, she or he *is finishing*)
Past progressive (I *was finishing*)
Future progressive (I *will be finishing*)
Present perfect progressive (I *have been finishing*)
Past perfect progressive (I *had been finishing*)
Future perfect progressive (I *will have been finishing*)

---

1 Using the Simple Tenses

The **simple tenses** include *present, past,* and *future.*

♦ The **present tense** usually indicates an action that is taking place at the time it is expressed in speech or writing. It can also indicate an action that occurs regularly.

I see your point. (an action taking place when it is expressed)

We wear wool in the winter. (an action that occurs regularly)

CLOSE-UP

SPECIAL USES OF THE PRESENT TENSE

The present tense has four special uses.

To Indicate Future Time: The grades arrive next Thursday.

To State a Generally Held Belief: Studying pays off.

To State a Scientific Truth: An object at rest tends to stay at rest.

To Discuss a Literary Work: *Family Installments* tells the story of a Puerto Rican family.

♦ The **past tense** indicates that an action has already taken place.

John Glenn <u>orbited</u> the earth three times on February 20, 1962. (an action completed in the past)

As a young man, Mark Twain <u>traveled</u> through the Southwest. (an action that occurred once or many times in the past but did not extend into the present)

♦ The **future tense** indicates that an action will or is likely to take place.

Halley's Comet <u>will reappear</u> in 2061. (a future action that will definitely occur)

The growth of community colleges <u>will</u> probably <u>continue</u>. (a future action that is likely to occur)

2 Using the Perfect Tenses

The **perfect tenses** designate actions that were or will be completed before other actions or conditions. The perfect tenses are formed with the appropriate tense form of the auxiliary verb *have* plus the past participle.

♦ The **present perfect** tense can indicate two types of continuing action beginning in the past.

Dr. Kim <u>has finished</u> studying the effects of BHA on rats. (an action that began in the past and is finished at the present time)

My mother <u>has invested</u> her money wisely. (an action that began in the past and extends into the present)

♦ The **past perfect** tense indicates an action occurring before a certain time in the past.

By 1946, engineers <u>had built</u> the first electronic digital computer.

♦ The **future perfect** tense indicates that an action will be finished by a certain future time.

By Tuesday, the transit authority <u>will have run</u> out of money.

CLOSE-UP

COULD HAVE, SHOULD HAVE, AND WOULD HAVE

Do not use the preposition *of* after *would, should, could,* and *might*. Use the auxiliary verb *have* after these words.

       have
I should ̭of left for class earlier.

3 Using the Progressive Tenses

The **progressive tenses** express continuing action. They are formed with the appropriate tense of the verb *be* plus the present participle.

♦ The **present progressive** tense indicates that something is happening at the time it is expressed in speech or writing.

The volcano <u>is erupting</u>, and lava <u>is flowing</u> toward the town.

♦ The **past progressive** tense indicates two kinds of past action.

Roderick Usher's actions <u>were becoming</u> increasingly bizarre. (a continuing action in the past)

The French revolutionary Marat was stabbed to death while he <u>was bathing</u>. (an action occurring at the same time in the past as another action)

♦ The **future progressive** tense indicates a continuing action in the future.

The treasury secretary <u>will be monitoring</u> the money supply regularly.

♦ The **present perfect progressive** tense indicates action continuing from the past into the present and possibly into the future.

Rescuers <u>have been working</u> around the clock.

♦ The **past perfect progressive** tense indicates that a past action went on until another one occurred.

Before President Kennedy was assassinated, he <u>had been working</u> on civil rights legislation.

♦ The **future perfect progressive** tense indicates that an action will continue until a certain future time.

By eleven o'clock we <u>will have been driving</u> for seven hours.

4 Using Verb Tenses in a Sentence

You use different tenses in a sentence to indicate that actions are taking place at different times. By choosing tenses that accurately express these times, you enable readers to follow the sequence of actions.

♦ *When a **verb** appears in a dependent clause, its tense depends on the tense of the main verb in the independent clause.* When the main verb in the independent clause is in the past tense, the verb in the dependent clause is usually in the past or past perfect tense. When the main verb in the independent clause is in the past perfect tense, the verb in the dependent clause is usually in the past tense. (When the main verb in the independent clause is in any tense except the past or past perfect, the verb in the dependent clause may be in any tense needed for meaning.)

Main Verb	Verb in Dependent Clause
George Hepplewhite <u>was</u> (past) an English cabinetmaker	who <u>designed</u> (past) distinctive chair backs.
The battle <u>had ended</u> (past perfect)	by the time reinforcements <u>arrived</u>. (past)

♦ When an **infinitive** appears in a verbal phrase, the tense it expresses depends on the tense of the sentence's main verb. The *present infinitive* (the *to* form of the verb) indicates an action happening at the same time as or later than the main verb. The *perfect infinitive* (*to have* plus the past participle) indicates action happening earlier than the main verb.

Main Verb	Infinitive
I <u>went</u>	<u>to see</u> the Rangers play last week. (The going and seeing occurred at the same time.)
I <u>want</u>	<u>to see</u> the Rangers play tomorrow. (Wanting occurs in the present, and seeing will occur in the future.)
I would <u>like</u>	<u>to have seen</u> the Rangers play. (Liking occurs in the present, and seeing would have occurred in the past.)

♦ When a **participle** appears in a verbal phrase, its tense depends on the tense of the sentence's main verb. The *present participle* indicates action happening at the same time as the action of the main verb. The *past participle* or the *present perfect participle* indicates action occurring before the action of the main verb.

Participle	Main Verb
<u>Addressing</u> the 1896 Democratic Convention,	William Jennings Bryan <u>delivered</u> his Cross of Gold speech. (The addressing and the delivery occurred at the same time.)
<u>Having written</u> her term paper,	Camille <u>studied</u> for her history final. (The writing occurred before the studying.)

EXERCISE 22.3

A verb is missing from each of the following sentences. Fill in the form of the verb indicated in parentheses.

Example: The Outer Banks ___*stretch*___ (stretch: present) along the North Carolina coast for more than 175 miles.

▶ 1. Many portions of the Outer Banks of North Carolina _____ (give: present) the visitor a sense of history and timelessness.

▶ 2. Many students of history _____ (read: present perfect) about the Outer Banks and its mysteries.

▶ 3. It was on Roanoke Island in the 1580s that English colonists
_____ (establish: past) the first settlement in the New World.
▶ 4. That colony vanished soon after it was settled, _____ (become: present participle) known as the famous "lost colony."
▶ 5. By 1718, the pirate Blackbeard _____ (made: past perfect) the Outer Banks a hiding place for his treasures.
6. It was at Ocracoke, in fact, that Blackbeard _____ (meet: past) his death.
7. Even today, fortune hunters _____ (search: present progressive) the Outer Banks for Blackbeard's hidden treasures.
8. The Outer Banks are also famous for Kitty Hawk and Kill Devil Hills; even as technology has advanced into the space age, the number of tourists flocking to the site of the Wright brothers' epic flight _____. (grow: present perfect progressive)
9. Long before that famous flight occurred, however, the Outer Banks _____ (claim: past perfect) countless ships along its ever-shifting shores, resulting in its nickname—the "Graveyard of the Atlantic."
10. If the Outer Banks continue to be protected from the ravages of overdevelopment and commercialization, visitors _____ (enjoy: future progressive) the mysteries of this tiny finger of land for years to come.

22c Understanding Mood

Mood is the form a verb takes to indicate whether a writer is making a statement or asking a question (*indicative mood*), giving a command (*imperative mood*), or expressing a wish or a contrary-to-fact statement (*subjunctive mood*).

♦ The **indicative** mood expresses an opinion, states a fact, or asks a question: *Jackie Robinson had a great impact on professional baseball.* The indicative is the mood used in most English sentences.
♦ The **imperative** mood is used in commands and direct requests. Usually, the imperative includes only the base form of the verb without a subject: *Use a dictionary.*
♦ The **subjunctive** mood was common in the past, but it now is used less and less often, and usually only in formal contexts.

1 Forming the Subjunctive Mood

The **present subjunctive** uses the base form of the verb, regardless of the subject. The **past subjunctive** has the same form as the past tense of the verb. (The auxiliary verb *be*, however, takes the form *were* regardless of the number or person of the subject.)

Dr. Gorman suggested that I study the Cambrian Period. (present subjunctive)

I wish I were going to Europe. (past subjunctive)

2 Using the Subjunctive Mood

The present subjunctive may be used in *that* clauses after words such as *ask, suggest, require, recommend,* and *demand.*

> The report recommended that juveniles <u>be</u> given mandatory counseling.
>
> Captain Ahab insisted that his crew <u>hunt</u> the white whale.

The past subjunctive may be used in **conditional statements** (statements beginning with *if* that are contrary to fact, including statements that express a wish).

> If John <u>were</u> here, he could see Marsha. (John is not here.)
>
> The father acted as if he <u>were</u> having the baby. (The father couldn't be having the baby.)
>
> I wish I <u>were</u> more organized. (expresses a wish)

Note: In many situations, the subjunctive mood can sound stiff or formal. To eliminate the need for a subjunctive construction, rephrase the sentence.

> The group asked ~~that~~ the city council ^to^ ban smoking in public places.

EXERCISE 22.4

Complete the sentences in the following paragraph by inserting the appropriate form (indicative, imperative, or subjunctive) of the verb in parentheses. Be prepared to explain your choices.

> Harry Houdini was a famous escape artist. ▶He _____ (perform) escapes from every type of bond imaginable: handcuffs, locks, straitjackets, ropes, sacks, and sealed chests underwater. ▶In Germany, workers _____ (challenge) Houdini to escape from a packing box. ▶If he _____ (be) to escape, they would admit that he _____ (be) the best escape artist in the world. Houdini accepted. Before getting into the box, he asked that the observers _____ (give) it a thorough examination. He then asked that a worker _____ (nail) him into the box. "_____ (place) a screen around the box," he ordered after he had been sealed inside. In a few minutes, Houdini _____ (step) from behind the screen. When the workers demanded that they _____ (see) the box, Houdini pulled down the screen. To their surprise, they saw the box with the lid still nailed tightly in place.

22d Understanding Voice

Voice is the form a verb takes to indicate whether its subject acts or is acted upon. When the subject of a verb does something—that is, acts—the verb is in the **active voice.** When the subject of a verb receives the action—that is, is acted upon—the verb is in the **passive voice.**

Active Voice: Hart Crane <u>wrote</u> *The Bridge.*

Passive Voice: *The Bridge* <u>was written</u> by Hart Crane.

CLOSE-UP

ACTIVE VERSUS PASSIVE VOICE

Because the active voice emphasizes the person or thing performing an action, it is usually briefer, clearer, and more emphatic than the passive voice. For this reason, you should usually use the active voice in your college writing.

Some situations, however, require use of the passive voice. For example, you should use passive constructions when the actor is unknown or unimportant or when the recipient of an action should logically receive the emphasis.

DDT <u>was found</u> in soil samples. (Passive voice emphasizes the discovery of DDT; who found it is not important.)

Grits <u>are eaten</u> throughout the South. (Passive voice emphasizes the fact that grits are eaten, not who eats them.)

---

1 Changing Verbs from Passive to Active Voice

You can change a verb from passive to active voice by making the subject of the passive verb the object of the active verb. The person or thing performing the action then becomes the subject of the new sentence.

Passive: The novel *Frankenstein* <u>was written</u> by Mary Shelley.

Active: Mary Shelley <u>wrote</u> the novel *Frankenstein.*

If a passive verb has no object, you must supply one that will become the subject of the active verb.

Passive: Baby elephants are taught to avoid humans. (By whom are baby elephants taught?)

Active: <u>Adult elephants</u> teach baby elephants to avoid humans.

EXERCISE 22.5

Determine which sentences in the following paragraph should be in the active voice, and rewrite those sentences.

▶Rockets were invented by the Chinese about AD 1000. ▶Gunpowder was packed into bamboo tubes and ignited by means of a fuse. ▶These rockets were fired by soldiers at enemy armies and usually caused panic. ▶In thirteenth-century England, an improved form of gunpowder was introduced by Roger Bacon. ▶As a result, rockets were used in battles and were a common—although unreliable—weapon. In the early eighteenth century, a twenty-pound rocket that traveled almost two miles was constructed by William Congreve, an English artillery expert. By the late nineteenth century, thought was given to supersonic speeds by the physicist Ernst Mach, and the sonic boom was predicted by him. The first liquid-fuel rocket was launched by the American Robert Goddard in 1926. A pamphlet written by him anticipated almost all future rocket developments. As a result of his pioneering work, he is called the father of modern rocketry.

2 Changing Verbs from Active to Passive Voice

You can change a verb from active to passive voice by making the object of the active verb the subject of the passive verb. The person or thing performing the action then becomes the object of the passive verb.

Active: Sir James Murray <u>compiled</u> *The Oxford English Dictionary.*

Passive: *The Oxford English Dictionary* <u>was compiled</u> by Sir James Murray.

Remember that an active verb must have an object or else it cannot be put into the passive voice. If an active verb has no object, supply one. This object will become the subject of the passive sentence.

Active: Jacques Cousteau invented.
         Cousteau invented _____?_____.

Passive: _____?_____was invented by Jacques Cousteau.
         The scuba was invented by Jacques Cousteau.

EXERCISE 22.6

Determine which sentences in the following paragraph should be in the passive voice, and rewrite those sentences.

> ▶The Regent Diamond is one of the world's most famous and coveted jewels. ▶A slave discovered the 410-carat diamond in 1701 in an Indian mine. ▶Over the years, people stole and sold the diamond several times. In 1717, the regent of France bought the diamond for an enormous sum, but during the French Revolution, it disappeared again. Someone later found it in a ditch in Paris. Eventually, Napoleon had the diamond set into his ceremonial sword. At last, when the French monarch fell, the government placed the Regent Diamond in the Louvre, where it remains today.

Using Adjectives and Adverbs
CHAPTER 23

23a Understanding Adjectives and Adverbs

Adjectives modify nouns and pronouns. **Adverbs** modify verbs, adjectives, or other adverbs—or entire phrases, clauses, or sentences. Both adjectives and adverbs describe, limit, or qualify other words, phrases, or clauses.

The *function* of a word in a sentence, not its *form,* determines whether it is an adjective or an adverb. Although many adverbs (such as *immediately* and *hopelessly*) end in *-ly,* others (such as *almost* and *very*) do not. Moreover, some words that end in *-ly* (such as *lively*) are adjectives.

> **ESL TIP**
>
> For information on correct placement of adjectives and adverbs in a sentence, **see 49d1.** For information on correct order of adjectives in a series, **see 49d2.**

23b Using Adjectives

Use an **adjective**—not an adverb—as a subject complement. A **subject complement** is a word that follows a linking verb and modifies the sentence's subject, not its verb. A <u>linking verb</u> does not show physical or emotional action. *Seem, appear, believe, become, grow, turn, remain, prove, look, sound, smell, taste, feel,* and the forms of the verb *be* are (or can be used as) linking verbs.

See 20c1

> Michelle seemed <u>brave</u>. (*Seemed* shows no action, so it is a linking verb. Because *brave* is a subject complement that modifies the subject *Michelle,* it takes the adjective form.)
>
> Michelle smiled <u>bravely</u>. (*Smiled* shows action, so it is not a linking verb. *Bravely* modifies *smiled,* so it takes the adverb form.)

Note: Sometimes the same verb can function as either a linking verb or an action verb: *He remained <u>stubborn</u>.* (He was still stubborn.) *He remained stubbornly.* (He remained, in a stubborn manner.)

Use an adjective—not an adverb—as an **object complement,** a word that follows a sentence's direct object and modifies that object and not the verb. Objects are nouns or pronouns, so their modifiers must be adjectives.

> Most people called him <u>timid</u>. (People consider him to be timid; here *timid* is an object complement that modifies *him,* the sentence's direct object, so the adjective form is correct.)
>
> Most people called him <u>timidly</u>. (People were timid when they called him; here *timidly* modifies the verb *called*—not the object—so the adverb form is correct.)

23c Using Adverbs

Use an **adverb**—not an adjective—to modify verbs, adjectives, or other adverbs—or entire phrases, clauses, or sentences.

$\overset{\textit{very well}}{\text{Most students did great}}$ on the midterm.

$\overset{\textit{conservatively}}{\text{My parents dress a lot more conservative}}$ than my friends do.

CLOSE-UP

USING ADJECTIVES AND ADVERBS

In informal speech, adjective forms such as *good, bad, sure, real, slow, quick,* and *loud* are often used to modify verbs, adjectives, and adverbs. Avoid these informal modifiers in college writing.

$\overset{\textit{really well}}{\text{The program ran real good}}$ the first time we tried it, but the new system
$\overset{\textit{badly}}{\text{performed bad.}}$

EXERCISE 23.1

Revise each of the incorrect sentences in the following paragraph so that only adjectives modify nouns and pronouns and only adverbs modify verbs, adjectives, or other adverbs.

▶A popular self-help trend in the United States today is downloadable motivational lectures. ▶These lectures, with titles like *How to Attract Love, Freedom from Acne,* and *I Am a Genius,* are intended to address every problem known to modern society—and to solve these problems quick and easy. ▶The lectures are said to work because they contain "hidden messages" that bypass conscious defense mechanisms. ▶The listener hears only music or relaxing sounds, like waves rolling slow and steady. ▶At decibel levels perceived only subconsciously, positive words and phrases are embedded, usually by someone who speaks deep and rhythmic. The top-selling lectures are those that help listeners lose weight or quit smoking. The popularity of such material is not hard to understand. They promise easy solutions to complex problems. But the main benefit of these lectures appears to be for the sellers, who are accumulating profits real fast.

EXERCISE 23.2

Being careful to use adjectives—not adverbs—as subject complements and object complements, write five sentences in imitation of each of the following sentences. Consult the list of linking verbs in **20c1,** and use a different linking verb in each of your sentences.

▶ 1. Julie looked worried.
   2. Dan considers his collection valuable.

23d Using Comparative and Superlative Forms

Most adjectives and adverbs have **comparative** and **superlative** forms that can be used to indicate degree.

COMPARATIVE AND SUPERLATIVE FORMS

Form	Function	Example
Positive	Describes a quality; does not indicate a comparison	big, easily
Comparative	Indicates a comparison between *two* qualities (greater or lesser)	bigger, more easily
Superlative	Indicates a comparison among *more than two* qualities (greatest or least)	biggest, most easily

Note: Some adverbs, particularly those indicating time, place, and degree (*almost, very, here,* and *immediately*), do not have comparative or superlative forms.

1 Regular Comparative Forms

To form the comparative, all one-syllable adjectives and many two-syllable adjectives (particularly those that end in *-y, -ly, -le, -er,* and *-ow*) add *-er*: *slower, funnier.* (Note that a final *y* becomes *i* before *-er* is added.)

Other two-syllable adjectives and all long adjectives form the comparative with *more*: *more famous, more incredible.*

Adverbs ending in *-ly* also form the comparative with *more*: *more slowly.* Other adverbs use the *-er* ending to form the comparative: *sooner.*

All adjectives and adverbs indicate a lesser degree with *less*: *less lovely, less slowly.*

2 Regular Superlative Forms

Adjectives that form the comparative with *-er* add *-est* to form the superlative: *nicest, funniest.* Adjectives that indicate the comparative with *more* use *most* to indicate the superlative: *most famous, most challenging.*

The majority of adverbs use *most* to indicate the superlative: *most quickly.* Others use the *-est* ending: *soonest.*

All adjectives and adverbs use *least* to indicate the least degree: *least interesting, least willingly.*

CLOSE-UP

USING COMPARATIVES AND SUPERLATIVES

♦ Never use both *more* and *-er* to form the comparative or both *most* and *-est* to form the superlative.

Nothing could have been ~~more~~ easier.

Jack is the ~~most~~ meanest person in town.

♦ Never use the superlative when comparing only two things.

Stacy is the ~~tallest~~ *taller* of the two sisters.

♦ Never use the comparative when comparing more than two things.

We chose the ~~earlier~~ *earliest* of the four appointments.

3 Irregular Comparatives and Superlatives

Some adjectives and adverbs have irregular comparative and superlative forms. Instead of adding a word or an ending to the positive form, they use different words to indicate the comparative and the superlative.

IRREGULAR COMPARATIVES AND SUPERLATIVES

	Positive	Comparative	Superlative
Adjectives:	good	better	best
	bad	worse	worst
	a little	less	least
	many, some, much	more	most
Adverbs:	well	better	best
	badly	worse	worst

CLOSE-UP

ILLOGICAL COMPARATIVE AND SUPERLATIVE FORMS

Many adjectives can logically exist only in the positive degree. For example, *perfect, unique, excellent, impossible, parallel, empty,* and *dead* can never be used in the comparative or superlative degree.

I saw ~~the most~~ *a* unique vase in the museum.

These words can, however, be modified by words that suggest approaching the absolute state—*nearly* or *almost,* for example.

He revised until his draft was <u>almost perfect</u>.

Note: Some adverbs, particularly those indicating time, place, and degree (*almost, very, here, immediately*), do not have comparative or superlative forms.

EXERCISE 23.3

Supply the correct comparative and superlative forms for each of the following adjectives or adverbs. Then, use each form in a sentence.

Example: strange   stranger   strangest

> The story had a *strange* ending.
> The explanation sounded *stranger* each time I heard it.
> This is the *strangest* gadget I have ever seen.

▶ 1. difficult
▶ 2. eccentric
▶ 3. confusing
▶ 4. bad
▶ 5. mysterious

6. softly
7. embarrassing
8. well
9. often
10. tiny

Revising Sentence Fragments

24a Recognizing Sentence Fragments

A **sentence fragment** is an incomplete sentence—a phrase or clause that is punctuated as if it were a complete sentence. A sentence may be incomplete for any of the following reasons:

◆ **It lacks a subject.**

Many astrophysicists now believe that galaxies are distributed in clusters. <u>And even form supercluster complexes.</u>

◆ **It lacks a verb.**

Every generation has its defining moments. <u>Usually the events with the most news coverage.</u>

◆ **It lacks both a subject and a verb.**

Researchers are engaged in a variety of studies. <u>Suggesting a link between alcoholism and heredity.</u> (*Suggesting* is a **verbal,** which cannot serve as a sentence's main verb.)

◆ **It is a dependent clause.**

Bishop Desmond Tutu was awarded the 1984 Nobel Peace Prize. <u>Because he fought to end apartheid.</u>

The pH meter and the spectrophotometer are two scientific instruments. <u>That changed the chemistry laboratory dramatically.</u>

Note: A sentence cannot consist of a single clause that begins with a subordinating conjunction (such as *because*) or a relative pronoun (such as *that*); moreover, unless it is a question, a sentence cannot consist of a single clause beginning with *when, where, who, which, what, why,* or *how.*

CLOSE-UP

IDENTIFYING FRAGMENTS

A fragment is especially confusing when it comes between two independent clauses and readers cannot tell which of the two clauses completes the fragment's thought. For instance, it is impossible to tell to which independent clause the underlined fragment in each of the following sequences belongs.

The course requirements were changed last year. <u>Because a new professor was hired at the very end of the spring semester</u>. I was unable to find out about this change until after preregistration.

In *The Ox-Bow Incident,* the crowd is convinced that the men are guilty. <u>Even though the men insist they are innocent and Davies pleads for their lives</u>. They are hanged.

GRAMMAR CHECKER

IDENTIFYING FRAGMENTS

Your grammar checker will identify many (although not all) sentence fragments. As you type, they will be highlighted, and you will be prompted to revise them. However, not every word group identified as a fragment will actually be a fragment. You, not your grammar checker, will have to make the final decision about whether or not a sentence is grammatically complete—and decide how to correct it.

EXERCISE 24.1

Identify each of the following word groups as either a sentence fragment or a complete sentence. Be prepared to explain why each fragment is not a complete sentence. When you have finished, type each sentence into your word-processing program, and use the grammar checker to check your responses.

▶ 1. Consisting of shortness of breath, a high fever, and a racing pulse.
▶ 2. Held in contempt of court by the presiding judge.
▶ 3. Walking to the end of the road and back is good exercise.
▶ 4. On her own at last, after many years of struggle for independence.
▶ 5. Because he felt torn between two cultures.
   6. With boundaries extending from the ocean to the bay.
   7. Although language study can be challenging.
   8. In addition, a new point guard will be a valuable addition to the team.
   9. Defeated by his own greed but not in the least regretful.
  10. Moreover, the continued presence of troops in Iraq.

CLOSE-UP

REVISING SENTENCE FRAGMENTS

If you identify a fragment in your writing, use one of the following two strategies to revise it:

1. Attach the fragment to an adjacent independent clause.

   According to German legend, Lohengrin is the son of Parzival, /And a knight of the Holy Grail. *and*

(continued)

> **REVISING SENTENCE FRAGMENTS** (*continued*)
> *because*
> Pioneers traveled west.~~/Because~~ they hoped to find a better life.
>
> 2. Turn the fragment into a sentence.
>
>   Lancaster County, Pennsylvania, is home to many Pennsylvania Dutch.
>   *They are descended*
>   ~~Descended~~ from German immigrants. (missing subject and verb added)
>   *City*
>   Property taxes rose sharply. ~~Although city~~ services declined. (subordinating
>   conjunction *although* deleted)

24b Revising Dependent Clause Fragments

A **dependent clause** contains both a subject and a verb, but it cannot stand alone as a sentence. Because it needs an independent clause to complete its meaning, a **dependent clause** (also called a *subordinate clause*) must always be attached to at least one independent clause to form a complete sentence. You can recognize a dependent clause because it is always introduced by a **subordinating conjunction** (*although, because,* and so on) or a **relative pronoun** (*that, which, who,* and so on).

See 14d

In most cases, the best way to correct a dependent clause fragment is to join the dependent clause to an adjacent independent clause, creating a complex sentence.

because
The United States declared war.~~/Because~~ the Japanese bombed Pearl Harbor. (Dependent clause has been attached to an independent clause, creating a complex sentence.)

, which
The battery is dead.~~/Which~~ means the car won't start. (Dependent clause has been attached to an independent clause, creating a complex sentence.)

Another way to correct a dependent clause fragment is to delete the subordinating conjunction or relative pronoun, turning the fragment into a complete sentence.

The
The United States declared war. ~~Because the~~ Japanese bombed Pearl Harbor. (Subordinating conjunction *because* has been deleted; the result is a new sentence.)

This
The battery is dead. ~~Which~~ means the car won't start. (Relative pronoun *which* has been replaced by *this;* the result is a new sentence.)

Note: Simply deleting or replacing the subordinating conjunction or relative pronoun, as in the two examples above, is usually the least desirable way to revise a dependent clause fragment because it is likely to create two choppy sentences and because it does not clearly indicate the logical relationship between the two clauses.

EXERCISE 24.2

Identify the sentence fragments in the following paragraph. Then, correct each fragment either by attaching the fragment to an independent clause or by deleting or replacing the subordinating conjunction or relative pronoun to create a sentence that can stand alone. (In some cases, you will have to replace a relative pronoun with another word that can serve as the subject.)

▶The drive-in movie came into being just after World War II. ▶When both movies and cars were central to the lives of many Americans. ▶Drive-ins were especially popular with teenagers and young families during the 1950s. ▶When cars and gas were relatively inexpensive. ▶Theaters charged by the carload. ▶Which meant that a group of teenagers or a family with several children could spend an evening at the movies for a few dollars. ▶In 1958, when the fad peaked, there were over four thousand drive-ins in the United States. ▶While today there are fewer than three thousand. Many of these are in the Sunbelt, with most in California. Although many Sunbelt drive-ins continue to thrive because of the year-round warm weather. Many northern drive-ins are in financial trouble. Because land is so expensive. Some drive-in owners break even only by operating flea markets or swap meets in daylight hours. While others, unable to attract customers, are selling their theaters to land developers. Soon, drive-ins may be a part of our nostalgic past. Which will be a great loss for many who enjoy them.

24c Revising Phrase Fragments

A **phrase** provides information—description, examples, and so on—about other words or word groups in a sentence. However, because it lacks a subject, a verb, or both, a phrase cannot stand alone as a sentence.

CLOSE-UP

FRAGMENTS INTRODUCED BY TRANSITIONS

Many phrase fragments are word groups that are introduced by <u>transitional words and phrases,</u> such as *also, finally, in addition,* and *now,* but are missing subjects and verbs. To correct such a fragment, you need to add the missing subject and verb.

See
5b2

It was also
~~Also~~ a step in the right direction.

he found
Finally, a new home for the family.

we need
In addition, three new keyboards for the computer lab.

I will explain
Now, the first step.

1 Prepositional Phrase Fragments

See
20f
ESL
49e

A <u>prepositional phrase</u> consists of a preposition, its object, and any modifiers of the object.

To correct a prepositional phrase fragment, attach it to the independent clause that contains the word or word group modified by the prepositional phrase.

President Lyndon Johnson did not seek reelection./ ~~For~~ ^{for} a number of reasons. (Prepositional phrase has been attached to an independent clause, creating a complete sentence.)

He ran sixty yards for a touchdown./ ~~In~~ ⁱⁿ the final minutes of the game. (Prepositional phrase has been attached to an independent clause, creating a complete sentence.)

EXERCISE 24.3

Read the following passage and identify the sentence fragments. Then, correct each one by attaching it to the independent clause that contains the word or word group it modifies.

▶Most college athletes are caught in a conflict. ▶Between their athletic and academic careers. ▶Sometimes college athletes' responsibilities on the playing field make it hard for them to be good students. ▶Often, athletes must make a choice. ▶Between sports and a degree. ▶Some athletes would not be able to afford college. ▶Without athletic scholarships. ▶Ironically, however, their commitments (training, exercise, practice, and travel to out-of-town games, for example) deprive athletes. ▶Of valuable classroom time. ▶The role of college athletes is constantly being questioned. Critics suggest that athletes exist only to participate in and promote college athletics. Because of the importance of this role to academic institutions, scandals occasionally develop. With coaches and even faculty members arranging to inflate athletes' grades to help them remain eligible. For participation in sports. Some universities even lower admissions standards. To help remedy this and other inequities. The controversial Proposition 48, passed at the NCAA convention in 1982, established minimum College Board scores and grade standards for student athletes. But many people feel that the NCAA remains overly concerned. With profits rather than with education. As a result, college athletic competition is increasingly coming to resemble pro sports. From the coaches' pressure on the players to win to the network television exposure to the wagers on the games' outcomes.

2 Verbal Phrase Fragments

A verbal phrase consists of a **verbal**—a present participle (*walking*), past participle (*walked*), infinitive (*to walk*), or gerund (*walking*)—plus related objects and modifiers (*walking along the lonely beach*). Because a verbal cannot serve as a sentence's main verb, a verbal phrase is not a complete sentence and should not be punctuated as one.

To correct a verbal phrase fragment, you can attach the verbal phrase to an adjacent independent clause that contains the words (a subject or verb or both) that are needed to make the fragment a sentence.

In 1948, India became an independent country/ ~~Divided~~ ^{divided} into the nations of India and Pakistan. (Verbal phrase has been attached to a related independent clause, creating a complete sentence.)

A familiar trademark can increase a product's sales/ ~~Reminding~~ ^{, reminding} shoppers that the product has a long-standing reputation. (Verbal phrase has been attached to a related independent clause, creating a complete sentence.)

Or, you can change the verbal to a verb and add a subject.

In 1948, India became an independent country. ^{It was divided} ~~Divided~~ into the nations of India and Pakistan. (Verb *was divided* has replaced verbal *divided,* and subject *it* has been added; the result is a complete sentence.)

A familiar trademark can increase a product's sales. ^{It reminds} ~~Reminding~~ shoppers that the product has a long-standing reputation. (Verb *reminds* has replaced verbal *reminding,* and subject *it* has been added; the result is a complete sentence.)

EXERCISE 24.4

Identify the sentence fragments in the following paragraph and correct each one. Either attach the fragment to a related independent clause, or add a subject and a verb to create a complete sentence.

▶Many food products have well-known trademarks. ▶Identified by familiar faces on product labels. ▶Some of these symbols have remained the same, while others have changed considerably. ▶Products like Sun-Maid Raisins, Betty Crocker potato mixes, Quaker Oats, and Uncle Ben's Rice use faces. ▶To create a sense of quality and tradition and to encourage shopper recognition of the products. ▶Many of the portraits have been updated several times. ▶To reflect changes in society. Betty Crocker's portrait, for instance, has changed many times since its creation in 1936. Symbolizing women's changing roles. The original Chef Boy-ar-dee has also changed. Turning from the young Italian chef Hector Boiardi into a white-haired senior citizen. Miss Sunbeam, trademark of Sunbeam Bread, has had her hairdo modified several times since her first appearance in 1942; the Blue Bonnet girl, also created in 1942, now has a more modern look, and Aunt Jemima has also been changed. Slimmed down a bit in 1965. Similarly, the Campbell's Soup kids are less chubby now than in the 1920s when they first appeared. Still, manufacturers are very careful about selecting a trademark or modifying an existing one. Typically spending a good deal of time and money on research before a change is made.

3 Appositive Fragments

An **appositive**—a noun or noun phrase that identifies or renames an adjacent noun or pronoun—cannot stand alone as a sentence.

To correct an appositive fragment, attach the appositive to the independent clause that contains the word the appositive renames.

Brian was the star forward of the Blue Devils, the team with the best record. (Appositive has been attached to an independent clause, creating a complete sentence.)

Piero della Francesca was a leader of the Umbrian school of painting, a school that remained close to the traditions of Gothic art. (Appositive has been attached to an independent clause, creating a complete sentence.)

See 34a1

CLOSE-UP

LISTS

When an appositive fragment takes the form of a list, add a colon to connect the list to the independent clause that introduces it.

Tourists often outnumber residents in four European cities: Venice, Florence, Canterbury, and Bath.

Sometimes an appositive consists of a word or phrase like *that is, for example, for instance, namely,* or *such as,* followed by an example.

To correct this kind of appositive fragment, attach the appositive to the preceding independent clause.

Fairy tales are full of damsels in distress, such as Cinderella and Rapunzel.

Note: Sometimes you can correct an appositive fragment by embedding the appositive within an independent clause.

Some popular novelists —for example, Charles Dickens and Mark Twain— are highly respected in later generations. ~~For example, Charles Dickens and Mark Twain.~~

EXERCISE 24.5

Identify the fragments in this paragraph, and correct them by attaching each one to the independent clause containing the word the appositive identifies or renames.

▶Until the early 1900s, communities in West Virginia, Tennessee, and Kentucky were isolated by the mountains that surrounded them. ▶The great chain of the Appalachian Mountains. ▶Set apart from the emerging culture of a growing America and American language, these communities retained a language rich with the dialect of Elizabethan English and sprinkled with hints of a Scotch-Irish influence. ▶In the 1910s and '20s, the communities in these mountains began to long for a better future for their children. ▶The key to that future, as they saw it, was education. In some communities, that education took the form of Settlement Schools. Schools led by idealistic young graduates of eastern women's colleges. These teachers taught the basic academic subjects. Such as reading, writing, and mathematics. They also schooled their students in the culture of the mountains. For example, the crafts, music, and folklore of the Appalachians. In addition, they taught them skills that would help them survive when the coal market began to decline. The Settlement Schools attracted artisans from around the world. Quilters, weavers, basketmakers, and carpenters. The schools also opened the mountains to the world, leading to the decline of the Elizabethan dialect.

24d   Revising Detached Compounds

The last part of a **compound predicate, compound object,** or **compound complement** cannot stand alone as a sentence.

To correct this type of fragment, connect the detached part of the compound to the sentence to which it belongs.

People with dyslexia have trouble reading, ~~And~~ *and* may also find it difficult to write. (Detached part of the compound predicate has been connected to the sentence to which it belongs.)

They took only a compass and a canteen, ~~And~~ *and* some trail mix. (Detached part of the compound object has been connected to the sentence to which it belongs.)

When their supplies ran out they were surprised, ~~And~~ *and* hungry. (Detached part of the compound complement has been connected to the sentence to which it belongs.)

EXERCISE 24.6

Identify the sentence fragments in this passage, and correct them by connecting each detached compound to the sentence to which it belongs.

▶As more and more Americans discover the pleasures of the wilderness, our national parks are feeling the stress. ▶Wanting to get away for a weekend or a week, hikers and backpackers stream from the cities into nearby state and national parks. ▶They bring with them a hunger for the wilderness. ▶But very little knowledge about how to behave ethically in the wild. ▶They also do not know how to keep themselves safe. ▶Some of them think of the national parks as inexpensive amusement parks. ▶Without proper camping supplies and lacking enough food and water for their trip, they are putting at risk their lives and the lives of those who will be called on to save them. ▶One family went for a hike up a desert canyon with an eight-month-old infant. ▶And their seventy-eight-year-old grandmother. Although the terrain was difficult, they were not wearing the proper shoes. Or good socks. They did not even carry a first aid kit. Or a map or compass. They were on an unmarked trail in a little-used section of Bureau of Land Management lands. And following vague directions from a friend. Soon, they were lost. They had not brought water or food. Or even rain gear or warm clothes. Luckily for them, they had brought a cell phone. By the time they called for help, however, it was getting dark and a storm was building. A rescue plane eventually located the family. And brought them to safety. Still, a little planning before they hiked in an inhospitable area, and a little awareness and preparedness for the terrain they were traveling in, would have saved this family much worry. And the taxpayers a lot of money.

24e Using Fragments Intentionally

Fragments are often used in speech and in personal email and other informal writing—as well as in journalism, political slogans, creative writing, bumper stickers, and advertising.

In professional and academic writing, however, sentence fragments are generally not acceptable.

CHECKLIST

USING FRAGMENTS INTENTIONALLY

In college writing, it is acceptable to use fragments in the following special situations:
- ❏ In lists
- ❏ In captions that accompany visuals
- ❏ In topic outlines
- ❏ In quoted dialogue
- ❏ In *PowerPoint* presentations
- ❏ In titles and subtitles of papers and reports

Revising Run-ons   CHAPTER 25

25a Recognizing Comma Splices and Fused Sentences

See 14b2 A **run-on** is an error that occurs when two <u>independent clauses</u> are joined incorrectly. There are two kinds of run-ons: *comma splices* and *fused sentences*.

A **comma splice** is a run-on that occurs when two independent clauses are joined by just a comma. A **fused sentence** is a run-on that occurs when two independent clauses are joined with no punctuation.

Comma Splice: Charles Dickens created the character of Mr. Micawber, he also created Uriah Heep.

Fused Sentence: Charles Dickens created the character of Mr. Micawber he also created Uriah Heep.

GRAMMAR CHECKER

REVISING COMMA SPLICES

Your grammar checker will highlight comma splices and prompt you to revise them. It may also highlight fused sentences, but it may identify them simply as long sentences that need revision. Moreover, it will not offer suggestions for revising fused sentences.

CLOSE-UP

REVISING COMMA SPLICES AND FUSED SENTENCES

To revise a comma splice or fused sentence, use one of thee following four strategies:

1. Add a period between the clauses, creating two separate sentences.
2. Add a semicolon between the clauses, creating a compound sentence.
3. Add a coordinating conjunction between the clauses, creating a compound sentence.
4. Subordinate one clause to the other, creating a complex sentence.

25b   Adding a Period

You can revise a comma splice or fused sentence by adding a period between the independent clauses, creating two separate sentences. This is a good strategy to use when the clauses are long or when they are not closely related.

In 1894, Frenchman Alfred Dreyfus was falsely convicted of
treason/ his struggle for justice made his case famous.
        . His

CLOSE-UP

COMMA SPLICES AND FUSED SENTENCES

Using a comma to punctuate an interrupted quotation that consists of two complete sentences creates a comma splice. Instead, use a period.

"This is a good course," Eric said/ "in fact, I wish I'd taken it sooner."
                               . "In

25c Adding a Semicolon

See
31a You can revise a comma splice or fused sentence by adding a <u>semicolon</u> between two closely related clauses that convey parallel or contrasting information. The result will be a compound sentence.

> In pre–World War II western Europe, only a small elite had access to
> a university education*;* however, this situation changed dramatically
> after the war.

See
5b2 *Note:* When you use a <u>transitional word or phrase</u> (such as *however, therefore,* or *for example*) to connect two independent clauses, the transitional element must be preceded by a semicolon and followed by a comma. If you link the two clauses with just a comma, you create a comma splice; if you omit punctuation entirely, you create a fused sentence.

25d Adding a Coordinating Conjunction

See
14c1 You can use a coordinating conjunction (*and, or, but, nor, for, so, yet*) to join two closely related clauses of equal importance into a <u>compound sentence</u>. The coordinating conjunction you choose indicates the relationship between the clauses: addition (*and*), contrast (*but, yet*), causality (*for, so*), or a choice of alternatives (*or, nor*). Be sure to include a comma before the coordinating conjunction.

> Elias Howe invented the sewing machine, *and* Julia Ward Howe was a poet
> and social reformer.

25e Creating a Complex Sentence

See
14d When the ideas in two independent clauses are not of equal importance, you can use a subordinating conjunction or relative pronoun to join the clauses into one <u>complex sentence</u>, placing the less important idea in the dependent clause. The subordinating conjunction or relative pronoun you choose indicates how the clauses are related.

> Stravinsky's ballet *The Rite of Spring* shocked Parisians in 1913, *because* its
> rhythms seemed erotic.
>
> Lady Mary Wortley Montagu*, who* had suffered from smallpox herself,
> ~~she~~ helped spread the practice of inoculation.

CLOSE-UP

ACCEPTABLE COMMA SPLICES

In a few special cases, comma splices are acceptable. For instance, a comma is conventionally used in dialogue between a statement and a tag question, even though each is a separate independent clause.

This is Ron's house, isn't it?

I'm not late, am I?

In addition, commas may be used to connect two short, balanced independent clauses or two or more short parallel independent clauses, especially when one clause contradicts the other.

Commencement isn't the end, it's the beginning.

EXERCISE 25.1

Identify the comma splices and fused sentences in the following paragraph. Correct each in two of the four possible ways listed in the Close-up box on page 233. If a sentence is correct, leave it alone.

Example: The fans rose in their seats, the game was almost over.

Revised: The fans rose in their seats; the game was almost over.
The fans rose in their seats because the game was almost over.

▶Entrepreneurship is the study of small businesses, college students are embracing it enthusiastically. ▶Many schools offer one or more courses in entrepreneurship these courses teach the theory and practice of starting a small business. ▶Students are signing up for courses, moreover, they are starting their own businesses. ▶One student started with a car-waxing business, now he sells condominiums. Other students are setting up catering services they supply everything from waiters to bartenders. One student has a thriving cake-decorating business, in fact, she employs fifteen students to deliver the cakes. All over the country, student businesses are selling everything from tennis balls to bagels, the student owners are making impressive profits. Formal courses at the graduate as well as undergraduate level are attracting more business students than ever, several schools (such as Baylor University, the University of Southern California, and Babson College) even offer degree programs in entrepreneurship. Many business school students are no longer planning to be corporate executives instead, they plan to become entrepreneurs.

EXERCISE 25.2

Combine each of the following sentence pairs into one sentence without creating comma splices or fused sentences. In each case, either connect the clauses into a compound sentence (with a semicolon or with a comma and a coordinating conjunction) or subordinate one clause to the other to create a complex sentence. You may have to add, delete, reorder, or change words or punctuation.

▶ 1. Several recent studies indicate that many American high school students have little knowledge of history. This is affecting our future as a democratic nation and as individuals.

▶ 2. Surveys show that nearly one-third of American seventeen-year-olds cannot identify the countries the United States fought against in World War II. One-third think Columbus reached the New World after 1750.

▶ 3. Several reasons have been given for this decline in historical literacy. The main reason is the way history is taught.

▶ 4. This problem is bad news. The good news is that there is increasing agreement among educators about what is wrong with current methods of teaching history.

▶ 5. History can be exciting and engaging. Too often, it is presented in a boring manner.

6. Students are typically expected to memorize dates, facts, and names. History as adventure—as a "good story"—is frequently neglected.

7. One way to avoid this problem is to use good textbooks. Textbooks should be accurate, lively, and focused.

8. Another way to create student interest in historical events is to use primary sources instead of so-called comprehensive textbooks. Autobiographies, journals, and diaries can give students insight into larger issues.

9. Students can also be challenged to think about history by taking sides in a debate. They can learn more about connections among historical events by writing essays than by taking multiple-choice tests.

10. Finally, history teachers should be less concerned about specific historical details. They should be more concerned about conveying the wonder of history.

Revising Agreement Errors

CHAPTER 26

ESL
49a1 **Agreement** is the correspondence between words in number, gender, and person. Subjects and verbs <u>agree</u> in **number** (singular or plural) and **person** (first, second, or third); pronouns and their antecedents agree in number, person, and **gender** (masculine, feminine, or neuter).

26a Making Subjects and Verbs Agree

Singular subjects take singular verbs, and plural subjects take plural verbs.

Singular: <u>Hydrogen peroxide</u> <u>is</u> an unstable compound.

Plural: <u>Characters</u> <u>are</u> not well developed in O. Henry's short stories.

ESL 49a2

See 26a4

Present tense verbs, except *be* and *have*, add -*s* or -*es* when the subject is third-person singular. Third-person singular subjects include nouns; the personal pronouns *he, she, it,* and *one;* and many indefinite pronouns.

The president has the power to veto congressional legislation.

She frequently cites statistics to support her assertions.

In every group, somebody emerges as a natural leader.

Present tense verbs do not add -*s* or -*es* when the subject is a plural noun, a first-person or second-person pronoun (*I, we, you*), or a third-person plural pronoun (*they*).

Experts recommend that dieters avoid salty processed meat.

In our Bill of Rights, we guarantee all defendants the right to a speedy trial.

At this stratum, you see rocks dating back fifteen million years.

They say that some wealthy people default on their student loans.

In the following special situations, subject-verb agreement can cause problems for writers.

1 When Words Come between Subject and Verb

If a modifying phrase comes between subject and verb, the verb should agree with the subject, not with a word in the modifying phrase.

The sound of the drumbeats builds in intensity in Eugene O'Neill's play *The Emperor Jones.*

The games won by the intramural team are usually few and far between.

Note: When phrases introduced by *along with, as well as, in addition to, including,* and *together with* come between subject and verb, these phrases do *not* change the subject's number: *Heavy rain, together with high winds, causes hazardous driving conditions.*

2 When Compound Subjects Are Joined by *And*

Compound subjects joined by *and* usually take plural verbs.

Navigation systems and antilock brakes are standard on many new cars.

There are, however, two exceptions to this rule. First, compound subjects joined by *and* that stand for a single idea or person are treated as a unit and take singular verbs.

Rhythm and blues is a forerunner of rock and roll.

Second, when *each* or *every* precedes a compound subject joined by *and,* the subject takes a singular verb.

Every desk and file cabinet was searched before the letter was found.

3 | When Compound Subjects Are Joined by *Or*

Compound subjects joined by *or* (or by *either . . . or* or *neither . . . nor*) may take either singular or plural verbs.

If both subjects are singular, use a singular verb; if both subjects are plural, use a plural verb.

> Either radiation or chemotherapy is combined with surgery for the most effective results. (Both *radiation* and *chemotherapy* are singular, so the verb is singular.)

> Either radiation treatments or chemotherapy sessions are combined with surgery for the most effective results. (Both *treatments* and *sessions* are plural, so the verb is plural.)

If one subject is singular and the other is plural, the verb agrees with the subject that is nearer to it.

> Either radiation treatments or chemotherapy is combined with surgery for the most effective results. (Singular verb agrees with *chemotherapy*.)

> Either chemotherapy or radiation treatments are combined with surgery for the most effective results. (Plural verb agrees with *treatments*.)

4 | When Indefinite Pronouns Serve as Subjects

ESL
49c3 Most indefinite pronouns—*another, anyone, everyone, one, each, either, neither, anything, everything, something, nothing, nobody,* and *somebody*—are singular and take singular verbs.

> Anyone is welcome to apply for this grant.

Some indefinite pronouns—*both, many, few, several, others*—are plural and take plural verbs.

> Several of the articles are useful.

A few indefinite pronouns—*some, all, any, more, most,* and *none*—can be singular or plural, depending on the noun they refer to.

> Of course, some of this trouble is to be expected. (*Some* refers to *trouble.*)

> Some of the spectators are getting restless. (*Some* refers to *spectators.*)

GRAMMAR CHECKER

SUBJECT-VERB AGREEMENT

Your grammar checker will highlight and offer revision suggestions for many subject-verb agreement errors, including errors in sentences that have indefinite pronoun subjects.

5 When Collective Nouns Serve as Subjects

A **collective noun** names a group of persons or things—for instance, *navy, union, association, band.* When a collective noun refers to a group as a unit (as it usually does), it takes a singular verb; when it refers to the individuals or items that make up the group, it takes a plural verb.

> To many people, the royal family symbolizes Great Britain. (The family, as a unit, is the symbol.)
>
> The family all eat at different times. (Each member eats separately.)

Note: If a plural verb sounds awkward with a collective noun, reword the sentence: *Family members all eat at different times.*

Phrases that name fixed amounts—*three-quarters, twenty dollars, the majority*—are treated like collective nouns. When the amount denotes a unit, it takes a singular verb; when it denotes part of the whole, it takes a plural verb.

> Three-quarters of his usual salary is not enough to live on. (*Three-quarters* denotes a unit.)
>
> Three-quarters of workshop participants improve dramatically. (*Three-quarters* denotes part of the group.)

Note: The number is always singular, and *a number* is always plural: *The number of voters has declined; A number of students have missed the opportunity to preregister.*

6 When Singular Subjects Have Plural Forms

A singular subject takes a singular verb, even if the form of the subject is plural.

> Politics makes strange bedfellows.
>
> Statistics deals with the collection, classification, analysis, and interpretation of data.

When such a word has a plural meaning, however, use a plural verb.

> Her politics are too radical for her parents. (*Politics* refers not to the science of political government but, rather, to political principles or opinions.)
>
> The statistics prove him wrong. (*Statistics* denotes not a body of knowledge but the numerical facts or data themselves.)

Note: Some words retain their Latin plural forms, which do not look like English plural forms. Be particularly careful to use the correct verbs with such words: *criterion is, criteria are; medium is, media are; bacterium is, bacteria are; datum is, data are.*

ESL
49f

7 When Subject-Verb Order Is Inverted

Even when <u>word order</u> is inverted so that the verb comes before the subject (as it does in questions and in sentences beginning with *there is* or *there are*), the subject and verb must agree.

<u>Is</u> <u>either</u> answer correct?

There <u>is</u> a <u>monument</u> to Emiliano Zapata in Mexico City.

There <u>are</u> currently thirteen federal <u>circuit courts</u> of appeals.

See
20c1

8 With Linking Verbs

A <u>linking verb</u> should agree with its subject, not with the subject complement.

The <u>problem</u> <u>was</u> termites.

Here, the verb *was* correctly agrees with the subject *problem,* not with the subject complement *termites.* If *termites* were the subject, the verb would be plural: *<u>Termites</u> <u>were</u> the problem.*

See
20b

9 With Relative Pronouns

When you use a <u>relative pronoun</u> (*who, which, that,* and so on) to introduce a dependent clause, the verb in that clause should agree in number with the pronoun's **antecedent** (the word to which the pronoun refers).

The farmer is among the <u>ones</u> who <u>suffer</u> during a grain embargo.
(Verb *suffer* agrees with plural antecedent *ones.*)

The farmer is the only <u>one</u> who <u>suffers</u> during the grain embargo.
(Verb *suffers* agrees with singular antecedent *one.*)

EXERCISE 26.1

Some of the following sentences are correct, but others contain common errors in subject-verb agreement. If a sentence is correct, mark it with a *C*; if it has an error, correct it.

▶ 1. *I Love Lucy* is one of those television shows that almost all Americans have seen at least once.
▶ 2. The committee presented its findings to the president.
▶ 3. Neither Western novels nor science fiction appeal to me.
▶ 4. Stage presence and musical ability makes a rock performer successful today.
▶ 5. *It's a Wonderful Life,* like many old Christmas movies, seems to be shown on television every year.
6. Hearts are my grandmother's favorite card game.

7. The best part of B. B. King's songs are the guitar solos.
8. Time and tide waits for no man.
9. Sports are my main pastime.
10. *Vincent and Theo* is Robert Altman's movie about the French Impressionist painter Vincent van Gogh and his brother.

26b Making Pronouns and Antecedents Agree

See 20b ESL 49c

A <u>pronoun</u> must agree with its **antecedent**—the word or word group to which the pronoun refers. Singular pronouns—such as *he, him, she, her, it, me, myself,* and *oneself*—should refer to singular antecedents. Plural pronouns—such as *we, us, they, them,* and *their*—should refer to plural antecedents.

In the following special situations, pronoun-antecedent agreement can cause problems for writers.

1 With Compound Antecedents

In most cases, use a plural pronoun to refer to a **compound antecedent** (two or more antecedents connected by *and*).

<u>Mormonism and Christian Science</u> were influenced in <u>their</u> beginnings by Shaker doctrines.

However, this rule has several exceptions:

♦ If a compound antecedent denotes a single unit—one person, thing, or idea—use a singular pronoun to refer to the compound antecedent.

In 1904, <u>the husband and father</u> brought <u>his</u> family from Germany to the United States.

♦ Use a singular pronoun when a compound antecedent is preceded by *each* or *every*.

<u>Every programming language and software package</u> has <u>its</u> limitations.

♦ Use a singular pronoun to refer to two or more singular antecedents linked by *or* or *nor*.

<u>Neither Thoreau nor Whitman</u> lived to see <u>his</u> work read widely.

♦ When one part of a compound antecedent is singular and one part is plural, the pronoun agrees in person and number with the closer antecedent.

<u>Neither the child nor her parents</u> had fastened <u>their</u> seatbelts.

2 With Collective Noun Antecedents

If the meaning of the collective noun antecedent is singular (as it will be in most cases), use a singular pronoun. If the meaning is plural, use a plural pronoun.

The nurses' <u>union</u> announced <u>its</u> plan to strike. (All the members acted as one.)

The <u>team</u> ran onto the court and took <u>their</u> positions. (Each member acted individually.)

3 With Indefinite Pronoun Antecedents

See
26a4
ESL
49c3
Most <u>indefinite pronouns</u>—*each, either, neither, one, anyone,* and the like—are singular and take singular pronouns.

<u>Neither</u> of the men had <u>his</u> proposal ready by the deadline.

<u>Each</u> of these neighborhoods has <u>its</u> own traditions and values.

CLOSE-UP

PRONOUN-ANTECEDENT AGREEMENT

In speech and in informal writing, many people use the plural pronouns *they* or *their* with singular indefinite pronouns that refer to people, such as *someone, everyone,* and *nobody.*

Informal: <u>Everyone</u> can present <u>their</u> own viewpoint.

In college writing, however, you should try to avoid using a plural pronoun to refer to a singular subject. Instead, you can use both the masculine and the feminine pronoun.

Correct: <u>Everyone</u> can present <u>his or her</u> own viewpoint.

Or, you can make the sentence's subject plural.

Correct: <u>All participants</u> can present <u>their</u> own viewpoints.

See
19e2
The use of *his* alone to refer to a singular indefinite pronoun (*Everyone can present his own viewpoint*) is considered <u>sexist language</u>.

GRAMMAR CHECKER

PRONOUN-ANTECEDENT AGREEMENT

Your grammar checker will highlight and offer revision suggestions for many pronoun-antecedent agreement errors.

EXERCISE 26.2

In the following sentences, find and correct any errors in subject-verb or pronoun-antecedent agreement.

▶ 1. The core of a computer is a collection of electronic circuits that are called the central processing unit.

▶ 2. Computers, because of advanced technology that allows the central processing unit to be placed on a chip, a thin square of semiconducting material about one-quarter of an inch on each side, has been greatly reduced in size.

▶ 3. Computers can "talk" to each other over phone lines through a modem, an acronym for *modulator-demodulator*.

▶ 4. Pressing keys on keyboards resembling typewriter keyboards generate electronic signals that are input for the computer.

▶ 5. Computers have built-in memory storage, and equipment such as disks or tapes provide external memory.

6. RAM (random-access memory), the erasable and reusable computer memory, hold the computer program, the computations executed by the program, and the results.

7. After computer programs are "read" from a disk or tape, the computer uses the instructions as needed to execute the program.

8. ROM (read-only memory), the permanent memory that is "read" by the computer but cannot be changed, are used to store programs that are needed frequently.

9. A number of video games with impressive graphics, sound, and color is available for home computers.

10. Although some computer users write their own programs, most buy ready-made software programs such as the ones that allows a computer to be used as a word processor.

Revising Misplaced and Dangling Modifiers
CHAPTER 27

A **modifier** is a word, phrase, or clause that describes, limits, or qualifies another word or word group in a sentence. A modifier should be placed close to the word it modifies.

Wendy watched the storm, <u>fierce and threatening</u>. (*fierce and threatening* modifies *storm*)

Faulty modification is the awkward or confusing placement of modifiers or the modification of nonexistent words.

GRAMMAR CHECKER

REVISING FAULTY MODIFICATION

Your grammar checker will identify some modification problems, including certain awkward **split infinitives**. However, the grammar checker will not offer revision suggestions. You will have to revise awkward split infinitives on your own, as illustrated in **27b**.

27a Revising Misplaced Modifiers

A **misplaced modifier** is a word or word group whose placement suggests that it modifies one word or word group when it is intended to modify another.

Wendy watched the storm, fierce
˄Fierce and threatening, ~~Wendy watched the storm.~~ (The storm, not Wendy, was fierce and threatening.)

The lawyer argued that the defendant, with
˄With an IQ of just 52, ~~the lawyer argued that the defendant~~ should not get the death penalty. (The defendant, not the lawyer, had an IQ of 52.)

1 Placing Modifying Words Precisely

Limiting modifiers—such as *almost, only, even, hardly, merely, nearly, exactly, scarcely, simply,* and *just*—should always immediately precede the words they modify. A different placement will change the meaning of the sentence.

Nick *just* set up camp at the edge of town. (He did it just now.)

Just Nick set up camp at the edge of town. (He did it alone.)

Nick set up camp *just* at the edge of town. (His camp was precisely at the edge.)

When a limiting modifier is placed so that it is not clear whether it modifies a word before it or one after it, it is called a **squinting modifier.**

The life that everyone thought would fulfill her <u>totally</u> bored her.

To correct a squinting modifier, place the modifier so that it is clear which word it modifies.

The life that everyone thought would <u>totally</u> fulfill her bored her. (Everyone expected her to be totally fulfilled.)

The life that everyone thought would fulfill her bored her <u>totally</u>. (She was totally bored.)

EXERCISE 27.1

In the following sentence pairs, the modifier in each sentence points to a different word. Underline the modifier and draw an arrow to the word it modifies. Then, explain the meaning of each sentence.

Example: She just came in wearing a hat. (She just now entered.)

She came in wearing just a hat. (She wore only a hat.)

▶ 1. He wore his almost new jeans.
   He almost wore his new jeans.
▶ 2. He had only three dollars in his pocket.
   Only he had three dollars in his pocket.
 3. I don't even like freshwater fish.
   I don't like even freshwater fish.
 4. I go only to the beach on Saturdays.
   I go to the beach only on Saturdays.
 5. He simply hated driving.
   He hated simply driving.

2 Relocating Misplaced Phrases

Placing a modifying phrase incorrectly can change the meaning of a sentence or create an unclear or confusing (or even unintentionally humorous) construction.

To avoid ambiguity, place phrases as close as possible to the words they modify.

◆ Place **verbal phrase** modifiers directly before or directly after the words or word groups they modify.

Roller-skating along the shore,
 Jane watched the boats, ~~roller skating along the shore.~~

◆ Place **prepositional phrase** modifiers immediately after the words they modify.

                              with no arms
Venus de Milo is a statue created by a famous artist, ~~with no arms.~~

EXERCISE 27.2

Underline the modifying verbal phrases or prepositional phrases in each sentence, and draw arrows to the words they modify.

Example: Calvin is the Democrat running for town council.

▶ 1. The bridge across the river swayed in the wind.
▶ 2. The spectators on the shore were involved in the action.

▶ 3. Mesmerized by the spectacle, they watched the drama unfold.
▶ 4. The spectators were afraid of a disaster.
▶ 5. Within the hour, the state police arrived.
6. They closed off the area with roadblocks.
7. Drivers approaching the bridge were asked to stop.
8. Meanwhile, on the bridge, the scene was chaos.
9. Motorists in their cars were paralyzed with fear.
10. Struggling against the weather, the police managed to rescue everyone.

EXERCISE 27.3

Use the phrase that follows each sentence as a modifier in that sentence. Then, underline the modifier, and draw an arrow to indicate the word it modifies.

Example: He approached the lion. (with fear in his heart)

With fear in his heart, he approached the lion.

▶ 1. The lion paced up and down in his cage, ignoring the crowd. (watching Jack)
▶ 2. Jack stared back at the lion. (in terror)
3. The crowd around them grew. (anxious to see what would happen)
4. Suddenly, Jack heard a terrifying growl. (from deep in the lion's throat)
5. Jack ran from the zoo, leaving the lion behind. (scared to death)

3 Relocating Misplaced Dependent Clauses

A dependent clause that serves as a modifier must be clearly related to the word it modifies.

♦ An **adjective clause** appears immediately *after* the word it modifies.

During the Civil War, Lincoln was the president who governed the United States.

♦ An **adverb clause** can appear in any of several positions, as long as its relationship to the word or word group it modifies is clear.

When Lincoln was president, the Civil War raged.

The Civil War raged when Lincoln was president.

EXERCISE 27.4

Relocate the misplaced verbal phrases, prepositional phrases, or dependent clauses so that they clearly point to the words or word groups they modify.

Example: *Silent Running* is a film about a scientist left alone in space, with Bruce Dern.

▶ 1. She realized that she had married the wrong man after the wedding.

▶ 2. *The Prince and the Pauper* is a novel about an exchange of identities by Mark Twain.
3. The energy was used up in the ten-kilometer race that he was saving for the marathon.
4. He loaded the bottles and cans into his new car, which he planned to leave at the recycling center.
5. The manager explained the sales figures to the board members using a graph.

27b   Revising Intrusive Modifiers

An **intrusive modifier** awkwardly interrupts a sentence, making it difficult to understand.

◆ Revise when a long modifying phrase comes between an auxiliary verb and a main verb.

Without
She had, without giving it a second thought or considering the conse-
she had
quences, planned to reenlist.

◆ Revise when an adverb phrase or clause comes between a subject and a verb (or between a verb and its object or complement).

was contested
The election because officials discovered that some people had voted more than once, was contested.

◆ Revise when a modifier creates an awkward **split infinitive**—that is, when a modifier comes between the word *to* and the base form of the verb.

defeat his opponent
He hoped to quickly and easily defeat his opponent.

Note: A split infinitive is acceptable when the intervening modifier is short, especially if the alternative would be awkward or ambiguous: *She expected to almost beat her previous record.*

EXERCISE 27.5

Revise these sentences so that the modifying phrases or clauses do not interrupt an infinitive, separate an auxiliary verb from a main verb, or separate a subject from a verb or a verb from its object or complement.

Despite the playwright's best efforts, a
Example: A play can sometimes be, despite the playwright's best efforts, mystifying to the audience.

▶ 1. The people in the audience, when they saw the play was about to begin and realized the orchestra had finished tuning up and had begun the overture, finally quieted down.

▶ 2. They settled into their seats, expecting to very much enjoy the first act.

3. However, most people were, even after watching and listening for twenty minutes and paying close attention to the drama, completely baffled.

4. In fact, the play, because it had nameless characters, no scenery, and a rambling plot that did not seem to be heading anywhere, puzzled even the drama critics.

5. Finally, one of the three major characters explained, speaking directly to the audience, what the play was really about.

27c Revising Dangling Modifiers

A **dangling modifier** is a word or phrase that cannot logically modify any word in the sentence.

Dangling: Using this drug, many undesirable side effects are experienced. (Who is using this drug?)

♦ One way to correct a dangling modifier is to **create a new subject** by adding a word or word group that the modifier can logically modify.

Revised: Using this drug, patients experience many undesirable side effects.

♦ Another way to correct a dangling modifier is to **create a dependent clause.**

Revised: Many undesirable side effects are experienced when this drug is used.

These two options for correcting dangling modifiers are further illustrated below.

1 Creating a New Subject

the technician lifted
Using a pair of forceps, the skin of the rat's abdomen ~~was lifted~~. (Modifier cannot logically modify *skin.*)

Meg found
With fifty more pages to read, War and Peace ~~was~~ absorbing. (Modifier cannot logically modify *War and Peace.*)

2 Creating a Dependent Clause

Before   *was implemented,*
~~To implement~~ a plus/minus grading system, all students were polled. (Modifier cannot logically modify *students.*)

Because the magazine had been on
~~On~~ the newsstands only an hour, its sales surprised everyone. (Modifier cannot logically modify *sales.*)

> ### CLOSE-UP
>
> **DANGLING MODIFIERS AND THE PASSIVE VOICE**
>
> Most sentences that include dangling modifiers are in the passive voice. Changing the <u>passive voice</u> to <u>active voice</u> often corrects the dangling modifier.
>
> See
> 22d
> ESL
> 49a6

EXERCISE 27.6

Eliminate the dangling modifier from each of the following sentences. Either supply a word or word group the dangling modifier can logically modify, or change the dangling modifier into a dependent clause.

Example: Skiing down the mountain, my hat flew off. (dangling modifier)

Revised: Skiing down the mountain, <u>I</u> lost my hat. (new subject added)
<u>As I skied down the mountain</u>, my hat flew off. (dependent clause)

▶ 1. Writing for eight hours every day, her lengthy books are published every year or so.
▶ 2. As an out-of-state student without a car, it was difficult to get to off-campus cultural events.
▶ 3. To build a campfire, kindling is necessary.
▶ 4. With every step upward, the trees became sparser.
▶ 5. Being an amateur tennis player, my backhand is weaker than my forehand.
6. When exiting the train, the station will be on your right.
7. Driving through the Mojave, the bleak landscape was oppressive.
8. By requiring auto manufacturers to further improve emission-control devices, the air quality will get better.
9. Using a piece of filter paper, the ball of sodium is dried as much as possible and placed in a test tube.
10. Having missed work for seven days straight, my job was in jeopardy.

Revising Awkward or Confusing Sentences CHAPTER 28

The most common causes of awkward or confusing sentences are *unwarranted shifts, mixed constructions, faulty predication,* and *illogical comparisons.*

28a Revising Unwarranted Shifts

1 Shifts in Tense

See 22b ESL 49a2

Verb <u>tense</u> in a sentence (or in a related group of sentences) should only shift for a good reason—to indicate changes of time, for example. Unwarranted shifts in tense can be confusing.

> I registered for the advanced philosophy seminar because I wanted a
> *started*
> challenge. However, after the first week I start having trouble
> understanding the reading. (unwarranted shift from past to present)

> Jack Kerouac's novel *On the Road* follows a group of friends who
> *drive*
> drove across the United States. (unwarranted shift from present to past)

See 8b

Note: Discussions of <u>literary works</u> generally use the present tense.

2 Shifts in Voice

See 22d ESL 49a6

Unwarranted shifts from active to passive <u>voice</u> (or from passive to active) can be confusing.

> *wrote*
> F. Scott Fitzgerald wrote *This Side of Paradise,* and later *The*
> *Great Gatsby* was written. (unwarranted shift from active to passive)

3 Shifts in Mood

See 22c

Unnecessary shifts in <u>mood</u> also create awkward sentences.

> *be*
> Next, heat the mixture in a test tube, and you should make sure
> it does not boil. (unwarranted shift from imperative to indicative)

4 Shifts in Person and Number

ESL 49a1

<u>Person</u> indicates who is speaking (first person—*I, we*), who is spoken to (second person—*you*), and who is spoken about (third person—*he, she, it,* or *they*). Most unwarranted shifts occur between second and third person.

> *you*
> When someone looks for a car loan, you should compare the interest
> rates of several banks. (shift from third to second person)

ESL 49a1

See 26b1

<u>Number</u> indicates one (singular—*novel, it*) or more than one (plural—*novels, they, them*). Singular pronouns should refer to singular <u>antecedents</u> and plural pronouns to plural antecedents.

he or she
If a person does not study regularly, ~~they~~ will have a difficult
time passing a course.

5 Shifts from Direct to Indirect Discourse

Direct discourse reports the exact words of a speaker or writer. It is always
enclosed in quotation marks and is often accompanied by an **identifying
tag** (*he says, she said*).

Indirect discourse summarizes the words of a speaker or writer. No quotation marks are used, and the reported words are often introduced with the
word *that* or, in the case of questions, with *who, what, why, whether, how,*
or *if.*

> **Direct Discourse:** My instructor said, "I want your paper by this
> Friday."

> **Indirect Discourse:** My instructor said that he wanted my paper by
> this Friday.

Unwarranted shifts between indirect and direct discourse are often confusing.

> During the trial, John Brown repeatedly defended his actions and
> *he was*
> said that ~~I am~~ not guilty. (shift from indirect to direct discourse)

> "*Are you* ?"
> My mother asked, ~~was I~~ ever going to get a job/ (shift from direct to
> indirect discourse)

EXERCISE 28.1

Read the following sentences, and eliminate any shifts in tense, voice, mood,
person, or number. Some sentences are correct, and some can be revised in
more than one way.

you
Example: When ~~one~~ examines the history of the women's movement, you see
that it had many different beginnings.

▶ 1. Some historians see World War II and women's work in the factories as
the beginning of the push toward equal rights for women.

▶ 2. Women went to work in the textile mills of Lowell, Massachusetts, in the
late 1800s, and her efforts at reforming the workplace are seen by many
as the beginning of the equal rights movement.

▶ 3. Farm girls from New Hampshire, Vermont, and western Massachusetts
came to Lowell to make money, and they wanted to experience life in
the city.

▶ 4. The factories promised the girls decent wages, and parents were
promised by them that their daughters would live in a safe, wholesome
environment.

▶ 5. Dormitories were built by the factory owners; they are supposed to ensure a safe environment for the girls.
6. First, visit the loom rooms at the Boot Mills Factory, and then you should
tour a replica of a dormitory.
7. When one visits the working loom room at the factory, you are overcome
with a sense of the risks and dangers the girls faced in the mills.
8. For a mill girl, moving to the city meant freedom and an escape from
the drudgery of farm life; it also meant they had to face many new social
situations for which they were not always prepared.
9. Harriet Robinson wrote *Loom and Spindle*, the story of her life as a mill girl,
and then a book of poems was published.
10. When you look at the lives of the loom girls, one can see that their work
laid part of the foundation for women's later demands for equal rights.

28b Revising Mixed Constructions

A **mixed construction** is created when a dependent clause, prepositional
phrase, or independent clause is incorrectly used as the subject of a sentence.

Because she studies every day, explains why she gets good grades.
(dependent clause incorrectly used as subject)

, you can
By calling for information is the way to learn more about the
benefits of ROTC. (prepositional phrase incorrectly used as subject)

Being
He was late made him miss the first act of the play. (independent
clause incorrectly used as subject)

EXERCISE 28.2

Revise the following mixed constructions so their parts fit together both grammatically and logically.

Investing
Example: By investing in commodities made her rich.

▶ 1. In implementing the "motor voter" bill has made it easier for people to
register to vote.
▶ 2. She sank the basket was the reason they won the game.
3. Just because situations change, does not change the characters' hopes
and dreams.
4. By dropping the course would be his only chance to avoid a low GPA.
5. Even though she works for a tobacco company does not mean that she is
against laws prohibiting smoking in restaurants.

28c Revising Faulty Predication

Faulty predication occurs when a sentence's predicate does not logically complete its subject.

1 Incorrect Use of *Be*

Faulty predication is especially common in sentences that contain a <u>linking verb</u>—a form of the verb *be*, for example—and a subject complement. *See 20c1*

Mounting costs and decreasing revenues ^*caused* ~~were~~ the downfall of the hospital.

This sentence incorrectly states that mounting costs and decreasing revenues *were* the downfall of the hospital when, in fact, they were the *reasons* for its downfall.

2 *Is When* or *Is Where*

Faulty predication occurs when a one-sentence definition includes the construction *is where* or *is when.* (In a definition, *is* must be preceded and followed by a noun or a noun phrase.)

Taxidermy is ^*the construction of* ~~where you construct~~ a lifelike representation of an animal from its preserved skin.

3 *The Reason . . . Is Because*

Faulty predication occurs when the phrase *the reason is* precedes *because.* In this situation, *because* (which means "for the reason that") is redundant and should be deleted.

The reason we drive is ^*that* ~~because~~ we are afraid to fly.

GRAMMAR CHECKER

REVISING FAULTY PREDICATION

Your grammar checker will highlight certain instances of faulty predication and offer suggestions for revision. However, the grammar checker will miss many unwarranted shifts, mixed constructions, and incomplete or illogical comparisons.

EXERCISE 28.3

Revise the following sentences to eliminate faulty predication. Keep in mind that each sentence may be revised in more than one way.

Example: ~~The reason traffic~~ jams occur at 9 a.m. and 5 p.m. ~~is because~~ too many
      Traffic
      people work traditional rather than staggered hours.

▶ 1. Inflation is when the purchasing power of currency declines.
▶ 2. Hypertension is where blood pressure is elevated.
  3. Television and the Internet were the decline in students' reading scores.
  4. Some people say the reason for the increasing violence in American cities is because guns are too easily available.
  5. The reason for all the congestion in American cities is because too many people live too close together.

28d Revising Incomplete or Illogical Comparisons

A comparison tells how two things are alike or unlike. When you make a comparison, be sure that it is *complete* (that it identifies which two items are being compared) and *logical* (that it equates two comparable items).

My chemistry course is harder. (What two things are being compared?)
                than Nina's

A pig's intelligence is greater than a ~~dog~~. (illogically compares
                      dog's
intelligence to *a dog*)

EXERCISE 28.4

Revise the following sentences to correct any incomplete or illogical comparisons.

Example: Technology-based industries are concerned about inflation as much
      as service industries/
            are.

▶ 1. Opportunities in technical writing are more promising than business writing.
▶ 2. Technical writing is more challenging.
  3. In some ways, technical writing requires more attention to detail and is, therefore, more difficult.
  4. Business writers are concerned about clarity as much as technical writers.
  5. Technology-based industries may one day create more writing opportunities than any other industry.

PART 5

Understanding
Punctuation

Understanding Punctuation

Using End Punctuation CHAPTER 29

29a Using Periods

1 Ending a Sentence

Use a period to signal the end of a statement, a mild command or polite request, or an indirect question.

Something is rotten in Denmark. (statement)

Be sure to have the oil checked before you start out. (mild command)

When the bell rings, please exit in an orderly fashion. (polite request)

They wondered whether the water was safe to drink. (indirect question)

2 Marking an Abbreviation

Use a period in most abbreviations.

Mr. Spock	1600 Pennsylvania Ave.	9 p.m.
Dr. Who	Aug.	etc.

If an abbreviation ends the sentence, do not add another period.

He promised to be there at 6 a.m./

However, do add a question mark if the sentence is a question.

Did he arrive at 6 p.m.?

If the abbreviation falls *within* a sentence, use normal punctuation after the period.

He promised to be there at 6 p.m., but he forgot.

CLOSE-UP

ABBREVIATIONS WITHOUT PERIODS

Abbreviations composed of all capital letters do not usually require periods unless they are the initials of people's names (E. B. White).

MD	RN	USA	DC

(continued)

257

ABBREVIATIONS WITHOUT PERIODS (*continued*)

Familiar abbreviations of the names of corporations or government agencies and abbreviations of scientific and technical terms do not require periods.

| IBM | EPA | DNA | CD-ROM |

Acronyms—new words formed from the initial letters or first few letters of a series of words—do not include periods.

| modem | op-ed | scuba | radar |
| OSHA | AIDS | NAFTA | CAT scan |

Clipped forms (commonly accepted shortened forms of words, such as *flu, dorm, math,* and *fax*) do not include periods.
Postal abbreviations do not include periods.

| NY | CA | MS | FL | TX |

3 Marking Divisions in Dramatic, Poetic, and Biblical References

Use periods to separate act, scene, and line numbers in plays; book and line numbers in long poems; and chapter and verse numbers in biblical references. (Do not space between the periods and the elements they separate.)

Dramatic Reference: *Hamlet* 2.2.1–5

Poetic Reference: *Paradise Lost* 7.163–67

Biblical Reference: Judges 4.14

See 47a1 *Note:* In <u>MLA parenthetical references</u>, titles of literary and biblical works are often abbreviated: (*Ham.* 2.2.1-5); (**Judg. 4.14**).

4 Marking Divisions in Electronic Addresses

Periods, along with other punctuation marks (such as slashes and colons), are frequently used in electronic addresses (URLs).

http://cengage.com/english/kirsznermandell

Note: When you type a URL, do not end it with a period; do not add spaces after periods within the address.

EXERCISE 29.1

Correct these sentences by adding missing periods and deleting unnecessary ones. If a sentence is correct, mark it with a C.

Example: Their mission changed the war.

▶ 1. Julius Caesar was killed in 44 B.C.

▶ 2. Dr. McLaughlin worked hard to earn his Ph.D..

3. Carmen was supposed to be at A.F.L.-C.I.O. headquarters by 2 p.m.; however, she didn't get there until 10 p.m.

4. After she studied the fall lineup proposed by N.B.C., she decided to work for C.B.S.

5. Representatives from the U.M.W. began collective bargaining after an unsuccessful meeting with Mr. L Pritchard, the coal company's representative.

29b Using Question Marks

1 Marking the End of a Direct Question

Use a question mark to signal the end of a direct question.

Who was at the door?

2 Marking Questionable Dates or Numbers

Use a question mark in parentheses to indicate uncertainty about a date or number.

Aristophanes, the Greek playwright, was born in 448 (?) BC and died in 380 (?) BC.

3 Editing Misused Question Marks

Do not use question marks in the following situations.

After an Indirect Question   Use a period, not a question mark, with an **indirect question** (a question that is not quoted directly).

The personnel officer asked whether he knew how to type?

With Other Punctuation   Do not use question marks along with other punctuation (except for closing quotation marks).

"Can it be true?," he asked.

With Another Question Mark   Do not use more than one question mark to end a sentence.

You did what?? Are you crazy??

To Convey Sarcasm   Do not use question marks to convey sarcasm. Instead, suggest your attitude through word choice.

         not very
I refused his generous (?) offer.

In an Exclamation   Do not use a question mark after an exclamation that is phrased as a question.

Will you please stop that at once?ᐱ ^!

EXERCISE 29.2

Correct the use of question marks and other punctuation in the following sentences.

Example: She asked whether Freud's theories were accepted during his lifetime?ᐱ

- ▶ 1. He wondered whether he should take a nine o'clock class?
- ▶ 2. The instructor asked, "Was the Spanish-American War a victory for America."
  3. Are they really going to China??!!
  4. He took a modest (?) portion of dessert—half a pie.
  5. "Is *data* the plural of *datum?*," he inquired.

29c   Using Exclamation Points

Use an exclamation point to signal the end of an emotional or emphatic statement, an emphatic interjection, or a forceful command.

Remember the *Maine*!

"No! Don't leave!"

Finish this job at once!

Note: Except for recording dialogue, exclamation points are almost never appropriate in college writing. Even in informal writing, use exclamation points sparingly—and never use two or more in a row.

Using Commas   CHAPTER 30

30a   Setting Off Independent Clauses

Use a comma when you form a compound sentence by linking two independent clauses with a **coordinating conjunction** (*and, but, or, nor, for, yet, so*) or with a pair of <u>correlative conjunctions</u>.

See 20g

The House approved the bill, <u>but</u> the Senate rejected it.

<u>Either</u> the hard drive is full, <u>or</u> the modem is too slow.

Note: You may omit the comma if two clauses connected by a coordinating conjunction are very short: *Seek and ye shall find; Love it or leave it.*

EXERCISE 30.1

Combine each of the following sentence pairs into one compound sentence, adding commas where necessary.

Example: Emergency medicine became an approved medical specialty in
1979. ~~Now~~ , and now pediatric emergency medicine is becoming
increasingly important. (and)

▶ 1. The Pope did not hesitate to visit Cuba. He did not hesitate to meet with President Fidel Castro. (nor)
▶ 2. Advertisers place brand-name products in prominent positions in films. The products are seen and recognized by large audiences. (and)
   3. Unisex insurance rates may have some drawbacks for women. These rates may be very beneficial. (or)
   4. Cigarette advertising no longer appears on television. It does appear in print media. (but)
   5. Dorothy Day founded the Catholic Worker movement in the 1930s. Her followers still dispense free food, medical care, and legal advice to the needy. (and)

30b Setting Off Items in a Series

1 Coordinate Elements

Use commas between items in a series of three or more **coordinate elements** (words, phrases, or clauses joined by a coordinating conjunction).

Chipmunk, *raccoon*, and *Mugwump* are Native American words.

You may pay by check, with a credit card, or in cash.

Brazilians speak Portuguese, Colombians speak Spanish, and Haitians speak French and Creole.

See 31c

Note: If phrases or clauses in a series already contain commas, use semicolons to separate the items.

Do not use a comma to introduce or to close a series.

Three important criteria are fat content, salt content, and taste.

Quebec, Ontario, and Alberta are Canadian provinces.

Note: To avoid ambiguity, always use a comma before the *and* (or other coordinating conjunction) that separates the last two items in a series: *He was inspired by his parents, the Dalai Lama, and Mother Teresa.*

2 Coordinate Adjectives

Use a comma between items in a series of two or more **coordinate adjectives**—adjectives that modify the same word or word group—unless they are joined by a conjunction.

She brushed her <u>long</u> , <u>shining</u> hair.

The baby was <u>tired</u> and <u>cranky</u> and <u>wet</u>. (no commas required)

CHECKLIST

PUNCTUATING ADJECTIVES IN A SERIES

❑ If you can reverse the order of the adjectives or insert *and* between the adjectives without changing the meaning, the adjectives are coordinate, and you should use a comma.

She brushed her <u>long</u> , <u>shining</u> hair.
She brushed her <u>shining</u> , <u>long</u> hair.
She brushed her <u>long</u> [and] <u>shining</u> hair.

❑ If you cannot reverse the order of the adjectives or insert *and,* the adjectives are not coordinate, and you should not use a comma.

<u>Ten red</u> balloons fell from the ceiling.
<u>Red ten</u> balloons fell from the ceiling.
<u>Ten</u> [and] <u>red</u> balloons fell from the ceiling.

Note: Numbers—such as *ten*—are not coordinate with other adjectives.

ESL TIP

If you have difficulty determining the order of adjectives in a series, **see 49d2.**

EXERCISE 30.2

Correct the use of commas in the following sentences, adding or deleting commas where necessary. If a sentence is punctuated correctly, mark it with a C.

Example: Neither dogs, snakes, bees, nor dragons frighten her.

▶ 1. Seals, whales, dogs, lions, and horses, all are mammals.
▶ 2. Mammals are warm-blooded vertebrates that bear live young, nurse them, and usually have fur.

3. Seals are mammals, but lizards, and snakes, and iguanas are reptiles, and salamanders are amphibians.
4. Amphibians also include frogs, and toads and newts.
5. Eagles geese ostriches turkeys chickens and ducks are classified as birds.

30c Setting Off Introductory Elements

1 Dependent Clauses

An introductory **dependent clause** is generally set off from the rest of the sentence by a comma.

> <u>Although the CIA used to call undercover agents *penetration agents*</u>, they now routinely refer to them as *moles*.

> <u>When war came to Baghdad</u>, many victims were children.

If a dependent clause is short and designates time, you may omit the comma—provided the sentence will be clear without it.

> <u>When I exercise</u> I drink plenty of water.

Note: Do not use a comma to set off a dependent clause at the *end* of a sentence: *I drink plenty of water⁄ when I exercise.*

2 Verbal and Prepositional Phrases

An introductory verbal phrase is usually set off by a comma.

> <u>Thinking that this might be his last chance</u>, Peary struggled toward the North Pole. (participial phrase)

> <u>To write well</u>, one must read a lot. (infinitive phrase)

CLOSE-UP

USING COMMAS WITH VERBAL PHRASES

A <u>verbal phrase</u> that serves as a subject of a sentence is not set off by a comma.

> Laughing out loud⁄ can release tension. (gerund phrase)

> To know him⁄ is to love him. (infinitive phrase)

See
14b1

An introductory **prepositional phrase** is also usually set off by a comma.

> <u>During the Depression</u>, movie attendance rose. (prepositional phrase)

However, if an introductory prepositional phrase is short and no ambiguity is possible, you may omit the comma.

> <u>After lunch</u> I took a four-hour nap.

3 **Transitional Words and Phrases**

See 5b2 When a <u>transitional word or phrase</u> begins a sentence, it is usually set off from the rest of the sentence with a comma.

> <u>However</u> , any plan that is enacted must be fair.
>
> <u>In other words</u> , we cannot act hastily.

EXERCISE 30.3

Add commas in the following paragraph where necessary to set off an introductory element from the rest of a sentence.

> ▶While childhood is shrinking adolescence is expanding. ▶Whatever the reason girls are maturing earlier. ▶The average onset of puberty is now two years earlier than it was only forty years ago. ▶What's more both boys and girls are staying in the nest longer. ▶At present, it is not unusual for children to stay in their parents' home until they are twenty or twenty-one, delaying adulthood and extending adolescence. To some who study the culture this increase in adolescence portends dire consequences. With teenage hormones running amuck for longer the problems of teenage pregnancy and sexually transmitted diseases loom large. Young boys' spending long periods of their lives without responsibilities is also a recipe for disaster. However others see this "youthing" of American culture in a more positive light. Without a doubt adolescents are creative, lively, and more willing to take risks. If we channel their energies carefully they can contribute, even in their extended adolescence, to American culture and technology.

30d Setting Off Nonessential Material

Sometimes words, phrases, or clauses *contribute* to the meaning of a sentence but are not *essential* for conveying the sentence's main point. Use commas to set off such **nonessential material** whether it appears at the beginning, in the middle, or at the end of a sentence.

1 Nonrestrictive Modifiers

Use commas to set off **nonrestrictive modifiers,** which supply information that is not essential to the meaning of the word or word group they modify. (Do *not* use commas to set off **restrictive modifiers,** which supply information that is essential to the meaning of the word or word group they modify.)

> **Nonrestrictive (commas required):** Actors , <u>who have inflated egos</u> , are often insecure. (*All* actors—not just those with inflated egos—are insecure.)
>
> **Restrictive (no commas):** Actors <u>who have inflated egos</u> are often insecure. (Only those actors with inflated egos—not all actors—are insecure.)

In the following examples, commas set off only nonrestrictive modifiers—those that supply nonessential information. Commas do not set off restrictive modifiers, which supply essential information.

Adjective Clauses

Nonrestrictive: He ran for the bus , <u>which was late as usual</u>.

Restrictive: Speaking in public is something <u>that most people fear</u>.

Prepositional Phrases

Nonrestrictive: The clerk , <u>with a nod</u> , dismissed me.

Restrictive: The man <u>with the gun</u> demanded their money.

Verbal Phrases

Nonrestrictive: The marathoner , <u>running her fastest</u> , beat her previous record.

Restrictive: The candidates <u>running for mayor</u> have agreed to a debate.

Appositives

Nonrestrictive: *Citizen Kane* , <u>Orson Welles's first film</u> , made him famous.

Restrictive: The film *Citizen Kane* made Orson Welles famous.

CHECKLIST

RESTRICTIVE AND NONRESTRICTIVE MODIFIERS

To determine whether a modifier is restrictive or nonrestrictive, ask yourself these questions:

- ❏ Is the modifier essential to the meaning of the noun it modifies (*The man <u>with the gun</u>,* not just any man)? If so, it is restrictive and does not take commas.
- ❏ Is the modifier introduced by *that* (*something <u>that most people fear</u>*)? If so, it is restrictive. *That* cannot introduce a nonrestrictive clause.
- ❏ Can you delete the relative pronoun without causing ambiguity or confusion (*something <u>[that] most people fear</u>*)? If so, the clause is restrictive.
- ❏ Is the appositive more specific than the noun that precedes it (*the film <u>Citizen Kane</u>*)? If so, it is restrictive.

CLOSE-UP

USING COMMAS WITH *THAT* AND *WHICH*

- ◆ *That* introduces only restrictive clauses, which are not set off by commas.
  I bought a used car <u>that</u> cost $2,000.
- ◆ *Which* introduces only nonrestrictive clauses, which are set off by commas.
  The used car I bought, <u>which</u> cost $2,000, broke down after a week.

> **GRAMMAR CHECKER**
>
> ***THAT* OR *WHICH***
>
> Your grammar checker may label *which* as an error when it introduces a restrictive clause. It will prompt you to add commas (using *which* to introduce a nonrestrictive clause) or to change *which* to *that.* Carefully consider the meaning of your sentence, and revise accordingly.

EXERCISE 30.4

Insert commas where necessary to set off nonrestrictive modifiers.

▶The Statue of Liberty which was dedicated in 1886 has undergone extensive renovation. ▶Its supporting structure whose designer was the French engineer Alexandre Gustave Eiffel is made of iron. The Statue of Liberty created over a period of nine years by sculptor Frédéric-Auguste Bartholdi stands 151 feet tall. The people of France who were grateful for American help in the French Revolution raised the money to pay the sculptor who created the statue. The people of the United States contributing over $100,000 raised the money for the pedestal on which the statue stands.

2 Transitional Words and Phrases

See 5b2 Transitional words and phrases—which include conjunctive adverbs such as *however, therefore, thus,* and *nevertheless* as well as expressions such as *for example* and *on the other hand*—qualify, clarify, and make connections. However, they are not essential to the sentence's meaning. For this reason, they are always set off by commas when they interrupt a clause or when they begin or end a sentence.

The Outward Bound program , for example , is considered safe.

In fact , Outward Bound has an excellent reputation.

Other programs are not so safe , however.

Note: When a transitional word or phrase joins two independent clauses, it must be preceded by a semicolon and followed by a comma: *Laughter is the best medicine; of course , penicillin also comes in handy sometimes.*

3 Contradictory Phrases

A phrase that expresses contradiction is usually set off by commas.

This medicine is taken after meals , never on an empty stomach.

Mark McGwire , not Sammy Sosa , was the first to break Roger Maris's home run record.

4 Absolute Phrases

An **absolute phrase,** which includes a noun or pronoun and a participle and modifies an entire independent clause, is always set off by a comma from the independent clause it modifies.

> <u>His fear increasing</u> , he waited to enter the haunted house.

> Many soldiers were lost in Southeast Asia , <u>their bodies never recovered</u>.

5 Miscellaneous Nonessential Material

Other nonessential material usually set off by commas includes tag questions, names in direct address, mild interjections, and *yes* and *no*.

> This is your first day on the job, <u>isn't it</u>?

> I wonder, <u>Mr. Honeywell</u> , whether Mr. Albright deserves a raise.

> <u>Well</u> , it's about time.

> <u>Yes</u> , that's what I thought.

EXERCISE 30.5

Set off the nonessential elements in these sentences with commas. If a sentence is correct, mark it with a C.

Example: Piranhas like sharks will attack and eat almost anything if the opportunity arises.

▶   1. Kermit the Frog is a Muppet a cross between a marionette and a puppet.
▶   2. The common cold a virus is frequently spread by hand contact not by mouth.
▶   3. The account in the Bible of Noah's Ark and the forty-day flood may be based on an actual deluge.
▶   4. Many US welfare recipients, such as children, the aged, and the severely disabled, are unable to work.
▶   5. The submarine *Nautilus* was the first to cross under the North Pole wasn't it?
  6. The 1958 Ford Edsel was advertised with the slogan "Once you've seen it, you'll never forget it."
  7. Superman was called Kal-El on the planet Krypton; on earth however he was known as Clark Kent not Kal-El.
  8. Its sales topping any of his previous singles "Heartbreak Hotel" was Elvis Presley's first million-seller.
  9. Two companies Nash and Hudson joined in 1954 to form American Motors.
  10. A firefly is a beetle not a fly and a prairie dog is a rodent not a dog.

30e Using Commas in Other Conventional Contexts

1 With Direct Quotations

In most cases, use commas to set off a direct quotation from the **identifying tag**—the phrase that identifies the speaker (*he said, she answered,* and so on).

> Emerson said to Whitman , "I greet you at the beginning of a great career."

> "I greet you at the beginning of a great career," Emerson said to Whitman.

> "I greet you ," Emerson said to Whitman , "at the beginning of a great career."

When the identifying tag comes between two complete sentences, however, the tag is introduced by a comma but followed by a period.

> "Winning isn't everything ," Coach Vince Lombardi once said . "It's the only thing."

If the first sentence of an interrupted quotation ends with a question mark or exclamation point, do not use commas.

> "Should we hold the front page ?" she asked. "It's a slow news day."

> "Hold the front page !" he cried. "There's breaking news !"

2 With Titles or Degrees Following a Name

> Hamlet , prince of Denmark , is Shakespeare's most famous character.

> Michael Crichton , MD, wrote *Jurassic Park.*

3 In Addresses and Dates

When a date or an address falls within a sentence, use a comma after the last element.

> On January 28 , 1986 , the space shuttle *Challenger* exploded.

Do not use a comma to separate the street number from the street or the state name from the ZIP code.

> Her address is 600 West End Avenue , New York , NY 10024.

Note: When only the month and year are given, do not use a comma to separate the month from the year: *August 1983.*

4 In Salutations and Closings

In informal correspondence, use commas following salutations and closings. Also use commas in both informal and business correspondence following the complimentary close.

Dear John,   Love,

Dear Aunt Sophie,   Sincerely,

Note: In business <u>letters</u>, always use a colon, not a comma, after the salutation. See 11a

5 In Long Numbers

For a number of four digits or more, place a comma before every third digit, counting from the right.

1,200   120,000

12,000   1,200,000

Note: Commas are not used in long page and line numbers, address numbers, telephone numbers, or ZIP codes (or in four-digit year numbers).

EXERCISE 30.6

Add commas where necessary to set off quotations, names, dates, addresses, and numbers.

▶ 1. India became independent on August 15 1947.
▶ 2. The UAW has more than 1500000 dues-paying members.
▶ 3. Nikita Khrushchev, former Soviet premier, once said "We will bury you!"
▶ 4. Mount St. Helens, northeast of Portland Oregon, began erupting on March 27 1980 and eventually killed at least thirty people.
▶ 5. Located at 1600 Pennsylvania Avenue Washington DC, the White House is a popular tourist attraction.
6. In 1956, playing before a crowd of 64519 fans in Yankee Stadium in New York New York, Don Larsen pitched the first perfect game in World Series history.
7. Lewis Thomas MD was born in Flushing New York and attended Harvard Medical School in Cambridge Massachusetts.
8. In 1967 2000000 people worldwide died of smallpox, but in 1977 only about twenty people died.
9. "The reports of my death" Mark Twain remarked "have been greatly exaggerated."
10. The French explorer Jean Nicolet landed at Green Bay Wisconsin in 1634, and in 1848 Wisconsin became the thirtieth state; it has 10355 lakes and a population of more than 4700000.

30g ʌ ☰ Using Commas

30f Using Commas to Prevent Misreading

In some cases, you need to use a comma to avoid ambiguity. For example, consider the following sentence:

Those who can, sprint the final lap.

Without the comma, *can* appears to be an auxiliary verb ("Those who can sprint . . ."), and the sentence seems incomplete. Because the comma tells readers to pause, it eliminates confusion.

Also use a comma to acknowledge the omission of a repeated word, usually a verb, and to separate words repeated consecutively.

Pam carried the box; Tim, the suitcase.

Everything bad that could have happened, happened.

EXERCISE 30.7

Add commas where necessary to prevent misreading.

Example: Whatever will be, will be.

▶ 1. According to Bob Frank's computer is obsolete.
▶ 2. Da Gama explored Florida; Pizarro Peru.
▶ 3. By Monday evening students must begin preregistration for fall classes.
▶ 4. Whatever they built they built with care.
   5. When batting practice carefully.
   6. Brunch includes warm muffins topped with whipped butter and freshly brewed coffee.
   7. Students go to school to learn not to play sports.
   8. Technology has made what once seemed not possible possible.

30g Editing Misused Commas

Do not use commas in the following situations.

1 To Join Two Independent Clauses

A comma alone cannot join two independent clauses; it must be followed by a coordinating conjunction. Using just a comma to connect two inde-
Ch. 25 pendent clauses creates a <u>comma splice</u>.

but
The season was unusually cool, the orange crop was not seriously harmed.

2 To Set Off Restrictive Modifiers

Commas are not used to set off <u>restrictive modifiers</u>.

See
30d1

Women⁄ who seek to be equal to men⁄ lack ambition.

The film⁄ *Malcolm X*⁄ was directed by Spike Lee.

3 Between Inseparable Grammatical Constructions

Do not place a comma between grammatical elements that cannot be logically separated: a subject and its predicate, a verb and its complement or direct object, a preposition and its object, or an adjective and the word or phrase it modifies.

A woman with dark red hair⁄ opened the door. (comma incorrectly placed between subject and predicate)

Louis Braille developed⁄ an alphabet of raised dots for the blind. (comma incorrectly placed between verb and object)

They relaxed somewhat during⁄ the last part of the obstacle course. (comma incorrectly placed between preposition and object)

Wind-dispersed weeds include the well-known and plentiful⁄ dandelions, milkweed, and thistle. (comma incorrectly placed between adjective and words it modifies)

4 Between a Verb and an Indirect Quotation or Indirect Question

Do not use commas between a verb and an indirect quotation or between a verb and an indirect question.

General Douglas MacArthur vowed⁄ that he would return. (comma incorrectly placed between verb and indirect quotation)

The landlord asked⁄ if we would sign a two-year lease. (comma incorrectly placed between verb and indirect question)

5 Between Phrases Linked by Correlative Conjunctions

Commas are not used to separate two phrases linked by <u>correlative conjunctions</u>.

See
20g

Forty years ago, most college students had access to neither photocopiers⁄ nor pocket calculators.

Both typewriters⁄ and tape recorders were generally available, however.

6 In Compounds That Are Not Composed of Independent Clauses

Do not use commas before coordinating conjunctions such as *and* or *but* when they join two elements of a compound subject, predicate, object, complement, or auxiliary verb.

Plagues⁄ and pestilence were common during the Middle Ages. (compound subject)

Many women thirty-five and older are returning to college⁄ and tend to be good students. (compound predicate)

Mattel has marketed a doctor's lab coat⁄ and an astronaut suit for its Barbie doll. (compound object)

People buy bottled water because it is convenient⁄ and fashionable. (compound complement)

She can⁄ and will be ready to run in the primary. (compound auxiliary verb)

7 Before a Dependent Clause at the End of a Sentence

Commas are generally not used before a dependent clause that falls at the end of a sentence.

Jane Addams founded Hull House⁄ because she wanted to help Chicago's poor.

EXERCISE 30.8

Unnecessary commas have been intentionally added to some of the sentences that follow. Delete any unnecessary commas. If a sentence is correct, mark it with a C.

Example: Spring fever⁄ is a common ailment.

▶ 1. A book is like a garden, carried in the pocket. (Arab proverb)
▶ 2. Like the iodine content of kelp, air freight, is something most Americans have never pondered. (*Time*)
   3. Charles Rolls, and Frederick Royce manufactured the first Rolls-Royce Silver Ghost, in 1907.
   4. The hills ahead of him were rounded domes of grey granite, smooth as a bald man's pate, and completely free of vegetation. (Wilbur Smith, *Flight of the Falcon*)
   5. Food here is scarce, and cafeteria food is vile, but the great advantage to Russian raw materials, when one can get hold of them, is that they are always fresh and untampered with. (Andrea Lee, *Russian Journal*)

A **semicolon** is used only between items of equal grammatical rank: two independent clauses, two phrases, and so on.

31a Separating Independent Clauses

Use a semicolon between closely related independent clauses that convey parallel or contrasting information but are not joined by a coordinating conjunction.

> Paul Revere's *The Boston Massacre* is traditional American protest art; Edward Hicks's paintings are socially conscious art with a religious strain.

Note: Using only a comma or no punctuation at all between independent clauses creates a <u>run-on</u>. See Ch. 25

EXERCISE 31.1

Add semicolons where necessary to separate independent clauses. Then, reread the paragraph to make certain no run-ons remain.

Example: *Birth of a Nation* was one of the earliest epic movies it was based on the book *The Klansman*.

▶During the 1950s movie attendance declined because of the increasing popularity of television. ▶As a result, numerous gimmicks were introduced to draw audiences into theaters. ▶One of the first of these was Cinerama, in this technique three pictures were shot side by side and projected onto a curved screen. ▶Next came 3-D, complete with special glasses, *Bwana Devil* and *The Creature from the Black Lagoon* were two early 3-D ventures. ▶*The Robe* was the first picture filmed in Cinemascope in this technique a shrunken image was projected on a screen twice as wide as it was tall. Smell-O-Vision (or Aroma-rama) enabled audiences to smell the scenes, it was a challenge to get one odor out of the theater in time for the next smell to be introduced. William Castle's *Thirteen Ghosts* introduced special glasses for cowardly viewers, the red part of the glasses was the "ghost viewer" and the green part was the "ghost remover." Perhaps the ultimate in movie gimmicks accompanied the film *The Tingler* seats in the theater were wired to generate mild electric shocks. Unfortunately, the shocks set off a chain reaction, leading to hysteria in the theater. During the 1960s, such gimmicks all but disappeared, viewers were able once again to simply sit back and enjoy a movie. In 1997, *Mr. Payback,* a short interactive film, introduced a new gimmick, it allowed viewers to vote on how they wanted the plot to unfold.

31b Separating Independent Clauses Introduced by Transitional Words and Phrases

See
5b2 Use a semicolon before a <u>transitional word or phrase</u> that joins two independent clauses. (The transitional element is followed by a comma.)

Thomas Jefferson brought two hundred vanilla beans and a recipe for vanilla ice cream back from France ; <u>thus</u>, he gave America its all-time favorite ice-cream flavor.

EXERCISE 31.2

Combine each of the following sentence groups into one sentence that contains only two independent clauses. Use a semicolon and the transitional word or phrase in parentheses to join the two clauses, adding commas within clauses where necessary. You will need to add, delete, relocate, or change some words. There is no one correct version; keep experimenting until you find the arrangement you feel is most effective.

Example: The Aleutian Islands are located off the west coast of Alaska. They
; in fact, they
are an extremely remote chain of islands. They are sometimes

called America's Siberia. (in fact)

▶ 1. The Aleutians lie between the North Pacific Ocean and the Bering Sea. The weather there is harsh. Dense fog, 100-mph winds, and even tidal waves and earthquakes are not uncommon. (for example)
▶ 2. These islands constitute North America's largest network of active volcanoes. The Aleutians boast some beautiful scenery. The islands are relatively unexplored. (still)
3. The Aleutians are home to a wide variety of birds. Numerous animals, such as fur seals and whales, are found there. These islands may house the largest concentration of marine animals in the world. (in fact)
4. During World War II, thousands of American soldiers were stationed on Attu Island. They were stationed on Adak Island. The Japanese eventually occupied both islands. (however)
5. The islands' original population of native Aleuts was drastically reduced in the eighteenth century by Russian fur traders. Today, the total population is only about 8,500. US military employees comprise more than half of this. (consequently)

(Adapted from *National Geographic*)

31c Separating Items in a Series

Use semicolons between items in a series when one or more of these items include commas.

Three papers are posted on the bulletin board outside the building: a description of the exams; a list of appeal procedures for students who fail; and an employment ad from an automobile factory, addressed specifically to candidates whose appeals are turned down. (Andrea Lee, *Russian Journal*)

Laramie, Wyoming; Wyoming, Delaware; and Delaware, Ohio, were three of the places they visited.

EXERCISE 31.3

Replace commas with semicolons where necessary to separate internally punctuated items in a series. (For information on the use of semicolons with quotation marks, see **33e2**.)

Example: Luxury automobiles have some strong selling points: they are status symbols/˔some, such as the Corvette, appreciate in value/˔and

they are usually comfortable and well appointed.

▶ 1. The history of modern art seems at times to be a collection of "isms": Impressionism, a term that applies to painters who attempted to depict contemporary life by reproducing an "impression" of what the eye sees, Abstract Expressionism, which applies to artists who stress emotion and the unconscious in their nonrepresentational works, and, more recently, Minimalism, which applies to painters and sculptors whose work reasserts the physical reality of the object.

▶ 2. Although the term *Internet* is widely used to refer only to the World Wide Web and email, the Internet consists of a variety of discrete elements, including newsgroups, which allow users to post and receive messages on an unbelievably broad range of topics, interactive communication forums, such as blogs, discussion forums, and chat rooms, and FTP, which allows users to download material from remote computers.

3. Three of rock and roll's best-known guitar heroes played with the "British Invasion" group The Yardbirds: Eric Clapton, the group's first lead guitarist, went on to play with John Mayall's Bluesbreakers, Cream, and Blind Faith, and then became a popular solo act, Jeff Beck, the group's second guitarist, though not as visible as Clapton, made rock history with the Jeff Beck Group and inventive solo albums, and Jimmy Page, the group's third and final guitarist, transformed the remnants of the original group into the premier heavy metal band, Led Zeppelin.

4. Some of the most commonly confused words in English are *aggravate,* which means "to worsen," and *irritate,* which means "to annoy," *continual,* which means "recurring at intervals," and *continuous,* which means "an action occurring without interruption," *imply,* which means "to hint, suggest," and *infer,* which means "to conclude from," and *compliment,* which means "to praise," and *complement,* which means "to complete or add to."

5. Tennessee Williams wrote *The Glass Menagerie,* which is about Laura Wingfield, a disabled young woman, and her family, *A Streetcar Named Desire,* which starred Marlon Brando, and *Cat on a Hot Tin Roof,* which won a Pulitzer Prize.

31d Editing Misused Semicolons

Do not use semicolons in the following situations.

1 Between a Dependent and an Independent Clause

Use a comma, not a semicolon, between a dependent and an independent clause.

Because new drugs can now suppress the body's immune reaction, fewer organ transplants are rejected by the body.

GRAMMAR CHECKER

EDITING MISUSED SEMICOLONS
Your grammar checker will highlight certain misused semicolons and frequently offer suggestions for revision.

---

2 Between a Phrase and a Clause

Use a comma, not a semicolon, between a phrase and a clause.

Increasing rapidly, computer crime poses a challenge for government, financial, and military agencies.

3 To Introduce a List

See
34a1 Use a colon, not a semicolon, to introduce a <u>list</u>.

Many people maintain a profile on one of three popular social networking sites: MySpace, Facebook, or LinkedIn.

Note: Always use a complete sentence followed by a colon to introduce a list.

4 To Introduce a Quotation

See
33a Do not use a semicolon to introduce <u>quoted speech or writing</u>.

Marie Antoinette may not have said, "Let them eat cake."

EXERCISE 31.4

Read the following paragraph carefully. Then, add semicolons where necessary, and delete incorrectly used ones, substituting other punctuation where necessary.

> ▶Barnstormers were aviators; who toured the country after World War I, giving people short airplane rides and exhibitions of stunt flying, in fact, the name *barnstormer* was derived from the use of barns as airplane hangars. ▶Americans' interest in airplanes had all but disappeared after the war. ▶The barnstormers helped popularize flying; especially in rural areas. ▶Some were pilots who had flown in the war; others were just young men with a thirst for adventure. They gave people rides in airplanes; sometimes charging a dollar a minute. For most passengers, this was their first ride in an airplane, in fact, sometimes it was their first sight of one. After Lindbergh's 1927 flight across the Atlantic; Americans suddenly needed no encouragement to embrace aviation. The barnstormers had outlived their usefulness; and an era ended. (Adapted from William Goldman, *Adventures in the Screen Trade*)

Using Apostrophes   C H A P T E R 32

Use an apostrophe to form the possessive case, to indicate omissions in contractions, and to form certain plurals.

32a   Forming the Possessive Case

The possessive case indicates ownership. In English, the possessive case of nouns and indefinite pronouns is indicated either with a phrase that includes the word *of* (the hands *of* the clock) or with an apostrophe and, in most cases, an *s* (the clock's hands).

1   Singular Nouns and Indefinite Pronouns

To form the possessive case of singular nouns and **indefinite pronouns,** add -'s.

"The Monk's Tale" is one of Chaucer's *Canterbury Tales.*

When we would arrive was anyone's guess.

2   Singular Nouns Ending in -s

To form the possessive case of **singular nouns that end in -s,** add -'s in most cases.

Reading Henry James's *The Ambassadors* was not Maris's idea of fun.

The class's time was changed to 8 a.m.

Note: With some singular nouns that end in -s, pronouncing the possessive ending as a separate syllable can sound awkward. In such cases, it is acceptable to use just an apostrophe: *Crispus Attucks' death, Aristophanes' Lysistrata, Achilles' left heel.*

Do not use an apostrophe to form the possessive case of a title that already contains an -'s ending; use a phrase instead.

The staging of
^*A Midsummer Night's Dream's* ~~staging~~ presents a challenge.

3 Plural Nouns Ending in -s

To form the possessive case of **regular plural nouns** (those that end in -s or -es), add only an apostrophe.

The Readers' Guide to Periodical Literature is available online.

Laid-off employees received two weeks' severance pay and three months' medical benefits.

The Lopezes' three children are triplets.

4 Irregular Plural Nouns

To form the possessive case of **nouns that have irregular plurals,** add -'s.

Long after they were gone, the geese's honking could still be heard.

The Children's Hour is a play by Lillian Hellman; *The Women's Room* is a novel by Marilyn French.

The two oxen's yokes were securely attached to the cart.

5 Compound Nouns or Groups of Words

To form the possessive case of **compound nouns** or of word groups, add -'s to the last word.

The editor-in-chief's position is open.

He accepted the Secretary of State's resignation under protest.

This is someone else's responsibility.

6 Two or More Items

To indicate **individual ownership** of two or more items, add -'s to each item.

Ernest Hemingway's and Gertrude Stein's writing styles have some similarities. (Hemingway and Stein have two separate writing styles.)

To indicate **joint ownership,** add -'s only to the last item.

Gilbert and Sullivan's operettas include *The Pirates of Penzance* and *The Mikado.* (Gilbert and Sullivan collaborated on both operettas.)

EXERCISE 32.1

Change each word or phrase in parentheses to its possessive form. In some cases, you may have to use a phrase to indicate the possessive.

Example: The (children) toys were scattered all over their (parents) bedroom.

The children's toys were scattered all over their parents' bedroom.

▶ 1. Jane (Addams) settlement house was called Hull House.
▶ 2. (*A Room of One's Own*) popularity increased with the rise of feminism.
  3. The (chief petty officer) responsibilities are varied.
  4. Vietnamese (restaurants) numbers have grown dramatically in ten (years) time.
  5. (Charles Dickens) and (Mark Twain) works have sold millions of copies.

32b Indicating Omissions in Contractions

1 Omitted Letters

Apostrophes replace omitted letters in contractions that combine a pronoun and a verb (*he + will = he'll*) or the elements of a verb phrase (*do + not = don't*).

FREQUENTLY USED CONTRACTIONS	
it's (it is, it has)	let's (let us)
he's (he is, he has)	we've (we have)
she's (she is, she has)	they're (they are)
who's (who is, who has)	we'll (we will)
isn't (is not)	I'm (I am)
wouldn't (would not)	we're (we are)
couldn't (could not)	you'd (you would)
don't (do not)	we'd (we would)
won't (will not)	they'd (they had)

Note: Contractions are very informal. Do not use contractions in college writing unless you are quoting a source that uses them.

GRAMMAR CHECKER

REVISING CONTRACTIONS

Your grammar checker will highlight contractions and offer suggestions for revision.

CLOSE-UP

USING APOSTROPHES

Be careful not to confuse contractions (which always include apostrophes) with the possessive forms of personal pronouns (which never include apostrophes).

Contractions	Possessive Forms
Who's on first?	Whose book is this?
They're playing our song.	Their team is winning.
It's raining.	Its paws were muddy.
You're a real pal.	Your résumé is very impressive.

2 Omitted Numbers

In informal writing, an apostrophe may be used to represent the century in a year.

    Crash of '29   class of '10   '57 Chevy

In college writing, however, write out the year in full: *the Crash of 1929, the class of 2010, a 1957 Chevrolet.*

EXERCISE 32.2

In the following sentences, correct any errors in the use of apostrophes. (Remember, apostrophes are used in contractions but not in possessive pronouns.) If a sentence is correct, mark it with a C.

              Whose
Example: ~~Who's~~ troops were sent to Afghanistan?

▶ 1. Its never easy to choose a major; whatever you decide, your bound to have second thoughts.

▶ 2. Olive Oyl asked, "Whose that knocking at my door?"

▶ 3. Their watching too much television; in fact, they're eyes are glazed.

▶ 4. Whose coming along on the backpacking trip?

▶ 5. The horse had been badly treated; it's spirit was broken.

   6. Your correct in assuming its a challenging course.

   7. Sometimes even you're best friends won't tell you your boring.

   8. They're training had not prepared them for the hardships they faced.

   9. It's too early to make a positive diagnosis.

  10. Robert Frost wrote the poem that begins, "Who's woods these are I think I know."

32c Forming Plurals

In a few special situations, add -'s to form plurals.

FORMING PLURALS WITH APOSTROPHES

Plurals of Letters

The Italian language has no *j*'s, *k*'s, or *w*'s.

Plurals of Words Referred to as Words

The supervisor would accept no *if*'s, *and*'s, or *but*'s.

Note: Elements spoken of as themselves (letters, numerals, or words) are set
in italic type; the plural ending, however, is not.

See
37c

Note: Apostrophes are not used in plurals of abbreviations (including acronyms) or numbers.

DVDs   WACs   1960s

EXERCISE 32.3

In the following sentences, form correct plurals for the letters and words in
parentheses. Underline to indicate italics where necessary.

Example: The word *bubbles* contains three (b).
The word *bubbles* contains three *b*'s.

▶ 1. She closed her letter with a row of (x) and (o) to indicate kisses and hugs.
▶ 2. The three (R) are reading, writing, and 'rithmetic.
   3. The report included far too many (maybe) and too few (definitely).
   4. The word bookkeeper contains two (o), two (k), and three (e).
   5. His letter included many (please) and (thank you).

32d Editing Misused Apostrophes

Do not use apostrophes with plural nouns that are not possessive.

The Thompson's are not at home.

Down vest's are very warm.

The Philadelphia 76er's have had good years and bad.

Do not use apostrophes to form the possessive case of personal pronouns.

This ticket must be your's or her's.

The next turn is their's.

Her doll had lost it's right eye.

The next great moment in history is our's.

See
32b1 **Note:** Be especially careful not to confuse the possessive forms of personal pronouns with contractions.

GRAMMAR CHECKER

EDITING MISUSED APOSTROPHES

Your grammar checker will highlight misused apostrophes in your writing and offer revision suggestions.

EXERCISE 32.4

In the following sentences, correct all errors in the use of apostrophes to form noun plurals or the possessive case of personal pronouns.

Example: Dr. Sampson's lecture's were more interesting than her's.

▶ 1. The Schaefer's seats are right next to our's.
▶ 2. Most of the college's in the area offer computer courses open to out-sider's as well as to their own students.
▶ 3. The network completely revamped it's daytime programming.
▶ 4. Is the responsibility for the hot dog concession Cynthia's or your's?
▶ 5. Romantic poets are his favorite's.
6. Debbie returned the books to the library, forgetting they were her's.
7. Cultural revolution's do not occur very often, but when they do they bring sweeping change's.
8. Roll-top desk's are eagerly sought by antique dealer's.
9. A flexible schedule is one of their priorities, but it isn't one of our's.
10. Is your's the red house or the brown one?

Using Quotation Marks   CHAPTER 33

Use quotation marks to set off brief passages of quoted speech or writing, to set off certain titles, and to set off words used in special ways. Do not use quotation marks when quoting long passages of prose or poetry.

33a Setting Off Quoted Speech or Writing

When you quote a word, phrase, or brief passage of someone else's speech or writing, enclose the quoted material in a pair of quotation marks.

> Gloria Steinem said, "We are becoming the men we once hoped to marry."

> Galsworthy writes that Aunt Juley is "prostrated by the blow" (329). (Note that in this example from a student paper, the end punctuation follows the parenthetical documentation.)

CLOSE-UP

USING QUOTATION MARKS WITH DIALOGUE

When you record **dialogue** (conversation between two or more people), enclose the quoted words in quotation marks. Begin a new paragraph each time a new speaker is introduced.

When you are quoting several paragraphs of dialogue by one speaker, begin each new paragraph with quotation marks. However, use closing quotation marks only at the end of the *entire quoted passage,* not at the end of each paragraph.

Special rules govern the punctuation of a quotation when it is used with an **identifying tag,** a phrase (such as *he said*) that identifies the speaker or writer. Punctuation guidelines for various situations involving identifying tags are outlined below.

1 Identifying Tag in the Middle of a Quoted Passage

Use a pair of commas to set off an identifying tag that interrupts a quoted passage.

> "In the future," pop artist Andy Warhol once said, "everyone will be world famous for fifteen minutes."

If the identifying tag follows a completed sentence but the quoted passage continues, use a period after the tag. Begin the new sentence with a capital letter, and enclose it in quotation marks.

> "Be careful," Erin warned. "Reptiles can be tricky."

2 Identifying Tag at the Beginning of a Quoted Passage

Use a comma after an identifying tag that introduces quoted speech or writing.

> The Raven repeated, "Nevermore."

Use a <u>colon</u> instead of a comma before a quotation if the identifying tag is a complete sentence.

See 34a3

> She gave her final answer: "No."

GRAMMAR CHECKER

CHECKING PUNCTUATION WITH QUOTATION MARKS

Your grammar checker will often highlight missing punctuation in sentences containing quotation marks and offer suggestions for revision.

---

3 Identifying Tag at the End of a Quoted Passage

Use a comma to set off a quotation from an identifying tag that follows it.

"Be careful out there," the sergeant warned.

If the quotation ends with a question mark or an exclamation point, use that punctuation mark instead of the comma. In this situation, the tag begins with a lowercase letter even though it follows end punctuation.

"Is Ankara the capital of Turkey?" she asked.

"Oh boy!" he cried.

Note: Commas and periods are always placed *before* quotation marks. For information on placement of other punctuation marks with quotation marks, **see 33e.**

EXERCISE 33.1

Add quotation marks to these sentences where necessary to set off quotations from identifying tags.

Example: Wordsworth's phrase "splendour in the grass" was used as the title of a movie about young lovers.

▶ 1. Few people can explain what Descartes's words I think, therefore I am actually mean.
▶ 2. Gertrude Stein said, You are all a lost generation.
3. Freedom of speech does not guarantee anyone the right to yell fire in a crowded theater, she explained.
4. There's no place like home, Dorothy insisted.
5. If everyone will sit down the teacher announced the exam will begin.

33b Setting Off Long Prose Passages and Poetry

1 Long Prose Passages

Do not enclose a **long prose passage** (a passage of more than four lines) in quotation marks. Instead, set it off by indenting the entire passage one inch from the left-hand margin. Double-space above and below the quoted passage, and double-space between lines within it. Introduce the passage with a colon, and place parenthetical documentation one space after the end punctuation.

> The following portrait of Aunt Juley illustrates several of the
> devices Galsworthy uses throughout *The Forsyte Saga,* such as a
> journalistic detachment that is almost cruel in its scrutiny, a subtle
> sense of the grotesque, and an ironic stance:
>
> > Aunt Juley stayed in her room, prostrated by the blow. Her
> > face, discoloured by tears, was divided into compartments by
> > the little ridges of pouting flesh which had swollen with
> > emotion. . . . At fixed intervals she went to her drawer,
> > and took from beneath the lavender bags a fresh pocket-
> > handkerchief. Her warm heart could not bear the thought that
> > Ann was lying there so cold. (329)
>
> Many similar portraits of characters appear throughout the novel.

CLOSE-UP

QUOTING LONG PROSE PASSAGES

When you quote a long prose passage that is a single paragraph, do not indent the first line. When quoting two or more paragraphs, however, indent the first line of each paragraph (including the first) an additional one-quarter inch. If the first sentence of the quoted passage does not begin a paragraph in the source, do not indent—but do indent the first line of each subsequent paragraph. If the long passage you are quoting includes material set in a pair of quotation marks, keep the quotation marks.

---

2 Poetry

Treat one line of poetry like a short prose passage: enclose it in quotation marks, and run it into the text.

> One of John Donne's best-known poems begins with the line, "Go and
> catch a falling star."

See 34e2

If you quote two or three lines of poetry, separate the lines with <u>slashes</u> (/), and run the quotation into the text. (Leave one space before and one space after the slash.)

> Alexander Pope writes, "True Ease in Writing comes from Art, not
> Chance, / As those move easiest who have learned to dance."

See
33b1 If you quote more than three lines of poetry, set them off like a <u>long prose passage</u>. (For special emphasis, you may set off fewer lines in this manner.) Do not use quotation marks, and be sure to reproduce punctuation, spelling, capitalization, and indentation *exactly* as they appear in the poem.

Wilfred Owen, a poet who was killed in action in World War I, expressed the horrors of war with vivid imagery:

Bent double, like old beggars under sacks.

Knock-kneed, coughing like hags, we cursed through sludge.

Till on the haunting flares we turned our backs

And towards our distant rest began to trudge. (lines 1-4)

33c Setting Off Titles

See
37a Titles of short works and titles of parts of long works are enclosed in quotation marks. Other titles are <u>italicized</u>.

TITLES REQUIRING QUOTATION MARKS

Articles in Magazines, Newspapers, and Professional Journals
  "Why Johnny Can't Write"

Essays, Short Stories, Short Poems, and Songs
  "Fenimore Cooper's Literary Offenses"   "Flying Home"
  "The Road Not Taken"   "The Star-Spangled Banner"

Chapters or Sections of Books
  "Miss Sharp Begins to Make Friends"

Episodes of Radio or Television Series
  "Lucy Goes to the Hospital"

  See 37a for a list of titles that require italics.

Note: MLA guidelines now recommend using italics rather than underlining to indicate italics.

33d Setting Off Words Used in Special Ways

Enclose a word used in a special or unusual way in quotation marks. (If you use the phrase *so-called* before an unusual usage, do not also use quotation marks.)

It was clear that adults approved of children who were "readers," but it was not at all clear why this was so. (Annie Dillard)

Also enclose a **coinage**—an invented word—in quotation marks.

After the twins were born, the minivan became a "babymobile."

33e Using Quotation Marks with Other Punctuation

At the end of a quotation, punctuation is sometimes placed before the quotation marks and sometimes placed after the quotation marks.

1 With Final Commas or Periods

At the end of a quotation, place a comma or period *before* the quotation marks.

Many, like the poet Robert Frost, think about "the road not taken," but not many have taken "the one less traveled by."

2 With Final Semicolons or Colons

At the end of a quotation, place a semicolon or colon *after* the quotation marks.

Students who do not pass the test receive "certificates of completion"; those who pass are awarded diplomas.

Taxpayers were pleased with the first of the candidate's promised "sweeping new reforms": a balanced budget.

3 With Question Marks, Exclamation Points, and Dashes

If a question mark, exclamation point, or dash is part of the quotation, place the punctuation mark *before* the quotation marks.

"Who's there?" she demanded.

"Stop!" he cried.

"Should we leave now, or—" Vicki paused, unable to continue.

If a question mark, exclamation point, or dash is *not* part of the quotation, place the punctuation mark *after* the quotation marks.

Did you finish reading "The Black Cat"?

Whatever you do, don't yell "Uncle"!

The first story—Updike's "A&P"— provoked discussion.

If both the quotation and the sentence are questions or exclamations, place the punctuation mark *after* the quotation marks.

Who asked, "Is Paris burning"?

CLOSE-UP

QUOTATIONS WITHIN QUOTATIONS

Use *single* quotation marks to enclose a quotation within a quotation.

> Claire noted, "Liberace always said, 'I cried all the way to the bank.'"

Also use single quotation marks within a quotation to indicate a title that would normally be enclosed in double quotation marks.

> I think what she said was, "Play it, Sam. Play 'As Time Goes By.'"

See 33b1

Use *double* quotation marks around quotations or titles within a <u>long prose passage</u>.

33f Editing Misused Quotation Marks

Quotation marks should not be used in the following situations.

1 To Convey Emphasis

Do not use quotation marks to convey emphasis.

William Randolph Hearst's ~~"fabulous"~~ home is a castle called San Simeon.

2 To Set Off Slang or Technical Terms

Do not use quotation marks to set off slang or technical terms. (Note that slang is almost always inappropriate in college writing.)

Dawn is ~~"into"~~ running.
                     ^very involved in^

~~"Biofeedback"~~ is sometimes used to treat migraine headaches.

3 To Enclose Titles of Long Works

See 37a <u>Titles</u> of long works are italicized, not set in quotation marks.

The classic novel ~~"~~*War and Peace*~~"~~ is even longer than the epic poem ~~"~~*Paradise Lost.*~~"~~

Note: Do not use quotation marks (or italics) to set off titles of your own papers.

4 To Set Off Terms Being Defined

Terms being defined are italicized.

> The word *"tintinnabulation,"* meaning the ringing sound of bells, is used by Poe in his poem "The Bells."

5 To Set Off Indirect Quotations

Quotation marks should not be used to set off **indirect quotations** (someone else's written or spoken words that are not quoted exactly).

> Freud wondered *"what a woman wanted."*

EXERCISE 33.2

Correct the use of quotation marks in the following sentences. If a sentence is correct, mark it with a C.

Example: The *"Watergate"* incident brought many new expressions into the English language.

▶ 1. Kilroy was here and Women and children first are two expressions *Bartlett's Familiar Quotations* attributes to "Anon."

▶ 2. Neil Armstrong said he was making a small step for man but a giant leap for mankind.

▶ 3. "The answer, my friend", Bob Dylan sang, "is blowin' in the wind".

▶ 4. The novel was a real "thriller," complete with spies and counterspies, mysterious women, and exotic international chases.

▶ 5. The sign said, Road liable to subsidence; it meant that we should look out for potholes.

   6. One of William Blake's best-known lines—To see a world in a grain of sand—opens his poem Auguries of Innocence.

   7. In James Thurber's short story The Catbird Seat, Mrs. Barrows annoys Mr. Martin by asking him silly questions like Are you tearing up the pea patch? Are you scraping around the bottom of the pickle barrel? and Are you lifting the oxcart out of the ditch?

   8. I'll make him an offer he can't refuse, promised "the godfather" in Mario Puzo's novel.

   9. What did Timothy Leary mean by "Turn on, tune in, drop out?"

   10. George, the protagonist of Bernard Malamud's short story, A Summer's Reading, is something of an "underachiever."

34a Using Colons

The **colon** is a strong punctuation mark that points readers ahead. When a colon introduces a list or series, explanatory material, or a quotation, it must be preceded by a complete sentence.

1 Introducing Lists or Series

Use colons to set off lists or series, including those introduced by phrases such as *the following* or *as follows*.

> Waiting tables requires three skills: memory, speed, and balance.

2 Introducing Explanatory Material

Use colons to introduce material that explains, exemplifies, or summarizes. Frequently, this material is presented as an **appositive,** a word group that identifies or renames an adjacent noun or pronoun.

> Diego Rivera painted a controversial mural: the one commissioned for Rockefeller Center in the 1930s.

> She had one dream: to play professional basketball.

Sometimes a colon separates two independent clauses, the second illustrating or explaining the first.

> A *U.S. News & World Report* survey revealed a surprising fact: Americans spend more time at malls than anywhere else except at home and at work.

CLOSE-UP

USING COLONS

When a complete sentence follows a colon, it may begin with either a capital or a lowercase letter. However, if the sentence is a quotation, the first word is always capitalized (unless it was not capitalized in the source).

---

3 Introducing Quotations

See 33b1

When you quote a <u>long prose passage</u>, always introduce it with a colon. Also use a colon before a short quotation when it is introduced by a complete sentence.

> With dignity, Bartleby repeated the familiar words: "I prefer not to."

OTHER CONVENTIONAL USES OF COLONS

To Separate a Title from a Subtitle

Family Installments: Memories of Growing Up Hispanic

To Separate Minutes from Hours

6:15 a.m.

After the Salutation in a Business <u>Letter</u>

See
11a

Dear Dr. Evans:

See
47a2

To Separate Place of Publication from Name of Publisher in a <u>Works-Cited</u> List

Boston: Wadsworth, 2010

---

4 Editing Misused Colons

Do not use colons in the following situations.

After Expressions Like Such As *and* For Example Do not use colons after the expressions *such as, namely, for example,* and *that is.* (Remember that when a colon introduces a list or series, a complete sentence must precede the colon.)

The Eye Institute treats patients with a wide variety of conditions, such as: myopia, glaucoma, and cataracts.

In Verb and Prepositional Constructions Do not place colons between verbs and their objects or complements or between prepositions and their objects.

James A. Michener wrote: *Hawaii, Centennial, Space,* and *Poland.*

Hitler's armies marched through: the Netherlands, Belgium, and France.

EXERCISE 34.1

Add colons where appropriate in the following sentences, and delete any misused colons.

Example: There was one thing he really hated: getting up at 7:00 every morning.

▶ 1. Books about the late John F. Kennedy include the following *A Hero for Our Time; Johnny, We Hardly Knew Ye; One Brief Shining Moment;* and *JFK: Reckless Youth.*

▶ 2. Only one task remained to tell his boss he was quitting.

3. The story closed with a familiar phrase "And they all lived happily ever after."

4. The sergeant requested: reinforcements, medical supplies, and more ammunition.

5. She kept only four souvenirs a photograph, a matchbook, a theater program, and a daisy pressed between the pages of *William Shakespeare The Complete Works.*

34b Using Dashes

1 Setting Off Nonessential Material

See 30d

Like commas, **dashes** can set off <u>nonessential material,</u> but unlike commas, dashes call attention to the material they set off. Indicate a dash with two unspaced hyphens (which your word-processing program will automatically convert to a dash).

For emphasis, you may use dashes to set off explanations, qualifications, examples, definitions, and appositives.

Neither of the boys—both nine-year-olds—had any history of violence.

Too many parents learn the dangers of swimming pools the hard way—after their toddler has drowned.

2 Introducing a Summary

Use a dash to introduce a statement that summarizes a list or series before it.

"Study hard," "Respect your elders," "Don't talk with your mouth full"—Sharon had often heard her parents say these things.

3 Indicating an Interruption

In dialogue, a dash can mark a hesitation or an unfinished thought.

"I think—no, I know—this is the worst day of my life," Julie sighed.

CLOSE-UP

EDITING OVERUSED DASHES

Too many dashes can make your writing seem disorganized and out of control, so you should be careful not to overuse them.

Registration was a nightmare—*. Most* most of the courses I wanted to take—geology and conversational Spanish, for instance—met at inconvenient times—*.* or were closed by the time I tried to sign up for them—*. It* it was really depressing—*,* even for registration.

EXERCISE 34.2

Add dashes where needed in the following sentences. If a sentence is correct, mark it with a C.

Example: World War I, called "the war to end all wars", was, unfortunately, no such thing.

▶ 1. Tulips, daffodils, hyacinths, lilies all these flowers grow from bulbs.
▶ 2. St. Kitts and Nevis two tiny island nations are now independent after 360 years of British rule.
   3. "But it's not" She paused and thought about her next words.
   4. He considered several different majors history, English, political science, and business before deciding on journalism.
   5. The two words added to the Pledge of Allegiance in the 1950s "under God" remain part of the Pledge today.

34c   Using Parentheses

1   Setting Off Nonessential Material

Use **parentheses** to enclose material that expands, clarifies, illustrates, or supplements.

> In some European countries (notably Sweden and France), high-quality day care is offered at little or no cost to parents.

When a complete sentence set off by parentheses falls within another sentence, it should not begin with a capital letter or end with a period.

> The region is so cold (temperatures average in the low twenties) that it is virtually uninhabitable.

When the parenthetical sentence does *not* fall within another sentence, it must begin with a capital letter and end with appropriate punctuation.

> The region is very cold. (Temperatures average in the low twenties.)

CLOSE-UP

USING PARENTHESES WITH OTHER PUNCTUATION

When parentheses fall within a sentence, punctuation never immediately precedes the opening parenthesis. Punctuation may follow the closing parenthesis, however.

> George Orwell's *1984* (1949), which focuses on the dangers of a totalitarian society, is required reading.

2 Using Parentheses in Other Situations

Parentheses are used around letters and numbers that identify points on a list, dates, cross-references, and documentation.

All reports must include the following components: (1) an opening summary, (2) a background statement, and (3) a list of conclusions.

Russia defeated Sweden in the Great Northern War (1700–1721).

Other scholars also make this point (see p. 54).

One critic has called the novel "puerile" (Arvin 72).

EXERCISE 34.3

Add parentheses where appropriate in the following sentences. If a sentence is correct, mark it with a C.

Example: The greatest battle of the War of 1812 (the Battle of New Orleans) was fought after the war was declared over.

▶ 1. During the Great War 1914–1918, Britain censored letters written from the front lines.
▶ 2. Those who lived in towns on the coast such as Dover could often hear the mortar shells across the channel in France.
3. Wilfred Owen wrote his most famous poem "Dulce et Decorum Est" in the trenches in France.
4. The British uniforms with bright red tabs right at the neck were responsible for many British deaths.
5. It was difficult for the War Poets as they are now called to return to writing about subjects other than the horrors of war.

34d Using Brackets

1 Setting Off Comments within Quotations

Brackets within quotations tell readers that the enclosed words are yours and not those of your source. You can bracket an explanation, a clarification, a correction, or an opinion.

"Even at Princeton he [F. Scott Fitzgerald] felt like an outsider."

If a quotation contains an error, indicate that the error is not yours by following the error with the Latin word *sic* ("thus") in brackets.

"The octopuss [sic] is a cephalopod mollusk with eight arms."

Note: See 44d1 Use brackets to indicate changes that you make in order to fit a <u>quotation</u> smoothly into your sentence.

2 Replacing Parentheses within Parentheses

When one set of parentheses falls within another, use brackets in place of the inner set.

> In her classic study of American education between 1945 and 1960 (*The Trouble Crusade* [New York: Basic, 1963]), Diane Ravitch addresses issues such as progressive education, race, educational reforms, and campus unrest.

34e Using Slashes

1 Separating One Option from Another

When separating one option from another with a **slash,** do not leave a space before or after the slash.

> The either/or fallacy is a common error in logic.
> Writer/director Spike Lee will speak at the film festival.

2 Separating Lines of Poetry Run Into the Text

When separating lines of poetry run into the text, leave one space before and one space after the slash.

> The poet James Schevill writes, "I study my defects / And learn how to perfect them."

34f Using Ellipses

1 Indicating an Omission in Quoted Prose

Use an **ellipsis**—three *spaced* periods—to indicate that you have omitted words from a prose quotation. Note that an ellipsis in the middle of a quoted passage can indicate the omission of a word, a sentence or two, or even a whole paragraph or more. When deleting material from a quotation, be careful not to change the meaning of the original passage.

> **Original:** "When I was a young man, being anxious to distinguish myself, I was perpetually starting new propositions." (Samuel Johnson)
>
> **With Omission:** "When I was a young man, . . . I was perpetually starting new propositions."

Note that when you delete words immediately after an internal punctuation mark (such as the comma in the above example), you retain the punctuation before the ellipsis.

When you delete material at the end of a sentence, place the ellipsis *after* the sentence's period or other end punctuation.

According to humorist Dave Barry, "from outer space Europe appears to be shaped like a large ketchup stain. . . ." (period followed by ellipsis)

 Never begin a quoted passage with an ellipsis.

When you delete material between sentences, place the ellipsis *after* any punctuation that appears in the original passage.

Deletion from Middle of One Sentence to End of Another: According to Donald Hall, "Everywhere one meets the idea that reading is an activity desirable in itself. . . . People surround the idea of reading with piety and do not take into account the purpose of reading." (period followed by ellipsis)

Deletion from Middle of One Sentence to Middle of Another: "When I was a young man, . . . I found that generally what was new was false." (**Samuel Johnson**) (comma followed by ellipsis)

Note: If a quoted passage already contains ellipses, MLA recommends that you enclose any ellipses of your own in brackets to distinguish them from those that appear in the original quotation.

CLOSE-UP

USING ELLIPSES

If a quotation ending with an ellipsis is followed by parenthetical documentation, the final punctuation comes *after* the documentation.

As Jarman argues, "Compromise was impossible . . ." (161) .

---

2   Indicating an Omission in Quoted Poetry

Use an ellipsis when you omit a word or phrase from a line of poetry. When you omit one or more lines of poetry, use a line of spaced periods. (The length may be equal either to the line above it or to the missing line—but it should not be longer than the longest line of the poem.)

Original:

Stitch! Stitch! Stitch!
In poverty, hunger, and dirt,
And still with a voice of dolorous pitch,
Would that its tone could reach the Rich,
She sang this "Song of the Shirt!"

(Thomas Hood)

With Omission:

Stitch! Stitch! Stitch!

In poverty, hunger, and dirt,

. . . .

She sang this "Song of the Shirt!"

EXERCISE 34.4

Read the following paragraph, and follow the instructions after it, taking care in each case not to delete essential information.

> The most important thing about research is to know when to stop. How does one recognize the moment? When I was eighteen or thereabouts, my mother told me that when out with a young man I should always leave a half-hour before I wanted to. Although I was not sure how this might be accomplished, I recognized the advice as sound, and exactly the same rule applies to research. One must stop *before* one has finished; otherwise, one will never stop and never finish. (Barbara Tuchman, *Practicing History*)

- ▶ 1. Delete words from the middle of one sentence, marking the omission with an ellipsis.
- ▶ 2. Delete words from the middle of one sentence to the middle of another, marking the omission with an ellipsis.
-   3. Delete words at the end of any sentence, marking the omission with an ellipsis.
-   4. Delete one complete sentence from the middle of the passage, marking the omission with an ellipsis.

EXERCISE 34.5

Add appropriate punctuation—colons, dashes, parentheses, brackets, or slashes—to the following sentences. If a sentence is correct, mark it with a C.

Example: There was one thing she was sure of if she did well at the interview, the job would be hers.

- ▶ 1. Mark Twain Samuel L. Clemens made the following statement "I can live for two months on a good compliment."
- ▶ 2. Liza Minnelli, the actress singer who starred in several films, is the daughter of legendary singer Judy Garland.
- ▶ 3. Saudi Arabia, Oman, Yemen, Qatar, and the United Arab Emirates all these are located on the Arabian Peninsula.
- ▶ 4. John Adams 1735–1826 was the second president of the United States; John Quincy Adams 1767–1848 was the sixth.
- ▶ 5. The sign said, "No tresspassing sic."
-   6. *Checkmate* a term derived from the Persian phrase meaning "the king is dead" announces victory in chess.

7. The following people were present at the meeting the president of the board of trustees, three trustees, and twenty reporters.
8. Before the introduction of the potato in Europe, the parsnip was a major source of carbohydrates in fact, it was a dietary staple.
9. In the well-researched book *Crime Movies* (New York Norton, 1980), Carlos Clarens studies the gangster genre in film.
10. I remember reading though I can't remember where that Upton Sinclair sold plots to Jack London.

PART 6

Understanding Spelling and Mechanics

Understanding Spelling and Mechanics

Improving Spelling

Knowing when and how to use a dictionary can help you improve your spelling. In addition, memorizing a few rules and their exceptions and learning the correct spelling of the most commonly misspelled words can make a big difference.

35a Using a Dictionary

To fit a lot of information into a small space, dictionaries use a system of symbols, abbreviations, and typefaces (see Figure 35.1 below). Consult the preface of your dictionary to determine how its system operates.

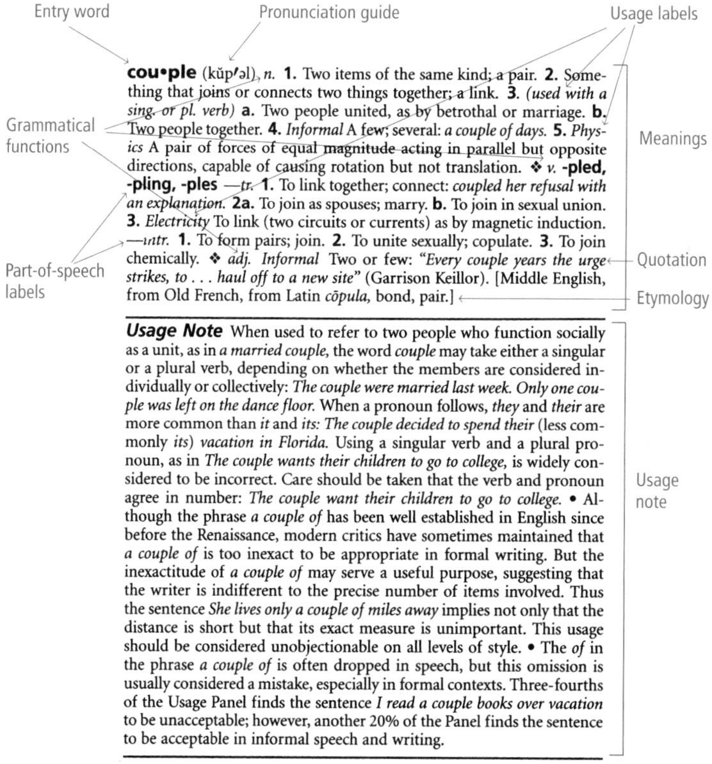

Entry word   Pronunciation guide   Usage labels

cou•ple (kŭp′əl), *n.* **1.** Two items of the same kind; a pair. **2.** Something that joins or connects two things together; a link. **3.** *(used with a sing. or pl. verb)* **a.** Two people united, as by betrothal or marriage. **b.** Two people together. **4.** *Informal* A few; several: *a couple of days.* **5.** *Physics* A pair of forces of equal magnitude acting in parallel but opposite directions, capable of causing rotation but not translation. ❖ *v.* **-pled, -pling, -ples** —*tr.* **1.** To link together; connect: *coupled her refusal with an explanation.* **2a.** To join as spouses; marry. **b.** To join in sexual union. **3.** *Electricity* To link (two circuits or currents) as by magnetic induction. —*intr.* **1.** To form pairs; join. **2.** To unite sexually; copulate. **3.** To join chemically. ❖ *adj. Informal* Two or few: *"Every couple years the urge strikes, to . . . haul off to a new site"* (Garrison Keillor). [Middle English, from Old French, from Latin *cōpula,* bond, pair.]

Grammatical functions

Part-of-speech labels

Meanings

Quotation

Etymology

Usage Note When used to refer to two people who function socially as a unit, as in *a married couple,* the word *couple* may take either a singular or a plural verb, depending on whether the members are considered individually or collectively: *The couple were married last week. Only one couple was left on the dance floor.* When a pronoun follows, *they* and *their* are more common than *it* and *its: The couple decided to spend their* (less commonly *its*) *vacation in Florida.* Using a singular verb and a plural pronoun, as in *The couple wants their children to go to college,* is widely considered to be incorrect. Care should be taken that the verb and pronoun agree in number: *The couple want their children to go to college.* • Although the phrase *a couple of* has been well established in English since before the Renaissance, modern critics have sometimes maintained that *a couple of* is too inexact to be appropriate in formal writing. But the inexactitude of *a couple of* may serve a useful purpose, suggesting that the writer is indifferent to the precise number of items involved. Thus the sentence *She lives only a couple of miles away* implies not only that the distance is short but that its exact measure is unimportant. This usage should be considered unobjectionable on all levels of style. • The *of* in the phrase *a couple of* is often dropped in speech, but this omission is usually considered a mistake, especially in formal contexts. Three-fourths of the Usage Panel finds the sentence *I read a couple books over vacation* to be unacceptable; however, another 20% of the Panel finds the sentence to be acceptable in informal speech and writing.

Usage note

FIGURE 35.1 Entry from *The American Heritage Dictionary of the English Language,* Fourth Edition.

35b Understanding Spelling and Pronunciation

Because pronunciation often provides few clues to English spelling, you need to pay particular attention to the three problem areas that cause the most misspellings.

1 Words That Are Often Pronounced Carelessly

Most of us pronounce words rather carelessly in everyday speech. Consequently, when spelling, we may leave out, add, or transpose letters.

candidate	library	recognize
environment	lightning	specific
February	nuclear	supposed to
government	perform	surprise
hundred	quantity	used to

2 American and British Spellings

Some words are spelled one way in the United States and another way in Great Britain and the Commonwealth nations.

American	**British**
color	colour
defense	defence
honor	honour
judgment	judgement
theater	theatre
toward	towards
traveled	travelled

3 Homophones

Homophones are words—such as *accept* and *except*—that are pronounced alike but spelled differently.

accept	to receive
except	other than
affect	to have an influence on (*verb*)
effect	result (*noun*); to cause (*verb*)
its	possessive of *it*
it's	contraction of *it is*
principal	most important (*adjective*); head of a school (*noun*)
principle	a basic truth; rule of conduct

For a full list of these and other homophones, along with their meanings and sentences illustrating their use, **see the Glossary of Usage.**

RUNNING A SPELL CHECK

Even if you run a spell check, you still have to proofread your papers. Remember that a spell checker will not recognize the following kinds of errors:

♦ A word that is spelled correctly but used incorrectly—*accept* for *except* or *there* for *their*, for example.
♦ A typo that creates another word—*form* for *from* or *then* for *than*, for example.
♦ Many capitalization errors—*president Lincoln* instead of *President Lincoln*, for example.

35c Learning Spelling Rules

Knowing a few reliable rules can help you overcome problems caused by the inconsistency between pronunciation and spelling.

1 The *ie*/*ei* Combinations

The old rule still stands: use *i* before *e* except after *c* (or when pronounced *ay*, as in *neighbor*).

i before *e*	*ei* after *c*	*ei* pronounced *ay*
belief	ceiling	weigh
chief	deceit	freight
niece	receive	eight

Exceptions: *either, neither, foreign, leisure, weird,* and *seize.* In addition, if the *ie* combination is not pronounced as a unit, the rule does not apply: *atheist, science.*

EXERCISE 35.1

Fill in the blanks with the proper *ie* or *ei* combination. After completing the exercise, use your dictionary or spell checker to check your answers.

Example: conc __*ei*__ ve

▶ 1. rec_____pt
▶ 2. var_____ty
▶ 3. caff_____ne
▶ 4. ach_____ve
▶ 5. kal_____doscope

6. misch_____f
7. effic_____nt
8. v_____n
9. spec_____s
10. suffic_____nt

2 Doubling Final Consonants

The only words that double their consonants before a suffix that begins with a vowel (*-ed, -ing*) are those that pass the following three tests:

1. They have one syllable or are stressed on the last syllable.
2. They contain only one vowel in the last syllable.
3. They end in a single consonant.

The word *tap* satisfies all three conditions: it has only one syllable, it contains only one vowel (*a*), and it ends in a single consonant (*p*). Therefore, the final consonant doubles before a suffix beginning with a vowel (*tapped, tapping*).

The word *relent* meets two of the three conditions: it is stressed on the last syllable, and it has one vowel in the last syllable, but it does not end in a single consonant. Therefore, its final consonant is not doubled (*relented, relenting*).

3 Prefixes

The addition of a prefix never affects the spelling of the root (*mis + spell = misspell*). Some prefixes can cause spelling problems, however, because they are pronounced alike although they are not spelled alike: *ante-/anti-, en-/in-, per-/pre-,* and *de-/di-.*

<u>ante</u>bellum	<u>anti</u>aircraft
<u>en</u>circle	<u>in</u>tegrate
<u>per</u>ceive	<u>pre</u>scribe
<u>de</u>duct	<u>di</u>rect

4 Silent *e* before a Suffix

When a suffix that begins with a consonant is added to a word ending in silent *e*, the *e* is generally kept: *hope/hopeful; lame/lamely; bore/boredom.* **Exceptions:** *argument, truly, ninth, judgment,* and *acknowledgment.*

When a suffix that starts with a vowel is added to a word that ends in a silent *e,* the *e* is generally dropped: *hope/hoping; trace/traced; grieve/grievance; love/lovable.* **Exceptions:** *changeable, noticeable,* and *courageous.*

EXERCISE 35.2

Combine the following words with the suffixes in parentheses. Keep or drop the silent *e* as you see fit; be prepared to explain your choices.

Example:　fate (al)
　　　　　　fatal

▶　1. surprise (ing)　　　　6. outrage (ous)
▶　2. sure (ly)　　　　　　7. service (able)
▶　3. force (ible)　　　　　8. awe (ful)
▶　4. manage (able)　　　　9. shame (ing)
▶　5. due (ly)　　　　　　10. shame (less)

5　*y* before a Suffix

When a word ends in a consonant plus *y,* the *y* generally changes to an *i* when a suffix is added (*beauty + ful = beautiful*). The *y* is kept, however, when the suffix -*ing* is added (*tally* + *ing* = *tallying*) and in some one-syllable words (*dry* + *ness* = *dryness*).

When a word ends in a vowel plus *y*, the *y* is retained (*joy* + *ful* = *joyful*; *employ* + *er* = *employer*). **Exception:** *day* + *ly* = *daily*.

EXERCISE 35.3

Add the endings in parentheses to the following words. Change or keep the final *y* as you see fit; be prepared to explain your choices.

Example: party (ing)
     partying

▶ 1. journey (ing)   6. sturdy (ness)
▶ 2. study (ed)   7. merry (ment)
▶ 3. carry (ing)   8. likely (hood)
▶ 4. shy (ly)   9. plenty (ful)
▶ 5. study (ing)   10. supply (er)

6 *seed* Endings

Endings with the sound *seed* are nearly always spelled *cede*, as in *precede, intercede, concede*, and so on. **Exceptions:** *supersede, exceed, proceed*, and *succeed*.

7 *-able, -ible*

If the root of a word is itself an independent word, the suffix -*able* is most often used. If the root of a word is not an independent word, the suffix -*ible* is most often used.

*comfor*able   *compat*ible
*agree*able   *incred*ible
*dry*able   *plaus*ible

8 Plurals

Most nouns form plurals by adding -*s*: *savage/savages, tortilla/tortillas, boat/boats*. There are, however, a number of exceptions.

Words Ending in -f *or* -fe   Some words ending in -*f* or -*fe* form plurals by changing the *f* to *v* and adding -*es* or -*s*: *life/lives, self/selves*. Others add just -*s*: *belief/beliefs, safe/safes*. Words ending in -*ff* take -*s* to form plurals: *tariff/tariffs*.

Words Ending in -y   Most words that end in a consonant followed by *y* form plurals by changing the *y* to *i* and adding -*es*: *baby/babies*. **Exceptions:** proper nouns, such as the *Kennedys* (never the *Kennedies*).

Words that end in a vowel followed by a *y* form plurals by adding -*s*: *day/days, monkey/monkeys*.

Words Ending in -o   Words that end in a vowel followed by *o* form the plural by adding -*s*: *radio/radios, stereo/stereos, zoo/zoos*. Most words that end in a consonant followed by *o* add *-es* to form the plural: *tomato/ tomatoes, hero/heroes.* **Exceptions:** *silo/silos, piano/pianos, memo/memos,* and *soprano/sopranos.*

Words Ending in -s, -ss, -sh, -ch, -x, *and* -z   These words form plurals by adding *-es: Jones/Joneses, mass/masses, rash/rashes, lunch/lunches, box/ boxes, buzz/buzzes.* **Exceptions:** Some one-syllable words that end in *-s* or *-z* double their final consonants when forming plurals: *quiz/quizzes.*

Compound Nouns   **Compound nouns**—nouns formed from two or more words—usually form the plural with the last word in the compound construction: *welfare state/welfare states; snowball/snowballs.* However, where the first word of the compound noun is more important than the others, form the plural with the first word: *sister-in-law/sisters-in-law, attorney general/attorneys general, hole in one/holes in one.*

Foreign Plurals   Some words, especially those borrowed from Latin or Greek, keep their foreign plurals. Look up a foreign word's plural form in a dictionary if you do not know it.

Singular	Plural
basis	bases
criterion	criteria
datum	data
larva	larvae
medium	media
memorandum	memoranda
stimulus	stimuli

Knowing When to Capitalize

C H A P T E R 36

REVISING CAPITALIZATION ERRORS

In *Microsoft Word,* the AutoCorrect tool will automatically capitalize certain words—such as the first word of a sentence or the days of the week. You can also designate additional words to be automatically capitalized for you as you type. To do this, select the AutoCorrect option, and type in the words you want to capitalize. Be sure to proofread your documents after using the AutoCorrect tool, though, since it may introduce capitalization errors into your writing.

36a Capitalizing the First Word of a Sentence

Capitalize the first word of a sentence, including a sentence of quoted speech or writing.

As Shakespeare wrote, "Who steals my purse steals trash."

Do not capitalize a sentence set off within another sentence by dashes or parentheses.

Finding the store closed—it was a holiday—they went home.

The candidates are Frank Lester and Jane Lester (they are not related).

Capitalization is optional when a complete sentence is introduced by a colon.

See 34a

> **CLOSE-UP**
>
> **USING CAPITAL LETTERS IN POETRY**
>
> The first word of a line of poetry is generally capitalized. If the poet uses a lower-case letter to begin a line, however, you should follow that style when you quote the line.

36b Capitalizing Proper Nouns

Proper nouns—the names of specific persons, places, or things—are capitalized, and so are adjectives formed from proper nouns.

> **ESL TIP**
>
> If you are not sure whether a noun should be capitalized, look it up in a dictionary. Do not capitalize a word simply because you want to emphasize its importance.

1 Specific People's Names

Always capitalize people's names: Olympia Snowe, Barack Obama.

Capitalize a title when it precedes a person's name (Senator Olympia Snowe) or is used instead of the name (Dad). Do not capitalize titles that *follow* names (Olympia Snowe, the senator from Maine) or those that refer to the general position, not the particular person who holds it (a stay-at-home dad).

You may, however, capitalize titles that indicate very high-ranking positions even when they are used alone or when they follow a name: the Pope; Barack Obama, President of the United States. Never capitalize a title denoting a family relationship when it follows an article or a possessive pronoun (an uncle, his mom).

Capitalize titles that represent academic degrees or abbreviations of those degrees even when they follow a name: <u>D</u>r. Sanjay Gupta; Sanjay Gupta, <u>MD</u>.

2 Names of Particular Structures, Special Events, Monuments, and So On

the Brooklyn Bridge	the Taj Mahal
the Eiffel Tower	Mount Rushmore
the World Series	the *Titanic*

Note: Capitalize a common noun, such as *bridge, river, county,* or *lake,* when it is part of a proper noun (<u>L</u>ake Erie, Kings <u>C</u>ounty).

3 Places and Geographical Regions

Saturn	the Straits of Magellan
Budapest	the Fiji Islands
Walden Pond	the Western Hemisphere

Capitalize *north, south, east,* and *west* when they denote particular geographical regions but not when they designate directions.

There are more tornadoes in Kansas than in the <u>East</u>. (*East* refers to a specific region.)

Turn <u>west</u> at Broad Street and continue <u>north</u> to Market. (*West* and *north* refer to directions, not specific regions.)

4 Days of the Week, Months, and Holidays

Saturday	Cinco de Mayo
January	Diwali

5 Historical Periods, Events, Documents, and Names of Legal Cases

the Industrial Revolution	the Treaty of Versailles
the Reformation	the Voting Rights Act
the Battle of Gettysburg	*Brown v. Board of Education*

Note: Names of court cases are italicized in the text of your papers, but not in works-cited entries.

6 Philosophic, Literary, and Artistic Movements

Naturalism	Dadaism
Neoclassicism	Expressionism

7 Races, Ethnic Groups, Nationalities, and Languages

African American   Korean
Latino/Latina   Farsi

Note: When the words *black* and *white* denote races, they have traditionally not been capitalized. Current usage is divided on whether or not to capitalize *black*.

8 Religions and Their Followers; Sacred Books and Figures

Islam   the Qur'an   Buddha
the Talmud   Jews   God

Note: It is not necessary to capitalize pronouns referring to God (although some people do so as a sign of respect).

9 Specific Groups and Organizations

the Democratic Party
the International Brotherhood of Electrical Workers
the New York Yankees
the American Civil Liberties Union
the National Council of Teachers of English
the Rolling Stones

Note: When the name of a group or organization is abbreviated, the <u>abbreviation</u> uses capital letters in place of the capitalized words.

See 39b

IBEW   ACLU   NCTE

10 Businesses, Government Agencies, and Other Institutions

General Electric   Lincoln High School
the Environmental Protection Agency   the University of Maryland

11 Brand Names and Words Formed from Them

Velcro   Coke   Post-it   Rollerblades   Astroturf

Note: Brand names that over long use have become synonymous with the product—for example, *nylon* and *aspirin*—are no longer capitalized. (Consult a dictionary to determine whether or not to capitalize a familiar brand name.)

USING BRAND NAMES

In general, use generic references, not brand names, in college writing—*photocopy*, not *Xerox*, for example. These generic names are not capitalized.

12 Specific Academic Courses

Sociology 201   English 101

Note: Do not capitalize a general subject area (sociology, zoology) unless it is the name of a language (English, Spanish).

13 Adjectives Formed from Proper Nouns

Freudian slip   Elizabethan era
Platonic ideal   Shakespearean sonnet
Aristotelian logic   Marxist ideology

When words derived from proper nouns have lost their original associations, do not capitalize them: *china bowl, french fries*.

GRAMMAR CHECKER

CHECKING PROPER NOUNS

Your spell checker may not recognize many of the proper nouns you use in your documents, particularly those that have irregular capitalization, such as *Leonardo da Vinci*, and therefore will identify these nouns as spelling errors. It may also fail to recognize certain discipline-specific proper nouns.

To solve this problem, click Ignore Once to instruct the spell checker to ignore the word one time and Ignore All to instruct the spell checker to ignore all uses of the word in your document.

36c Capitalizing Important Words in Titles

In general, capitalize all words in titles with the exception of articles (*a, an,* and *the*), prepositions, coordinating conjunctions, and the *to* in infinitives (unless they are the first or last word in the title or subtitle).

"Dover Beach"   *On the Waterfront*
The Declaration of Independence   *Madame Curie: A Biography*
Across the River and into the Trees "What Friends Are For"

36d Capitalizing the Pronoun *I*, the Interjection *O*, and Other Single Letters in Special Constructions

Always capitalize the pronoun *I* even if it is part of a contraction (*I'm, I'll, I've*).

Sam and I finally went to Mexico, and I'm glad we did.

Always capitalize the interjection *O*.

Give us peace in our time, O Lord.

However, capitalize the interjection *oh* only when it begins a sentence.

Note: Many other single letters are capitalized in certain usages: an A in history, vitamin B, C major. Check your dictionary to determine whether or not to use a capital letter.

36e Capitalizing Salutations and Closings of Letters

Always capitalize the first word of the salutation of a personal or business letter. See 11a

Dear Fred,   Dear Mr. Reynolds:

Always capitalize the first word of the complimentary close.

Sincerely,   Very truly yours,

36f Editing Misused Capitals

Do not capitalize words for emphasis or as an attention-getting strategy. If you are uncertain about whether or not a word should be capitalized, consult a dictionary.

1 Seasons

Do not capitalize the names of the seasons—summer, fall, winter, spring—unless they are personified, as in *Old Man Winter*.

2 Centuries and Loosely Defined Historical Periods

Do not capitalize the names of centuries or general historical periods.

seventeenth-century poetry   the automobile age

Do, however, capitalize names of specific historical, anthropological, and geological periods: *Iron Age; Renaissance; Paleozoic Era*.

3 Diseases and Other Medical Terms

Do not capitalize names of diseases or medical tests or conditions unless a proper noun is part of the name or unless the name of the disease is an
See 29a2 **acronym.**

smallpox	Apgar test	AIDS
Lyme disease	mumps	SIDS

EXERCISE 36.1

Capitalize words where necessary in these sentences.

Example: John F. Kennedy won the pulitzer prize for his book *profiles in courage.*

▶ 1. Two of the brontë sisters wrote *jane eyre* and *wuthering heights,* nineteenth-century novels that are required reading in many english classes that focus on victorian literature.

▶ 2. It was a beautiful day in the spring—it was april 15, to be exact—but all Ted could think about was the check he had to write to the internal revenue service and the bills he had to pay by friday.

▶ 3. Traveling north, they hiked through british columbia, planning a leisurely return on the cruise ship *canadian princess.*

▶ 4. Alice liked her mom's apple pie better than aunt nellie's rhubarb pie, but she liked grandpa's punch best of all.

▶ 5. A new elective, political science 30, covers the vietnam war from the gulf of tonkin to the fall of saigon, including the roles of ho chi minh, the viet cong, and the buddhist monks; the positions of presidents johnson and nixon; and the influence of groups like the student mobilization committee and vietnam veterans against the war.

6. When the central high school drama club put on a production of shaw's *pygmalion,* the director xeroxed extra copies of the parts for eliza doolittle and professor henry higgins so he could give them to the understudies.

7. Shaking all over, Bill admitted, "driving on the los angeles freeway is a frightening experience for a kid from brooklyn, even in a bmw."

8. The new united federation of teachers contract guarantees teachers many paid holidays, including columbus day, veterans day, and presidents' day; a week each at christmas and easter; and two full months (july and august) in the summer.

9. The sociology syllabus included the books *beyond the best interests of the child, regulating the poor: the functions of public welfare,* and *a welfare mother;* in anthropology, we were to begin by studying the stone age; and in geology, we were to focus on the Mesozoic era.

10. Winners of the nobel peace prize include lech walesa, former leader of the polish trade union solidarity; the reverend dr. martin luther king jr., founder of the southern christian leadership conference; and archbishop desmond tutu of south africa.

37a Setting Off Titles and Names

Use italics for the titles and names listed in the following box. Most other titles are set off with **quotation marks**.

See 33c

TITLES AND NAMES SET IN ITALICS

Books: *Twilight, Harry Potter and the Deathly Hallows*

Newspapers: the *Washington Post*, the *Philadelphia Inquirer*
(In MLA style, the word *the* is not italicized in titles of newspapers.)

Magazines and Journals: *Rolling Stone, Scientific American*

Online Magazines and Journals: *salon.com, theonion.com*

Web Sites or Home Pages: *urbanlegends.com, movie-mistakes.com*

Pamphlets: *Common Sense*

Films: *The Matrix, Citizen Kane*

Television Programs: *60 Minutes, The Bachelorette, Fear Factor*

Radio Programs: *All Things Considered, A Prairie Home Companion*

Long Poems: *John Brown's Body, The Faerie Queen*

Plays: *Macbeth, A Raisin in the Sun*

Long Musical Works: *Rigoletto, Eroica*

Software Programs: *Microsoft Word, PowerPoint*

Search Engines and Web Browsers: *Google, Safari, Internet Explorer*

Databases: *Academic Search Premier, Expanded Academic ASAP Plus*

Paintings and Sculpture: *Guernica, Pietà*

Ships: *Lusitania,* U.S.S. *Saratoga* (S.S. and U.S.S. are not italicized.)

Trains: *City of New Orleans, The Orient Express*

Aircraft: *The Hindenburg, Enola Gay* (Only particular aircraft, not makes or types such as Piper Cub or Airbus, are italicized.)

Spacecraft: *Challenger, Enterprise*

Note: Names of sacred books, such as the Bible and the Qur'an, and well-known documents, such as the Constitution and the Declaration of Independence, are neither italicized nor placed within quotation marks.

> **CLOSE-UP**
>
> **USING ITALICS**
>
> Current MLA guidelines recommend that you use italics instead of underlining to indicate italics.

37b Setting Off Foreign Words and Phrases

Italics are often used to set off foreign words and phrases that have not become part of the English language.

"*C'est la vie,*" Madeline said when she saw the long line for the concert.

Spirochaeta plicatilis is a corkscrewlike bacterium.

If you are not sure whether a foreign word has been assimilated into English, consult a dictionary.

37c Setting Off Elements Spoken of as Themselves and Terms Being Defined

Use italics to set off letters, numerals, and words that refer to the letters, numerals, and words themselves.

Is that a *p* or a *g*?

I forget the exact address, but I know it has a *3* in it.

Does *through* rhyme with *cough*?

Also use italics to set off words and phrases that you go on to define.

A *closet drama* is a play meant to be read, not performed.

Note: When you quote a dictionary definition, put the word you are defining in italics and the definition itself in quotation marks.

To *infer* means "to draw a conclusion"; to *imply* means "to suggest."

37d Using Italics for Emphasis

Italics may occasionally be used for emphasis.

Initially, poetry might be defined as a kind of language that says *more* and says it *more intensely* than does ordinary language. (Lawrence Perrine, *Sound and Sense*)

However, overuse of italics is distracting. Instead of italicizing, try to indicate emphasis with word choice and sentence structure.

EXERCISE 37.1

Underline to indicate italics where necessary, and delete any italics that are incorrectly used. If a sentence is correct, mark it with a C.

Example: <u>However</u> is a conjunctive adverb, not a coordinating conjunction.

▶ 1. I said Carol, not Darryl.
▶ 2. A *deus ex machina,* an improbable device used to resolve the plot of a fictional work, is used in Charles Dickens's novel Oliver Twist.
▶ 3. He dotted every i and crossed every t.
▶ 4. The Metropolitan Opera's production of Carmen was a tour de force for the principal performers.
▶ 5. *Laissez-faire* is a doctrine holding that government should not interfere with trade.
6. Antidote and anecdote are often confused because their pronunciations are similar.
7. Hawthorne's novels include Fanshawe, The House of the Seven Gables, The Blithedale Romance, and The Scarlet Letter.
8. Words like mailman, policeman, and fireman have been replaced by non-sexist terms like letter carrier, police officer, and firefighter.
9. A classic black tuxedo was considered de rigueur at the charity ball, but Jason preferred to wear his *dashiki.*
10. Thomas Mann's novel Buddenbrooks is a bildungsroman.

Using Hyphens CHAPTER 38

Hyphens have two conventional uses: to break a word at the end of a line and to link words in certain compounds.

38a Breaking a Word at the End of a Line

A computer never breaks a word at the end of a line; if the full word will not fit, it is brought down to the next line. Sometimes, however, you will want to break a word with a hyphen—for example, to fill in excessive space at the end of a line when you want to increase a document's visual appeal.

When you break a word at the end of a line, divide it only between syllables, consulting a dictionary if necessary. Never divide a word at the end of a page, and never hyphenate a one-syllable word. In addition, never leave a single letter at the end of a line or carry only one or two letters to the next line.

See
38b
If you divide a <u>compound word</u> at the end of a line, place the hyphen between the elements of the compound (*snow-mobile*, not *snowmo-bile*).

CLOSE-UP

DIVIDING ELECTRONIC ADDRESSES (URLS)

Never insert a hyphen to divide an electronic address (URL) at the end of a line. (Readers might think the hyphen is part of the address.) MLA style recommends that you break the URL after a slash. If this is not possible, break it in a logical place—after a period, for example—or avoid the problem altogether by moving the entire URL to the next line.

38b Dividing Compound Words

A **compound word** consists of two or more words. Some familiar compound words are always hyphenated: *no-hitter, helter-skelter*. Other compounds are always written as one word: *fireplace, peacetime*. Finally, some compounds are always written as two separate words: *labor relations, bunk bed*. Your dictionary can tell you whether a particular compound requires a hyphen.

GRAMMAR CHECKER

HYPHENATING COMPOUND WORDS

Your grammar checker will highlight certain compound words with incorrect or missing hyphenation and offer suggestions for revision.

---

1 Hyphenating with Compound Adjectives

A **compound adjective** is a series of two or more words that function together as an adjective. When a compound adjective *precedes* the noun it modifies, use hyphens to join its elements.

> The research team tried to use <u>nineteenth-century</u> technology to design a <u>space-age</u> project.

When a compound adjective *follows* the noun it modifies, do not use hyphens to join its elements.

> The three <u>government-operated</u> programs were run smoothly, but the one that was not <u>government operated</u> was short of funds.

Note: A compound adjective formed with an adverb ending in *-ly* is not hyphenated, even when it precedes the noun: *Many <u>upwardly mobile</u> families are on tight budgets.*

Use **suspended hyphens**—hyphens followed by a space or by appropriate punctuation and a space—in a series of compounds that have the same principal elements.

Graduates of two- and four-year colleges were eligible for the grants.

The exam called for sentence-, paragraph-, and essay-length answers.

2 Hyphenating with Certain Prefixes and Suffixes

Use a hyphen between a prefix and a proper noun or proper adjective.

mid-July   pre-Columbian

Use a hyphen to connect the prefixes *all-*, *ex-*, *half-*, *quarter-*, *quasi-*, and *self-* and the suffix *-elect* to a noun.

ex-senator   self-centered   president-elect

Note: The words *selfhood*, *selfish*, and *selfless* do not include hyphens. In these words, *self* is the root, not a prefix.

3 Hyphenating in Compound Numerals and Fractions

Hyphenate compounds that represent numbers below one hundred (even if they are part of a larger number).

the twenty-first century   three hundred sixty-five days

Also hyphenate the written form of a fraction when it modifies a noun.

a two-thirds share of the business

4 Hyphenating for Clarity

Hyphenate to prevent readers from misreading one word for another.

Before we can reform criminals, we must re-form our ideas about prisons.

Hyphenate to avoid certain hard-to-read combinations, such as two *i*'s (*semi-illiterate*) or more than two of the same consonant (*shell-less*).

In most cases, hyphenate between a capital initial and a word when the two combine to form a compound: *A-frame, T-shirt, D-day*.

5 Hyphenating in Coined Compounds

A **coined compound,** one that uses a new combination of words as a unit, requires hyphens.

He looked up with a who-do-you-think-you-are expression.

EXERCISE 38.1

Add hyphens to the compounds in these sentences wherever they are required. Consult a dictionary if necessary.

Example: Alaska was the forty‑ninth state to join the United States.

▶ 1. One of the restaurant's blue plate specials is chicken fried steak.
▶ 2. Virginia and Texas are both right to work states.
▶ 3. He stood on tiptoe to see the near perfect statue, which was well hidden by the security fence.
▶ 4. The five and ten cent store had a self service makeup counter and stocked many up to the minute gadgets.
▶ 5. The so called Saturday night special is opposed by pro gun control groups.
6. He ordered two all beef patties with special sauce, lettuce, cheese, pickles, and onions on a sesame seed bun.
7. The material was extremely thought provoking, but it hardly presented any earth shattering conclusions.
8. The Dodgers Phillies game was rained out, so the long suffering fans left for home.
9. Bone marrow transplants carry the risk of what is known as a graft versus host reaction.
10. The state funded child care program was considered a highly desirable alternative to family day care.

Using Abbreviations CHAPTER 39

Generally speaking, **abbreviations** are not appropriate in college writing except in tables, charts, and works-cited lists. Some abbreviations are acceptable only in scientific, technical, or business writing, or only in a particular discipline. If you have any questions about the appropriateness of a particular abbreviation, check a style manual in your field.

CLOSE-UP

ABBREVIATIONS IN ELECTRONIC COMMUNICATIONS

Like emoticons and acronyms, which are popular in email and instant messages, shorthand abbreviations and symbols—such as GR8 (great) and 2NITE (tonight)—are common in text messages. Although they are acceptable in informal electronic communication, such abbreviations are not appropriate in college writing or in business communication.

39a Abbreviating Titles

Titles before and after proper names are usually abbreviated.

Mr. Homer Simpson   Rep. Loretta Sanchez
Henry Kissinger, PhD   Prof. Elie Weisel

Do not, however, use an abbreviated title without a name.

   doctor
The ~~Dr.~~ diagnosed tuberculosis.

39b Abbreviating Organization Names and Technical Terms

Well-known businesses and government, social, and civic organizations are frequently referred to by capitalized initials. These <u>abbreviations</u> fall into two categories: those in which the initials are pronounced as separate units (MTV) and **acronyms,** in which the initials are pronounced as a word (FEMA). See 29a2

To save space, you may use accepted abbreviations for complex technical terms that are not well known, but be sure to spell out the full term the first time you mention it, followed by the abbreviation in parentheses.

> Citrus farmers have been using ethylene dibromide (EDB), a chemical pesticide, for more than twenty years. Now, however, EDB has contaminated water supplies.

CLOSE-UP

ABBREVIATIONS IN MLA DOCUMENTATION

<u>MLA documentation style</u> requires abbreviations of publishers' company names— for example, **Columbia UP** for *Columbia University Press*—in the works-cited list. Do not, however, use such abbreviations in the body of your paper. See 47a

MLA style also permits the use of abbreviations that designate parts of written works (**ch. 3, sec. 7**)—but only in the works-cited list and parenthetical documentation.

Finally, MLA recommends abbreviating literary works and books of the Bible in parenthetical citations: *Oth.* (*Othello*), **Exod.** (*Exodus*). These words should not be abbreviated in the text of your paper or in the works-cited list.

39c Abbreviating Dates, Times of Day, and Temperatures

Dates, times of day, and temperatures are often abbreviated.

50 BC (*BC* follows the date)   AD 432 (*AD* precedes the date)
6 a.m.   3:03 p.m.
20°C (Centigrade or Celsius)   180°F (Fahrenheit)

Always capitalize *BC* and *AD*. (The alternatives *BCE*, for "before the common era," and *CE*, for "common era," are also capitalized.) Use lowercase letters for *a.m.* and *p.m.*, but use these abbreviations only when they are accompanied by numbers.

> *morning.*
> We will see you in the ~~a.m.~~

Note: Avoid the abbreviation *no.* (written either *no.* or *No.*), except in technical writing, and then use it only before a specific number: *The unidentified substance was labeled <u>no.</u> 52.*

39d   Editing Misused Abbreviations

In college writing, abbreviations are not used in the following cases.

1 Names of Days, Months, or Holidays

Do not abbreviate days of the week, months, or holidays.

> *Saturday, December   Christmas*
> On ~~Sat., Dec.~~ 23, I started my ~~Xmas~~ shopping.

2 Names of Streets and Places

In general, do not abbreviate names of streets and places.

> *Drive   New York City.*
> He lives on Riverside ~~Dr.~~ in ~~NYC.~~

Exceptions: The abbreviation *US* is often acceptable (*US Coast Guard*), as is *DC* in *Washington, DC*. Also permissible are *Mt.* before the name of a mountain (*Mt. Etna*) and *St.* in a place name (*St. Albans*).

3 Names of Academic Subjects

Do not abbreviate names of academic subjects.

> *Psychology   literature*
> ~~Psych.~~ and English ~~lit.~~ are required courses.

4 Names of Businesses

Write company names exactly as the firms themselves write them, including the distinction between the ampersand (&) and the word *and*: *AT&T, Charles Schwab & Co., Inc.* Abbreviations for *company, corporation,* and the like are used only along with a company name.

> *corporation   company*
> The ~~corp.~~ merged with a ~~co.~~ in Ohio.

5 Latin Expressions

Abbreviations of common Latin phrases such as *i.e.* ("that is"), *e.g.* ("for example"), and *etc.* ("and so forth") are not appropriate in college writing except in notes and bibliographic citations.

Other musicians (~~e.g.,~~ *for example,* Bruce Springsteen) have also been influenced by Bob Dylan.

Poe wrote "The Raven," "Annabel Lee," *and other poems.* ~~etc.~~

6 Units of Measurement

In technical and business writing, some units of measurement are abbreviated when they are preceded by a numeral.

The hurricane had winds of 35 mph.

One new hybrid car gets over 50 mpg.

However, MLA style requires that you write out units of measurement and spell out words such as *inches, feet, years, miles, pints, quarts,* and *gallons.*

7 Symbols

The symbols =, +, and # are acceptable in technical and scientific writing but not in nontechnical college writing. The symbols % and $ are acceptable only when used with <u>numerals</u> (15%, $15,000), not with spelled-out numbers.

See
40b4,7

EXERCISE 39.1

Correct any incorrectly used abbreviations in the following sentences, assuming that all are intended for a college audience. If a sentence is correct, mark it with a C.

Example: *Romeo* ~~&~~ *and Juliet* is a play by Shakespeare.

▶ 1. The committee meeting, attended by representatives from Action for Children's Television (ACT) and NOW, Sen. Putnam, & the pres. of ABC, convened at 8 A.M. on Mon. Feb. 24 at the YWCA on Germantown Ave.

▶ 2. An econ. prof. was suspended after he encouraged his students to speculate on securities issued by a corp. under investigation by the SEC.

▶ 3. Benjamin Spock, who wrote *Baby and Child Care,* was a respected dr. known throughout the USA.

▶ 4. The FDA banned the use of Red Dye no. 2 in food in 1976, but other food additives are still in use.

▶ 5. The Rev. Dr. Martin Luther King Jr., leader of the SCLC, led the famous Selma, Ala., march.

6. Wm. Golding, a novelist from the U.K., won the Nobel Prize in lit.
7. The adult education center, financed by a major computer corp., offers courses in basic subjects like introductory bio. and tech. writing as well as teaching HTML and XML.
8. All the brothers in the fraternity agreed to write to Pres. Dexter appealing their disciplinary probation under Ch. 4, Sec. 3, of the IFC constitution.
9. A 4 qt. (i.e., 1 gal.) container is needed to hold the salt solution.
10. According to Prof. Morrison, all those taking the exam should bring two sharpened no. 2 pencils to the St. Joseph's University auditorium on Sat.

Using Numbers

CHAPTER 40

Convention determines when to use a **numeral** (22) and when to spell out a number (twenty-two). Numerals are commonly used in scientific and technical writing and in journalism, but they are used less often in the humanities.

Note: The guidelines in this chapter are based on the *MLA Handbook for Writers of Research Papers,* 7th ed. (2009). APA style, however, requires that all numbers below ten be spelled out if they do not represent specific measurements and that numbers ten and above be expressed in numerals.

40a Spelled-Out Numbers versus Numerals

Unless a number falls into one of the categories listed in **40b,** spell it out if you can do so *in one or two words.*

The Hawaiian alphabet has only <u>twelve</u> letters.

Class size stabilized at <u>twenty-eight</u> students.

The subsidies are expected to total about <u>two million</u> dollars.

Numbers *more than two words* long are expressed in figures.

The dietitian prepared <u>125</u> sample menus.

The developer of the community purchased <u>300,000</u> doorknobs and <u>153,000</u> faucets.

Never begin a sentence with a numeral. If necessary, reword the sentence.

Faulty: 250 students are currently enrolled in World History 106.

Revised: Current enrollment in World History 106 is 250 students.

Note: When one number immediately precedes another in a sentence, spell out the first, and use a numeral for the second: *five 3-quart containers.*

> **GRAMMAR CHECKER**
>
> **SPELLED-OUT NUMBERS VERSUS NUMERALS**
>
> Your grammar checker will often highlight numerals in your writing and suggest that you spell them out. Before clicking Change, be sure that the number does not fall into one of the categories listed in **40b**.

40b Conventional Uses of Numerals

1 Addresses

1920 Walnut Street, Philadelphia, PA 19103

2 Dates

January 15, 1929   1914–1919

3 Exact Times

9:16   10 a.m. (or 10:00 a.m.)

Exceptions: Spell out times of day when they are used with *o'clock: eleven o'clock,* not <u>11</u> *o'clock.* Also spell out times expressed in quarter and half hours: *half-past eight, a quarter to ten.*

4 Exact Sums of Money

$25.11 $6,752.00

Note: Always use a numeral (not a spelled-out number) with a $ symbol. You may spell out a round sum of money if you use sums infrequently in your paper, provided you can do so in two or three words: *five dollars; two thousand dollars.*

5 Divisions of Written Works

Use arabic (not roman) numerals for chapter and volume numbers; acts, scenes, and lines of plays; chapters and verses of the Bible; and line numbers of long poems.

6 Measurements before an Abbreviation or Symbol

12″   55 mph
32°   15 cc

7 Percentages and Decimals

80%   3.14

Note: You may spell out a percentage (*eighty percent*) if you use percentages infrequently in your paper, provided the percentage can be expressed in two or three words. Always use a numeral (not a spelled-out number) with a % symbol.

8 Ratios, Scores, and Statistics

See Ch. 48 In a paper that follows <u>APA</u> style, use numerals for numbers presented as a comparison.

Children preferred Fun Flakes over Graino by a ratio of 20 to 1.

The Orioles defeated the Phillies 6 to 0.

The median age of the patients was 42; the mean age was 40.

9 Identification Numbers

Route 66   Track 8   Channel 12

Note: When writing out large numbers, insert a comma every three digits from the right, beginning after the third digit.

3,000   25,000   6,751,098

Do not, however, use commas in four-digit page and line numbers, addresses, or year numbers.

page 1202   3741 Laurel Ave.   1968

EXERCISE 40.1

Following MLA guidelines, revise the use of numbers in these sentences, making sure usage is correct and consistent. If a sentence uses numbers correctly, mark it with a C.

Example: The Empire State Building is ~~one hundred and two~~ 102 stories high.

▶ 1. 1984, a novel by George Orwell, is set in a totalitarian society.

▶ 2. The English placement examination included a 30-minute personal-experience essay, a 45-minute expository essay, and a 150-item objective test of grammar and usage.

▶ 3. In a control group of two hundred forty-seven patients, almost three out of four suffered serious adverse reactions to the new drug.

▶ 4. Before the Thirteenth Amendment to the Constitution, slaves were counted as 3/5 of a person.

▶ 5. The intensive membership drive netted 2,608 new members and additional dues of over 5 thousand dollars.

6. They had only 2 choices: either they could take the yacht at Pier Fourteen, or they could return home to the penthouse at Twenty-seven Harbor View Drive.

7. The atomic number of lithium is three.

8. Approximately 3 hundred thousand schoolchildren in District 6 were given hearing and vision examinations between May third and June 26.

9. The United States was drawn into the war by the Japanese attack on Pearl Harbor on December seventh, 1941.

10. An upper-middle-class family can spend over 250,000 dollars to raise each child up to age 18.

PART 7

Doing Research and Documenting Sources

Doing Research and Documenting Sources

Research is the systematic investigation of a topic outside your own knowledge and experience. However, doing research means more than just reading other people's ideas. When you undertake a research project, you become involved in a process that requires you to **think critically**: to evaluate and interpret the ideas explored in your sources and to develop ideas of your own. Although the research process is much richer and more complex than suggested by the list of activities in the following box, your research will be most efficient if you follow a systematic process. (As an added benefit, following such a process will make it easier for you to identify and correct unintended **plagiarism**.)

See Ch. 6

See Ch. 46

THE RESEARCH PROCESS		
Activity	**Date Due**	**Date Completed**
Move from an Assignment to a Topic, **41a**	_____	_____
Do Exploratory Research and Formulate a Research Question, **41b**	_____	_____
Assemble a Working Bibliography, **41c**	_____	_____
Develop a Tentative Thesis, **41d**	_____	_____
Do Focused Research, **41e**	_____	_____
Take Notes, **41f**	_____	_____
Fine-Tune Your Thesis, **41g**	_____	_____
Outline Your Paper, **41h**	_____	_____
Draft Your Paper, **41i**	_____	_____
Revise Your Paper, **41j**	_____	_____
Prepare Your Final Draft, **41k**	_____	_____

41a Moving from Assignment to Topic

1 Understanding Your Assignment

Every research paper begins with an assignment. Before you can find a direction for your research, you must be sure you understand the exact requirements of the specific assignment.

UNDERSTANDING YOUR ASSIGNMENT

Asking questions like the following will help you focus on your assignment:

❑ Has your instructor provided a list of possible topics, or are you expected to select a topic on your own?

❑ Is your purpose to explain, to persuade, or to do something else?

❑ Is your audience your instructor? Your fellow students? Both? Someone else?

❑ Can you assume that your audience knows a lot (or just a little) about your topic?

❑ When is the completed research paper due?

❑ About how long should it be?

❑ Will you be given a specific research schedule to follow, or are you expected to set your own schedule?

❑ Is peer review permitted? Is it encouraged? If so, at what stages of the writing process?

❑ Does your instructor expect you to prepare a formal outline?

❑ Are instructor–student conferences required? Are they encouraged?

❑ Will your instructor review notes, outlines, or drafts with you at regular intervals?

❑ Does your instructor require you to keep a research notebook?

❑ What manuscript guidelines and documentation style are you to follow?

❑ What help is available to you—from your instructor, from other students, from experts on your topic, from community resources, from your library staff?

In Chapters 2–4 of this text, you followed the writing process of Rebecca James as she planned, drafted, and revised a short essay for her first-semester composition course. In her second-semester composition class, Rebecca was given the following assignment:

> Write a ten- to fifteen-page research paper that takes a position on any issue related to the Internet. Keep a research notebook that traces your progress.

Throughout this chapter, you will see examples of the work Rebecca did as she completed this assignment.

2 Choosing a Topic

Once you understand the requirements and scope of your assignment, you need to decide on a topic. In many cases, your instructor will help you choose a topic, either by providing a list of suitable topics or by suggesting a general subject area—for example, a famous trial, an event that happened on the day you were born, a problem on college campuses. Keep in mind, though, that you will still need to narrow your topic to one you can write about: one trial, one event, one problem.

If your instructor requires you to select a topic on your own, you should consider several possible topics and weigh both their suitability for research and your interest in them. You decide on a topic for your research paper in much the same way you decide on a topic for a short essay: you read, brainstorm, talk to people, and ask questions. Specifically, you talk to friends and family, coworkers, and perhaps your instructor; read magazines and newspapers; take stock of your interests; consider possible topics suggested by your other courses (historical events, scientific developments, and so on); and, of course, browse the Internet. (Your search engine's <u>subject guides</u> can be particularly helpful to you as you look for a promising topic for your research or try to narrow a broad subject area.)

See 43a2

3 Starting a Research Notebook

Keeping a **research notebook,** a combination journal of your reactions and log of your progress, is an important part of the research process. A research notebook maps out your direction and keeps you on track; throughout the research process, it helps you define and redefine the boundaries of your assignment.

In your research notebook (which can be an actual notebook or a computer file), you can record lists of things to do, sources to check, leads to follow up on, appointments, possible community contacts, questions to which you would like to find answers, stray ideas, possible thesis statements or titles, and so on. (Be sure to date your entries and to check off and date work completed.)

As she began her research, Rebecca set up a computer file in which she planned to keep all the electronic documents for her paper. In a *Word* document that she labeled "Research Notebook," she outlined her schedule and explored some preliminary ideas.

Here is an example of an entry from Rebecca's research notebook in which she discusses how she chose a topic for her research paper.

Excerpt from Research Notebook

Last semester, I wrote an essay about using *Wikipedia* for college-level research. In class, we'd read *Wikipedia*'s statement "Researching with *Wikipedia*," which helped me to understand *Wikipedia*'s specific limitations for college research. In that paper, I used a sample *Wikipedia* entry related to my accounting class to support my points about the site's strengths and weaknesses. For this research paper, which has to be about the Internet, I want to expand the paper I wrote for Professor Burks's first-semester composition course about using *Wikipedia* for college research assignments. This time, I want to talk more about the academic debate surrounding

Wikipedia. (I asked Professor Burks if I could use this topic for her class this semester, and she said I could. In fact, she really liked the idea.)

EXERCISE 41.1

Enter information about your assignment and your schedule in your research notebook. Next, using your instructor's guidelines for selecting a research topic, begin thinking of possible topics for your paper. Then, explore some preliminary ideas about these topics in your research notebook, and decide which one you want to write about.

41b Doing Exploratory Research and Formulating a Research Question

During **exploratory research,** you develop an overview of your topic, searching the Internet and perhaps also looking through general reference works such as encyclopedias, bibliographies, and specialized dictionaries (either in print or online). Your goal at this stage is to formulate a **research question** that you want your research paper to answer. A research question helps you to decide which sources to seek out, which to examine first, which to examine in depth, and which to skip entirely. (The answer to your research question will be your paper's <u>thesis statement</u>.)

See 41d

Rebecca began her exploratory research with a preliminary search on *Google* (see Figure 41.1). When she entered the keywords *Wikipedia and*

FIGURE 41.1 *Google* search engine.

academia, they generated millions of hits, but she wasn't overwhelmed. She had learned in her library orientation that the first ten to twenty items would be most useful to her because the results of a *Google* search are listed in order of relevance to the topic, with the most relevant sites listed first. After a quick review of these items, she moved on to a keyword search on *Info-Trac College Edition,* a database her library subscribed to (see Figure 41.2).

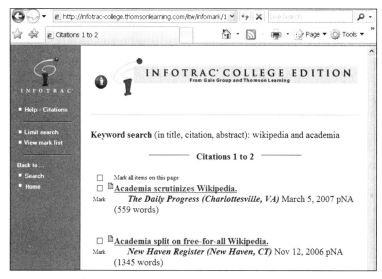

FIGURE 41.2 *InfoTrac College Edition.*

When she finished her exploratory research, Rebecca decided on the following research question:

> What are the most recent developments in the academic debate surrounding *Wikipedia*?

41c Assembling a Working Bibliography

During your exploratory research, you begin to assemble a **working bibliography** for your paper. This working bibliography will be the basis for your works-cited list, which will include all the sources you cite in your paper. See 47a2

As you consider each potential source, record full and accurate bibliographic information in a separate computer file designated "Bibliography" (or, if you prefer, on individual index cards). Keep records of interviews (including telephone and email interviews), meetings, lectures, films, and electronic sources as well as articles and books. For each source, include not only basic identifying details—such as the date of an interview, the call number of a library book, the URL of an Internet source and the date you downloaded it, or the author of an article accessed from a database—but also a brief evaluation that includes comments about the kind of information the source contains, the amount of information offered, its relevance to your topic, and its limitations.

CLOSE-UP

ASSEMBLING A WORKING BIBLIOGRAPHY

As you record bibliographic information for your sources, include the following information:

♦ **Article** Author(s); title of article (in quotation marks); title of journal (italicized in computer file, underlined on index card); volume and issue numbers; date; inclusive page numbers; medium; date downloaded (if applicable); URL (if applicable); brief evaluation

♦ **Book** Author(s); title (italicized in computer file, underlined on index card); call number (for future reference); city of publication; publisher; date of publication; medium; brief evaluation

---

Figure 41.3 shows two of the sources Rebecca found as she put together her working bibliography.

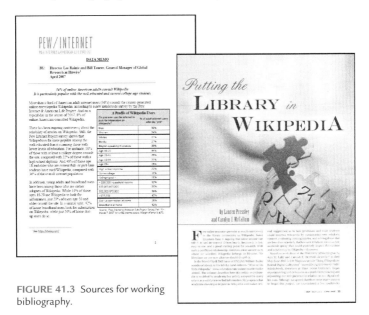

FIGURE 41.3 Sources for working bibliography.

On the facing page are examples of records Rebecca kept for her working bibliography. In the library, she copied her source information on index cards. When she returned to her dorm room, she transferred the information from her cards into a computer file.

Information for Working Bibliography (on Index Card)

Authors —— Rainie, Lee, and Bill Tancer

Title —— "Online Activities & Pursuits: Wikipedia Users"

Publication —— Data memo
information
and medium
Web

24 Apr. 2007

Accessed April 7, 2009

Evaluation —— Reports on nationwide survey by the Pew Internet & American Life Project on Wikipedia users

Information for Working Bibliography (in Computer File)

Author — Badke, William

Title — "What to Do with *Wikipedia*"

Publication — *Online* Mar.-Apr. 2008: 48-50. *Academic Search Elite*. Web.
information
and medium
Accessed April 7, 2009.

Evaluation — Argues that it's important for the academic community to be involved in *Wikipedia*'s development.

EXERCISE 41.2

Do some exploratory research to find a research question for your paper, carefully evaluating the relevance and usefulness of each source. Then, compile a working bibliography. When you have finished, reevaluate the usefulness of your sources and plan additional research if necessary.

41d Developing a Tentative Thesis

Your **tentative thesis** is a preliminary statement of the main point you think your research will support. This statement, which you will eventually refine into your paper's <u>thesis statement</u>, should answer your research question. Rebecca's progress from assignment to tentative thesis appears below.

See 41g

Assignment	Topic	Research Question
Issue related to the Internet	Using *Wikipedia* for college-level research	What are the most recent developments in the academic debate surrounding *Wikipedia*?

Tentative Thesis: The debate surrounding *Wikipedia* has helped people in the academic community to consider how college-level research has changed in recent years.

Because your tentative thesis suggests the specific direction your research will take as well as the scope and emphasis of your argument, it can help you generate a list of the main points you plan to develop in your paper. This list can help you narrow the focus of your research so you can zero in on a few specific categories to explore as you read and take notes.

Rebecca used her tentative thesis to help her generate the following list of points to explore further.

Tentative thesis: The debate surrounding *Wikipedia* has helped people in the academic community to consider how college-level research has changed in recent years.

- Give background about *Wikipedia;* explain its benefits and drawbacks.
- Talk about who uses *Wikipedia* and for what purposes.
- Explain possible future enhancements to the site.
- Explain college professors' resistance to *Wikipedia.*
- Talk about efforts made by librarians and others to incorporate *Wikipedia* into academic research.

EXERCISE 41.3

Following your instructor's guidelines, develop a tentative thesis for your research paper, and compile a list of the points you plan to develop.

41e Doing Focused Research

During exploratory research, you consult general reference works to get an overview of your topic. During **focused research,** however, you consult periodical articles, books, and other sources (in print and online) to find the specific information—facts, examples, statistics, definitions, quotations—you need to support your points. Once you have decided on a tentative thesis and made a list of the points you plan to explore, you are ready to begin your focused research.

1 Reading Sources

As you look for information, try to explore as many sources as possible. It makes sense to examine more sources than you actually intend to use so that you can proceed even if one or more of your sources turns out to be biased, outdated, unreliable, superficial, or irrelevant—in other words, not suitable.

As you explore various sources, quickly evaluate each source's potential usefulness. For example, if your source is a journal article, read the abstract; if your source is a book, skim the table of contents and the index. Then, if an article or a section of a book seems useful, photocopy it for future reference. As you explore sources online, you may find you have multiple windows open at once. If this is the case, be especially careful not to paste material you see onscreen directly into your paper. (This practice can lead to plagiarism.) Instead, print out promising material (or send it to yourself as an email attachment) so you can evaluate it further later on. (For information on evaluating print and electronic sources, **see 42c** and **43d.**)

See Ch. 46

2 Balancing Primary and Secondary Sources

During your focused research, you will encounter both <u>primary sources</u> (original documents and observations) and <u>secondary sources</u> (interpretations of original documents and observations).

See 42b4

For some research projects, primary sources are essential; however, most research projects in the humanities rely heavily on secondary sources, which provide scholars' insights and interpretations. Remember, though, that the further you get from the primary source, the more chances exist for inaccuracies caused by misinterpretations or distortions.

41f Taking Notes

As you locate information in the library and on the Internet, take notes (either by hand or on a computer) to create a record of exactly what you found and where you found it.

1 Recording Source Information

Each piece of information you record in your notes (whether <u>summarized</u>, <u>paraphrased</u>, or <u>quoted</u> from your sources) should be accompanied by a short descriptive heading that indicates its relevance to one of the points you will develop in your paper. Because you will use these headings to guide you as you organize your notes, you should make them as specific as possible. For example, labeling every note for a paper on *Wikipedia* **Wikipedia** or **Internet** will not prove very helpful later on. More focused headings—for instance, *Wikipedia's* **growth potential** or **college professors' objections**—will be much more useful.

See Ch. 44

Also include brief comments that make clear your reasons for recording the information. These comments (enclosed in brackets so you will know they are your own ideas, not those of your source) should establish the purpose of your note—what you think it can explain, support, clarify, describe, or contradict—and perhaps suggest its relationship to other notes or other sources. Any questions you have about the information or its source can also be included in your comment.

Finally, each note should fully and accurately identify the source of the information you are recording. You do not have to write out the complete citation, but you do have to include enough information to identify your source. For example, **Rainie and Tancer** would be enough to send you back to your working bibliography card or file, where you would be able to find the complete documentation for the authors' online memo "Online Activities and Pursuits: *Wikipedia* Users."

Following are examples of notes that Rebecca took.

Notes (on Index Card)

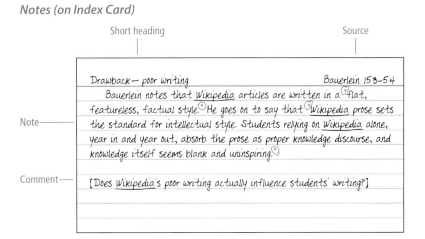

Short heading   Source

Note ———

Comment ———

Drawback — poor writing   Bauerlein 153–54
    Bauerlein notes that Wikipedia articles are written in a "flat,
featureless, factual style." He goes on to say that "Wikipedia prose sets
the standard for intellectual style. Students relying on Wikipedia alone,
year in and year out, absorb the prose as proper knowledge discourse, and
knowledge itself seems blank and uninspiring."

[Does Wikipedia's poor writing actually influence students' writing?]

Notes (in Computer File)

Short heading   Source

Note
(quotation) ———

Comment ———

Note
(paraphrase) ———

Growth potential   Spinellis and Louridas 71

"the apparently chaotic *Wikipedia* development process delivers
growth at a sustainable rate."

**[Does this mean *Wikipedia* will eventually become a reliable
research source?]**

Unreliability—vandalism   Spinellis and Louridas 68

In 2006, 11% of *Wikipedia*'s articles were vandalized at least once,
but only 0.13% of at-risk articles were locked.

Comment — [Are *Wikipedia*'s current control measures sufficient to prevent vandalism?]

Benefit—stubs   Spinellis and Louridas 71

Note
(summary)
"Stub" articles have the potential to become complete articles. Data show that, over time, the coverage of various topics in *Wikipedia* tends to even out.

Comment — [Do the benefits of stubs outweigh their drawbacks?]

CLOSE-UP

TAKING NOTES

When you take notes, your goal is flexibility: you want to be able to arrange and rearrange information easily and efficiently as your paper takes shape.

If you take notes at your computer, type each individual note (accompanied by source information) under a specific heading rather than listing all information from a single source under the same heading, and be sure to divide notes from one another with extra space or horizontal lines, as illustrated above. (As you revise, you can move notes around so notes on the same topic are grouped together.)

If you take notes by hand, use the time-tested index-card system, taking care to write on only one side of the card and to use a separate index card for each individual note rather than running several notes together on a single card. (Later, you can enter the information from these notes into your computer file.)

CHECKLIST

TAKING NOTES

❏ **Identify the source of each piece of information.**

❏ **Include everything now that you will need later** to understand your note—names, dates, places, connections with other notes—and to remember why you recorded it.

❏ **Distinguish quotations from paraphrases and summaries and your own ideas from those of your sources.** If you copy a source's words, place them in quotation marks. (If you take notes by hand, circle the quotation marks; if you type your notes, put the quotation marks in boldface.) If you write down your own ideas, enclose them in brackets—and, if you are typing, boldface them as well. These techniques will help you avoid accidental plagiarism in your paper.

See
Ch. 46

(*continued*)

TAKING NOTES (*continued*)

❏ **Put an author's ideas into your own words whenever possible,** summarizing and paraphrasing material as well as adding your own observations and analyses.

❏ **Copy quoted material accurately,** using the exact words, spelling, punctuation marks, and capitalization of the original.

❏ **Never paste information from a source directly into your paper.** This practice can lead to plagiarism.

ESL TIP

Taking notes in English (rather than in your native language) will make it easier for you to transfer the notes into a draft of your paper. However, you may find it faster and more effective to use your native language when writing your own comments about each note.

2 **Managing Photocopies and Printouts**

Much of the information you gather will be in the form of photocopies (of articles, book pages, and so on) and material printed out from the Internet or from a library database. Learning to manage this source information efficiently will save you a lot of time.

First, do not use the ease of copying and downloading as an excuse to postpone decisions about the usefulness of your sources. After all, you can easily accumulate so many pages that it will be almost impossible for you to keep track of all your information.

Also keep in mind that photocopies and printouts are just raw material, not information that you have already interpreted and evaluated. Making copies of sources is only the first step in the process of taking thorough, careful notes. You still have to evaluate, paraphrase, and summarize your sources' ideas and make connections among them.

Moreover, photocopies and printouts do not have much flexibility. For example, a single page of text may include information that should be earmarked for several different sections of your paper. This lack of flexibility makes it almost impossible for you to arrange source material into any meaningful order. Just as you would with any source, you will have to take notes on the information you read. These notes will give you the flexibility you need to write your paper.

See Ch. 46

CLOSE-UP

AVOIDING PLAGIARISM

To avoid the possibility of accidental **plagiarism,** be sure to keep all downloaded material in a separate file—not in your Notes file. After you read this material and decide how to use it, you can move the information you use into your Notes file (along with full source information).

CHECKLIST

WORKING WITH PHOTOCOPIES AND COMPUTER PRINTOUTS

To get the most out of photocopies and material printed out from the Internet, follow these guidelines:

❑ Record full and accurate source information, including the inclusive page numbers, electronic address (URL), and any other relevant information, on the first page of each copy.

❑ Clip or staple together consecutive pages of a single source.

❑ Do not photocopy or print out a source without reminding yourself—*in writing*—why you are doing so. In pencil or on removable self-stick notes, record your initial responses to the source's ideas, jot down cross-references to other works or notes, and highlight important sections.

❑ Photocopying can be time-consuming and expensive, so try to avoid copying material that is only marginally relevant to your paper.

❑ Keep photocopies and printouts in a separate file so you will be able to find them when you need them.

EXERCISE 41.4

Begin focused research for your paper, reading sources carefully and taking notes as you read. Your notes should include paraphrase, summary, and your own observations and analysis as well as quotations.

41g Fine-Tuning Your Thesis

After you have finished your focused research and note-taking, you should be ready to refine your tentative thesis into a carefully worded statement that expresses a conclusion your research can support. This <u>thesis state-</u> <u>ment</u> should be more precise than your tentative thesis, accurately conveying the direction, emphasis, and scope of your paper.

See 3a–b

Compare Rebecca's tentative thesis with her final thesis statement.

Tentative Thesis	Thesis Statement
The debate surrounding *Wikipedia* has helped people in the academic community to consider how college-level research has changed in recent years.	Despite its contentious nature, the debate surrounding *Wikipedia* has overall been a positive development because it has led the academic community to confront the evolving nature of college-level research in the twenty-first century.

EXERCISE 41.5

Review the tentative thesis you developed for Exercise 41.3. Carefully read all the notes you have collected during your focused research, and develop a thesis statement for your paper.

41h Constructing an Outline

Once you have a thesis statement, you are ready to make an outline to guide you as you write your rough draft.

A formal outline is different from a list of the main points you tentatively plan to develop in your paper. A **formal outline**—which may be either a **topic outline** or a **sentence outline**—includes all the points you will develop. It indicates both the exact order in which you will present your ideas and the relationship between main points and supporting details.

Note: The outline you construct at this stage is only a guide for you to follow as you draft your paper. During the revision process, you may want to construct another outline to help you check the logic of your paper's organization.

CHECKLIST

CONSTRUCTING A FORMAL OUTLINE

When you construct a formal outline for your research paper, follow these guidelines:

❑ Write your thesis statement at the top of the page.

❑ Review your notes to make sure each note expresses only one general idea. If this is not the case, recopy any unrelated information to create a separate note.

❑ Check that the heading for each note specifically characterizes that note's information. If it does not, change the heading.

❑ Sort your notes according to their headings, keeping a miscellaneous file for notes that do not seem to fit into any category. Irrelevant notes, those unrelated to your paper's thesis, should be set aside (but not discarded).

❑ Check your categories for balance. If most of your notes fall into just one or two categories, revise some of your headings to create narrower, more focused categories. If you have only one or two notes in a category, you may need to do additional research or treat that topic only briefly (or not at all).

❑ Organize the individual notes within each group, adding more specific subheads to your headings as needed. Arrange your notes in an order that highlights the most important points and subordinates lesser ones.

❑ Decide on a logical order in which to discuss your paper's major points.

❑ Construct your formal outline, using divisions and subdivisions that correspond to your headings.

❑ Review your completed outline to make sure you have not placed too much emphasis on a relatively unimportant idea, ordered ideas illogically, or created sections that overlap with others.

Rebecca made the following topic outline to guide her as she wrote the first draft of her research paper.

Formal (Topic) Outline

<u>Thesis statement</u>: Despite its contentious nature, the debate surrounding *Wikipedia* has overall been a positive development because it has led the academic community to confront the evolving nature of college-level research in the twenty-first century.

I. Definition of wiki and explanation of *Wikipedia*
   A. Fast and easy
   B. Range of topics
II. Introduction to *Wikipedia*'s drawbacks
   A. Warnings on "Researching with *Wikipedia*" page
   B. Middlebury College history department example
III. *Wikipedia*'s unreliability
   A. Lack of citations, factual inaccuracy, and bias
   B. Vandalism
IV. *Wikipedia*'s poor writing
   A. *Wikipedia*'s coding system
   B. Bauerlein's point about *Wikipedia*'s influence on students' writing
V. *Wikipedia*'s popularity and benefits
   A. Pew report statistic and table
   B. Comprehensive abstracts, internal and external links, and current and comprehensive bibliographies
VI. *Wikipedia*'s benefits over professionally edited online encyclopedias
   A. Current and popular culture topics
   B. "Stub" articles
VII. *Wikipedia*'s growth potential
   A. *Wikipedia*'s control measures
   B. Users as editors
   C. "Talk" page
VIII. Spinellis and Louridas
   A. Summary of their study
   B. Graph showing *Wikipedia*'s topic coverage
IX. Academia's reluctance to work with *Wikipedia*
   A. Academics' failure to keep up with technology
   B. Academics' qualifications to improve *Wikipedia*

X. Librarians' efforts to use and improve *Wikipedia*

    A. Badke and Bennington's support of *Wikipedia*

    B. Pressley, McCallum, and other librarians' success stories

EXERCISE 41.6

Carefully review your notes. Then, sort and group them into categories, and construct a topic outline for your paper.

CLOSE-UP

OUTLINING

Before you begin writing, create a separate file for each major section of your outline. Then, copy your notes into these files in the order in which you intend to use them.

    Make sure that you name the files clearly for later reference. Each file name should include a reference to the class and assignment for which it was written. For instance, Rebecca's file for the section of her English 102 essay on *Wikipedia*'s growth potential is called "102 Wikipedia Growth Potential." The individual files relating to this paper are all collected in a folder titled "Eng 102 Wikipedia." By organizing your files in this way, you can print out each file as you need it and use it as a guide as you write.

41i　Writing a Rough Draft

See 4a
When you are ready to write your **rough draft,** check to be sure you have arranged your notes in the order in which you intend to use them. Follow your outline as you write, using your notes as needed. As you draft, you can write notes to yourself in brackets, jotting down questions and identifying points that need further clarification and areas that need more development.

    As you move along, leave space for material you plan to add, and identify phrases or whole sections that you think you may later decide to move or delete. In other words, lay the groundwork for revision.

    As your draft takes shape, be sure to supply transitions between sentences and paragraphs to indicate how your points are related. To make it easy for you to revise later on, you might want to triple-space your draft. Be careful to copy source information fully and accurately on this and every subsequent draft, placing documentation as close as possible to the material it identifies.

1　Shaping the Parts of the Paper

Like any other essay, a research paper has an introduction, a body, and a conclusion. In your rough draft, as in your outline, you focus on the body of your paper. Don't spend too much time planning your introduction or conclusion at this stage; your ideas will change as you write, and you will need to revise and expand your opening and closing paragraphs later to reflect those changes.

Introduction   In your **introduction,** you identify your topic and establish how you will approach it, perhaps presenting an overview of the problem you will discuss or summarizing research already done on your topic. Your introduction also includes your thesis statement, which presents the position you will support in the rest of the paper.

See 5e2

Body   As you draft the **body** of your paper, you lead readers through your discussion with strong topic sentences that correspond to the divisions of your outline.

See 5a1

> Without a professional editorial board to oversee its development, *Wikipedia* has several shortcomings that ultimately limit its trustworthiness as a research source.

You can also use headings if they are a convention of the discipline in which you are writing.

See 12b

> *Wikipedia's* Advantages
>
> *Wikipedia* has advantages over other, professionally edited online encyclopedias.

At this stage, carefully worded topic sentences and headings will help you keep your discussion under control.

Use different patterns of development to shape the individual sections of your paper, and be sure to connect your sentences and paragraphs with clear transitions. If necessary, connect two sections of your paper with a transitional paragraph that shows their relationship.

See 5d

See 5e1

Conclusion   In the **conclusion** of your research paper, you may want to restate your thesis. This is especially important in a long paper because by the time your readers get to the end, they may have lost sight of your paper's main idea. Your conclusion can also include a summary of your key points, a call for action, or perhaps an apt quotation. (Remember, however, that in your rough draft, your concluding paragraph is usually very brief.)

See 5e3

2   Working Source Material into Your Paper

In the body of your paper, you evaluate and interpret your sources, comparing different ideas and assessing various points of view. As a writer, your job is to draw your own conclusions, blending information from various sources into a paper that coherently and forcefully presents your own original viewpoint.

See
44d Be sure to **integrate source material** smoothly into your paper, clearly and accurately identifying the relationships among various sources (and between those sources' ideas and your own). If two sources present conflicting interpretations, you should be especially careful to use precise language and accurate transitions to make the contrast apparent (for instance, **Although some academics believe that** *Wikipedia* **should not be a part of college-level research, Pressley and McCallum argue . . .**). When two sources agree, you should make this clear (for example, **Like Badke, Bennington claims . . .** or **Spinellis and Louridas's findings support Pressley and McCallum's point**). Such phrasing will provide a context for your own comments and conclusions. If different sources present complementary information about a subject, blend details from the sources carefully, keeping track of which details come from which source.

3 Integrating Visuals

See
12d Photographs, diagrams, graphs, and other **visuals** can be very useful in your research paper because they can provide additional support for the points you make. You may be able to create a visual on your own (for example, by taking a photograph or creating a bar graph). You may also be able to scan an appropriate visual from a book or magazine or access an image database.

When Rebecca searched *Google*'s image database, she was able to find a visual to include in her paper (see Figure 41.4).

FIGURE 41.4 Image database search results.

EXERCISE 41.7

Write a rough draft of your paper, being careful to incorporate source material and visuals smoothly and to record source information accurately. Begin by drafting the section for which you have the most material.

41j Revising Your Drafts

1 Outlining

As you review your drafts, you follow the <u>revision</u> procedures that apply to any paper. In addition, you should review the questions in the checklist on pages 349–50, which apply specifically to research papers.

See 4b–c

A good way to begin revising is to make a formal **outline** of your draft to check the logic of its organization and the relationships among sections. When Rebecca began to revise, the first thing she did was construct a **sentence outline** to check the structure of her paper. An excerpt from her sentence outline is shown below.

See 4c4, 41h

Sentence Outline (Excerpt)

Thesis statement: Despite its contentious nature, the debate surrounding *Wikipedia* has overall been a positive development because it has led the academic community to confront the evolving nature of college-level research in the twenty-first century.

  I. *Wikipedia* is the most popular wiki.

   A. Users can edit existing articles and add new articles using *Wikipedia*'s editing tools.

   B. *Wikipedia* has grown into a huge collection of articles on a vast range of topics.

 II. *Wikipedia* has several shortcomings that ultimately limit its trustworthiness as a research source.

   A. Many *Wikipedia* articles lack reliability.

    1. Many *Wikipedia* articles do not supply citations to the sources that support their claims.

    2. *Wikipedia* articles can be factually inaccurate, biased, and even targeted for vandalism.

2 Instructor's Comments

Your instructor's revision suggestions can come in a conference or in handwritten comments on your paper. Your instructor can also use *Microsoft*

Word's Comment tool to make comments electronically on a draft that you email to him or her. When you revise, you can incorporate these suggestions into your paper, as Rebecca did.

Draft with Instructor's Comments (Excerpt)

Emory University English professor Mark Bauerlein asserts that *Wikipedia* articles are written in a "flat, featureless, factual style" (153). *Wikipedia* has instituted a coding system in which it labels the shortcomings of its less-developed articles, but a warning about an article's poor writing style is likely to go unnoticed by the typical user.

> **Comment [JB1]:**
> You need a transition sentence before this one to show that this ¶ is about a new idea. See 5b2.

> **Comment [JB2]:**
> Wordy. See 17a.

Revision Incorporating Instructor's Suggestions

Because their content is open to public editing, *Wikipedia* articles also often suffer from poor writing. Emory University English professor Mark Bauerlein asserts that *Wikipedia* articles are written in a "flat, featureless, factual style" (153). *Wikipedia* has instituted a coding system to label the shortcomings of its less developed articles, but a warning about an article's poor writing style is likely to go unnoticed by the typical user.

 3 Peer Review

See 4c2 Feedback you get from <u>peer review</u>—other students' comments, handwritten or electronic—can also help you revise. As you incorporate your classmates' suggestions, as well as your own changes and any suggested by your instructor, you can use *Microsoft Word*'s Track Changes tool to help you keep track of the revisions you make on your draft.

Following are two versions of an excerpt from Rebecca's paper. The first version includes comments (inserted with *Microsoft Word*'s Comment tool) from two peer reviewers. The second uses the Track Changes tool to show the revisions Rebecca made in response to these comments.

Draft with Peer Reviewers' Comments (Excerpt)

Because users can update articles in real time from any location, *Wikipedia* offers up-to-the-minute coverage of political and cultural events as well as timely information on popular culture topics that receive little or no attention from other sources. Even when the available information on a particular topic is sparse, *Wikipedia* allows users to create "stub"

> **Comment [RS1]:** I think you need a better transition here.

> **Comment [TG2]:** I think an example here would really help.

> **Comment [DL3]:** I agree. Maybe talk about a useful *Wikipedia* article you found recently.

articles, which provide minimal information that users can expand over time. According to a 2008 study, approximately 20% of *Wikipedia*'s articles are classified as stubs. Thus, *Wikipedia* can be a valuable first step in finding reliable research sources.

Comment [RS4]: Which study?

Comment [DL5]: Do you need a pg. #?

Comment [RS6]: I think you need a better transition here.

Revision with Track Changes

Wikipedia has advantages over other, professionally edited online encyclopedias. Because users can update articles in real time from any location, *Wikipedia* offers up-to-the-minute coverage of political and cultural events as well as timely information on popular culture topics that receive little or no attention from other sources. For example, a student researching the history of video gaming would find *Wikipedia*'s "Wii" article, with its numerous pages of information and nearly 150 external links to additional sources, to be a valuable resource. *Encyclopaedia Britannica Online* does not contain a comparable article on this popular game console. Even when the available information on a particular topic is sparse, *Wikipedia* allows users to create "stub" articles, which provide minimal information that users can expand over time. According to a 2008 Spinellis and Louridas's study, approximately 20% of *Wikipedia*'s articles are classified as stubs. Thus (70). By offering immediate access to information on relatively obscure topics, *Wikipedia* can be a valuable first step in finding reliable research sources on such topics.

CHECKLIST

REVISING A RESEARCH PAPER

As you revise your research paper, consider these questions:

- ❏ Should you do more research to find support for certain points?
- ❏ Do you need to reorder the major sections of your paper?
- ❏ Should you rearrange the order in which you present your points within sections?
- ❏ Do you need to add section headings? transitional paragraphs?
- ❏ Have you integrated source material smoothly into your paper?
- ❏ Have you chosen visuals carefully and integrated them smoothly into your paper?
- ❏ Are quotations blended with paraphrase, summary, and your own observations and reactions?
- ❏ Have you avoided plagiarism by carefully documenting all borrowed ideas?

(continued)

REVISING A RESEARCH PAPER (*continued*)

❑ Have you analyzed and interpreted the ideas of others rather than simply stringing those ideas together?

❑ Do your own ideas—not those of your sources—define the focus of your discussion?

Note: You will probably take your paper through several drafts, changing different parts of it each time or working on one part over and over again. After revising each draft thoroughly, print out a corrected version and make additional corrections by hand on that draft before typing in your changes to create the next draft.

CLOSE-UP

PREPARING YOUR WORKS-CITED LIST

When you finish revising your paper, copy the file that contains your working bibliography and insert it at the end of your paper. Keep the original file for your working bibliography as a backup in case any data is lost in the process. Delete any irrelevant entries, and then create your works-cited list. (Make sure the format of the entries in your works-cited list conforms to the documentation style you are using.)

If you save multiple drafts of your works-cited list, be sure to name each file with the date or other label so that it is readily identifiable. Keep all files pertaining to a single project in a folder dedicated to that paper or assignment.

EXERCISE 41.8

Following the guidelines in 41j and 4c, revise your research paper until you are ready to prepare your final draft.

41k Preparing a Final Draft

See 4d

Before you print out the final version of your paper, **edit and proofread** hard copy of both your paper and your works-cited list. Next, consider (or reconsider) your paper's **title.** It should be descriptive enough to tell your readers what your paper is about, and it should create interest in your

See 1a

subject. Your title should also be consistent with the **purpose** and tone of your paper. (You would hardly want a humorous title for a paper about the death penalty or world hunger.) Finally, your title should be engaging and to the point—and perhaps even provocative. Often, a quotation from one of your sources will suggest a likely title.

When you are satisfied with your title, read your paper one last time, proofreading for grammar, spelling, or typing errors you may have missed.

Pay particular attention to parenthetical documentation and works-cited entries. (Remember that every error undermines your credibility.) Once you are satisfied that your paper is as accurate as you can make it, print out your final draft. Then, fasten the pages with a paper clip (do not staple the pages or fold the corners together), and hand it in. Some instructors will allow you to email your final draft. (For the final draft of Rebecca's research paper, along with her works-cited list, **see 47c.**)

EXERCISE 41.9

> Prepare a works-cited list for your research paper. Then, edit your paper and your works-cited list; decide on a title; and check to make sure your paper follows the format your instructor requires. Proofread your final draft carefully before you hand it in.

Using and Evaluating Library Sources CHAPTER 42

A modern, networked college library offers you resources that you cannot find anywhere else—even on the <u>Internet.</u> In the long run, you will save a great deal of time and effort, as well as gain a deeper understanding of your topic, if you begin your research with a survey of your library's print and electronic resources.

See
Ch. 43

42a Doing Exploratory Library Research

During **exploratory research,** your goal is to formulate a **research question**—the question you want your paper to answer. At this stage, you search the library's print and electronic resources to get a general sense of what they contain. (Later, during your <u>focused research,</u> you will look for specific material to use in your paper.)

See
42b

   The best way to start your exploratory research is to search your college or university library's **online catalog** to see what kind of information is available about your topic. You can then look at *general reference works* and consult the library's *electronic databases.*

1 Using Online Catalogs

The library's **online catalog** is a computer database that lists all the books, articles, and other materials held by the library. Figure 42.1 on page 352 shows the home page of a university library's online catalog.

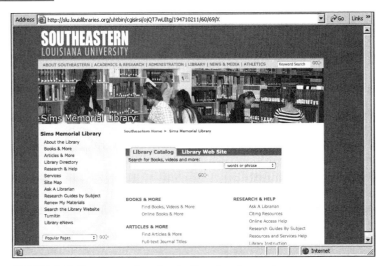

FIGURE 42.1 Home page of a university library's online catalog.

You access an online catalog through the library's Web site (or by using one of the computer terminals located throughout the library) and typing in specific words or phrases that enable you to find the information you need.

When you search the online catalog for information about your topic, you may conduct either a *keyword search* or a *subject search*. (Later on, when you know exactly what you are looking for, you can search for a particular book by entering its title, author, or call number.)

Conducting a Keyword Search   When you carry out a **keyword search,** you enter into the Search box of the online catalog a word or words associated with your topic. The screen then displays a list of articles that contain those words in their bibliographic citations or abstracts. The more precise your keywords are, the more specific and useful the information you retrieve will be. (Combining keywords with AND, OR, and NOT allows you to narrow or broaden your search. This technique is called conducting See 43a3 a <u>Boolean search</u>.)

CHECKLIST

KEYWORD DOS AND DON'TS

When conducting a keyword search, remember the following hints:

❏ Use precise, specific keywords to distinguish your topic from similar topics.

❏ Enter both singular and plural keywords when appropriate—*printing press* and *printing presses,* for example.

❏ Enter both abbreviations and their full-word equivalents (for example, *US* and *United States*).

❏ Try variant spellings (for example, *color* and *colour*).
❏ Don't use too long a string of keywords. (If you do, you will retrieve large amounts of irrelevant material.)

Conducting a Subject Search   When you carry out a **subject search,** you enter specific subject headings into the online catalog. Although it may be possible to guess at a subject heading, your search will be more successful if you consult the *Library of Congress Subject Headings,* held at the reference desk of your library, to help you identify the exact words you need. Figure 42.2 shows the results of a subject search in a library's online catalog.

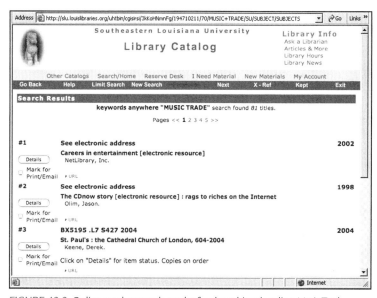

FIGURE 42.2 Online catalog search results for the subject heading *Music Trade.*

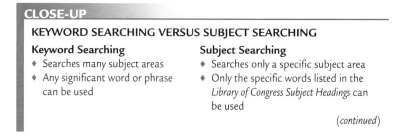

CLOSE-UP

KEYWORD SEARCHING VERSUS SUBJECT SEARCHING

Keyword Searching	Subject Searching
♦ Searches many subject areas	♦ Searches only a specific subject area
♦ Any significant word or phrase can be used	♦ Only the specific words listed in the *Library of Congress Subject Headings* can be used

(continued)

KEYWORD SEARCHING VERSUS SUBJECT SEARCHING (*continued*)

Keyword Searching	Subject Searching
♦ Retrieves large number of items	♦ Retrieves small number of items
♦ May retrieve many irrelevant items	♦ Retrieves few irrelevant items

2 Consulting the Library's General Reference Works

General reference works—encyclopedias, bibliographies, and so on—are available both in print and online. They provide broad overviews of particular subjects that can be helpful when you are doing exploratory research. From these sources, you can learn key facts and specific terminology as well as find dates, places, and names. In addition, general reference works often include bibliographies that you can use later on when you do focused research.

CLOSE-UP

GENERAL REFERENCE WORKS

General Encyclopedias A general encyclopedia presents information about a wide range of subjects. Although they are a good place to start your research, articles in general encyclopedias are usually not comprehensive or detailed enough for a college-level research paper. Articles in specialized encyclopedias, however, are more likely to be appropriate for your research.

Specialized Encyclopedias, Dictionaries, and Bibliographies These specialized reference works contain in-depth articles focusing on a single subject area.

General Bibliographies General bibliographies—such as *Books in Print* and *The Bibliographic Index*—list books available in a wide variety of fields.

General Biographical References Biographical reference books—such as *Who's Who in America, Who's Who,* and *Dictionary of American Biography*—provide information about people's lives as well as bibliographic listings.

---

3 Using Library Databases

The same Web site that enables you to access the online catalog also enables you to access a variety of other electronic databases.

Online Databases **Online databases** are collections of digital information—citations of books, reports, and journal, magazine, and newspaper articles (and sometimes the full text of articles)—arranged for easy access and retrieval by computer. Different libraries subscribe to different databases and make them available in different ways. Most libraries subscribe to information service companies, such as DIALOG or Gale Group Databases, that provide online access to hundreds of databases not available on the free Internet. One of your first tasks should be to determine what subscription databases your library offers. Visit your library's Web site, or ask a reference librarian for more information. Figure 42.3 shows a partial list of databases to which one college library subscribes.

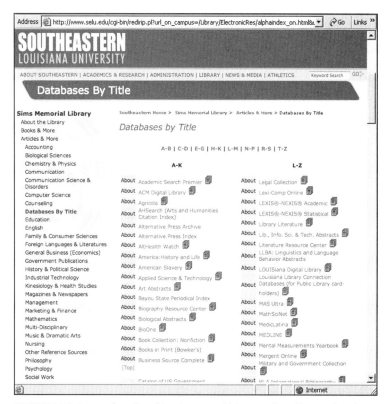

FIGURE 42.3 Excerpt from list of databases to which one college library subscribes.

Some library databases cover many subject areas (*Expanded Academic ASAP* and *LexisNexis Academic Universe,* for example); others cover just one subject area in great detail (*PsycINFO* and *Sociological Abstracts,* for example). Assuming that your library offers a variety of databases, how do you know which ones will be best for your research topic? One strategy is to begin by searching a general database that includes full-text articles and then move on to a more specialized database that covers your subject in more detail. The specialized databases are more likely to include scholarly and professional sources, but they are also less likely to include full text. They will, however, include **abstracts** (short summaries) that can help you determine the usefulness of a source. (Figure 42.4 on page 356 shows a printout from a library subscription database.)

Note: You search the library's subscription databases the same way you search the library's online catalog: you conduct either a keyword search or a subject search (**see 43a2**).

Date   Volume   Issue   First page   Total number
       number   number   of article   of pages

Title: The Supply Side of the Digital Divide: Is There Equal Availability in the Broadband Internet Access Market?

Periodical: *Economic Inquiry,* April 2003 v41 i2 p346(18).

Author: James E. Prieger

Author's Abstract: The newest dimension of the digital divide is access to broadband (high-speed) Internet service. Using comprehensive US data covering all forms of access technology (chiefly DSL and cable modem), I look for evidence of unequal broadband availability in areas with high concentrations of poor, minority, or rural households. There is little evidence of unequal availability based on income or on black or Hispanic concentration. There is mixed evidence concerning availability based on Native American or Asian concentration. Other findings: Rural location decreases availability; market size, education, Spanish language use, commuting distance, and Bell presence increase availability. (JEL L96, J78, L51)

Subjects: Digital Divide (Technology) = Demographic Aspects

Internet = Usage

Features: tables; figures

FIGURE 42.4 Library subscription database printout.

42b Doing Focused Library Research

Once you have completed your exploratory research and formulated your research question, it is time to move to focused research. During **focused research,** you examine the specialized reference works, books, and articles devoted specifically to your topic.

1 Consulting Periodicals

A **periodical** is a newspaper, magazine, scholarly journal, or other publication published at regular intervals (weekly, monthly, or quarterly). Articles in **scholarly journals** are often the best, most reliable sources you can find on a subject; they provide current information and are written by experts on the topic. And, because these journals focus on a particular subject area, they can provide in-depth analysis. However, because journal articles are written for experts, they can be difficult to understand.

Note: You cannot access most scholarly journals on the free Internet. Although you may occasionally find individual articles on the Internet, the easiest and most reliable way to access scholarly journals is through one of the subscription databases in your college library.

Periodical indexes are databases that list articles from a selected group of magazines, newspapers, or scholarly journals. Most libraries offer these indexes online. They are updated frequently and provide the most current information available.

CLOSE-UP

FREQUENTLY USED PERIODICAL INDEXES

Academic libraries usually subscribe to the following periodical indexes. (Be sure to check your library's Web site or ask a librarian about those available to you.)

General Indexes	Description
EBSCOhost	Database system for thousands of periodical articles on many subjects
Expanded Academic ASAP	A largely full-text database covering all subjects in thousands of magazines and scholarly journals
FirstSearch	Full-text articles from many popular and scholarly periodicals
LexisNexis Academic Universe	Includes full-text articles from national, international, and local newspapers. Also includes large legal and business sections.
Readers' Guide to Periodical Literature	Index to popular periodicals

Specialized Indexes	Description
Dow Jones Interactive	Full-text articles from US newspapers and trade journals
ERIC	Largest database of education-related journal articles and reports in the world
General BusinessFile ASAP	A full-text database covering business topics
PubMed (MEDLINE)	Covers articles in medical journals. Some may be available in full text.
PsycINFO	Covers psychology and related fields
Sociological Abstracts	Covers the social sciences

---

2 Consulting Specialized Reference Works

During your exploratory research, you used general reference works to help you narrow your topic and formulate your research question. Now, you can access **specialized reference works**—unabridged dictionaries, special dictionaries, yearbooks, almanacs, atlases, and so on—to find facts, examples, statistics, definitions, and expert opinion. (Note that many of these works are available online as well as in print.)

3 Consulting Books

The online catalog gives you the information you need—the call numbers—for locating specific titles. A **call number** is like a book's address in the library: it tells you exactly where to find the book you are looking for.

Once you become familiar with the physical layout of the library and the classification system your library uses, you should find it quite simple to locate the books you need.

CHECKLIST

TRACKING DOWN A MISSING BOOK

Problem	Possible Solution
1. Book has been checked out of library.	❑ Consult person at circulation desk. ❑ Check other nearby libraries.
2. Book is not in library's collection.	❑ Ask instructor if he or she owns a copy. ❑ Arrange for interlibrary loan (if time permits).
3. Journal is not in library's collection/article is ripped out of journal.	❑ Arrange for interlibrary loan (if time permits). ❑ Check to see whether article is available in a full-text database. ❑ Ask librarian whether article has been reprinted as part of a collection.

---

4 Finding Primary and Secondary Sources

Primary sources are original documents and observations. They include diaries, letters, speeches, manuscripts, memoirs, autobiographies, records of governments or organizations, newspaper articles, and books. Primary sources also include photographs, maps, films, tape recordings, statistics and other research data, novels, short stories, poems, and plays.

CHECKLIST

FINDING PRIMARY SOURCES

❑ Do a keyword search of your online catalog. Use keywords that combine your topic with additional terms that describe the format of the primary source—for example, *slaves* AND *narratives.*

❑ See if the online catalog lists any bibliographies that might include primary sources. For example, a bibliography might list works *by* an author (primary sources) as well as works *about* the author (secondary sources).

❑ Check with a reference librarian to see if your library subscribes to any databases that contain full-text primary sources.

❑ Check with a reference librarian to see if your library houses government publications that may include primary sources.

❑ Check with a reference librarian to see if your library houses any manuscripts.

❏ Use the Internet to find digitized collections of primary source materials—for example, documents that relate to US history, transcripts of television shows, or videos of significant events.

Note: The US government makes available a good deal of primary source material, much of it on the Web—for example, statistical information collected by government agencies; reports issued by government agencies such as the Environmental Protection Agency, the Department of Education, and NASA; US Supreme Court decisions; and presidential papers, political speeches, treaties, and US patents. A good Web site for locating government publications is <http://www.firstgov.gov>.

Secondary sources are interpretations of original documents and observations. In many cases, their purpose is to analyze primary sources. Secondary sources include textbooks, literary criticism, and encyclopedias.

CHECKLIST

FINDING SECONDARY SOURCES

❏ Search your library's online catalog for books. Combine a term that describes your topic with terms such as *interpretation, criticism,* or *bibliography.*

❏ Search your library's subscription databases for articles in scholarly journals, popular magazines, and newspapers that discuss and interpret the causes and effects of events.

❏ Check the notes, bibliographies, and works-cited lists that appear in books and articles.

❏ Do a keyword search on the Internet—but be sure to evaluate any information you find.

EXERCISE 42.1

Which library research sources would you consult to find the following information?

▶ 1. A discussion of the movie *Brick Lane* (2008) based on Monica Ali's 2003 novel

▶ 2. A government publication about how to heat your home with solar energy

▶ 3. Biographical information about the American anthropologist Margaret Mead

▶ 4. Books about Margaret Mead and her work

▶ 5. Information about what is being done to prevent the killing of wolves in North America

 6. Information about the theories of Albert Einstein

 7. Current information about the tobacco lobby

8. The address at which to contact Edward P. Jones, an American writer
9. Whether your college library has *The Human Use of Human Beings* by Norbert Wiener
10. Current information about AmeriCorps

42c Evaluating the Library's Print and Electronic Sources

Whenever you find a source (print or electronic), take the time to **evaluate** it—to assess its usefulness and its reliability. To determine the usefulness of a library source, ask the following questions:

♦ **Does the source treat your topic in enough detail?** To be of any real help, a book should include a section or chapter on your topic, not simply a footnote or a brief reference. For articles, either read the abstract or skim the entire article for key facts, looking closely at section headings, information set in boldface type, and topic sentences. An article should have your topic as its central subject (or at least one of its main concerns).

♦ **Is the source current?** The date of publication tells you whether the information in a book or article is up to date. A source's currency is particularly important for scientific and technological subjects, but even in the humanities, new discoveries and new ways of thinking lead scholars to reevaluate and modify their ideas.

♦ **Is the source respected?** A contemporary review of a source can help you make this assessment. *Book Review Digest,* available in print and online, lists popular books that have been reviewed in at least three newspapers or magazines and includes excerpts from representative reviews as well as abstracts.

♦ **Is the source reliable?** Is the source largely fact or unsubstantiated opinion? Does the writer support his or her conclusions? Does the writer include documentation? Is the writer objective, or does he or she have a particular agenda to advance? Compare a few statements with a neutral source—a textbook or an encyclopedia, for instance—to see whether a writer seems to be slanting facts.

Note: In general, **scholarly publications**—books and journals aimed at an audience of expert readers—are more respected and reliable than **popular publications**—books, magazines, and newspapers aimed at an audience of general readers. However, assuming they are current, written by reputable authors, and documented, articles from some popular publications (such as the *Atlantic* and *Harper's*) may be appropriate for your research. Check with your instructor to be sure.

CLOSE-UP

SCHOLARLY VERSUS POPULAR PUBLICATIONS

Scholarly Publications	**Popular Publications**
Report the results of research	Entertain and inform
Are often published by a university press or have some connection with a university or academic organization	Are published by commercial presses
Are usually **refereed;** that is, a group of expert reviewers determines what will be published	Are usually not refereed
Are usually written by someone who is a recognized authority in the field about which he or she is writing	May be written by experts in a particular field, but more often they are written by freelance or staff writers
Are written for a scholarly audience, so they often use technical vocabulary and include challenging content	Are written for general readers, so they usually use an accessible vocabulary and do not include challenging content
Nearly always contain extensive documentation as well as a bibliography of works consulted	Rarely cite sources or use documentation
Are published primarily because they make a contribution to a particular field of study	Are published primarily to make a profit

---

EXERCISE 42.2

Read the following paragraphs carefully, paying close attention to the information provided about their sources and authors as well as to their content. Decide which sources would be most useful and reliable in supporting the thesis "Winning the right to vote has (or has not) significantly changed the role of women in national politics." Which sources, if any, should be disregarded? Which would you examine first? Why?

▶ 1. Woman has been the great unpaid laborer of the world, and although within the last two decades a vast number of new employments have been opened to her, statistics prove that in the great majority of these, she is not paid according to the value of the work done, but according to sex. The opening of all industries to women, and the wage question as connected with her, are the most subtle and profound questions of political economy, closely interwoven with the rights of self-government. (Susan B. Anthony; first appeared in Vol. I of *The History of Woman Suffrage;* reprinted in *Voices from Women's Liberation,* ed. Leslie B. Tanner,

NAL, 1970. *An important figure in the battle for women's suffrage, Susan B. Anthony [1820–1906] also lectured and wrote on abolition and temperance.*)

▶ 2. With women as half the country's elected representatives, and a woman President once in a while, the country's machismo problems would be greatly reduced. The old-fashioned idea that manhood depends on violence and victory is, after all, an important part of our troubles. . . . I'm not saying that women leaders would eliminate violence. We are not more moral than men; we are only uncorrupted by power so far. When we do acquire power, we might turn out to have an equal impulse toward aggression. (Gloria Steinem, "What It Would Be Like If Women Win," *Time,* 1970. *Steinem, a well-known feminist and journalist, was one of the founders of* Ms. *magazine.*)

3. Nineteen eighty-two was the year that time ran out for the proposed equal rights amendment. Eleanor Smeal, president of the National Organization for Women, the group that headed the intense 10-year struggle for the ERA, conceded defeat on June 24. Only 24 words in all, the ERA read simply: "Equality of rights under the law shall not be denied or abridged by the United States or by any state on account of sex." Two major opinion polls had reported just weeks before the ERA's defeat that a majority of Americans continued to favor the amendment. (June Foley, "Women 1982: The Year That Time Ran Out," *The World Almanac & Book of Facts,* 1983.)

4. It won't happen this year. But the next chance at the White House is only four years away, and more women than you might think are already laying the groundwork for their own presidential bids. Bolstered by changing public attitudes, women in politics no longer assume that the Oval Office will always be a male bastion. In 1936, when George Gallup first asked people whether they would "vote for a woman for president if she qualified in every other respect," 65 percent said they would not. Back then, women were only slightly more open to the idea than men. Things are far different today. A recent poll shows that 90 percent of Americans, men included, say they could support a woman for president. (Eleanor Clift and Tom Brazaitis, *Madam President,* © 2000 by Eleanor Clift and Tom Brazaitis. *The authors profile the women who they say are positioning themselves to be president.*)

42d Doing Research Outside the Library

Interviews (conducted in person or by email) often give you material that you cannot always find in a library—for instance, biographical information, a firsthand account of an event, or the opinions of an expert.

The kinds of questions you ask in an interview depend on the information you want. **Open-ended questions**—questions designed to elicit general information—allow a respondent great flexibility in answering: *"Do you think students today are motivated? Why or why not?"* **Closed-ended**

questions—questions intended to elicit specific information—enable you to zero in on a particular detail about a subject: *"How much money did the government's cost-cutting programs actually save?"*

CHECKLIST

CONDUCTING AN INTERVIEW

❑ Always make an appointment.

❑ Prepare a list of specific questions tailored to the subject matter and the time limit of your interview.

❑ Do background reading about your topic. (Do not ask for information that you can easily find elsewhere.)

❑ Have a pen and paper with you. If you want to record the interview, get your subject's permission in advance.

❑ Allow the person you are interviewing to complete an answer before you ask another question.

❑ Take notes, but continue to pay attention as you do so.

❑ Pay attention to the reactions of your interview subject.

❑ Be willing to depart from your prepared list of questions to ask follow-up questions.

❑ At the end of the interview, thank your subject for his or her time and cooperation.

❑ Send a brief note of thanks.

Using and Evaluating Internet Sources

CHAPTER 43

The **Internet** is a vast system of networks that links millions of computers. Even with all its advantages, however, the Internet does not give you access to the high-quality print and electronic resources found in a typical college library. For this reason, you should consider the Internet a supplement to your library research, not a substitute for it.

CLOSE-UP

LIMITATIONS OF INTERNET RESEARCH

♦ Many important and useful publications are available only in print or through the library's subscription databases and not on the Internet.

♦ The information in your college library will almost always be more focused and more useful than much of what you will find on the Internet.

(continued)

LIMITATIONS OF INTERNET RESEARCH (*continued*)

♦ The information you see on an Internet site—unlike information in your library's subscription databases—may not be there when you try to access it at a later time. (For this reason, it is a good idea to print out all Internet documents you use in your research.)

♦ Because librarians screen the material in your college library, it is likely to meet academic standards of reliability.

♦ Although the authorship of Internet documents can often be difficult or impossible to determine, this is not usually the case with the sources in your college library.

43a   Using the World Wide Web for Research

To carry out a Web search, you need a **Web browser,** an application such as *Microsoft Internet Explorer, Mozilla Firefox,* or *Safari* that enables you to view Web documents.

Once you are connected to the Internet, you use your browser to access a **search engine,** a program (such as *Google* or *Ask.com*) that searches for and retrieves documents available on the Web. There are three ways to use search engines to find the information you want: *entering an electronic address, using subject guides,* and *doing a keyword search.*

1   Entering an Electronic Address

The most basic way to access information on the Web is to go directly to a specific electronic address, called a **URL** (uniform resource locator). Search engines and Web browsers enable you to enter a URL into the Location text field on your browser's **home page** (the page you see when you open your browser). Once you type in a URL and click on Search (or hit Enter or the return key), you will be connected to the Web site you want. (Figure 43.1 shows a location field.)

CHECKLIST

WHAT TO DO IF YOU CANNOT ACCESS A WEB SITE

If you cannot connect to the Web site that you want, do not give up. You can use the following strategies to help you connect:

❏ Wait a short period of time, and try again. If a Web site is extremely busy, it may block users.

❏ Make sure that you have typed in the URL correctly. Adding a space or omitting just a punctuation mark will send you to the wrong site—or to no site at all.

❏ If the URL is very long, delete a section of the end of the URL—from slash to slash—and try again.

❏ Try using just the base URL, deleting everything after *.com* or *.gov*. If this ab-breviated URL does not take you where you want to go, you have an incorrect address.

❏ If you are following a link from one document to another and cannot con-nect, type the URL of the link into the location field of your search engine, and try again.

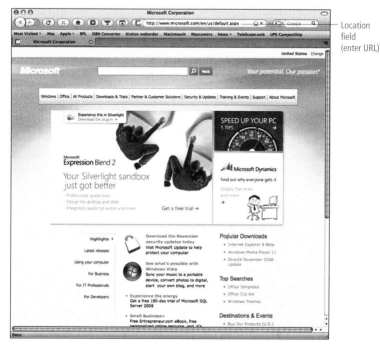

FIGURE 43.1 Entering an address in *Internet Explorer*.

For links to Web sites for **exploratory and focused research,** go to http://cengage.com/english/kirsznermandell ▶ *The Concise Wadsworth Handbook* ▶ Chapter 43 ▶ Using and Evaluating Internet Sources.

2 Using Subject Guides

You can also use subject guides to help you locate information. Some search engines, such as *Yahoo!, About.com,* and *Look Smart,* contain a **subject guide** (or **search directory**)—a list of general categories from which you can choose. Each general category will lead you to a more specific list of categories and subcategories until you get to the topic you want. For ex-ample, clicking on *Society and Culture* might lead you to *Activism* and then to *Animal Rights* and eventually to an article concerning cruelty to ani-mals on factory farms. Although using subject guides is a time-consuming

See
42a strategy for finding specific information, it can be an excellent tool during <u>exploratory research</u>, when you want to find or narrow a topic. (Figure 43.2 shows a home page of a search engine with a subject guide.)

FIGURE 43.2 *Yahoo!* home page showing a subject guide.

3 Doing a Keyword Search

Finally, you can locate information by doing a **keyword search.** You do this by entering a keyword (or words) into your search engine's search field. (Figure 43.3 shows a search engine's keyword search page.) The search engine will identify any site in its database on which the keyword (or words) you have typed appears. (These sites are called **hits.**) If, for example, you simply type *Civil War* (say, in hope of finding information on Fort Sumter during the Civil War), the search engine will generate an enormous list of hits—well over a million. This list will likely include, along with sites that might be relevant to your research, the Civil War Reenactors home page as well as sites that focus on Civil War music.

Because keyword searching this way can yield thousands of hits, you need to focus your search by using **search operators,** words and symbols that tell a search engine how to interpret your keywords. One way to focus your search is to put quotation marks around your search term (type "*Fort Sumter*" rather than *Fort Sumter*). This will direct the search engine to locate only documents containing this phrase.

Another way to focus your search is to carry out a **Boolean search,** combining keywords with AND, OR, NOT (typed in all capital letters), or a plus or minus sign, to eliminate irrelevant hits from your search. (To do this type of search, you may have to select a search engine's Advanced Search option.)

Search field

FIGURE 43.3 *Google* keyword search page.

CLOSE-UP

USING SEARCH OPERATORS

" " (quotation marks) Use quotation marks to search for a specific phrase: "*Baltimore Economy*"

AND Use AND to search for sites that contain both terms: *Baltimore* AND *Economy*

OR Use OR to search for sites that contain either term: *Baltimore* OR *Economy*

NOT Use NOT to exclude the term that comes after the NOT: *Baltimore* AND *Economy* NOT *Agriculture*

* (asterisk) Use an asterisk after a word to tell the search engine to look for a word plus any ending. For example, the term *photo** will yield *photograph, photographer, photojournalist, photoactive, photosynthesis,* and so on.

? (question mark) Use a question mark to tell the search engine to look for a group of letters plus one varying character. For example, *?at* will yield *hat, bat, cat, fat, mat,* and so on.

Note: Many search engines offer advanced options that allow you to tailor your search even further.

---

4 Choosing the Right Search Engine

General-Purpose Search Engines   The most widely used search engines are **general-purpose search engines** that focus on a wide variety of topics. Some of these search engines are more user-friendly than others; some allow for more sophisticated searching functions; some are updated more frequently; and some are more comprehensive than others. As you try out various search engines, you will probably settle on a favorite that you will turn to first whenever you need to find information.

CLOSE-UP

POPULAR SEARCH ENGINES

AltaVista <www.altavista.com>: Good, precise engine for focused searches. Fast and easy to use.

Ask.com <www.ask.com>: Allows you to narrow your search by asking questions, such as *Are dogs smarter than pigs?*

Excite <www.excite.com>: Good for general topics. Because it searches over 250 million Web sites, you often receive more information than you need.

Google <www.google.com>: Arguably the best search engine available. Accesses a large database that includes both text and graphics. It is easy to navigate, and searches usually yield a high percentage of useful hits.

HotBot <www.hotbot.com>: Excellent, fast search engine for locating specific information. Good search options allow you to fine-tune your searches.

Lycos <www.lycos.com>: Enables you to search for specific media (graphics, for example). A somewhat small index of Web pages.

Yahoo! <www.yahoo.com>: Good for exploratory research. Enables you to search using either subject headings or keywords. Searches its own indexes as well as the Web.

Because even the best search engines search only a fraction of what is on the Web, if you use only one search engine, you will most likely miss much valuable information. It is therefore a good idea to repeat each search with several different search engines or to use one of the **metasearch** or **metacrawler** engines that uses several search engines simultaneously.

CLOSE-UP

METASEARCH ENGINES

Dogpile <www.dogpile.com>

Ixquick <www.ixquick.com>

Metacrawler <www.metacrawler.com>

Zworks <www.zworks.com>

Specialized Search Engines   In addition to the popular general-purpose search engines and metasites, there are numerous **specialized search engines** devoted entirely to specific subject areas, such as literature, business, sports, and women's issues. Very often your college library will have lists of specialized search engines; you can also access them on the Web at a site such as *College Degree.com* <http://www.collegedegree.com/library/college-life/99-resources-to>. These sites are especially useful during See 42b focused research, when you are looking for in-depth information about your topic.

CLOSE-UP

GOOGLE RESOURCES

Google is the most-used search engine on the Internet. In fact, many people now say that they are going to "Google" a subject rather than search it. Few people who use *Google,* however, actually know its full potential. Following are just a few of the resources that *Google* offers:

- **Blog Search** Enables users to find blogs on specific subjects
- **Blogger** A tool for creating and posting blogs online
- **Book Search** A database that allows users to access the full text of thousands of books
- **Google Earth** A downloadable, dynamic global map that enables users to see satellite views of almost any place on the planet
- **Finance** Business information, news, and interactive charts
- **News** Enables users to search thousands of news stories
- **Patent Search** Enables users to search the full text of US patents
- **Google Scholar** Searches scholarly literature, including peer-reviewed papers, books, and abstracts

Note: You can access these tools by going to the *Google* home page and clicking on MORE in the top menu bar of your screen and then clicking on EVEN MORE on the pull-down menu.

CHECKLIST

TIPS FOR EFFECTIVE SEARCHING

❑ **Choose your keywords carefully.** A search engine is only as good as the keywords you enter. Use quotation marks and Boolean search operators to make your search more productive. Review the Close-up box, "Using Search Operators," on page 367 before you use any search engine.

❑ **Include enough terms.** If you are looking for information on housing, for example, search several variations of your keyword: *housing, houses, home buyer, buying houses, rental real estate,* and so on. Some search engines, like *AltaVista,* automatically search variants of your keyword; others require you to think of variants yourself.

❑ **Choose the right search engine.** No one all-purpose search engine exists. Make sure you evaluate the strengths and weaknesses of your search engine to make sure it suits your purpose. Check your college library's Web site to see if you can access comparisons of various search engines.

❑ **Use more than one search engine.** Because different search engines index different sites, try several. If one does not yield results after a few tries, switch to another. Also, don't forget to try a metasearch engine like *Metacrawler.*

❑ **Add useful sites to your Bookmarks or Favorites list.** Whenever you find a particularly useful Web site, **bookmark** it by selecting this option on the menu bar of your browser. If you add a site to your bookmark list, you can return to the site whenever you open the Bookmark menu and select it.

43b Evaluating Internet Sites

Web sites vary greatly in reliability. Because anyone can operate a Web site and thereby publish anything, regardless of quality, critical evaluation of Web-based material is even more important than evaluation of more traditional sources of information, such as books and journal articles.

Determining the quality of a Web site is crucial if you plan to use it as a source for your research. For this reason, you should evaluate the content of any Web site for *accuracy, credibility, objectivity, currency,* and *scope of coverage.*

Accuracy **Accuracy** refers to the reliability of the material itself and to the use of proper documentation. Factual errors—especially errors in facts that are central to the main idea of the source—should cause you to question the reliability of the material you are reading. To evaluate a site's accuracy, ask these questions:

♦ Is the text free of basic grammatical and mechanical errors?
♦ Does the site contain factual errors?
♦ Does the site provide a list of references?
♦ Are links available to other sources?
♦ Can information be verified by print or other sources?

Credibility **Credibility** refers to the credentials of the person or organization responsible for the site. Web sites operated by well-known institutions (the Smithsonian or the Library of Congress, for example) have a high degree of credibility. Those operated by individuals (personal Web pages or blogs, for example) are often less reliable. To evaluate a site's credibility, ask these questions:

♦ Does the site list an author (or authors)? Are credentials (for example, professional or academic affiliations) provided for the author?
♦ Is the author a recognized authority in his or her field?
♦ Is the site **refereed?** That is, does an editorial board or a group of experts determine what material appears on the Web site?
♦ Does the organization sponsoring the Web site exist apart from its Web presence?
♦ Can you determine how long the Web site has existed?

Objectivity **Objectivity** refers to the degree of bias that a Web site exhibits. Some Web sites make no secret of their biases. They openly advocate a particular point of view or action, or they are clearly trying to sell something. Other Web sites may try to hide their biases. For example, a Web site may present itself as a source of factual information when it is actually advocating a political point of view. To evaluate a site's objectivity, ask these questions:

♦ Does advertising appear in the text?
♦ Does a business, a political organization, or a special interest group sponsor the site?

♦ Does the site express a particular viewpoint?
♦ Does the site contain links to other sites that express a particular viewpoint?

CHECKLIST

DETERMINING THE LEGITIMACY OF AN ANONYMOUS OR QUESTIONABLE WEB SOURCE

When a Web source is anonymous (or has an author whose name is not familiar to you), you can take the following steps to determine its legitimacy:

❑ **Post a query.** If you subscribe to a newsgroup or listserv, ask others in the group what they know about the source and its author.

❑ **Follow the links.** Follow the hypertext links in a document to other documents. If the links take you to legitimate sources, you know that the author is aware of these sources of information.

❑ **Do a keyword search.** Do a search using the name of the sponsoring organization or the author as keywords. Other documents (or citations in other works) may identify the author.

❑ **Look at the URL.** The last part of a Web site's URL can tell you whether the site is sponsored by a commercial entity (.*com*), a nonprofit organization (.*org*), an educational institution (.*edu*), the military (.*mil*), or a government agency (.*gov*). Knowing this information can tell you whether an organization is trying to sell you something (.*com*) or just providing information (.*edu* or .*org*).

Currency   **Currency** refers to how up-to-date the Web site is. The easiest way to assess a site's currency is to see when it was last updated. Keep in mind, however, that even if the date on the site is current, the information that the site contains may not be. To evaluate a site's currency, ask these questions:

♦ Does the site include the date when it was last updated?
♦ Are all the links to other sites still functioning?
♦ Is the actual information on the page up-to-date?
♦ Does the site clearly identify the date it was created?

Scope of Coverage   **Scope of coverage** refers to the comprehensiveness of the information on a Web site. More coverage is not necessarily better, but some sites may be incomplete. Others may provide information that is no more than common knowledge. Still others may present discussions that may not be suitable for college-level research. To evaluate the scope of a site's coverage, ask these questions:

♦ Does the site provide in-depth coverage?
♦ Does the site provide information that is not available elsewhere?
♦ Does the site identify a target audience? Does this target audience suggest the site is appropriate for your research needs?

EXERCISE 43.1

Examine the home page for the *National Geographic* Web site (Figure 43.4). Use the criteria discussed in 43c to write a paragraph in which you evaluate its content in terms of accuracy, credibility, objectivity, currency, and scope of coverage.

FIGURE 43.4 *National Geographic* home page <www.nationalgeographic.com>.

Summarizing, Paraphrasing, and Quoting Sources   CHAPTER 44

See
41f

Although it may seem like a good strategy, copying down the words of a source is the least efficient way of **taking notes**. Experienced researchers know that a better strategy is to take notes that combine summary and paraphrase with direct quotation. By doing so, they make sure they understand the material and see its relevance to their research. (This, in turn, makes

See
Ch. 45

it possible for them to **synthesize sources**, combining borrowed material with their own original ideas.)

44a   Writing a Summary

A **summary** is a brief restatement, *in your own words*, of the main idea of a passage or an article.

When you summarize, use your own words, not the language or phrasing of your source. Remember that your summary should accurately represent the writer's ideas and should include only the ideas of your source, not your own interpretations or opinions. Finally, be sure to document the summary.

CLOSE-UP

SUMMARIES

- ✦ **Summaries are original.** They should use your own language and phrasing, not the language and phrasing of your source.
- ✦ **Summaries are concise.** They should always be much shorter than the original.
- ✦ **Summaries are accurate.** They should precisely express the main idea of your source.
- ✦ **Summaries are objective.** They should not include your opinions.

Compare the following three passages. The first is an original source; the second, an acceptable summary; and the third, an unacceptable summary.

Original Source

Today, the First Amendment faces challenges from groups who seek to limit expressions of racism and bigotry. A growing number of legislatures have passed rules against "hate speech"—[speech] that is offensive on the basis of race, ethnicity, gender, or sexual orientation. The rules are intended to promote respect for all people and protect the targets of hurtful words, gestures, or actions.

Legal experts fear these rules may wind up diminishing the rights of all citizens. "The bedrock principle [of our society] is that government may never suppress free speech simply because it goes against what the community would like to hear," says Nadine Strossen, president of the American Civil Liberties Union and professor of constitutional law at New York University Law School. In recent years, for example, the courts have upheld the right of neo-Nazis to march in Jewish neighborhoods; protected cross-burning as a form of free expression; and allowed protesters to burn the American flag. The offensive, ugly, distasteful, or repugnant nature of expression is not reason enough to ban it, courts have said.

But advocates of limits on hate speech note that certain kinds of expression fall outside of First Amendment protection. Courts have ruled that "fighting words"—words intended to provoke immediate violence—or speech that creates a clear and present danger are not protected forms of expression. As the classic argument goes, freedom of speech does not give you the right to yell "Fire!" in a crowded theater. (Phil Sudo, "Freedom of Hate Speech?")

The following acceptable summary gives an accurate, objective overview of the original without using its exact language or phrasing.

Acceptable Summary

The right to freedom of speech, guaranteed by the First Amendment, is becoming more difficult to defend. Some people think that stronger laws against the use of hate speech weaken the First

Amendment. But others argue that some kinds of speech should be exempt from this protection (Sudo 17).

The following unacceptable summary uses words and phrases from the original. In addition, the unacceptable summary includes the student writer's opinion (**Other people have the sense to realize . . .**).

Unacceptable Summary

Today, the First Amendment faces challenges from lots of people. Some of these people are legal experts who want to let Nazis march in Jewish neighborhoods. Other people have the sense to realize that some kinds of speech fall outside of First Amendment protection because they create a clear and present danger (Sudo 17).

CHECKLIST

WRITING A SUMMARY

❑ Reread your source until you understand it.

❑ Write a one-sentence restatement of the main idea.

❑ Write your summary, using the one-sentence restatement as your topic sentence. Use your own words and phrasing, not those of your source. Include quotation marks where necessary.

❑ Add appropriate documentation.

44b Writing a Paraphrase

A summary conveys just the main idea of a source; a **paraphrase** gives a *detailed* restatement of a source's important ideas. It not only indicates the source's main points, but it also reflects its tone and emphasis. Keep in mind that a paraphrase should convey only the ideas of the source—not the writer's analysis or interpretation of those ideas.

When you paraphrase, make certain that you use your own words, except when you want to quote to give readers a sense of the original. If you do include quotations, circle the quotation marks in your draft so that you will not think that they are your own words later on. Try not to look at the source as you write, use language and syntax that come naturally to you, and avoid duplicating the phrasing or sentence structure of the original. Whenever possible, use synonyms that accurately convey the meaning of the original word or phrase. If you cannot think of a synonym for an important term, quote it.

CLOSE-UP

PARAPHRASES

♦ **Paraphrases are original.** They should use your original language and phrasing, not the language and phrasing of your source.

> ♦ **Paraphrases are accurate.** They should precisely reflect both the ideas and the emphasis of your source.
> ♦ **Paraphrases are objective.** They should not include your opinions.
> ♦ **Paraphrases are complete.** They should include all the important ideas in your source.

Compare the following three passages. The first is an original source, the second is an acceptable paraphrase, and the third is an unacceptable paraphrase.

Original Passage

When you play a video game, you enter into the world of the programmers who made it. You have to do more than identify with a character on a screen. You must act for it. Identification through action has a special kind of hold. Like playing a sport, it puts people into a highly focused and highly charged state of mind. For many people, what is being pursued in the video game is not just a score, but an altered state.

The pilot of a race car does not dare to take . . . attention off the road. The imperative of total concentration is part of the high. Video games demand the same level of attention. They can give people the feeling of being close to the edge because, as in a dangerous situation, there is no time for rest and the consequences of wandering attention [are] dire. With pinball, a false move can be recuperated. The machine can be shaken, the ball repositioned. In a video game, the program has no tolerance for error, no margin for safety. Players experience their every movement as instantly translated into game action. The game is relentless in its demand that all other time stop and in its demand that the player take full responsibility for every act, a point that players often sum up [with] the phrase "One false move and you're dead." (Sherry Turkle, *The Second Self: Computers and the Human Spirit*)

The following acceptable paraphrase conveys the key ideas of the source and maintains an objective tone. Although it follows the emphasis of the original—and even quotes a key phrase—its wording and sentence structure are very different from those of the source.

Acceptable Paraphrase

According to Turkle, the programmer defines the reality of the video game. The game forces a player to merge with the character who is part of the game. The character becomes an extension of the player, who determines how he or she will think and act. Like sports, video games put a player into a very intense state of mind that is the most important part of the activity.

For Turkle, the total involvement video games demand is what attracts many people to them. These games can simulate the thrill of participating in a dangerous activity without any of the risks. There is no time for rest and no opportunity to correct errors of judgment. Unlike video games, pinball games are forgiving. A player can—within certain limits—manipulate a pinball game to correct minor mistakes. With video games, however, every move has immediate consequences. The game forces a player to adapt to its rules and to act carefully. One mistake can cause the death of the character on the screen and the end of the game (84).

The following unacceptable paraphrase simply echoes the phrasing and syntax of the original, borrowing words and expressions without enclosing them in quotation marks. This constitutes plagiarism. In addition, the paraphrase digresses into a discussion of the student writer's own views about the relative merits of pinball and video games (**That is why I like . . .**).

See Ch. 46

Unacceptable Paraphrase

Playing a video game, you enter into a new world—one the programmer of the game made. You can't just play a video game; you have to identify with it. Your mind goes to a new level, and you are put into a highly focused state of mind.

Just as you would if you were driving a race car or piloting a plane, you must not let your mind wander. Video games demand complete attention. But the sense that at any time you could make one false move and lose is their attraction—at least for me. That is why I like video games more than pinball. Pinball is just too easy. You can always recover. By shaking the machine or quickly operating the flippers, you can save the ball. Video games, however, are not so easy to control. Usually, one slip and you're dead (Turkle 83-84).

CHECKLIST

WRITING A PARAPHRASE

- ❑ Reread your source until you understand it.
- ❑ Write your paraphrase, following the order, tone, and emphasis of the original and making sure that you do not use the words or phrasing of the original without enclosing the borrowed material within quotation marks.
- ❑ Add appropriate documentation.

44c Quoting Sources

When you **quote,** you copy a writer's statements exactly as they appear in a source, word for word and punctuation mark for punctuation mark, enclosing the borrowed material in quotation marks.

As a rule, you should not quote extensively in a research paper. Numerous quotations interrupt the flow of your discussion and give readers the impression that your paper is just a collection of other people's ideas.

> **CHECKLIST**
>
> ### WHEN TO QUOTE
>
> Quote a source only in the following situations:
>
> ❑ Quote when a source's wording or phrasing is so distinctive that a summary or paraphrase would diminish its impact.
>
> ❑ Quote when a source's words will lend authority to your discussion.
>
> ❑ Quote when a writer's words are so concise that paraphrasing would change the meaning of the original.
>
> ❑ Quote when you go on to disagree with a source. Using a source's exact words helps convince readers you are being fair.
>
> *Note:* Remember to document all quotations that you use in your paper.

EXERCISE 44.1

Assume that in preparation for a paper on the effects of the rise of the suburbs, you read the following paragraph from the book *Great Expectations: America and the Baby Boom Generation,* by Landon Y. Jones. Reread the paragraph, and write a brief summary. Then, write a paraphrase of the paragraph, quoting only those words and phrases you consider especially distinctive.

> As an internal migration, the settling of the suburbs was phenomenal. In the twenty years from 1950 to 1970, the population of the suburbs doubled from 36 million to 72 million. No less than 83 percent of the total population growth in the United States during the 1950s was in the suburbs, which were growing fifteen times faster than any other segment of the country. As people packed and moved, the national mobility rate leaped by 50 percent. The only other comparable influx was the wave of European immigrants to the United States around the turn of the century. But as *Fortune* pointed out, more people moved to the suburbs every year than had ever arrived on Ellis Island.

44d Integrating Source Material into Your Writing

Weave quotations, paraphrases, and summaries smoothly into your discussion, adding your own analysis or explanation to increase coherence and to show the relevance of your source material to the points you are making.

> **CLOSE-UP**
>
> ### INTEGRATING SOURCE MATERIAL INTO YOUR WRITING
>
> To make sure your sentences do not all sound the same, experiment with different methods of integrating source material into your paper:
>
> *(continued)*

INTEGRATING SOURCE MATERIAL INTO YOUR WRITING (*continued*)

♦ Vary the verbs you use to introduce a source's words or ideas (instead of repeating *says*).

acknowledges	discloses	implies
suggests	observes	notes
concludes	believes	comments
insists	explains	claims
predicts	summarizes	illustrates
reports	finds	proposes
warns	concurs	speculates
admits	affirms	indicates

♦ Vary the placement of the **identifying tag** (the phrase that identifies the source), putting it in the middle or at the end of the quoted material instead of always at the beginning.

Quotation with Identifying Tag in Middle: "A serious problem confronting Amish society from the viewpoint of the Amish themselves," observes Hostetler, "is the threat of absorption into mass society through the values promoted in the public school system" (193).

Paraphrase with Identifying Tag at End: The Amish are also concerned about their children's exposure to the public school system's values, notes Hostetler (193).

1 Integrating Quotations

Be sure to work quotations smoothly into your sentences. Quotations should never be awkwardly dropped into your paper, leaving the relationship between the quoted words and your point unclear. Use a brief introductory remark to provide a context for the quotation, and quote only those words you need to make your point.

Acceptable: For the Amish, the public school system is a problem because it represents "the threat of absorption into mass society" (Hostetler 193).

Unacceptable: For the Amish, the public school system represents a problem. "A serious problem confronting Amish society from the viewpoint of the Amish themselves is the threat of absorption into mass society through the values promoted in the public school system" (Hostetler 193).

Whenever possible, use an identifying tag to introduce the source of the quotation.

Identifying Tag: As John Hostetler points out, the Amish see the public school system as a problem because it represents "the threat of absorption into mass society" (193).

PUNCTUATING IDENTIFYING TAGS

Whether or not to use a comma with an identifying tag depends on where you place the tag in the sentence. If the identifying tag immediately precedes a quotation, use a comma.

> As Hostetler points out, "The Amish are successful in maintaining group identity" (56).

If the identifying tag does not immediately precede a quotation, do not use a comma.

> Hostetler points out that the Amish frequently "use severe sanctions to preserve their values" (56).

Note: Never use a comma after *that*: Hostetler says that/ Amish society is "defined by religion" (76).

Substitutions or Additions within Quotations   Indicate changes or additions that you make to a quotation by enclosing your changes in brackets.

Original Quotation: "Immediately after her wedding, she and her husband followed tradition and went to visit almost everyone who attended the wedding" (Hostetler 122).

Quotation Edited to Make Verb Tenses Consistent: Nowhere is the Amish dedication to tradition more obvious than in the events surrounding marriage. Right after the wedding celebration, the Amish bride and groom "visit almost everyone who [has] attended the wedding" (Hostetler 122).

Quotation Edited to Supply an Antecedent for a Pronoun: "Immediately after her wedding, [Sarah] and her husband followed tradition and went to visit almost everyone who attended the wedding" (Hostetler 122).

Quotation Edited to Change an Uppercase to a Lowercase Letter: The strength of the Amish community is illustrated by the fact that "[i]mmediately after her wedding, she and her husband followed tradition and went to visit almost everyone who attended the wedding" (Hostetler 122).

Omissions within Quotations   When you delete unnecessary or irrelevant words, substitute an <u>ellipsis</u> (three spaced periods) for the deleted words. See 34f1

Original Quotation: "Not only have the Amish built and staffed their own elementary and vocational schools, but they have gradually organized on local, state, and national levels to cope with the task of educating their children" (Hostetler 206).

Quotation Edited to Eliminate Unnecessary Words: "Not only have the Amish built and staffed their own elementary and vocational schools, but they have gradually organized . . . to cope with the task of educating their children" (Hostetler 206).

CLOSE-UP

OMISSIONS WITHIN QUOTATIONS

Be sure you do not misrepresent or distort the meaning of quoted material when you shorten it. For example, do not say, "the Amish have managed to maintain . . . their culture" when the original quotation is "the Amish have managed to maintain *parts* of their culture."

Note: If the passage you are quoting already contains ellipses, MLA style requires that you place brackets around any ellipses you add.

See 33b **Long Quotations** Set off a quotation of more than four typed lines of prose (or more than three lines of **poetry**) by indenting it one inch from the margin. Double-space, and do not use quotation marks. If you are quoting a single paragraph, do not indent the first line. If you are quoting more than one paragraph, indent the first line of each complete paragraph an additional one-quarter inch. Integrate the quotation into your paper by introducing it with a complete sentence followed by a colon. Place parenthetical documentation one space after the end punctuation.

> According to Hostetler, the Amish were not always hostile to public education:
>
> > The one-room rural elementary school served the Amish community well in a number of ways. As long as it was a public school, it stood midway between the Amish community and the world. Its influence was tolerable, depending upon the degree of influence the Amish were able to bring to the situation. (196)

2 **Integrating Paraphrases and Summaries**

Introduce your paraphrases and summaries with identifying tags, and end them with appropriate documentation. By doing so, you make certain that your readers are able to differentiate your ideas from those of your sources.

Correct (Identifying Tag Differentiates Ideas of Source from Ideas of Writer): Art can be used to uncover many problems that children have at home, in school, or with their friends. For this reason, many therapists use art therapy extensively. According to William Alschuler in *Art and Self-Image*, children's views of themselves in society are often reflected by their art style. For example, a cramped, crowded art style using only a portion of the paper shows a child's limited role (260).

Misleading (Ideas of Source Blend with Ideas of Writer): Art can be used to uncover many problems that children have at home, in school, or with their friends. For this reason, many therapists use art therapy extensively. Children's views of themselves in society are often reflected by their art style. For example, a cramped, crowded art style using only a portion of the paper shows their limited role (Alschuler 260).

EXERCISE 44.2

Look back at the summary and paraphrase that you wrote for Exercise 44.1. Write three possible identifying tags for each, varying the verbs you use for attribution and the placement of the identifying tag. Be sure to include appropriate documentation at the end of each passage.

EXERCISE 44.3

Choose a debatable issue from the following list.

- Illegal immigrants' rights to free public education
- Helmet requirements for motorcycle riders
- Community service requirements for college students

Write a one-sentence summary of your own position on the issue. Then, interview a classmate and write a one-sentence summary of his or her position on the same issue. Finally, locate a source that discusses your issue, and write a paraphrase of the writer's position.

Synthesizing Sources   CHAPTER 45

In academic settings, writers must often synthesize information, combining borrowed material with their own ideas in order to express an original viewpoint. Synthesis allows writers to explore relationships among ideas and to arrange those ideas in a logical and meaningful way.

A **synthesis** integrates information from two or more sources. In a synthesis, you weave ideas from your sources together and show how these ideas are similar or different. In the process, you try to make sense of your sources and help readers understand them in some meaningful way. For this reason, knowing how to write a synthesis is an important skill.

45a Understanding Synthesis

Summaries and paraphrases rephrase a source's main ideas, and quotations reproduce a source's exact language. Synthesis combines summary, paraphrase, and quotation to create an essay or paragraph that expresses a writer's original viewpoint. Thus, an effective synthesis establishes a context for the source material it uses, showing the relevance of each source to the writer's points.

The following synthesis was written by a student as part of a research paper. The student effectively uses paraphrase and quotation to define the term *outsider art* and to explain it in relation to a particular artist's life and work.

Sample Student Synthesis

Topic sentence states student's main point	Bill Traylor is one of America's leading outsider artists. According to *Raw Vision* magazine, Traylor is one of the foremost
Summary of Karlins article	artists of the twentieth century (Karlins). Born on a cotton plantation as a slave in the 1850s and illiterate all his life, Traylor
Paraphrase from one-page Glueck article	was self-taught and did not consider himself an artist. He created work for himself rather than for the public (Glueck). The term

outsider art refers to works of art created by individuals who are by definition outside society. Because of their mental condition, lack of education, criminal behavior, or physical handicaps, they are not part of the mainstream of society. According to Louis-Dreyfus, outsider artists also possess the following characteristics:

Long quotation from introduction to exhibit pamphlet	Few have formal training of any kind. They do their work absent from the self-consciousness that necessarily comes from being an artist in the ordinarily accepted circumstance. The French call it "Art Brut." But here in America, "Outsider Art" also refers to work done by the poor, illiterate, and self-taught African Americans whose artistic product is not the result of a controlling mental or behavioral factor but of their untaught and impoverished social conditions. (iv)
Conclusion summarizes student writer's position	As a Southern African-American man with few resources and little formal training, Traylor fits the definition of an outsider artist whose works are largely defined by the hardships he faced.

As this example demonstrates, an effective synthesis weaves selected passages of source material into a discussion, establishing relationships between sources and the writer's own ideas.

45b Planning a Synthesis

To synthesize source material, you need to discover connections among sources that may seem unrelated. For this reason, you need to think critically about your topic and your sources, trying to understand both your topic and your own point of view.

The first step in synthesizing material is to determine how your sources are alike and different, where they agree and disagree, and whether they reach the same conclusions. As you identify connections between one source and another or between a source and your own ideas, you will develop your own perspective on your subject. It is this viewpoint, summarized in a thesis statement (in the case of an entire paper) or in a topic sentence (in the case of a paragraph), that becomes the focus of your synthesis.

CLOSE-UP

QUESTIONS FOR MAKING CONNECTIONS BETWEEN AND AMONG SOURCES

As you plan your synthesis, ask yourself these questions:

◆ What positions do the sources take on the issue?
◆ What key terms do the sources identify and define?
◆ What background information do the sources provide?
◆ How do the sources address their audiences?
◆ How do the sources agree?
◆ How do the sources disagree?
◆ What evidence do the sources use to support their assertions?
◆ How do the sources address opposing points of view?
◆ How do the sources organize their main ideas?

CHECKLIST

WRITING A SYNTHESIS

As you write your synthesis, follow these guidelines:

❏ Begin with a statement that sums up the main point of your synthesis.
❏ Develop your points one at a time, using your sources as support.
❏ Identify each source, naming its author(s) and title.
❏ Be sure to identify the similarities and differences among your sources.
❏ Carefully analyze and interpret source material.
❏ Use identifying tags as well as transitional words and phrases to help your readers follow your discussion.
❏ Be sure to differentiate your ideas from those of your sources.
❏ Document all summaries, paraphrases, and quotations that you use in your synthesis.

45c Writing a Synthesis

In a first-semester composition class, Jay Gilman, a computer science major, was given the following assignment:

> Choose an area related to your major that you think others would benefit from learning more about. Then, using three sources as support, write a paragraph that defines and explains this topic to an audience unfamiliar with the field. Summarize, paraphrase, and quote source material as appropriate, using MLA (Modern Language Association) documentation style.

After carefully reading his sources and thinking critically about them, Jay wrote the following synthesis.

Effective Synthesis

Computers have already changed our lives. They perform (at incredible speed) many of the everyday tasks that make our way of life possible. For example, computer billing, with all its faults, makes modern business possible, and without computers we would not have access to the cellular services and cable or satellite television that we take for granted.

Topic sentence states student's main point

But computers are more than fast calculators; they are also equipped with artificial intelligence (AI), which has transformed fields such as medicine, agriculture, and manufacturing. One technology writer defines artificial

Quotation from Havenstein article

intelligence as "a field that attempts to provide machines with humanlike reasoning and language-processing capabilities" (Havenstein). Farming is one

Paraphrase of unsigned article's text and visual content

Effective synthesis of source material to explain application of AI

industry that is now using AI technology: with new, high-tech agricultural sprayers that treat crops precisely and accurately, farmers are able to improve the output and quality of their yield

Source

> There's no precise definition of AI, but broadly, it's a field that attempts to provide machines with humanlike reasoning and language-processing capabilities.

Source

> Researchers at Oklahoma State University, meanwhile, have demonstrated the potential for adding machine intelligence to agricultural sprayers (photo). Enhanced with sensors and computers, the field sprayers dramatically increased the application efficiency by applying fertilizers and herbicides only where needed, reports John B. Solie, professor, power and machinery at Oklahoma State.

("More Machine Intelligence"). AI has also made possible
numerous medical advances—for example, helping scientists to
generate human tissue, bone, and organs for patients in need
(Howell). Given the importance of AI technology, it seems certain
that computers will change our lives even more in the future.

Summary of Howell article

Conclusion summarizes student writer's position

Source

> **Human 2.0**
> News that an artificial pancreas has been developed, which could help millions of diabetes patients, is only the tip of the iceberg as far as augmentation of the human body goes. We can already grow skin, cartilage, bone, ears and bladders.

This synthesis effectively defines the term *artificial intelligence* and uses information from three short articles to explain AI and briefly describe its use in various fields. The writer introduces his paragraph with a summary of computer applications familiar to his readers and then moves into a discussion of AI.

The sources selected for the above synthesis could have been used far less carefully and effectively. In the following ineffective explanatory synthesis, source material dominates the discussion, all but eliminating the writer's own voice.

Ineffective Synthesis

Heather Havenstein defines artificial intelligence (AI) as "a
field that attempts to provide machines with humanlike reasoning
and language-processing capabilities." As reported in *IndustryWeek*
magazine, the farming community is using AI technology by adding
machine intelligence to agricultural sprayers, dramatically
increasing their application efficiency and improving the output
and quality of crops ("More Machine Intelligence"). In the
medical field, scientists have used AI to "grow skin, cartilage,
bone, ears and bladders" (Howell). AI technology has changed
our lives in important ways, and it seems obvious that it will
continue to do so in the future.

Begins with out-of-context quotation from source, not student writer's own position

Source's exact words used without quotation marks, resulting in plagiarism

Quotation used where paraphrase is more appropriate

Vague conclusion

This example does not include a topic sentence that states the writer's position; it also lacks supporting examples and has a vague conclusion. Moreover, the paragraph inadvertently **plagiarizes** its source's words.

See Ch. 46

EXERCISE 45.1

Examine a group of advertisements (on television or in print or electronic media) that either target the same group of consumers (singles, for example) or focus on a similar product (weight-loss products, for example). Then, integrate the information from at least three ads in a paragraph-length synthesis that discusses the message the ads are trying to convey.

EXERCISE 45.2

Read the following three sources. Then, write an essay that synthesizes the sources. Summarize, paraphrase, and quote from the sources, using MLA documentation style.

Source A

The following excerpt comes from the introduction to a photo essay that depicts the complex nature of American girl culture today.

> Girl culture today is driven largely by commercial forces outside the family and local community. Peers seem to supplant parents as a source of authority; anxiety has replaced innocence. Despite the important and satisfying gains women have made in achieving greater access to education, power, and all forms of self-expression, including sexual, we have a sense of disquiet about what has happened to our girls.
>
> In the 1990s, a warning about girls was sounded by some bestselling books such as *Meeting at the Crossroads* by Lyn Mikel Brown and Carol Gilligan and *Reviving Ophelia* by Mary Pipher. These powerful discussions alerted the nation to the psychological difficulties of growing up female in a society that silences and stifles girls even in social and educational settings thought to be enlightened. Other studies confirmed that women really are the "stronger sex"—that is, until puberty, when their vulnerability to physical and mental health problems increases. In *The Body Project: An Intimate History of American Girls,* I argued that our current cultural environment is especially "toxic" for adolescent girls because of the anxieties it generates about the developing female body and sexuality. On the basis of my reading over one hundred personal diaries written by adolescent girls between 1830 and 1980, I concluded that as the twentieth century progressed, more and more young women grew up believing that "good looks"—rather than "good works"—were the highest form of female perfection. The body projects that currently absorb the attention of girls not only constitute a "brain drain," but can also threaten mental and physical health. (Brumberg, Joan Jacobs. Introduction. *Girl Culture.* By Lauren Greenfield. San Francisco: Chronicle, 2002. 5–8. Print.)

Source B

The following passage is excerpted from a book exploring the relationship between advertising and consumer behavior.

> The gap between boys and girls is closing, but this is not always for the best. According to a 1998 status report by a consortium of universities and research centers, girls have closed the gap with boys in math performance and are coming close in science. But they are also now smoking, drinking, and using drugs as often as boys their own age. And, although girls are not nearly as violent as boys, they are committing more crimes than ever before and are far more often physically attacking each other.

It is important to understand that these problems go way beyond individual psychological development and pathology. Even girls who are raised in loving homes by supportive parents grow up in a toxic cultural environment, at risk for self-mutilation, eating disorders, and addictions. The culture, both reflected and reinforced by advertising, urges girls to adopt a false self, to bury alive their real selves, to become "feminine," which means to be nice and kind and sweet, to compete with other girls for the attention of boys, and to value romantic relationships with boys above all else. Girls are put into a terrible double bind. They are supposed to repress their power, their anger, their exuberance and be simply "nice," although they also eventually must compete with men in the business world and be successful. They must be overtly sexy and attractive but essentially passive and virginal. It is not surprising that most girls experience this time as painful and confusing, especially if they are unconscious of these conflicting demands. (Kilbourne, Jean. *Can't Buy My Love: How Advertising Changes the Way We Think and Feel*. New York: Simon, 1999. 129-30. Print.)

Source C

The following is excerpted from a book about the impact of popular notions of feminine beauty.

When this book first came out [in 1991], general public opinion considered anorexia and bulimia to be anomalous marginal behavior, and the cause was not assumed to be society's responsibility, insofar as it created ideals and exerted pressure to conform to them—but rather personal crises, perfectionism, poor parenting, and other forms of individual psychological maladjustment. In reality, however, these diseases were widely suffered by many ordinary young women from unremarkable backgrounds, women and girls who were simply trying to maintain an unnatural "ideal" body shape and weight. I knew from looking around me in high school and at college that eating disorders were widespread among otherwise perfectly well balanced young women, and that the simple, basic social pressure to be thin was a major factor in the development of these diseases. . . . Disordered eating, which was understood to fit a disordered ideal, was one of the causes of the disease, and not necessarily, as popular opinion of the day held, a manifestation of an underlying neurosis.

Now, of course, education about the dangers of obsessive dieting or exercise is widespread, and information about eating disorders, their addictive nature, and how to treat them is available in every bookstore, as well as in middle schools, doctors' offices, gyms, high schools, and sororities. *This*, now, is progress.

Yet, on the down side, those very disorders are now so widespread, in fact, almost destigmatized by such intense publicity that they have become virtually normal. Not only do whole sororities take for granted that bulimia is mainstream behavior, but models now openly talk to *Glamour* magazine about their starvation regimes. A newspaper feature about a group of thin, ambitious young women talking about weight quotes one of them as saying, "Now what's wrong with throwing up?" And "pro-an" Web sites have appeared on the Internet, indicating a subculture of girls who are "pro-anorexia," who find the anorexic look appealing and validate it. This is definitely *not* progress. (Wolf, Naomi. *The Beauty Myth: How Images of Beauty Are Used against Women*. New York: Harper, 2002. 5-6. Print.)

46a Defining Plagiarism

Plagiarism is presenting another person's ideas or words as if they were your own. Most plagiarism is **unintentional plagiarism**—for example, inadvertently typing a quoted passage into a paper and forgetting to include the quotation marks and documentation.

There is a difference, however, between an honest mistake and **intentional plagiarism**—for example, copying sentences from a journal article or submitting a paper that someone else has written. The penalties for unintentional plagiarism may sometimes be severe, but intentional plagiarism is almost always dealt with harshly: students who intentionally plagiarize can receive a failing grade for the paper (or the course) or can even be expelled from school.

CLOSE-UP

DETECTING PLAGIARISM

The same technology that has made unintentional plagiarism more common has also made plagiarism easier to detect. By doing a *Google* search, an instructor can quickly find the source of a phrase that has been plagiarized from an Internet source. In addition, plagiarism detection services such as *Turnitin.com* can search subscription databases and identify plagiarized passages in student papers.

46b Avoiding Unintentional Plagiarism

The most common cause of unintentional plagiarism is sloppy research habits. To avoid this problem, start your research paper early. Do not cut and paste text from a Web site or full-text database directly into your paper. If you paraphrase, do so correctly by following the advice in **44b**.

ESL TIP

Because writing in a second language can be difficult, you may be tempted to closely follow the syntax and word choice of your sources. Be aware, however, that this practice constitutes plagiarism.

See
Chs.
47–48

Another cause of unintentional plagiarism is failure to use proper <u>docu-</u><u>mentation</u>. In general, you must document the following information:

♦ Words, ideas, and images that you borrow from a source (print or electronic)
♦ Facts and opinions that are another writer's original contributions
♦ Information that is the product of an author's original research
♦ Statistics, charts, graphs, or other compilations of data that are not yours

Of course, certain material need not be documented: **common knowledge** (information most readers probably know), facts available from a variety of reference sources, familiar sayings and well-known quotations, and your own original research (interviews and surveys, for example).

So, although you do not have to document the fact that John F. Kennedy graduated from Harvard in 1940 or that he was elected president in 1960, you do have to document information from a historian's evaluation of his presidency. The best rule to follow is if you have doubts, document.

Note: You should not submit a paper to one course that you have already received a grade for in another course. If you intend to substantially rework or expand the paper, however, you may be able to use it—but be sure to get permission from both instructors.

46c Revising to Eliminate Plagiarism

You can avoid plagiarism by using documentation wherever it is required and by following these guidelines:

1 Enclose Borrowed Words in Quotation Marks

Original: Historically, only a handful of families have dominated the fireworks industry in the West. Details such as chemical recipes and mixing procedures were cloaked in secrecy and passed down from one generation to the next. . . . One effect of familial secretiveness is that, until recent decades, basic pyrotechnic research was rarely performed, and even when it was, the results were not generally reported in scientific journals. (John A. Conkling, "Pyrotechnics")

Plagiarism: John A. Conkling points out that until recently, little scientific research was done on the chemical properties of fireworks, and when it was, the results were not generally reported in scientific journals (96).

Even though the student writer documents the source of his information, he uses the source's exact words without placing them in quotation marks.

Correct (Borrowed Words in Quotation Marks): John A. Conkling points out that until recently, little scientific research was done on the chemical properties of fireworks, and when it was, "the results were not generally reported in scientific journals" (96).

Correct (Paraphrase): John A. Conkling points out that the little research conducted on the chemical composition of fireworks was seldom reported in the scientific literature (96).

CLOSE-UP

PLAGIARISM AND INTERNET SOURCES

Any time you download text from the Internet, you run the risk of committing unintentional plagiarism. To avoid the possibility of plagiarism, follow these guidelines:

♦ Download information into individual files so that you can keep track of your sources.

♦ Do not simply cut and paste blocks of downloaded text into your paper; first summarize or paraphrase this material.

♦ If you record the exact words of your source, enclose them in quotation marks.

♦ Whether your information is from emails, online discussion groups, listservs, or Web sites, provide appropriate documentation.

♦ Always document figures, tables, charts, and graphs obtained from the Internet or from any other electronic source.

---

2 Do Not Imitate a Source's Syntax and Phrasing

Original: Let's be clear: this wish for politically correct casting goes only one way, the way designed to redress the injuries of centuries. When Pat Carroll, who is a woman, plays Falstaff, who is not, casting is considered a stroke of brilliance. When Josette Simon, who is black, plays Maggie in *After the Fall*, a part Arthur Miller patterned after Marilyn Monroe and which has traditionally been played not by white women, but by blonde white women, it is hailed as a breakthrough.

But when the pendulum moves the other way, the actors' union balks. (Anna Quindlen, "Error, Stage Left")

Plagiarism: Let us be honest. The desire for politically appropriate casting goes in only one direction, the direction intended to make up for the damage done over hundreds of years. When Pat Carroll, a female, is cast as Falstaff, a male, the decision is a brilliant one. When Josette Simon, a black woman, is cast as Maggie in *After the Fall*, a role that Arthur Miller based on Marilyn Monroe and that has usually been played by a woman who is not only white but also blonde, it is considered a major advance.

But when the shoe is on the other foot, the actors' union resists (Quindlen 21).

Although this student writer does not use the exact words of her source, she closely follows the original's syntax and phrasing, simply substituting synonyms for the author's words.

Correct (Paraphrase; One Distinctive Phrase Placed in Quotation Marks): According to Anna Quindlen, the actors' union supports "politically correct casting" (21) only when it means casting a woman or minority group member in a role created for a male or a Caucasian. Thus, it is acceptable for actress Pat Carroll to play Falstaff or for black actress Josette Simon to play Marilyn Monroe; in fact, casting decisions such as these are praised. But when it comes to casting a Caucasian in a role intended for an African American, Asian, or Hispanic, the union objects (21).

Note: Although the parenthetical documentation at the end identifies the passage's source, the quotation requires separate documentation.

3 Document Statistics Obtained from a Source

Although many people assume that statistics are common knowledge, they are usually the result of original research and must, therefore, be documented. Moreover, providing the source of the statistics helps readers to assess their validity.

Correct: According to Morton Schuman, male drivers between the ages of sixteen and twenty-four accounted for the majority of accidents. Of 303 accidents recorded, almost one half took place before the drivers were legally allowed to drive at eighteen (1027).

4 Differentiate Your Words and Ideas from Those of Your Source

Original: At some colleges and universities traditional survey courses of world and English literature . . . have been scrapped or diluted. At others they are in peril. At still others they will be. What replaces them is sometimes a mere option of electives, sometimes "multicultural" courses introducing material from Third World cultures and thinning out an already thin sampling of Western writings, and sometimes courses geared especially to issues of class, race, and gender. Given the notorious lethargy of academic decision-making, there has probably been more clamor than change; but if there's enough clamor, there will be change. (Irving Howe, "The Value of the Canon")

Plagiarism: Debates about expanding the literary canon take place at many colleges and universities across the United States. At many universities, the Western literature survey courses have been edged out by courses that emphasize minority concerns. These courses are "thinning out an already thin sampling of Western writings" in favor of courses geared especially to issues of "class, race, and gender" (Howe 40).

Because the student writer does not differentiate his ideas from those of his source, it appears that only the quotations in the last sentence are borrowed when, in fact, the first sentence also owes a debt to the original. The writer should have clearly identified the boundaries of the borrowed material by introducing it with an identifying tag and ending with documentation. (Note that a quotation *always* requires its own documentation.)

Correct: Debates about expanding the literary canon take place at many colleges and universities across the United States. According to critic Irving Howe, at many universities the Western literature survey courses have been edged out by courses that emphasize minority concerns (41). These courses, says Howe, are "thinning out an already thin sampling of Western writings" in favor of "courses geared especially to issues of class, race, and gender" (40).

CHECKLIST

AVOIDING PLAGIARISM

- ❏ **Take careful notes.** Be sure you have recorded information from your sources carefully and accurately.
- ❏ **In your notes, clearly identify borrowed material.** In handwritten notes, put all words borrowed from your sources inside circled quotation marks, and enclose your own comments within brackets. If you are taking notes on a computer, boldface all quotation marks.
- ❏ **In your paper, differentiate your ideas from those of your sources** by clearly introducing borrowed material with an identifying tag and by following it with documentation.
- ❏ **Enclose all direct quotations** used in your paper within quotation marks.
- ❏ **Review all paraphrases and summaries** in your paper to make certain they are in your own words and that any distinctive words and phrases from a source are quoted.
- ❏ **Document all quoted material and all paraphrases and summaries** of your sources.
- ❏ **Document all information** that is open to dispute or that is not common knowledge.
- ❏ **Document all opinions, conclusions, figures, tables, statistics, graphs, and charts** taken from a source.
- ❏ **Never submit the work of another person as your own.** Do not buy a paper from an online paper mill or use a paper written by a friend. In addition, never include in your paper passages that have been written by a friend, relative, or writing tutor.
- ❏ **Never use sources that you have not actually read (or invent sources that do not exist).**

EXERCISE 46.1

The following paragraph uses material from three sources, but its student author has neglected to cite them. After reading the paragraph and the three sources that follow it, identify the material that has been quoted directly from a source. Compare the wording to the original for accuracy, and insert quotation marks where necessary, making sure the quoted passages fit smoothly into the paragraph. Differentiate the ideas of the student from those of each of the three sources by using identifying tags to introduce any quotations. (If you think the student did not need to quote a passage, paraphrase it instead.) Finally, add parenthetical documentation for each piece of information that requires it.

Student Paragraph

Oral history is an important way of capturing certain aspects of the past that might otherwise be lost. While history books relate the stories of great men and great events, rarely do they include the experiences of ordinary people—slaves, concentration camp survivors, and the illiterate, for example. By providing information about the people and emotions of the past, oral history makes sense of the present and gives a glimpse of the likely future. But because any particular rendition of a life history relies heavily on personal memory, great care must be taken to evaluate and explain the context of an oral history. Like any other historical account, oral history is just one of many possible versions of an individual's past.

Source 1

Oral history relies heavily on memory, a notoriously malleable entity; people remake the past in light of present concerns and knowledge. Yet not all memories are false, and oral history gives us testimony that might otherwise be lost—stories of slaves, of concentration camp survivors, of the illiterate and the obscure, of the legion "ordinary people" who rarely find their way into the history books. Oral history gives us the human element, the thoughts and emotions and confusions that lie beneath the calm surface of written documents. Even when people remake the past because memories are faulty or unbearable, we can learn much about the ways in which the past affects the present. (Freedman, Jean R. "Never Underestimate the Power of a Bus: My Journey to Oral History." *Oral History Review* 29.2 [2002]: 30. Print.)

Source 2

[There is a] widely held view that history belongs to great men and great events, not ordinary people or ordinary life. Yet we know that "ordinary" people in our local districts have important stories to tell. . . . Local histories tell us, on the one hand, that things were done differently in the past, but on the other hand, that in essence people and emotions were much the same. We need to learn from the past to make sense of the present, and get a glimpse of the likely future. (Gregg, Alison. "Planning and Managing an Oral History Collection." *Aplis* 13.4 [2000]: 174. Print.)

Source 3

One aspect of oral history . . . concerns the way in which any particular rendition of a life history is a product of the personal present. It is well-recognized that chronicles of the past are invariably a product of the present, so that different "presents" inspire different versions of the past. Just as all historical accounts—the very questions posed or the interpretive framework imposed—are informed by the historian's present, so, too, is a life history structured by both the interviewer's and the narrator's present. . . . [O]ral history cannot be treated as a source of some narrative truth, but rather as one of many possible versions of an individual's past. . . . [and] the stories told in an oral history are not simply the source of explanation, but rather require explanation. (Honig, Emily. "Getting to the Source: Striking Lives: Oral History and the Politics of Memory." *Journal of Women's History* 9.1 [1997]: 139. Print.)

Directory of MLA Parenthetical References

Directory of MLA Works-Cited List Entries

PRINT SOURCES: *Entries for Articles*

Articles in Scholarly Journals

Articles in Magazines and Newspapers

PRINT SOURCES: *Entries for Books*

Authors

Editions, Multivolume Works, Graphic Narratives, Forewords, Translations, and Sacred Works

Parts of Books

Dissertations, Pamphlets, Government Publications, and Legal Sources

ENTRIES FOR MISCELLANEOUS PRINT AND NONPRINT SOURCES

Lectures and Interviews

Letters

Films, Videotapes, Radio and Television Programs, and Recordings

Paintings, Photographs, Cartoons, and Advertisements

ELECTRONIC SOURCES: *Entries for Sources from Internet Sites*

Internet-Specific Sources

Books, Articles, Reviews, Letters, and Reference Works on the Internet

Paintings, Photographs, Cartoons, and Maps on the Internet

ELECTRONIC SOURCES: *Entries for Sources from Online Databases*

Journal Articles, Magazine Articles, News Services, and Dissertations from Online Databases

73. A scholarly journal article (p. 420)
74. A monthly magazine article (p. 420)
75. A news service (p. 420)
76. A newspaper article (p. 420)
77. A published dissertation (p. 420)

OTHER ELECTRONIC SOURCES

DVD-ROMs and CD-ROMs

78. A nonperiodical publication on DVD-ROM or CD-ROM (p. 421)
79. A periodical publication on DVD-ROM or CD-ROM (p. 421)

Digital Files

80. A word-processing document (p. 421)
81. An MP3 file (p. 421)

MLA Documentation Style CHAPTER 47

Documentation is the formal acknowledgment of the sources you use in your paper. This chapter explains and illustrates the documentation style recommended by the Modern Language Association (MLA). Chapter 48 discusses the documentation style of the American Psychological Association (APA).

47a Using MLA Style

MLA style* is required by instructors of English and other languages as well as by many instructors in other humanities disciplines. MLA documentation has three parts:

---

*MLA documentation style follows the guidelines set in the *MLA Handbook for Writers of Research Papers,* 7th ed. (New York: MLA, 2009).

♦ Parenthetical references in the body of the paper (also known as **in-text citations**)
♦ A works-cited list
♦ Content notes

1 Parenthetical References

MLA documentation uses parenthetical references in the body of the paper keyed to a works-cited list at the end of the paper. A typical parenthetical reference consists of the author's last name and a page number.

The colony appealed to many idealists in Europe (Kelley 132).

If you state the author's name or the title of the work in your discussion, do not include it in the parenthetical reference.

Penn's political motivation is discussed by Joseph J. Kelley in *Pennsylvania, The Colonial Years, 1681–1776* (44).

To distinguish two or more sources by the same author, include a shortened title after the author's name. When you shorten a title, begin with the word by which the work is alphabetized in the list of works cited.

Penn emphasized his religious motivation (Kelley, *Pennsylvania* 116).

CLOSE-UP

PUNCTUATING WITH MLA PARENTHETICAL REFERENCES

Paraphrases and Summaries Parenthetical references are placed *before* the sentence's end punctuation.

Penn's writings epitomize seventeenth-century religious thought (Dengler and Curtis 72).

Quotations Run In with the Text Parenthetical references are placed *after* the quotation but *before* the end punctuation.

As Ross says, "Penn followed his conscience in all matters" (127).

According to Williams, "Penn's utopian vision was informed by his Quaker beliefs . . ." (72).

Quotations Set Off from the Text When you quote more than four lines of prose or more than three lines of poetry, parenthetical references are placed one space *after* the end punctuation.

See 33b

(continued)

> **PUNCTUATING WITH MLA PARENTHETICAL REFERENCES**
> (*continued*)
>
> According to Arthur Smith, William Penn envisioned a state based on
> his religious principles:
>
> > Pennsylvania would be a commonwealth in which all
> > individuals would follow God's truth and develop according
> > to God's law. For Penn, this concept of government was
> > self-evident. It would be a mistake to see Pennsylvania as
> > anything but an expression of Penn's religious beliefs. (314)

Sample MLA Parenthetical References

1. A Work by a Single Author

Fairy tales reflect the emotions and fears of children (Bettelheim 23).

2. A Work by Two or Three Authors

The historian's main job is to search for clues and solve mysteries (Davidson
and Lytle 6).

With the advent of behaviorism, psychology began a new phase of inquiry
(Cowen, Barbo, and Crum 31-34).

3. A Work by More Than Three Authors

List only the first author, followed by **et al.** ("and others").

Helping each family reach its goals for healthy child development and
overall family well-being was the primary approach of Project EAGLE
(Bartle et al. 35).

Or, list the last names of all authors in the order in which they appear on
the work's title page.

Helping each family reach its goals for healthy child development and
overall family well-being was the primary approach of Project EAGLE (Bartle,
Couchonnal, Canda, and Staker 35).

4. A Work in Multiple Volumes

If you list more than one volume of a multivolume work in your works-
cited list, include the appropriate volume and page number (separated by a
colon followed by a space).

Gurney is incorrect when he says that a twelve-hour limit is negotiable (6: 128).

5. A Work without a Listed Author
Use the full title (if brief) or a shortened version of the title (if long), beginning with the word by which it is alphabetized in the works-cited list.

> The group issued an apology a short time later ("Satire Lost" 22).

6. A Work That Is One Page Long
Do not include a page reference for a one-page article.

> Sixty percent of Arab Americans work in white-collar jobs (El-Badru).

7. An Indirect Source
If you use a statement by one author that is quoted in the work of another author, indicate that the material is from an indirect source with the abbreviation **qtd. in** ("quoted in").

> According to Valli and Lucas, "the form of the symbol is an icon or picture
> of some aspect of the thing or activity being symbolized" (qtd. in Wilcox 120).

8. More Than One Work
Cite each work as you normally would, separating one citation from another with a semicolon.

> The Brooklyn Bridge has been used as a subject by many American artists
> (McCullough 144; Tashjian 58).

Note: Long parenthetical references can distract readers. Whenever possible, present them as **content notes**.

See 47a3

9. A Literary Work
When citing a work of **fiction,** it may be helpful to include more than the author's name and the page number in the parenthetical citation. Follow the page number with a semicolon, and then add any other information that might be helpful.

> In *Moby-Dick,* Melville refers to a whaling expedition funded by Louis XIV of
> France (151; ch. 24).

Parenthetical references to **poetry** do not include page numbers. In parenthetical references to *long poems,* cite division and line numbers, separating them with a period.

> In the *Aeneid,* Virgil describes the ships as cleaving the "green woods
> reflected in the calm water" (8.124).

(In this citation, the reference is to book 8, line 124 of the *Aeneid.*)

When citing *short poems,* use line numbers in the citation.

In "A Song in the Front Yard," Brooks's speaker says, "I've stayed in the front yard all my life / I want a peek at the back" (lines 1-2).

Note: When citing lines of a poem, include the word **line** (or **lines**) in the first parenthetical reference; supply just the line numbers in subsequent references.

When citing a **play,** include the act, scene, and line numbers (in arabic numerals), separated by periods. Titles of well-known literary works (such as Shakespeare's plays) are often abbreviated (*Mac.* **2.2.14-16**).

10. Sacred Texts

When citing sacred texts, such as the Bible or the Qur'an, include the version (italicized) and the book (abbreviated if longer than four letters, but not italicized or enclosed in quotation marks), followed by the chapter and verse numbers (separated by a period).

The cynicism of the speaker is apparent when he says, "All things are wearisome; no man can speak of them all" (*New English Bible,* Eccles. 1.8).

Note: The first time you cite a sacred text, include the version in your parenthetical reference; after that, include only the book. If you are using more than one version of a sacred text, however, include the version in each in-text citation.

11. An Entire Work

When citing an entire work, include the author's name and the work's title in the text of your paper rather than in a parenthetical reference.

Lois Lowry's *Gathering Blue* is set in a technologically backward village.

12. Two or More Authors with the Same Last Name

To distinguish authors with the same last name, include their initials in your parenthetical references.

Recent increases in crime have caused thousands of urban homeowners to install alarms (L. Cooper 115). Some of these alarms use sophisticated sensors that were developed by the army (D. Cooper 76).

13. A Government Document or a Corporate Author

Cite such works using the organization's name (usually abbreviated) followed by the page number (**Amer. Automobile Assn. 34**). You can avoid long parenthetical references by working the organization's name (not abbreviated) into your discussion.

According to the President's Commission for the Study of Ethical Problems in Medicine and Biomedical and Behavioral Research, the issues relating to euthanasia are complicated (76).

14. A Legal Source

Titles of acts or laws that appear in the text of your paper or in the works-cited list should not be italicized or enclosed in quotation marks. In the parenthetical reference, titles are usually abbreviated, and the act or law is referred to by sections. Include the USC (United States Code) and the year the act or law was passed (if relevant).

Such research should include investigations into the cause, diagnosis, early detection, prevention, control, and treatment of autism (42 USC 284q, 2000).

Names of legal cases are usually abbreviated (**Roe v. Wade**). They are italicized in the text of your paper but not in the works-cited list.

In *Goodridge v. Department of Public Health,* the court ruled that the Commonwealth of Massachusetts had not adequately provided a reasonable constitutional cause for barring homosexual couples from civil marriages (2003).

15. An Electronic Source

If a reference to an electronic source includes paragraph numbers rather than page numbers, use the abbreviation **par.** or **pars.** followed by the paragraph number or numbers.

The earliest type of movie censorship came in the form of licensing fees, and in Deer River, Minnesota, "a licensing fee of $200 was deemed not excessive for a town of 1000" (Ernst, par. 20).

If the electronic source has no page or paragraph numbers, try to cite the work in your discussion rather than in a parenthetical reference. By consulting your works-cited list, readers will be able to determine that the source is electronic and therefore may not have page numbers.

In her article "Limited Horizons," Lynne Cheney observes that schools do best when students read literature not for practical information but for its insights into the human condition.

2 Works-Cited List

The **works-cited list,** which appears at the end of your paper, is an alphabetical listing of all the sources you cite. Double-space within and between entries on the list, and indent the second and subsequent lines of each entry one-half inch. (**See 47b** for full manuscript guidelines.)

MLA PRINT SOURCES ◆ Entries for Articles

Article citations include the author's name; the title of the article (in quotation marks); the title of the periodical (italicized); the volume and issue numbers (when applicable; see below); the year or date of publication; the pages on which the full article appears, without the abbreviation *p.* or *pp.*; and the publication medium (**Print, Web,** and so on). Figure 47.1 shows where you can find this information.

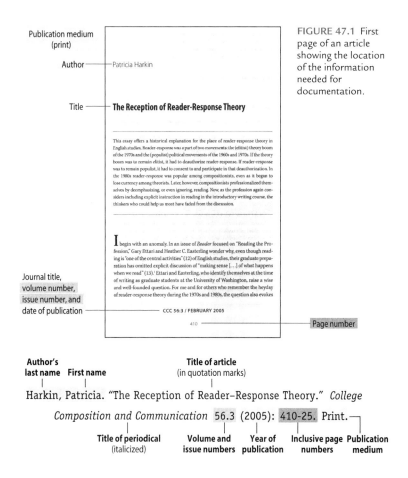

Publication medium (print)

Author — Patricia Harkin

Title — **The Reception of Reader-Response Theory**

This essay offers a historical explanation for the place of reader-response theory in English studies. Reader-response was a part of two movements: the (elitist) theory boom of the 1970s and the (populist) political movements of the 1960s and 1970s. If the theory boom was to remain elitist, it had to deauthorize reader-response. If reader-response was to remain populist, it had to consent to and participate in that deauthorization. In the 1980s reader-response was popular among compositionists, even as it began to lose currency among theorists. Later, however, compositionists professionalized themselves by deemphasizing, or even ignoring, reading. Now, as the profession again considers including explicit instruction in reading in the introductory writing course, the thinkers who could help us most have faded from the discussion.

I begin with an anomaly. In an issue of *Reader* focused on "Reading the Profession," Gary Ettari and Heather C. Easterling wonder why, even though reading is "one of the central activities" (12) of English studies, their graduate preparation has omitted explicit discussion of "making sense [...] of what happens when we read" (13).¹ Ettari and Easterling, who identify themselves at the time of writing as graduate students at the University of Washington, raise a wise and well-founded question. For me and for others who remember the heyday of reader-response theory during the 1970s and 1980s, the question also evokes

Journal title, volume number, issue number, and date of publication — CCC 56:3 / FEBRUARY 2005

410 — Page number

FIGURE 47.1 First page of an article showing the location of the information needed for documentation.

Author's last name   First name

Title of article (in quotation marks)

Harkin, Patricia. "The Reception of Reader–Response Theory." *College Composition and Communication* 56.3 (2005): 410-25. Print.

Title of periodical (italicized)   Volume and issue numbers   Year of publication   Inclusive page numbers   Publication medium

Articles in Scholarly Journals

1. An Article in a Scholarly Journal

MLA guidelines now recommend that you include both the volume number and the issue number (separated by a period) for all scholarly journal articles that you cite, regardless of whether they are paginated continuously through an annual volume or separately in each issue. Follow the volume and issue numbers with the year of publication (in parentheses), the inclusive page numbers, and the publication medium.

> Siderits, Mark. "Perceiving Particulars: A Buddhist Defense." *Philosophy East and West* 54.3 (2004): 367-83. Print.

Articles in Magazines and Newspapers

2. An Article in a Weekly Magazine (Signed)
For signed articles, start with the author, last name first. In dates, the day precedes the month (abbreviated except for May, June, and July).

> Corliss, Richard. "His Days in Hollywood." *Time* 14 June 2004: 56-62. Print.

3. An Article in a Weekly Magazine (Unsigned)
For unsigned articles, start with the title of the article.

> "Ronald Reagan." *National Review* 28 June 2004: 14-17. Print.

4. An Article in a Monthly Magazine

> Thomas, Evan. "John Paul Jones." *American History* Aug. 2003: 22-25. Print.

5. An Article That Does Not Appear on Consecutive Pages
When, for example, an article begins on page 120 and then skips to page 186, include only the first page number, followed by a plus sign.

> Di Giovanni, Janine. "The Shiites of Iraq." *National Geographic* June 2004: 62+. Print.

6. An Article in a Newspaper (Signed)

> Krantz, Matt. "Stock Success Not Exactly Unparalleled." *Wall Street Journal* 11 June 2004: B1+. Print.

7. An Article in a Newspaper (Unsigned)

> "A Steadfast Friend on 9/11 Is Buried." *New York Times* 6 Aug. 2002, late ed.: B8. Print.

Note: Omit the article *the* from the title of a newspaper even if the newspaper's actual title includes the article.

8. An Editorial in a Newspaper

> "The Government and the Web." Editorial. *New York Times* 25 Aug. 2009, late ed.: A20. Print.

9. A Letter to the Editor of a Newspaper

> Chang, Paula. Letter. *Philadelphia Inquirer* 10 Dec. 2006, suburban ed.: A17. Print.

10. A Book Review in a Newspaper

Straw, Deborah. "Thinking about Tomorrow." Rev. of *Planning for the 21st Century: A Guide for Community Colleges,* by William A. Wojciechowski and Dedra Manes. *Community College Week* 7 June 2004: 15. Print.

11. An Article with a Title within Its Title

If the article you are citing contains a title that is normally enclosed in quotation marks, use single quotation marks for the interior title.

Zimmerman, Brett. "Frantic Forensic Oratory: Poe's 'The Tell-Tale Heart.'" *Style* 35 (2001): 34-50. Print.

If the article you are citing contains a title that is normally italicized, use italics for the title in your works-cited entry.

Lingo, Marci. "Forbidden Fruit: The Banning of *The Grapes of Wrath* in the Kern County Free Library." *Libraries and Culture* 38 (2003): 351-78. Print.

MLA PRINT SOURCES ◆ Entries for Books

Book citations include the author's name; book title (italicized); and publication information (place, publisher, date, publication medium). Figures 47.2 and 47.3 show where you can find this information.

In each works-cited entry, capitalize all major words of the book's title except articles, coordinating conjunctions, prepositions, and the *to* of an infinitive (unless such a word is the first or last word of the title or subtitle). Do not italicize the period that follows a book's title.

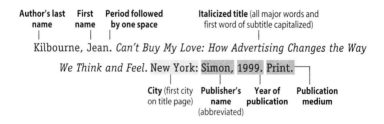

Author's last | First | Period followed | Italicized title (all major words and
name | name | by one space | first word of subtitle capitalized)

Kilbourne, Jean. *Can't Buy My Love: How Advertising Changes the Way We Think and Feel.* New York: Simon, 1999. Print.

City (first city on title page) | Publisher's name (abbreviated) | Year of publication | Publication medium

---

CLOSE-UP

PUBLISHERS' NAMES

MLA requires that you use abbreviated forms of publishers' names in the works-cited list. In general, omit articles; abbreviations, such as *Inc.* and *Corp.*; and words such as *Publishers, Books,* and *Press.* If the publisher's name includes a person's name, use the last name only. Finally, use standard abbreviations whenever you can—*UP* for University Press and *P* for Press, for example.

Name	Abbreviation
Basic Books	Basic
Government Printing Office	GPO
The Modern Language Association of America	MLA
Oxford University Press	Oxford UP
Alfred A. Knopf, Inc.	Knopf
Random House, Inc.	Random
University of Chicago Press	U of Chicago P

FIGURE 47.2 Title page from a book showing the location of the information needed for documentation.

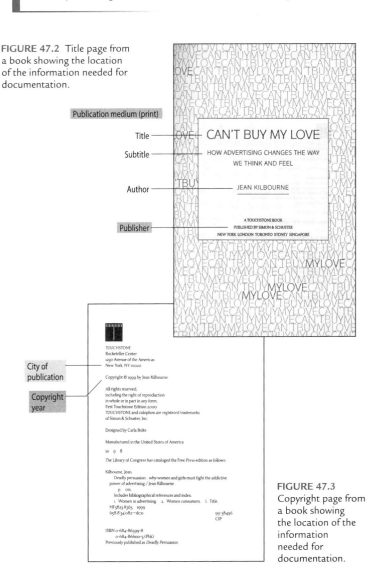

Publication medium (print)

Title

Subtitle

Author

Publisher

City of publication

Copyright year

FIGURE 47.3 Copyright page from a book showing the location of the information needed for documentation.

Authors

12. A Book by One Author

> Bettelheim, Bruno. *The Uses of Enchantment: The Meaning and Importance of Fairy Tales.* New York: Knopf, 1976. Print.

13. A Book by Two or Three Authors

List the first author with last name first. List subsequent authors with first name first in the order in which they appear on the title page.

> Peters, Michael A., and Nicholas C. Burbules. *Poststructuralism and Educational Research.* Lanham: Rowman, 2004. Print.

14. A Book by More Than Three Authors

List the first author only, followed by **et al.** ("and others").

> Badawi, El Said, et al. *Modern Written Arabic.* London: Routledge, 2004. Print.

Or, include all the authors in the order in which they appear on the title page.

> Badawi, El Said, Daud A. Abdu, Mike Carfter, and Adrian Gully. *Modern Written Arabic.* London: Routledge, 2004. Print.

15. Two or More Books by the Same Author

List books by the same author in alphabetical order by title. After the first entry, use three unspaced hyphens followed by a period in place of the author's name.

> Ede, Lisa. *Situating Composition: Composition Studies and the Politics of Location.* Carbondale: Southern Illinois UP, 2004. Print.
>
> ---. *Work in Progress.* 6th ed. Boston: Bedford, 2004. Print.

Note: If the author is the editor or translator of the second entry, place a comma and the appropriate abbreviation after the hyphens (---**, ed.**). See entry 17 for more on edited books and entry 25 for more on translated books.

16. A Book by a Corporate Author

A book is cited by its corporate author when individual members of the association, commission, or committee that produced it are not identified on the title page.

> American Automobile Association. *Western Canada and Alaska.* Heathrow: AAA, 2004. Print.

17. An Edited Book

An edited book is a work prepared for publication by a person other than the author. If your focus is on the *author's* work, begin your citation with the author's name. After the title, include the abbreviation **Ed.** ("Edited by"), followed by the editor or editors.

Twain, Mark. *Adventures of Huckleberry Finn*. Ed. Michael Patrick Hearn.

New York: Norton, 2001. Print.

If your focus is on the *editor's* work, begin your citation with the editor's name followed by the abbreviation **ed.** ("editor") if there is one editor or **eds.** ("editors") if there are more than one. After the title, give the author's name, preceded by the word **By.**

Hearn, Michael Patrick, ed. *Adventures of Huckleberry Finn*. By Mark Twain.

New York: Norton, 2001. Print.

Editions, Multivolume Works, Graphic Narratives, Forewords, Translations, and Sacred Works

18. A Subsequent Edition of a Book

When citing an edition other than the first, include the edition number that appears on the work's title page.

Wilson, Charles Banks. *Search for the Native American Purebloods*. 3rd ed.

Norman: U of Oklahoma P, 2000. Print.

19. A Republished Book

Include the original publication date after the title of a republished book— for example, a paperback version of a hardcover book.

Wharton, Edith. *The House of Mirth*. 1905. New York: Scribner's, 1975. Print.

20. A Book in a Series

If the title page indicates that the book is a part of a series, include the series name, neither italicized nor enclosed in quotation marks, and the series number, followed by a period, after the publication information. Use the abbreviation **Ser.** if *Series* is part of the series name.

Davis, Bertram H. *Thomas Percy*. Boston: Twayne, 1981. Print. Twayne's

English Authors Ser. 313.

21. A Multivolume Work

When all volumes of a multivolume work have the same title, include the number of the volume you are using.

Fisch, Max H., ed. *Writings of Charles S. Peirce: A Chronological Edition*.

Vol. 4. Bloomington: Indiana UP, 2000. Print.

If you use two or more volumes that have the same title, cite the entire work.

Fisch, Max H., ed. *Writings of Charles S. Peirce: A Chronological Edition.*

6 vols. Bloomington: Indiana UP, 2000. Print.

When the volume you are using has an individual title, you may cite the title without mentioning any other volumes.

Mareš, Milan. *Fuzzy Cooperative Games: Cooperation with Vague Expectations.*

New York: Physica-Verlag, 2001. Print.

If you wish, however, you may include supplemental information, such as the number of the volume, the title of the entire work, the total number of volumes, or the inclusive publication dates.

22. An Illustrated Book or a Graphic Narrative

An **illustrated book** is a work in which illustrations accompany the text. If your focus is on the *author's* work, begin your citation with the author's name. After the title, include the abbreviation **Illus.** ("Illustrated by") followed by the publication information.

Frost, Robert. *Stopping by Woods on a Snowy Evening.* Illus. Susan Jeffers.

New York: Dutton-Penguin, 2001. Print.

If your focus is on the *illustrator's* work, begin your citation with the illustrator's name followed by the abbreviation **illus.** ("illustrator"). After the title, give the author's name, preceded by the word **By.**

Jeffers, Susan, illus. *Stopping by Woods on a Snowy Evening.* By Robert Frost.

New York: Dutton-Penguin, 2001. Print.

A **graphic narrative** is a work in which text and illustrations work together to tell a story. Cite a graphic narrative as you would cite a book.

Bechdel, Alison. *Fun Home: A Family Tragicomic.* Boston: Houghton, 2006.

Print.

23. The Foreword, Preface, or Afterword of a Book

Campbell, Richard. Preface. *Media and Culture: An Introduction to Mass*

Communication. By Bettina Fabos. Boston: Bedford, 2005. vi-xi. Print.

24. A Book with a Title within Its Title

If the book you are citing contains a title that is normally italicized (a novel, play, or long poem, for example), do not italicize the interior title.

Fulton, Joe B. *Mark Twain in the Margins: The Quarry Farm Marginalia*

and A Connecticut Yankee in King Arthur's Court. Tuscaloosa: U of

Alabama P, 2000. Print.

If the book you are citing contains a title that is normally enclosed in quotation marks, keep the quotation marks.

> Hawkins, Hunt, and Brian W. Shaffer, eds. *Approaches to Teaching Conrad's "Heart of Darkness" and "The Secret Sharer."* New York: MLA, 2002. Print.

25. A Translation

> García Márquez, Gabriel. *One Hundred Years of Solitude*. Trans. Gregory Rabassa. New York: Avon, 1991. Print.

26. The Bible

> *The New English Bible with the Apocrypha*. Oxford Study ed. New York: Oxford UP, 1976. Print.

27. The Qur'an

> *Holy Qur'an*. Trans. M. H. Shakir. Elmhurst: Tahrike Tarsile Qur'an, 1999. Print.

Parts of Books

28. A Short Story, Play, or Poem in an Anthology

> Chopin, Kate. "The Storm." *Literature: Reading, Reacting, Writing*. Ed. Laurie G. Kirszner and Stephen R. Mandell. 7th ed. Boston: Wadsworth, 2010. 313-17. Print.

> Shakespeare, William. *Othello, the Moor of Venice*. *Shakespeare: Six Plays and the Sonnets*. Ed. Thomas Marc Parrott and Edward Hubler. New York: Scribner's, 1956. 145-91. Print.

29. A Short Story, Play, Poem, or Essay in a Collection of an Author's Work

> Bukowski, Charles. "lonely hearts." *The Flash of Lightning behind the Mountain: New Poems*. New York: Ecco, 2004. 115-16. Print.

Note: The title of the poem in the entry above is not capitalized because it appears in lowercase letters in the original.

30. A Work in an Anthology

> Crevel, René. "From *Babylon*." *Surrealist Painters and Poets: An Anthology*. Ed. Mary Ann Caws. Cambridge: MIT P, 2001. 175-77. Print.

Note: Supply inclusive page numbers for the entire work, not just for the page or pages you cite in your paper.

31. More Than One Work from the Same Anthology

List each work from the same anthology separately, followed by a cross-reference to the entire anthology. Also list complete publication information for the anthology itself.

> Agar, Eileen. "Am I a Surrealist?" Caws 3-7.
>
> Caws, Mary Ann, ed. *Surrealist Painters and Poets: An Anthology*. Cambridge:
>
> MIT P, 2001. Print.
>
> Crevel, René. "From *Babylon*." Caws 175-77.

32. A Scholarly Article in a Collection

> Booth, Wayne C. "Why Ethical Criticism Can Never Be Simple." *Style* 32.2
>
> (1998): 351-64. Rpt. in *Mapping the Ethical Turn: A Reader in Ethics,*
>
> *Culture, and Literary Theory*. Ed. Todd F. Davis and Kenneth Womack.
>
> Charlottesville: UP of Virginia, 2001. 16-29. Print.

33. An Article in a Reference Book (Signed/Unsigned)

For a **signed** article, begin with the author's name. For unfamiliar reference books, include full publication information.

> Drabble, Margaret. "Expressionism." *The Oxford Companion to English*
>
> *Literature*. 6th ed. New York: Oxford UP, 2000. Print.

If the article is **unsigned,** begin with the title. For familiar reference books, do not include full publication information.

> "Cubism." *The Encyclopedia Americana*. 2004 ed. Print.

Note: Omit page numbers when the reference book lists entries alphabetically. If you are listing one definition among several from a dictionary, include the abbreviation **Def.** ("Definition") along with the letter and/or number that corresponds to the definition.

> "Justice." Def. 2b. *The Concise Oxford Dictionary*. 10th ed. 1999. Print.

Dissertations, Pamphlets, Government Publications, and Legal Sources

34. A Dissertation (Published)

Cite a published dissertation the same way you would cite a book, but add relevant dissertation information before the publication information.

> Rodriguez, Jason Anthony. *Bureaucracy and Altruism: Managing the*
>
> *Contradictions of Teaching*. Diss. U of Texas at Arlington, 2003. Ann
>
> Arbor: UMI, 2004. Print.

Note: University Microfilms, which publishes most of the dissertations in the United States, is also available online by subscription. For the proper format for citing online databases, see entries 73–77.

35. A Dissertation (Unpublished)

Use quotation marks for the title of an unpublished dissertation.

> Bon Tempo, Carl Joseph. "Americans at the Gate: The Politics of American
>
> Refugee Policy." Diss. U of Virginia, 2004. Print.

36. A Pamphlet

Cite a pamphlet as you would a book. If no author is listed, begin with the title (italicized).

> *Choosing the Right Digital Camera*. Rochester: Kodak, 2004. Print.

37. A Government Publication

If the publication has no listed author, begin with the name of the government, followed by the name of the agency. You may use an abbreviation if its meaning is clear: **United States. Cong. Senate.**

> United States. Office of Consumer Affairs. *2003 Consumer's Resource*
>
> *Handbook*. Washington: GPO, 2003. Print.

When citing two or more publications by the same government, use three unspaced hyphens (followed by a period) in place of the name for the second and subsequent entries. When you cite more than one work from the same agency of that government, use an additional set of unspaced hyphens in place of the agency name.

> United States. FAA. *Passenger Airline Safety in the Twenty-First Century*.
>
> Washington: GPO, 2003. Print.
>
> ---. ---. *Recycled Air in Passenger Airline Cabins*. Washington: GPO, 2002.
>
> Print.

38. A Legal Source

In general, you do not need a works-cited entry for familiar historical documents. Parenthetical references in the text are sufficient—for example, (**US Const., art. 3, sec. 2**). If you cite an act in the works-cited list, include the name of the act, its Public Law (Pub. L.) number, its Statutes at Large (Stat.) cataloging number, its enactment date, and its publication medium.

> Children's Health Act. Pub. L. 106-310. 114 Stat. 1101. 17 Oct. 2000. Print.

In works-cited entries for legal cases, abbreviate names of cases, but spell out the first important word of each party's name. Include the volume number, abbreviated name (not italicized), and inclusive page numbers of the law report; the name of the deciding court; the decision year; and publication information for the source. Do not italicize the case name in the works-cited list.

> Abbott v. Blades. 544 US 929. Supreme Court of the US. 2005. *United States Reports*. Washington: GPO, 2007. Print.

MLA ENTRIES FOR MISCELLANEOUS PRINT AND NONPRINT SOURCES

Lectures and Interviews

39. A Lecture

> Grimm, Mary. "An Afternoon with Mary Grimm." Visiting Writers Program. Dept. of English, Wright State U, Dayton. 16 Apr. 2004. Lecture.

40. A Personal Interview

> West, Cornel. Personal interview. 28 Dec. 2008.
> Tannen, Deborah. Telephone interview. 8 June 2008.

41. A Published Interview

> Huston, John. "The Outlook for Raising Money: An Investment Banker's Viewpoint." *NJBIZ* 30 Sept. 2002: 2-3. Print.

Letters

42. A Personal Letter

Include the abbreviation **TS** (for "typescript") after the date of a typed letter.

> Tan, Amy. Letter to the author. 7 Apr. 2008. TS.

43. A Published Letter

> Joyce, James. "Letter to Louis Gillet." 20 Aug. 1931. *James Joyce*. By Richard Ellmann. New York: Oxford UP, 1965. 631. Print.

44. A Letter in a Library's Archives

Include the abbreviation **MS** (for "manuscript") after the date of a handwritten letter.

> Stieglitz, Alfred. Letter to Paul Rosenberg. 5 Sept. 1923. MS. Stieglitz Archive. Yale U Arts Lib., New Haven.

Films, Videotapes, Radio and Television Programs, and Recordings

45. A Film

Include the title of the film (italicized), the distributor, and the date, along with other information that may be useful to readers, such as the names of the performers, the director, and the screenwriter. Conclude with the publication medium.

> *Citizen Kane.* Dir. Orson Welles. Perf. Welles, Joseph Cotten, Dorothy
> Comingore, and Agnes Moorehead. RKO, 1941. Film.

If you are focusing on the contribution of a particular person, begin with that person's name.

> Welles, Orson, dir. *Citizen Kane.* Perf. Welles, Joseph Cotten, Dorothy
> Comingore, and Agnes Moorehead. RKO, 1941. Film.

46. A Videotape, DVD, or Laser Disc
Cite a videotape, DVD, or laser disc as you would cite a film, but include the original release date (when available).

> *Bowling for Columbine.* Dir. Michael Moore. 2002. United Artists and Alliance
> Atlantis, 2003. DVD.

47. A Radio or Television Program
> "War Feels Like War." *P.O.V.* Dir. Esteban Uyarra. PBS. WPTD, Dayton, 6 July
> 2004. Television.

48. A Recording
List the composer, conductor, or performer (whomever you are focusing on), followed by the title, publisher, year of issue, and publication medium.

> Boubill, Alain, and Claude-Michel Schönberg. *Miss Saigon.* Perf. Lea
> Salonga, Claire Moore, and Jonathan Pryce. Cond. Martin Koch.
> Geffen, 1989. Audiocassette.
> Marley, Bob. "Crisis." *Kaya.* Kava Island, 1978. LP.

Paintings, Photographs, Cartoons, and Advertisements

49. A Painting
> Hopper, Edward. *Railroad Sunset.* 1929. Oil on canvas. Whitney Museum of
> American Art, New York.

50. A Photograph
Cite a photograph in a museum's collection in the same way you cite a painting.

> Stieglitz, Alfred. *The Steerage.* 1907. Photograph. Los Angeles County
> Museum of Art, Los Angeles.

51. A Cartoon or Comic Strip

Trudeau, Garry "Doonesbury." Comic strip. *Philadelphia Inquirer* 15 Sept.

2003, late ed.: E13. Print.

52. An Advertisement

Microsoft. Advertisement. *National Review* 8 June 2004: 17. Print.

MLA ELECTRONIC SOURCES ◆
Entries for Sources from Internet Sites

MLA style* recognizes that full source information for Internet sources is not always available. Include in your citation whatever information you can reasonably obtain: the author or editor of the site (if available); the name of the site (italicized); the version number of the source (if applicable); the name of any institution or sponsor (if unavailable, include the abbreviation **N.p.** for "no publisher"); the date of electronic publication or update (if unavailable, include the abbreviation **n.d.** for "no date of publication"); the publication medium (**Web**); and the date you accessed the source. MLA recommends omitting the URL from the citation unless it is necessary to find the source (as in entry 56). Figure 47.4 shows where you can find information you need for documentation.

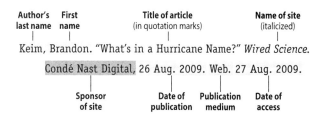

If an electronic address (URL) is necessary, MLA requires that you enclose the URL within angle brackets to distinguish the address from the punctuation in the rest of the citation. If a URL will not fit on a line, the entire URL will be automatically carried over to the next line. If you prefer to divide the URL, divide it after a slash. (Do not insert a hyphen.)

Internet-Specific Sources

53. An Entire Web Site

Nelson, Cary, ed. *Modern American Poetry*. Dept. of English, U of Illinois,

Urbana-Champaign, 2002. Web. 26 May 2008.

---

*The documentation style for Internet sources presented here conforms to the most recent guidelines published in the *MLA Handbook for Writers of Research Papers* (7th ed.) and found online at <http://www.mlahandbook.org>.

Publication medium (Web)

Name of site

Title of article

Author

Date

Sponsor of site

FIGURE 47.4 Part of an online article showing the location of the information needed for documentation.

54. A Document within a Web Site

"D-Day: June 6, 1944." *History.com*. History Channel, 1999. Web. 7 June 2002.

55. A Home Page for a Course

Walker, Janice R. Home page. *Georgia Southern University*. Dept. of Writing and Linguistics, Georgia Southern U, 5 June 2008. Web. 30 Mar. 2009.

56. A Personal Home Page

Gainor, Charles. Home page. U of Toronto, 22 July 2005. Web. 10 Nov. 2005. <http://www.chass.utoronto.ca:9094/~char>.

57. A Radio Program Accessed from an Internet Archive

"Teenage Skeptic Takes on Climate Scientists." Narr. David Kestenbaum. *Morning Edition*. Natl. Public Radio. WNYC, New York, 15 Apr. 2008. Transcript. *NPR*. Web. 30 Mar. 2009.

58. An Email

Mauk, Karen R. Message to the author. 28 June 2008. E-mail.

59. An Online Posting (Online Forum or Blog)

Schiller, Stephen. "Paper Cost and Publishing Costs." *New York Times.*

New York Times, 24 Apr. 2002. Web. 17 May 2002. <www.nytimes.com/

webin/webx?13A^41356.ee765e/0>.

Merry. "The Way We Roll. . . ." *EnviroMom.* EnviroMom, 27 June 2008. Web.

3 July 2008.

Books, Articles, Reviews, Letters, and Reference Works on the Internet

60. A Book

Douglass, Frederick. *My Bondage and My Freedom.* Boston, 1855. *Google Book*

Search. Web. 8 June 2005.

61. An Article in a Scholarly Journal

When you cite information from an electronic source that has a print version, include the publication information for the print source, the inclusive page numbers (if available), the publication medium, and the date you accessed it.

DeKoven, Marianne. "Utopias Limited: Post-Sixties and Postmodern

American Fiction." *Modern Fiction Studies* 41.1 (1995): 75-97. Web.

20 Jan. 2005.

62. An Article in a Magazine

Weiser, Jay. "The Tyranny of Informality." *Time.* Time, 26 Feb. 1996. Web.

1 Mar. 2008.

63. An Article in a Newspaper

Wyatt, Edward. "Electronic Device Stirs Unease at Book Fair." *New York*

Times. New York Times, 2 June 2008. Web. 12 June 2008.

64. An Article in a Newsletter

Sullivan, Jennifer S., comp. "Documentation Preserved, New Collections."

AIP Center for History of Physics 39.2 (2007): 2-3. Web. 26 Feb. 2008.

65. A Review

Ebert, Roger. Rev. of *Star Wars: Episode I—The Phantom Menace,* dir. George

Lucas. *Chicago Sun-Times.* Digital Chicago, 8 June 2000. Web. 22 June

2007.

66. A Letter to the Editor

> Chen-Cheng, Henry H. Letter. *New York Times*. New York Times, 19 July
>> 1999. Web. 1 Jan. 2009.

67. An Article in an Encyclopedia

Include the article's title, the title of the database (italicized), the version number (if available), the sponsor, the date of electronic publication, the publication medium, and the date of access.

> "Hawthorne, Nathaniel." *Encyclopaedia Britannica Online*. Encyclopaedia
>> Britannica, 2008. Web. 16 May 2008.

68. A Government Publication

Cite an online government publication as you would cite a print version; end with the information required for an electronic source.

> United States. Dept. of Justice. Office of Justice Programs. *Violence against*
>> *Women: Estimates from the Redesigned National Crime Victimization*
>> *Survey*. By Ronet Bachman and Linda E. Saltzman. Aug. 1995. *Bureau*
>> *of Justice Statistics*. Web. 10 July 2007.

Paintings, Photographs, Cartoons, and Maps on the Internet

69. A Painting

> Seurat, Georges-Pierre. *Evening, Honfleur*. 1886. Museum of Mod. Art,
>> New York. *MoMA.org*. Web. 8 Jan. 2004.

70. A Photograph

> Brady, Mathew. *Ulysses S. Grant 1822–1885*. 1864. *Mathew Brady's National*
>> *Portrait Gallery*. Web. 2 Oct. 2008.

71. A Cartoon

> Stossel, Sage. "Star Wars: The Next Generation." Cartoon. *Atlantic Unbound*.
>> Atlantic Monthly Group, 2 Oct. 2002. Web. 14 Nov. 2007.

72. A Map

> "Philadelphia, Pennsylvania." Map. *U.S. Gazetteer*. US Census Bureau, n.d.
>> Web. 17 July 2009.

MLA ELECTRONIC SOURCES ◆
Entries for Sources from Online Databases

To cite information from an online database, supply the publication information (including page numbers, if available; if unavailable, use **n. pag.**)

followed by the name of the database (italicized), the publication medium (**Web**), and the date of access.

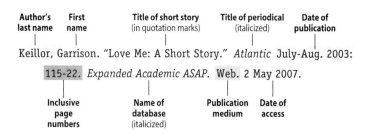

Journal Articles, Magazine Articles, News Services, and Dissertations from Online Databases

73. A Scholarly Journal Article

Schaefer, Richard J. "Editing Strategies in Television News Documentaries."

Journal of Communication 47.4 (1997): 69-89. InfoTrac OneFile Plus.

Web. 2 Oct. 2008.

74. A Monthly Magazine Article

Livermore, Beth. "Meteorites on Ice." Astronomy July 1993: 54-58. Expanded

Academic ASAP Plus. Web. 12 Nov. 2007.

Wright, Karen. "The Clot Thickens." Discover Dec. 1999: n. pag. MasterFILE

Premier. Web. 10 Oct. 2007.

75. A News Service

Ryan, Desmond. "Some Background on the Battle of Gettysburg." Knight

Ridder/Tribune News Service 7 Oct. 1993: n. pag. InfoTrac OneFile Plus.

Web. 16 Nov. 2009.

76. A Newspaper Article

Meyer, Greg. "Answering Questions about the West Nile Virus." Dayton

Daily News 11 July 2002: Z3-7. LexisNexis. Web. 17 Feb. 2006.

77. A Published Dissertation

Rodriguez, Jason Anthony. Bureaucracy and Altruism: Managing the

Contradictions of Teaching. Diss. U of Texas at Arlington, 2003.

ProQuest. Web. 4 Mar. 2006.

MLA OTHER ELECTRONIC SOURCES

DVD-ROMs and CD-ROMs

78. A Nonperiodical Publication on DVD-ROM or CD-ROM

Cite a nonperiodical publication on DVD-ROM or CD-ROM the same way you would cite a book, but include the appropriate medium of publication.

"Windhover." *The Oxford English Dictionary*. 2nd ed. Oxford: Oxford UP,

2001. DVD-ROM.

"Whitman, Walt." *DiskLit: American Authors*. Boston: Hall, 2000. CD-ROM.

79. A Periodical Publication on DVD-ROM or CD-ROM

Zurbach, Kate. "The Linguistic Roots of Three Terms." *Linguistic Quarterly*

37 (1994): 12-47. CD-ROM. *InfoTrac: Magazine Index Plus*. Information

Access. Jan. 2009.

Digital Files

80. A Word-Processing Document

Russell, Brad. "Work Trip Notes." File last modified on 22 Mar. 2009.

Microsoft Word file.

81. An MP3 File

U2. "Beautiful Day." *All That You Can't Leave Behind*. Universal-Island, 2000.

MP3 file.

EXERCISE 47.1

The following notes identify sources used in a paper on censorship and the Internet. Following the proper format for MLA parenthetical documentation, create a parenthetical reference for each source, and then create a works-cited list, arranging the sources in the proper order.

1. Page 72 in a book called Banned in the USA by Herbert N. Foerstel. The book has 231 pages and was published in a third edition in 2006 by Greenwood Press, located in Westport, Connecticut. The author's name appears in the text of your paper.
2. A statement made by Esther Dyson in her keynote address at the News-papers 1996 Conference. Her statement is quoted in an article by Jodi B. Cohen called Fighting Online Censorship. The speech has not been printed in any other source. The article is in the April 13, 1996, edi-tion of the weekly business journal Editor & Publisher. Dyson's quotation appears on page 44. The article begins on page 44 and continues on page 60. Dyson's name is mentioned in the text of your paper.

3. If You Don't Love It, Leave It, an essay by Esther Dyson in the New York Times Magazine, July 15, 1995, on pages 26 and 27. Your quotation comes from the second page of the essay. No author's name is mentioned in the text of your paper.
4. An essay by Nat Hentoff titled Speech Should Not Be Limited on pages 22–26 of the book Censorship: Opposing Viewpoints, edited by Terry O'Neill. The book is published by Greenhaven Press in St. Paul, Minnesota. The publication year is 2005. The quotation you have used is from page 24, and the author is mentioned in the text of your paper.
5. An essay by Robert Cannon on the Internet called A Parent's Guide to Supervising a Child Online. The essay appeared on the Web site Internet Issues, which was updated May 10, 2002. Although the essay prints out on four pages, the pages are not numbered. In your paper, you summarize information from the second and third pages of the document. You accessed the information on January 20, 2006, from the online database *Expanded Academic ASAP Plus*.

3 Content Notes

Content notes—multiple bibliographical citations or other material that does not fit smoothly into your paper—are indicated by a **superscript** (raised numeral) in the text.

Notes can appear either as footnotes at the bottom of the page or as endnotes on a separate sheet titled **Notes,** placed after the last page of the paper and before the works-cited list. Content notes are double-spaced within and between entries. The first line is indented one-half inch, and subsequent lines are typed flush left.

For Multiple Citations

In the Paper

Many researchers emphasize the necessity of having dying patients share their experiences.[1]

In the Note

1. Kübler-Ross 27; Stinnette 43; Poston 70; Cohen and Cohen 31-34; Burke 1: 91-95.

For Other Material

In the Paper

The massacre during World War I is an event the survivors could not easily forget.[2]

In the Note

2. For a firsthand account of these events, see Bedoukian 178-81.

47b MLA-Style Manuscript Guidelines

Although MLA papers do not usually include abstracts or internal headings, this situation is changing. Be sure you know what your instructor expects.

The following guidelines are based on the latest version of the *MLA Handbook for Writers of Research Papers.*

CHECKLIST

TYPING YOUR PAPER

When typing your paper, use the student paper in **47c** as your model.

❏ Type your paper with a one-inch margin at the top and bottom and on both sides. Double-space your paper throughout.

❏ If your instructor requires a title page, use the one on page 425 as a guide. If no title page is required, your first page should follow the format of page 54.

❏ Capitalize all important words in your title, but not prepositions, articles, coordinating conjunctions, or the *to* in infinitives (unless one of these words begins or ends the title or subtitle). Do not underline your title or enclose it in quotation marks. Never put a period after the title, even if it is a sentence.

❏ Number all pages of your paper consecutively—including the first—in the upper right-hand corner, one-half inch from the top, flush right. Type your last name followed by a space before the page number on every page.

❏ Set off quotations of more than four lines of prose or more than three lines of poetry by indenting the whole quotation one inch. If you quote a single paragraph or part of a paragraph, do not indent the first line beyond one inch. If you quote two or more paragraphs, however, indent the first line of each paragraph an additional quarter inch. (If the first sentence does not begin a paragraph, do not indent it. Indent the first line only in successive paragraphs.)

❏ If you use source material in your paper, follow <u>MLA documentation style</u>. See 47a

---

CHECKLIST

USING VISUALS

❏ Insert <u>visuals</u> into the text as close as possible to where they are discussed. See 12d

❏ Above each table, type the word **Table** followed by an arabic numeral (for instance, **Table 1**). Double-space, and type a descriptive caption, with the first line flush with the left-hand margin; indent subsequent lines one-quarter inch. Capitalize the caption as if it were a title.

Below the table, type the word **Source,** followed by a colon and all source information. Type the first line of the source information flush with the left-hand margin; indent subsequent lines one-quarter inch.

(continued)

USING VISUALS (*continued*)

❏ Label other types of visual material—graphs, charts, photographs, clip art, drawings, and so on—**Fig.** (Figure) followed by an arabic numeral (for example, **Fig. 2**). Directly below the visual, type the label and a title or caption on the same line, followed by source information. Type all lines flush with the left-hand margin.

❏ Do not include the source of the visual in the works-cited list unless you use other material from that source elsewhere in the paper.

CHECKLIST

PREPARING THE MLA WORKS-CITED LIST

When typing your works-cited list, follow these guidelines:

See
47a3

❏ Begin the works-cited list on a new page after the last page of text or **content notes,** numbered as the next page of the paper.

❏ Center the title **Works Cited** one inch from the top of the page. Double-space between the title and the first entry.

❏ Each entry in the works-cited list has three divisions: author, title, and publication information. Separate divisions with a period and one space.

❏ List entries alphabetically, with last name first. Use the author's full name as it appears on the title page. If a source has no listed author, alphabetize it by the first word of the title (not counting the article).

❏ Type the first line of each entry flush with the left-hand margin; indent subsequent lines one-half inch.

❏ Double-space within and between entries.

47c Sample MLA-Style Research Paper

The following student paper, "The Great Debate: *Wikipedia* and College-Level Research," by Rebecca James, uses MLA documentation style. It includes MLA-style in-text citations, a line graph, a notes page, and a works-cited list. Although MLA does not require a title page, Rebecca's instructor required her class to include one. See page 54 for an example of the first page of an MLA-style paper without a title page.

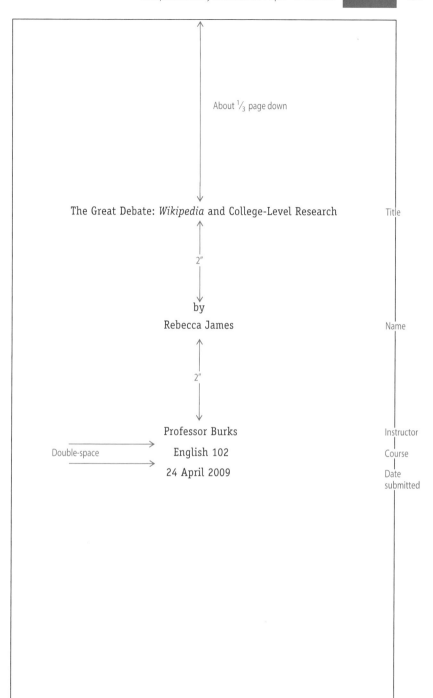

About ⅓ page down

The Great Debate: *Wikipedia* and College-Level Research — Title

2″

by
Rebecca James — Name

2″

Professor Burks — Instructor
English 102 — Course
24 April 2009 — Date submitted

Double-space

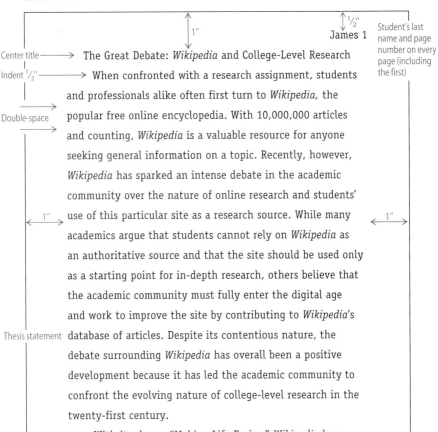

James 1

The Great Debate: *Wikipedia* and College-Level Research

When confronted with a research assignment, students and professionals alike often first turn to *Wikipedia,* the popular free online encyclopedia. With 10,000,000 articles and counting, *Wikipedia* is a valuable resource for anyone seeking general information on a topic. Recently, however, *Wikipedia* has sparked an intense debate in the academic community over the nature of online research and students' use of this particular site as a research source. While many academics argue that students cannot rely on *Wikipedia* as an authoritative source and that the site should be used only as a starting point for in-depth research, others believe that the academic community must fully enter the digital age and work to improve the site by contributing to *Wikipedia*'s database of articles. Despite its contentious nature, the debate surrounding *Wikipedia* has overall been a positive development because it has led the academic community to confront the evolving nature of college-level research in the twenty-first century.

With its slogan "Making Life Easier," *Wikipedia* has positioned itself as the most popular wiki, an open-source Web site that allows users to edit as well as contribute content. Derived from a Hawaiian word meaning "quick," the term *wiki* conveys the swiftness and ease with which users can access information on and contribute content to such a site ("Wiki"). In accordance with the site's policies, users can edit existing articles and add new articles using *Wikipedia*'s editing tools, which do not require specialized programming knowledge or expertise. Since its creation in 2001, *Wikipedia* has grown into a huge collection of articles on topics ranging from contemporary rock bands to obscure scientific and

Labels (margin annotations):
- Center title
- Indent ½″
- Double-space
- 1″
- Thesis statement
- Parenthetical documentation refers to material accessed from a Web site
- Student's original conclusions; no documentation necessary
- Student's last name and page number on every page (including the first)
- ½″
- 1″
- 1″
- 1″

James 2

technical concepts. Because anyone can edit or add content to the site, however, *Wikipedia* has been criticized as unreliable by many members of the academic community.

Without a professional editorial board to oversee its development, *Wikipedia* has several shortcomings that ultimately limit its trustworthiness as a research source. As *Wikipedia*'s own "Researching with *Wikipedia*" page concedes, "not everything in *Wikipedia* is accurate, comprehensive, or unbiased." Referring to the collaborative, open-source nature of the wiki format, Bart Ehrman, professor of religious studies at the University of North Carolina at Chapel Hill, observes, "Democratization isn't necessarily good for scholarship" (qtd. in Philips). Similarly, Middlebury College history department chairman Don J. Wyatt notes the danger of relying on the information in *Wikipedia* articles—even as he acknowledges the appeal of online research: "*Wikipedia* is very seductive: We all are sort of enamored of the convenience and speed of the Web. From the standpoint of access, it's a marvelous thing. But from the standpoint of maintaining quality, it's much less so" (qtd. in Read). In fact, Middlebury's history department instituted a policy in 2007 that prohibits students from citing *Wikipedia* as a research source.

Most academics agree that many *Wikipedia* articles lack reliability. Although many *Wikipedia* articles include citations, many others—especially those that are underdeveloped—do not supply citations to the sources that support their claims. In addition, because anyone can create or edit them, *Wikipedia* articles can be factually inaccurate, biased, and even targeted for vandalism. Some *Wikipedia* users tamper with the biographies of especially high-profile political or cultural figures.[1] According to a 2008 study that examines

Quotations from Internet source, introduced by author's name, are not followed by a paragraph or page number because this information was not provided in the electronic text

Qtd. in indicates that Ehrman's comments were quoted in Philips's article

Superscript number identifies content note

Wikipedia data from 2006, 11% of *Wikipedia*'s articles were vandalized at least once (Spinellis and Louridas 68). *Wikipedia* administrators can lock articles that are likely to be vandalized, preventing the ordinary user from editing them, but Spinellis and Louridas's study found that only 0.13% of at-risk articles were locked (68). As William Badke, associate librarian at Trinity Western University, notes, *Wikipedia* can be "an environment for shallow thinking, debates over interpretation, and the settling of scores" (50).

Because their content is open to public editing, *Wikipedia* articles also often suffer from poor writing. Emory University English professor Mark Bauerlein asserts that *Wikipedia* articles are written in a "flat, featureless, factual style" (153). *Wikipedia* has instituted a coding system to label the shortcomings of its less-developed articles, but a warning about an article's poor writing style is likely to go unnoticed by the typical user. Bauerlein argues that the poor writing of many *Wikipedia* articles reaffirms to students that sloppy writing and grammatical errors are acceptable in their own writing as well: "*Wikipedia* prose sets the standard for intellectual style. Students relying on *Wikipedia* alone, year in and year out, absorb the prose as proper knowledge discourse, and knowledge itself seems blank and uninspiring" (153-54). Thus, according to Bauerlein, *Wikipedia* articles have actually set a new, lower standard for what constitutes acceptable college-level writing.

Despite *Wikipedia*'s drawbacks, there is no denying the popularity of the site among both college students and professionals. According to a 2007 report by the Pew Internet & American Life Project, 36% of American adults use *Wikipedia,* with the majority of users having or pursuing

James 4

higher-education degrees (Rainie and Tancer 1). Table 1
shows a breakdown of the people who most commonly consult
Wikipedia.

Table 1

Wikipedia User Profile

A Profile of Wikipedia Users	
Do you ever use the internet to look for information on Wikipedia?	% of adult internet users who say "yes"
Men	39%
Women	34%
Whites	37%
Blacks	27%
English-speaking Hispanics	36%
Age 18-29	44%
Age 30-49	38%
Age 50-64	31%
Age 65+	26%
High school diploma	22%
Some college	36%
College grad +	50%
< $30,000 household income	32%
$30,000-$50,000	35%
$50,000-$75,000	39%
>$75,000	42%
Dial-up connection at home	26%
Broadband at home	42%

Table summarizes
relevant data.
Source information
is typed directly
below the table.

Source: Lee Rainie and Bill Tancer; "Online Activities & Pursuits:
  Wikipedia Users"; data memo; 24 Apr. 2007; Web; 7 Apr. 2009; 1.

There are good reasons to explain why so many educated
adults are using *Wikipedia*. The site offers numerous benefits
to researchers seeking information on a topic. Longer
Wikipedia articles often include comprehensive abstracts
that summarize their content. *Wikipedia* articles also often
include hyperlinks, or "wikilinks," to other *Wikipedia* articles,
allowing users to navigate quickly through related content.
In addition, many *Wikipedia* articles contain external links

James 5

to other print and online sources, including reliable peer-reviewed sources. Another benefit, noted by Middlebury College history department chairman Don J. Wyatt, is the inclusion of current and comprehensive bibliographies in some *Wikipedia* articles (Read). Assuming that *Wikipedia* users make the effort to connect their articles' content with more reliable, traditional research sources (including print sources), *Wikipedia* can provide real value to serious researchers.

Wikipedia has advantages over other, professionally edited online encyclopedias. Because users can update articles in real time from any location, *Wikipedia* offers up-to-the-minute coverage of political and cultural events as well as timely information on popular culture topics that receive little or no attention from other sources. For example, a student researching the history of video gaming would find *Wikipedia*'s "Wii" article, with its numerous pages of information and nearly 150 external links to additional sources, to be a valuable resource. *Encyclopaedia Britannica Online* does not contain a comparable article on this popular game console. Even when the available information on a particular topic is sparse, *Wikipedia* allows users to create "stub" articles, which provide minimal information that users can expand over time. According to Spinellis and Louridas's study, approximately 20% of *Wikipedia*'s articles are classified as stubs (70). By offering immediate access to information on relatively obscure topics, *Wikipedia* can be a valuable first step in finding reliable research sources on such topics.

As Spinellis and Louridas's study suggests, *Wikipedia* is poised to become an even more comprehensive database of information that could eventually gain acceptance in the academic community. *Wikipedia*'s "About" page claims

James 6

that the site's articles "are continually edited and improved
over time, and in general, this results in an upward trend
of quality and a growing consensus over a fair and balanced
representation of information." In fact, *Wikipedia* has
instituted control measures to help weed out inaccurate or
biased information and to make its content more reliable.
For example, using the criteria of accuracy, neutrality,
completeness, and style, the site ranks its best articles as
"featured" and its second-best articles as "good."[2] Although
no professional editorial board oversees the development of
content within *Wikipedia,* users may be nominated into an
editor role that allows them to manage the process by which
content is added and updated. Users may also use the "Talk"
page to discuss an article's content and make suggestions
for improvement. With such control measures in place, some
Wikipedia articles are comparable in scope and accuracy to
articles in professionally edited online encyclopedias.

    Although some critics argue that the collaborative
nature of the wiki format does not necessarily help improve
content, Spinellis and Louridas's study seems to confirm just
the opposite. In examining trends of content development in
Wikipedia, Spinellis and Louridas affirm that the coverage of
various topics in *Wikipedia* tends to even out over time:

> *Wikipedia*'s topic coverage has been criticized
> as too reflective of and limited to the interests
> of its young, tech-savvy contributors, covering
> technology and current affairs disproportionately
> more than, say, world history or the arts. We
> hypothesize that the addition of new *Wikipedia*
> articles is not a purely random process following
> the whims of its contributors but that references

Superscript number identifies content note

Quotation of more than four lines is typed as a block, indented 1", and double spaced, with no quotation marks

James 7

to nonexistent articles trigger the eventual creation of a corresponding article. Although it is difficult to claim that this process guarantees even and unbiased coverage of topics (adding links is also a subjective process), such a mechanism could eventually force some kind of balance in *Wikipedia* coverage. (71)

Spinellis and Louridas summarize their findings with a positive conclusion: "the apparently chaotic *Wikipedia* development process delivers growth at a sustainable rate" (71). Fig. 1 supports this conclusion, illustrating how, in recent years, *Wikipedia* has achieved a relative balance between complete and incomplete (or stub) articles.

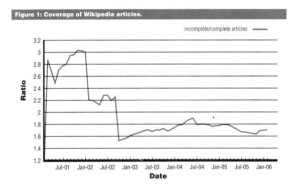

Fig. 1. Diomidis Spinellis and Panagiotis Louridas, "The Collaborative Organization of Knowledge"; *Communications of the ACM* 51.8 (2008): 71; *Academic Search Elite*; Web; 3 Apr. 2009.

In offering increasingly more consistent (as well as broader) coverage, *Wikipedia* is positioning itself as a more reliable source of information than some critics might like to admit.

James 8

Some argue that the academic community's rejection of *Wikipedia* has less to do with *Wikipedia*'s shortcomings and more to do with academia's resistance to emergent digital research technologies. Harvard Law professor Jonathan L. Zittrain suggests that academia has, in effect, fallen behind:

> It's to academia's enduring disappointment that *Wikipedia* had to be invented by a [private entrepreneur] named Jimbo. So many projects by universities and libraries are about knowledge and information online, and they just couldn't get *Wikipedia* going, or anything like it. I don't see academia rising to the challenge and trying to figure out how this wonderful network can meet its goals of bringing information to the world. (qtd. in Foster)

William Badke, associate librarian at Trinity Western University, agrees, stating, "*Wikipedia* is an affront to academia, because it undercuts what makes academics the elite in society. . . . *Wikipedia* doesn't depend on elite scholars" (49). Although he acknowledges that *Wikipedia* should serve only as a starting point for more in-depth research, Jimmy Wales, cofounder of *Wikipedia,* calls for the academic community to recognize *Wikipedia* as one of several new, important digital platforms that change the way people learn and disseminate knowledge: "Instead of fearing the power, complexity, and extraordinary potential of these new platforms, we should be asking how we can gain from their success" (qtd. in Goldstein). As Badke and others argue, members of the academic community are uniquely qualified to improve *Wikipedia* by expanding stub articles and writing new articles about their areas of expertise. As Badke suggests,

Ellipsis indicates that the student has omitted words from the quotation

"The most daring solution would be for academia to enter the world of *Wikipedia* directly. Rather than throwing rocks at it, the academy has a unique opportunity to engage *Wikipedia* in a way that marries the digital generation with the academic enterprise" (50). According to Badke, academics should not be asking whether or not college students should use *Wikipedia* in their research but rather how academia can work to improve this bank of information that is, and will continue to be, consulted before any other research source.

In recent years, librarians across the country have committed their time and resources to enhancing *Wikipedia* articles that pertain to their own special collections and areas of expertise. Like William Badke, Adam Bennington, a librarian at the State Farm Insurance Corporate Library in Bloomington, Illinois, argues that the *Wikipedia* phenomenon presents a "teachable moment" in which librarians and other members of the academic community can help develop students' information literacy skills (47). In their article "Putting the Library in *Wikipedia*," Wake Forest University librarians Lauren Pressley and Carolyn J. McCallum explain their own learning curve in contributing content to *Wikipedia* that directs users back to their library's special collections. Pressley and McCallum argue that librarians can play a pivotal role in making *Wikipedia* a more reliable and scholarly source of information, as demonstrated by their own contributions as well as by those made by librarians at the University of Washington Digital Initiatives, the University of North Texas, and Villanova University. "Through this type of collaboration," Pressley and McCallum suggest, "perhaps we will reach a whole new group of users that wouldn't have come through our doors another way. We may not have

James 10

resolved the issue of putting *Wikipedia* in libraries, but
we think we've found an effective way to put libraries in
Wikipedia" (42). Badke, Bennington, Pressley, McCallum, and
other librarians believe that it is the responsibility of the
academic community to bridge the divide between traditional
research sources and the digital tools and technologies
students are increasingly using to conduct college-level
research.

Paragraph
synthesizes several
sources cited in
paper

    With emerging research on *Wikipedia* use, and with
new efforts by colleges and universities around the country
to incorporate *Wikipedia* into academic research, the
debate surrounding *Wikipedia* has shifted. While previously
instructors tended to seek ways to prevent students from
using *Wikipedia* as a research source, the academic community
now seems to be acknowledging not only the undeniable
pervasiveness, but also the importance and usefulness of
this online resource in students' lives. Moreover, *Wikipedia*
offers academics an opportunity to participate in emergent
digital technologies that have changed the ways students
conduct research. In an interview with the *Chronicle of
Higher Education,* Jimmy Wales explains future proposed
enhancements to *Wikipedia,* including a "flagging" feature
that would allow instructors to approve certain *Wikipedia*
articles as acceptable research sources (Young). Eventually,
Wikipedia may become an approved college-level research
source. At the very least, it will have provided new insight
into the evolving nature of college-level research in the
twenty-first century.

Conclusion
restates the thesis
and summarizes
key points

James 11

Center title —————————→ Notes

Indent ½" —————→ 1. In one well-known example, the reputation of
American journalist John Seigenthaler was tarnished when a

Double-space *Wikipedia* user edited his biography to inaccurately claim that
Seigenthaler was involved in the Kennedy assassination, a lie
that spread to other online sources.

2. In addition, *Wikipedia*'s policies state that the
information in its articles must be verifiable and must be
based on documented, preexisting research.

James 12

Works Cited

"About." *Wikipedia.* Wikimedia Foundation, 2009. Web.
25 Mar. 2009.

Badke, William. "What to Do with *Wikipedia.*" *Online* Mar.-Apr.
2008: 48-50. *Academic Search Elite.* Web. 3 Apr. 2009.

Bauerlein, Mark. *The Dumbest Generation: How the Digital Age
Stupefies Young Americans and Jeopardizes Our Future
(or, Don't Trust Anyone Under 30).* New York: Penguin,
2008. Print.

Bennington, Adam. "Dissecting the Web through *Wikipedia.*"
American Libraries Aug. 2008: 46-48. Print.

Foster, Andrea L. "Professor Predicts Bleak Future for the
Internet." *Chronicle of Higher Education* 18 Apr. 2008:
A29. *Academic Search Elite.* Web. 3 Apr. 2009.

Goldstein, Evan R. "The Dumbing of America?" *Chronicle of
Higher Education* 21 Mar. 2008: B4. *Academic Search
Elite.* Web. 3 Apr. 2009.

Philips, Matthew. "God's Word, According to *Wikipedia.*"
Newsweek 23 June 2008: 14. Print.

Pressley, Lauren, and Carolyn J. McCallum. "Putting the
Library in *Wikipedia.*" *Online* Sept.-Oct. 2008: 39-42.
Academic Search Elite. Web. 3 Apr. 2009.

Rainie, Lee, and Bill Tancer. "Online Activities & Pursuits:
Wikipedia Users." Data memo. 24 Apr. 2007. Web. 7 Apr.
2009.

Read, Brock. "Middlebury College History Department
Limits Students' Use of *Wikipedia.*" *Chronicle of Higher
Education* 16 Feb. 2007: n. pag. *Academic Search Elite.*
Web. 3 Apr. 2009.

"Researching with *Wikipedia.*" *Wikipedia.* Wikimedia
Foundation, 2009. Web. 25 Mar. 2009.

Center title

Double-space

1″

1″

↑ 1″

↑ ½″

1″

Newspaper
article accessed
from an online
database

Signed article
in a weekly
magazine

Online memo

Newspaper
article without
pagination
accessed from
an online
database

Unsigned
document within
a Web site

James 13

Spinellis, Diomidis, and Panagiotis Louridas. "The Collaborative
    Organization of Knowledge." *Communications of the ACM*
    51.8 (2008): 68-73. *Academic Search Elite*. Web. 3 Apr.
    2009.

Article in
an online
encyclopedia
"Wiki." *Encyclopaedia Britannica Online*. Encyclopaedia
    Britannica, 2009. Web. 25 Mar. 2009.

Young, Jeffrey R. "*Wikipedia*'s Co-Founder Wants to Make It
    More Useful to Academe." *Chronicle of Higher Education*
    13 June 2008: n. pag. *Academic Search Elite*. Web. 3 Apr.
    2009.

Directory of APA In-Text Citations

Directory of APA Reference List Entries

PRINT SOURCES: *Entries for Articles*

Articles in Scholarly Journals

Articles in Magazines and Newspapers

PRINT SOURCES: *Entries for Books*

Authors

Editions, Multivolume Works, and Forewords

48a   Using APA Style

APA style* is used extensively in the social sciences. APA documentation has three parts:

♦ Parenthetical references in the body of the paper
♦ A reference list
♦ Content footnotes

1   Parenthetical References

APA documentation uses short parenthetical references in the body of the paper keyed to an alphabetical list of references that follows the paper. A typical parenthetical reference consists of the author's last name (followed by a comma) and the year of publication.

> Many people exhibit symptoms of depression after the death of a pet
>
> (Russo, 2000).

If the author's name appears in an introductory phrase, include the year of publication there as well.

> According to Russo (2000), many people exhibit symptoms of depression
>
> after the death of a pet.

When quoting directly, include the page number in parentheses after the quotation.

> According to Weston (1996), children from one-parent homes read at
>
> "a significantly lower level than those from two-parent homes" (p. 58).

Note: A long quotation (forty words or more) is not enclosed in quotation marks. It is typed as a block, and the entire quotation is double-spaced and indented one-half inch from the left margin. Parenthetical documentation is placed one space after the final punctuation.

---

*APA documentation format follows the guidelines set in the *Publication Manual of the American Psychological Association*, 6th ed., Washington, DC: APA, 2010.

Sample APA In-Text Citations

1. A Work by a Single Author

Many college students suffer from sleep deprivation (Anton, 2008).

2. A Work by Two Authors

There is growing concern over the use of psychological testing in elementary schools (Albright & Glennon, 2007).

3. A Work by Three to Five Authors

If a work has more than two but fewer than six authors, mention all the authors' names in the first reference; in subsequent references in the same paragraph, cite only the first author followed by **et al.** ("and others"). When the reference appears in later paragraphs, include the year.

First Reference

(Sparks, Wilson, & Hewitt, 2008)

Subsequent References in the Same Paragraph

(Sparks et al.)

References in Later Paragraphs

(Sparks et al., 2008)

4. A Work by Six or More Authors

When a work has six or more authors, cite the name of the first author followed by **et al.** and the year in all references.

(Miller et al., 2006)

CLOSE-UP

CITING WORKS BY MULTIPLE AUTHORS

When referring to multiple authors in the text of your paper, join the last two names with **and.**

According to Rosen, Wolfe, and Ziff (2008) . . . .

In-text citations (as well as reference list entries) require an **ampersand (&).**

(Rosen, Wolfe, & Ziff, 2008)

---

5. Works by Authors with the Same Last Name

If your paper cites works by two or more authors with the same last name, use each author's initials in all in-text citations.

F. Bor (2008) and S. D. Bor (2007) concluded that no further study was needed.

6. A Work by a Corporate Author

If the name of a corporate author is long, abbreviate it after the first citation.

First Reference

> (National Institute of Mental Health [NIMH], 2008)

Subsequent Reference

> (NIMH, 2008)

7. A Work with No Listed Author

If a work has no listed author, cite the first two or three words of the title (followed by a comma) and the year. Use quotation marks around titles of periodical articles and chapters of books; use italics for titles of books, periodicals, brochures, reports, and the like.

> ("New Immigration," 2007)

8. A Personal Communication

Cite letters, memos, telephone conversations, personal interviews, emails, messages from electronic bulletin boards, and so on only in the text—*not* in the reference list.

> (R. Takaki, personal communication, October 17, 2008)

9. An Indirect Source

> Cogan and Howe offer very different interpretations of the problem (cited in
>
> Swenson, 2008).

10. A Specific Part of a Source

Use abbreviations for the words *page* (**p.**), *pages* (**pp.**), but spell out *chapter* and *section*.

> These theories have an interesting history (Lee, 2006, Chapter 2).

11. An Electronic Source

For an electronic source that does not show page numbers, use the paragraph number preceded by the abbreviation **para.**

> Conversation at the dinner table is an example of a family ritual (Kulp,
>
> 2008, para. 3).

In the case of an electronic source that has neither page nor paragraph numbers, cite both the heading in the source and the number of the paragraph following the heading in which the material is located.

> Healthy eating is a never-ending series of free choices (Shapiro, 2008,
>
> Introduction section, para. 2).

If the source has no headings, you may not be able to specify an exact location.

12. Two or More Works by Different Authors

List works by different authors in alphabetical order, separated by semicolons.

> This theory is supported by several studies (Barson & Roth, 1995; Rose,
> 2001; Tedesco, 2008).

13. Two or More Works by the Same Author

List two or more works by the same author or authors in order of date of publication (separated by commas), with the earliest date first.

> This theory is supported by several studies (Rhodes & Dollek, 2006, 2007,
> 2008).

For two or more works by the same author published in the same year, designate the work whose title comes first alphabetically *a*, the one whose title comes next *b*, and so on; repeat the year in each citation.

> This theory is supported by several studies (Shapiro, 2008a, 2008b).

14. A Table

If you use a table from a source, give credit to the author in a note at the bottom of the table. Do *not* include this information in the reference list.

> *Note.* From "Predictors of Employment and Earnings Among JOBS
> Participants," by P. A. Neenan and D. K. Orthner, 1996, *Social Work
> Research, 20*(4), p. 233.

2 Reference List

The **reference list** gives the publication information for all the sources you cite. It should appear at the end of your paper on a new numbered page titled **References.**

Entries in the reference list should be arranged alphabetically. Double-space within and between reference list entries. The first line of each entry should start at the left margin, with the second and subsequent lines indented one-half inch. (**See 48b** for full manuscript guidelines.)

APA PRINT SOURCES ◆ Entries for Articles

Article citations include the author's name (last name first); the date of publication (in parentheses); the title of the article; the title of the periodical (italicized); the volume number (italicized); the issue number, if any (in parentheses); and the inclusive page numbers (including all digits). Figure 48.1 shows where you can find this information.

Capitalize the first word of the article's title and subtitle as well as any proper nouns. Do not underline or italicize the title of the article or enclose it in quotation marks. Give the periodical title in full, and capitalize all words except articles, prepositions, and conjunctions of fewer than four letters. Use **p.** or **pp.** when referring to page numbers in newspapers, but omit this abbreviation when referring to page numbers in journals and popular magazines.

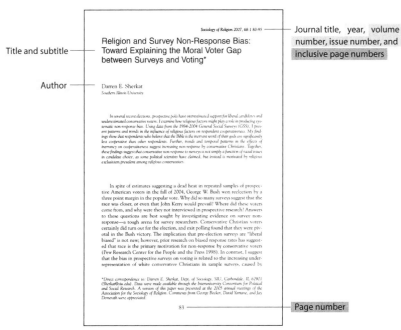

FIGURE 48.1 First page of an article showing the location of the information needed for documentation.

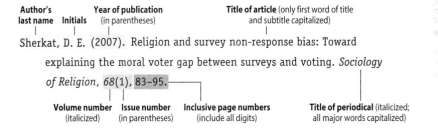

Articles in Scholarly Journals

1. An Article in a Scholarly Journal with Continuous Pagination throughout an Annual Volume

Miller, W. (1969). Violent crimes in city gangs. *Journal of Social Issues, 27,*

581–593.

2. An Article in a Scholarly Journal with Separate Pagination in Each Issue

> Williams, S., & Cohen, L. R. (1984). Child stress in early learning
> situations. *American Psychologist, 21*(10), 1–28.

 Note: Do not leave a space between the volume and issue numbers.

3. A Book Review in a Scholarly Journal (Unsigned)

A review with no author should be listed by title, followed by a description of the reviewed work in brackets.

> Coming of age and joining the cult of thinness [Review of the book *The cult*
> *of thinness,* by Sharlene Nagy Hesse-Biber]. (2008, June). *Psychology of*
> *Women Quarterly, 32*(2), 221–222.

Articles in Magazines and Newspapers

4. A Magazine Article

> McCurdy, H. G. (1983, June). Brain mechanisms and intelligence. *Psychology*
> *Today, 46,* 61–63.

5. A Newspaper Article

If an article appears on nonconsecutive pages, give all page numbers, separated by commas (for example, **A1, A14**). If the article appears on consecutive pages, indicate the full range of pages (for example, **A7–A9**).

> James, W. R. (1993, November 16). The uninsured and health care. *Wall*
> *Street Journal,* pp. A1, A14.

6. A Newspaper Editorial (Unsigned)

An editorial with no author should be listed by title, followed by the label **Editorial** in brackets.

> The plight of the underinsured [Editorial]. (2008, June 12). *The New York*
> *Times,* p. A30.

7. A Letter to the Editor of a Newspaper

> Williams, P. (2006, July 19). Self-fulfilling stereotypes [Letter to the
> editor]. *Los Angeles Times,* p. A22.

APA PRINT SOURCES ♦ Entries for Books

Book citations include the author's name (last name first); the year of publication (in parentheses); the book title (italicized); and publication information. Figures 48.2 and 48.3 show where you can find this information.

Capitalize only the first word of the title and subtitle and any proper nouns. Include any additional necessary information—edition, report number, or volume number, for example—in parentheses after the title. In the publication information, write out in full the names of associations, corporations, and university presses. Include the words **Book** and **Press,** but do not include terms such as **Publishers, Co.,** or **Inc.**

Author's last
name   Initials   Year of publication   Title (italicized, with only first word
                            (in parentheses)   of title and subtitle capitalized)

Schwartz, J. M., & Begley, S. (2002). *The mind and the brain:*

Neuroplasticity and the power of mental force. New York, NY:

ReganBooks.   City and State

Publisher (not including
terms *Publisher, Co.,* or *Inc.*)

FIGURE 48.2 Title page from
a book showing the location
of the information needed for
documentation.

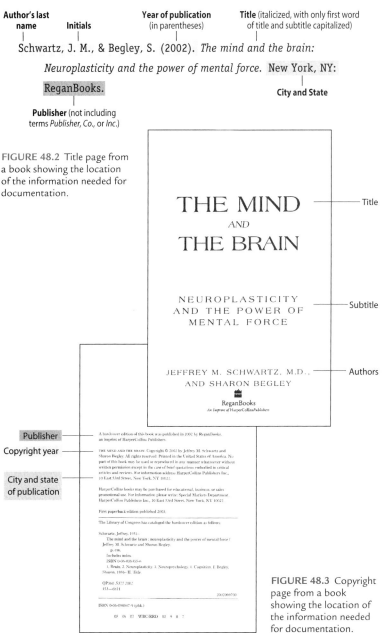

FIGURE 48.3 Copyright
page from a book
showing the location of
the information needed
for documentation.

Authors

8. A Book with One Author

Maslow, A. H. (1974). *Toward a psychology of being*. Princeton, NJ: Van Nostrand.

9. A Book with More Than One Author

List up to seven authors by last name and initials, using an ampersand (&) to connect the last two names. For more than seven authors, insert an ellipsis (three spaced periods) and add the last author's name.

Wolfinger, D., Knable, P., Richards, H. L., & Silberger, R. (2007). *The chronically unemployed*. New York, NY: Berman Press.

10. A Book with No Listed Author or Editor

Writing with a computer. (2006). Philadelphia, PA: Drexel Press.

11. A Book with a Corporate Author

When the author and the publisher are the same, include the word **Author** at the end of the citation instead of repeating the publisher's name.

League of Women Voters of the United States. (2008). *Local league handbook*. Washington, DC: Author.

12. An Edited Book

Lewin, K., Lippitt, R., & White, R. K. (Eds.). (1985). *Social learning and imitation*. New York, NY: Basic Books.

Editions, Multivolume Works, and Forewords

13. A Work in Several Volumes

Jones, P. R., & Williams, T. C. (Eds.). (1990–1993). *Handbook of therapy* (Vols. 1–2). Princeton, NJ: Princeton University Press.

14. The Foreword, Preface, or Afterword of a Book

Taylor, T. (1979). Preface. In B. B. Ferencz, *Less than slaves* (pp. ii–ix). Cambridge, MA: Harvard University Press.

Parts of Books

15. A Selection from an Anthology

Give inclusive page numbers preceded by **pp.** (in parentheses) after the title of the anthology. The title of the selection is not enclosed in quotation marks.

Lorde, A. (1984). Age, race, and class. In P. S. Rothenberg (Ed.), *Racism and sexism: An integrated study* (pp. 352–360). New York, NY: St. Martin's Press.

Note: If you cite two or more selections from the same anthology, give the full citation for the anthology in each entry.

16. An Article in a Reference Book

Edwards, P. (Ed.). (2006). Determinism. In *The encyclopedia of philosophy* (Vol. 2, pp. 359–373). New York, NY: Macmillan.

Government and Technical Reports

17. A Government Report

U.S. Department of Health and Human Services, National Institutes of Health, National Institute of Mental Health. (1987). *Motion pictures and violence: A summary report of research* (DHHS Publication No. ADM 91-22187). Washington, DC: Government Printing Office.

18. A Technical Report

Attali, Y., & Powers, D. (2008). *Effect of immediate feedback and revision on psychometric properties of open-ended GRE® subject test items* (ETS GRE Board Research Report No. 04-05). Princeton, NJ: Educational Testing Service.

APA ENTRIES FOR MISCELLANEOUS PRINT SOURCES

Letters

19. A Personal Letter

References to unpublished personal letters, like references to all other personal communications, should be included only in the text of the paper, not in the reference list.

20. A Published Letter

Joyce, J. (1931). Letter to Louis Gillet. In Richard Ellmann, *James Joyce* (p. 631). New York, NY: Oxford University Press.

APA ENTRIES FOR OTHER SOURCES

Television Broadcasts, Films, CDs, Audiocassette Recordings, and Computer Software

21. A Television Broadcast

Murphy, J. (Executive Producer). (2002, March 4). *The CBS evening news* [Television broadcast]. New York, NY: Columbia Broadcasting Service.

22. A Television Series

Sorkin, A., Schlamme, T., & Wells, J. (Executive Producers). (2002). *The west wing* [Television series]. Los Angeles, CA: Warner Bros. Television.

23. A Film

Spielberg, S. (Director). (1994). *Schindler's list* [Motion picture]. United States: Universal.

24. A CD Recording

Marley, B. (1977). Waiting in vain. On *Exodus* [CD]. New York, NY: Island Records.

25. An Audiocassette Recording

Skinner, B. F. (Speaker). (1972). *Skinner on Skinnerism* [Cassette recording]. Hollywood, CA: Center for Cassette Studies.

26. Computer Software

Sharp, S. (1995). Career Selection Tests (Version 5.0) [Software]. Chico, CA: Avocation Software.

APA ELECTRONIC SOURCES ◆
Entries for Sources from Internet Sites

APA guidelines for documenting electronic sources focus on Web sources, which often do not include all the bibliographic information that print sources do. For example, Web sources may not include page numbers or a place of publication. At a minimum, a Web citation should have a title, a date (the date of publication, update, or retrieval), and a Digital Object Identifier (DOI) (when available) or an electronic address (URL). If possible, also include the author(s) of a source. Figure 48.4 shows where you can find this information.

When you need to divide a URL at the end of a line, break it after a double slash or before most other punctuation (do not add a hyphen). Do not add a period at the end of the URL.

Author's last name | Initials   Year of publication (in parentheses)   Title of article (only first word of title and subtitle as well as proper nouns capitalized)

Yip, T., Gee, G. C., & Takeuchi, D. T. (2008). Racial discrimination and psychological distress: The impact of ethnic identity and age among immigrant and United States-born Asian adults. *Developmental Psychology*, *44*(3), 787–800. doi:10.1037/0012-1649.44.3.787

Volume number (italicized)   Issue number (in parentheses)   Inclusive page numbers (include all digits)   DOI (without period at end)   Title of periodical (italicized)

Journal title, year, volume number, issue number, and inclusive page numbers

DOI

Title and subtitle

Authors

Page number

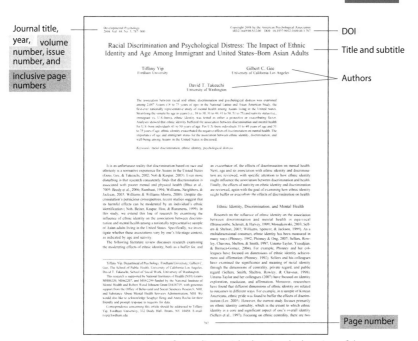

FIGURE 48.4 Part of an online article showing the location of the information needed for documentation.

Internet-Specific Sources

27. An Internet Article Based on a Print Source

If the article has a DOI, it is unnecessary to include the retrieval date or the URL. Always include the volume number (italicized) and the issue number (in parentheses, if available).

> Rutledge, P. C., Park, A., & Sher, K. J. (2008). 21st birthday drinking:
>
> Extremely extreme. *Journal of Consulting and Clinical Psychology, 76*(3),
>
> 511–516. doi:10.1037/0022-006X.76.3.511

28. An Article in an Internet-Only Journal

If the article does not have a DOI, include the URL. When available, always include the URL for the archived version of the article. If you accessed the article through a subscription database, include the URL for the home page of the journal. If, as in the following example, the article appears within frames and a single URL links to multiple articles, include the URL for the journal's home page. No retrieval date is needed for content that is not likely to be changed or updated—for example, a journal article or a book.

> Hill, S. A., & Laugharne, R. (2006). Patient choice survey in general
>
> adult psychiatry. *Psychiatry On-Line*. Retrieved from http://www
>
> .priory.co.uk/psych.htm

29. A Document from a University Web Site

> Beck, S. E. (2008, April 3). *The good, the bad & the ugly: Or, why it's a good idea to evaluate web sources.* Retrieved July 7, 2008, from New Mexico State University Library website: http://lib.nmsu.edu/instruction/ evalcrit.html

30. A Web Document (No Author Identified, No Date)

A document with no author or date should be listed by title, followed by the abbreviation **n.d.** (for "no date"), the retrieval date, and the URL.

> *The stratocaster appreciation page.* (n.d.). Retrieved July 27, 2008, from http://members.tripod.com/~AFH

31. An Email

As with all other personal communications, references to personal email should be included only in the text of your paper, not in the reference list.

32. A Message Posted to a Newsgroup

List the author's full name—or, if that is not available, the screen name. In brackets after the title, provide information that will help readers access the message.

> Silva, T. (2007, March 9). Severe stress can damage a child's brain [Online forum comment]. Retrieved from http://groups.google.com/group/sci .psychology.psychotherapy.moderated

33. A Message Posted to a Blog

> Jamie. (2008, June 26). Re: Trying to lose 50 million pounds [Web log comment]. Retrieved from http://blogs.wsj.com/numbersguy

34. A Searchable Database

Include the database name only if the material you are citing is obscure, out of print, or otherwise difficult to locate. No retrieval date is needed when citing archived material.

> Murphy, M. E. (1940, December 15). When war comes. *Vital Speeches of the Day, 7*(5), 139–144. Retrieved from http://www.vsotd.com

Abstracts and Newspaper Articles

35. An Abstract

> Qiong, L. (2008, July). After the quake: Psychological treatment following the disaster. *China Today, 57*(7), 18–21. Abstract retrieved from http://www.chinatoday.com.cn/ctenglish/index.htm

36. An Article in a Daily Newspaper

Fountain, H. (2008, July 1). In sleep, we are birds of a feather. *The New York Times*. Retrieved from http://www.nytimes.com

3 Content Footnotes

APA format permits content notes, indicated by **superscripts** in the text. The notes are listed on a separate numbered page, titled **Footnotes,** after the reference list and before any appendices. Double-space all notes, indenting the first line of each note one-half inch and beginning subsequent lines flush left. Number the notes with superscripts that correspond to the numbers in your text.

48b APA-Style Manuscript Guidelines

Social science papers label sections with headings. Sections may include an introduction (untitled), followed by headings like **Background, Method, Results,** and **Conclusion.** Each section of a social science paper is a complete unit with a beginning and an end so that it can be read separately and still make sense out of context. The body of the paper may include charts, graphs, maps, photographs, flowcharts, or tables.

CHECKLIST

TYPING YOUR PAPER

When typing your paper, use the student paper in **48c** as your model.

❑ Leave one-inch margins at the top and bottom and on both sides. Double-space your paper throughout.

❑ Indent the first line of every paragraph and the first line of every content footnote one-half inch from the left-hand margin.

❑ Set off a **long quotation** (more than forty words) in a block format by indenting the entire quotation one-half inch from the left-hand margin. Do not indent the first line further.

❑ Number all pages consecutively. Each page should include a **page header** (an abbreviated title) and a page number typed one-half inch from the top and one inch from the right-hand edge of the page. Leave one-half inch between the page header and the page number.

❑ Center major headings, and type them with uppercase and lowercase letters. Place minor headings flush left, typed with uppercase and lowercase letters. Use boldface for both major and minor heads. *See 12b*

❑ Format items in a series as a numbered list. *See 12c*

(continued)

TYPING YOUR PAPER (*continued*)

❑ Arrange the pages of the paper in the following order:

♦ **Title page** (page 1) with a page header, page number, title, your name, and the name of your school. (Your instructor may require additional information.)
♦ **Abstract** (page 2)
♦ **Text of paper** (beginning on page 3)
♦ **Reference list** (new page)
♦ **Content footnotes** (new page)
♦ **Appendices** (start each on a new page)

See 48a ❑ If you use source material in your paper, citations should be consistent with APA documentation style.

CHECKLIST

USING VISUALS

APA style distinguishes between two types of visuals: **tables** and **figures** (charts, graphs, photographs, and diagrams). In manuscripts not intended for publication, tables and figures are included in the text. A short table or figure should appear on the page where it is discussed; a long table or figure should be placed on a separate page just after the page where it is discussed.

Tables

Number all **tables** consecutively. Each table should have a *label* and a *title*.

❑ The **label** consists of the word **Table** (not in italics), along with an arabic numeral, typed flush left above the table.

❑ Double-space and type a brief explanatory **title** for each table (in italics) flush left below the label. Capitalize the first letters of principal words of the title.

Table 7

Frequency of Negative Responses of Dorm Students to Questions

Concerning Alcohol Consumption

Figures

Number all **figures** consecutively. Each figure should have a *label* and a *caption*.

❑ The **label** consists of the word **Figure** (typed flush left below the figure) followed by the figure number (both in italics).

❑ The **caption** explains the figure and serves as a title. Double-space the caption, but do not italicize it. Capitalize only the first word, and end the caption with a period. The caption follows the label (on the same line).

Figure 1. Duration of responses measured in seconds.

Note: If you use a table or figure from an outside source, include full source information in a note at the bottom of the table or figure. This information does not appear in your reference list.

CLOSE-UP
ARRANGING ENTRIES IN THE APA REFERENCE LIST

♦ Single-author entries precede multiple-author entries that begin with the same name.

Field, S. (1987).

Field, S., & Levitt, M. P. (1984).

♦ Entries by the same author or authors are arranged according to date of publication, starting with the earliest date.

Ruthenberg, H., & Rubin, R. (1985).

Ruthenberg, H., & Rubin, R. (1987).

♦ Entries with the same author or authors and date of publication are arranged alphabetically according to title. Lowercase letters (*a, b, c,* and so on) that indicate the order of publication are placed within parentheses.

Wolk, E. M. (1996a). Analysis . . .

Wolk, E. M. (1996b). Hormonal . . .

48c   Sample APA-Style Research Paper

The following student paper, "Sleep Deprivation in College Students," uses APA documentation style. It includes a title page, an abstract, a reference list, a table, and a bar graph.

Title   Sleep Deprivation in College Students

Your name   Andrew J. Neale

School   University of Texas

Course title   Psychology 215, Section 4

Instructor's name   Dr. Reiss

Date   April 12, 2009

1″   Abstract   Center heading

A survey of 50 first-year college students in an introductory
biology class was conducted. The survey consisted of
5 questions regarding the causes and results of sleep
deprivation and specifically addressed the students' study
methods and the grades they received on the fall midterm.
The study's hypothesis was that although students believe
that forgoing sleep to study will yield better grades, sleep
deprivation may actually cause a decrease in performance.
The study concluded that while only 43% of the students
who received either an A or a B on the fall midterm deprived
themselves of sleep in order to cram for the test, 90% of
those who received a C or a D were sleep deprived.

Abstract typed
as a single
paragraph in
block format
(not indented)

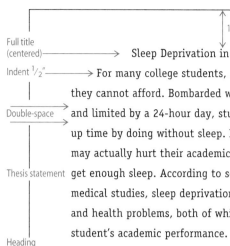

Full title (centered)———————→

Sleep Deprivation   3

Sleep Deprivation in College Students

Indent ½"————→ For many college students, sleep is a luxury they feel   Introduction

they cannot afford. Bombarded with tests and assignments

Double-space ——→ and limited by a 24-hour day, students often attempt to make

up time by doing without sleep. Ironically, however, students

may actually hurt their academic performance by failing to

Thesis statement get enough sleep. According to several psychological and

medical studies, sleep deprivation can lead to memory loss

and health problems, both of which are likely to harm a

student's academic performance.

Heading (centered and boldfaced)
Background

Sleep is often overlooked as an essential part of a

|←——1"——→| healthy lifestyle. Millions of Americans wake up daily to |←—1"—→|

alarm clocks when their bodies have not gotten enough sleep.

Literature review (paras. 2–7)
This indicates that for many people, sleep is viewed as a

luxury rather than a necessity. As National Sleep Foundation

Executive Director Richard L. Gelula observes, "Some of the

Quotation requires its own documentation and a page number (or a paragraph number for Internet sources)
problems we face as a society—from road rage to obesity—

may be linked to lack of sleep or poor sleep" (National Sleep

Foundation, 2002, para. 3). In fact, according to the National

Sleep Foundation, "excessive sleepiness is associated with

reduced short-term memory and learning ability, negative

mood, inconsistent performance, poor productivity and loss of

some forms of behavioral control" (2000, para. 2).

Sleep deprivation is particularly common among college

students, many of whom have busy lifestyles and are required

to memorize a great deal of material before their exams. It

is common for college students to take a quick nap between

classes or fall asleep while studying in the library because

they are sleep deprived. Approximately 44% of young adults

1"

Sleep Deprivation 4

experience daytime sleepiness at least a few days a month (National Sleep Foundation, 2002, para. 6). Many students face daytime sleepiness on the day of an exam because they stayed up all night studying. These students believe that if they read and review immediately before taking a test—even though this usually means losing sleep—they will remember more information and thus get better grades. However, this is not the case.

A study conducted by professors Mary Carskadon at Brown University in Providence, Rhode Island, and Amy Wolfson at the College of the Holy Cross in Worcester, Massachusetts, showed that high school students who got adequate sleep were more likely to do well in their classes (Carpenter, 2001). According to their study of the correlation between grades and sleep, students who went to bed earlier on both weeknights and weekends earned mainly A's and B's. The students who received D's and F's averaged about 35 minutes less sleep per day than the high achievers (cited in Carpenter). Apparently, then, sleep is essential to high academic achievement.

Once students reach college and have the freedom to set their own schedules, however, many believe that sleep is a luxury they can do without. For example, students believe that if they use the time they would normally sleep to study, they will do better on exams. A recent survey of 144 undergraduate students in introductory psychology classes contradicted this assumption. According to this study, "long sleepers," those individuals who slept 9 or more hours out of a 24-hour day, had significantly higher grade point averages (GPAs) than "short sleepers," individuals who slept less than

Student uses past tense when discussing other researchers' studies

Cited in indicates an indirect source

7 hours out of a 24-hour day. Therefore, contrary to the belief of many college students, more sleep is often required to achieve a high GPA (Kelly, Kelly, & Clanton, 2001).

Many students believe that sleep deprivation is not the cause of their poor performance, but rather that a host of other factors might be to blame. A study in the *Journal of American College Health* tested the effect that several factors have on a student's performance in school, as measured by students' GPAs. Some of the factors considered included exercise, sleep, nutritional habits, social support, time management techniques, stress management techniques, and spiritual health (Trockel, Barnes, & Egget, 2000). The most significant correlation discovered in the study was between GPA and the sleep habits of students. Sleep deprivation had a more negative impact on GPAs than any other factor did (Trockel et al.).

Despite these findings, many students continue to believe that they will be able to remember more material if they do not sleep at all before an exam. They fear that sleeping will interfere with their ability to retain information. Pilcher and Walters (1997), however, showed that sleep deprivation actually impaired learning skills. In this study, one group of students was sleep deprived, while the other got 8 hours of sleep before the exam. Each group estimated how well it had performed on the exam. The students who were sleep deprived believed their performance on the test was better than did those who were not sleep deprived, but actually the performance of the sleep-deprived students was significantly worse than that of those who got 8 hours of sleep prior to the test (Pilcher & Walters, 1997, cited in Bubolz, Brown, & Soper,

First reference includes all three authors; *et al.* replaces second and third authors in subsequent reference in same paragraph

Sleep Deprivation   6

2001). This study confirms that sleep deprivation harms cognitive performance even though many students believe that the less sleep they get, the better they will do.

A survey of students in an introductory biology class at the University of Texas demonstrated the effects of sleep deprivation on academic performance and supported the hypothesis that despite students' beliefs, forgoing sleep does not lead to better test scores.

Student uses past tense when discussing his own research study

Method

To determine the causes and results of sleep deprivation, a study of the relationship between sleep and test performance was conducted. A survey of 50 first-year college students in an introductory biology class was completed, and their performance on the fall midterm was analyzed.

Each student was asked to complete a survey consisting of the following five questions about their sleep patterns and their performance on the fall midterm:

1. Do you regularly deprive yourself of sleep when studying for an exam?

2. Did you deprive yourself of sleep when studying for the fall midterm?

3. What was your grade on the exam?

4. Do you feel your performance was helped or harmed by the amount of sleep you had?

5. Will you deprive yourself of sleep when you study for the final exam?

List is indented $\frac{1}{2}$" and set in block format

To maintain confidentiality, the students were asked not to put their names on the survey. Also, to determine whether the students answered question 3 truthfully, the group grade distribution from the surveys was compared to the number of A's, B's, C's, and D's shown in the instructor's record of the test results. The two frequency distributions were identical.

Results

Analysis of the survey data indicated a significant difference between the grades of students who were sleep deprived and the grades of those who were not. The results of the survey are presented in Table 1.

Table 1 introduced

The grades in the class were curved so that out of 50 students, 10 received A's, 20 received B's, 10 received C's, and 10 received D's. For the purposes of this survey, an A or B on the exam indicates that the student performed well. A grade of C or D on the exam is considered a poor grade.

Table 1

Table placed on page where it is discussed

Results of Survey of Students in University of Texas Introduction to Biology Class Examining the Relationship between Sleep Deprivation and Academic Performance

Table created by student; no documentation necessary

Grade totals	Sleep deprived	Not sleep deprived	Usually sleep deprived	Improved	Harmed	Continue sleep deprivation?
A = 10	4	6	1	4	0	4
B = 20	9	11	8	8	1	8
C = 10	10	0	6	5	4	7
D = 10	8	2	2	1	3	2
Total	31	19	17	18	8	21

Statistical findings in table discussed

Of the 50 students in the class, 31 (or 62%) said they deprived themselves of sleep when studying for the fall midterm. Of these students, 17 (or 34% of the class) answered yes to the second question, reporting they regularly deprive themselves of sleep before an exam.

Of the 31 students who said they deprived themselves of sleep when studying for the fall midterm, only 4 earned A's, and the majority of the A's in the class were received by those students who were not sleep deprived. Even more significant was the fact that of the 4 students who were sleep deprived and got A's, only one student claimed to usually be sleep deprived on the day of an exam. Thus, assuming the students who earn A's in a class do well in general, it is possible that sleep deprivation did not help or harm these students' grades. Not surprisingly, of the 4 students who received A's and were sleep deprived, all said they would continue to use sleep deprivation to enable them to study for longer hours.

The majority of those who used sleep deprivation in an effort to obtain a higher grade received B's and C's on the exam. A total of 20 students earned a grade of B on the exam. Of those students, only 9, or 18% of the class, said they were deprived of sleep when they took the test.

Students who said they were sleep deprived when they took the exam received the majority of the poor grades. Ten students got C's on the midterm, and of these 10 students, 100% said they were sleep deprived when they took the test. Of the 10 students (20% of the class) who got D's, 8 said they were sleep deprived. Figure 1 shows the significant relationship that was found between poor grades on the exam and sleep deprivation.

Figure 1 introduced

Conclusion

For many students, sleep is viewed as a luxury rather than as a necessity. Particularly during the exam period, students use the hours in which they would normally sleep to study. However, this method does not seem to be effective.

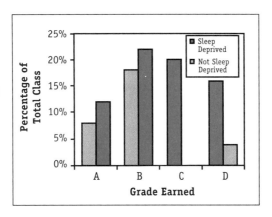

Figure placed as close as possible to discussion in paper

Label and caption

(No source information needed for graph based on student's original data)

Figure 1. Results of a survey of students in a University of Texas Introduction to Biology class, examining the relationship between sleep deprivation and academic performance.

The survey discussed here reveals a clear correlation between sleep deprivation and lower exam scores. In fact, the majority of students who performed well on the exam, earning either an A or a B, were not deprived of sleep. Therefore, students who choose studying over sleep should rethink their approach and consider that sleep deprivation may actually lead to impaired academic performance.

References

Bubolz, W., Brown, F., & Soper, B. (2001). Sleep habits and patterns of college students: A preliminary study. *Journal of American College Health, 50,* 131–135.

Carpenter, S. (2001). Sleep deprivation may be undermining teen health. *Monitor on Psychology, 32*(9). Retrieved from http://www.apa.org/monitor/oct01/sleepteen.html

Kelly, W. E., Kelly, K. E., & Clanton, R. C. (2001). The relationship between sleep length and grade-point average among college students. *College Student Journal, 35*(1), 84–90.

National Sleep Foundation. (2000). *Adolescent sleep needs and patterns: Research report and resource guide.* Retrieved from http://www.sleepfoundation.org

National Sleep Foundation. (2002, April 2). *Epidemic of daytime sleepiness linked to increased feelings of anger, stress and pessimism.* Retrieved from http://www.sleepfoundation.org

Trockel, M., Barnes, M., & Egget, D. (2000). Health-related variables and academic performance among first-year college students: Implications for sleep and other behaviors. *Journal of American College Health, 49,* 125–131.

PART 8

Bilingual and ESL Writers

Bilingual and ESL Writers

C H A P T E R 49

For ESL writers (as for many native English writers), grammar can be a persistent problem. Grammatical knowledge in a second language usually develops slowly, with time and practice, and much about English is idiomatic (not subject to easy-to-learn rules). This chapter is designed to provide you with the tools you will need to address some of the most common grammatical problems ESL writers face.

49a Using Verbs

1 Subject-Verb Agreement

English <u>verbs</u> change their form according to person, number, and tense. See Ch. 22
The verb in a sentence must **agree** with the subject in both person and number. Person refers to *who* or *what* is performing the action of the verb (for example, **I, you,** or someone else), and number refers to *how many* people or things are performing the action (one or more than one). See 26a
In English, the rules for <u>subject-verb agreement</u> are very important. Unless you use the correct person and number in the verbs in your sentences, you will confuse your English-speaking audience by communicating meanings you do not intend.

CLOSE-UP

SUBJECT-VERB AGREEMENT

Follow these basic guidelines when selecting verbs for your sentences:

♦ If the subject consists of only one noun or pronoun, use a singular verb.

He <u>is</u> at the park.

♦ If the subject consists of two or more nouns or pronouns connected with the word *and,* use a plural verb.

Bob and Carol <u>are</u> at the park.

♦ If the subject contains both a singular and a plural noun or pronoun connected with the word *or,* the verb should agree with the noun that is nearer to it.

Bob or <u>the boys</u> <u>are</u> at the park.
<u>The boys</u> or <u>Bob</u> <u>is</u> at the park.

Note: Don't be confused by phrases that come between the subject and the verb. The verb should agree with the subject of the sentence, not with a noun that appears within an intervening phrase.

(continued)

> **SUBJECT-VERB AGREEMENT** (*continued*)
>
> The woman with all of the children is at the park.
> The coach, as well as the players, is nervous.
>
> For information on subject-verb agreement with **indefinite pronouns,** such as *each, everyone,* and *nobody,* see **26a4.**

2 Verb Tense

See 22b
See 22a2

Tense refers to *when* the action of the verb takes place. One problem that many nonnative speakers of English have with English verb tenses results from the large number of irregular verbs in English. For example, the first-person singular present tense of *be* is not "I be" but "I am," and the past tense is not "I beed" but "I was."

Note: ESL writers whose first language is Chinese, Japanese, Korean, Russian, Thai, or Vietnamese are especially likely to have difficulty with verb tenses.

CLOSE-UP

CHOOSING THE SIMPLEST VERB FORMS

Some nonnative English speakers use verb forms that are more complicated than they need to be. They may do this because their native language uses more complicated verb forms than English does or because they "overcorrect" their verbs into complicated forms. Specifically, nonnative speakers tend to use progressive and perfect verb forms instead of simple verb forms. To communicate your ideas clearly to an English-speaking audience, choose the simplest possible verb form.

3 Auxiliary Verbs

The **auxiliary verbs** (also known as **helping verbs**) *be, have,* and *do* are used to create some present, past, and future forms of verbs in English: "Julio is taking a vacation"; "I have been tired lately"; "He does not need a license." The auxiliary verbs *be, have,* and *do* change form to reflect the time frame of the action or situation and to agree with the subject.

Note: ESL writers whose first language is Arabic, Chinese, Creole, Haitian, or Russian may have difficulty with auxiliary verbs because their first language sometimes omits the *be* verb.

See
20c1

CLOSE-UP

AUXILIARY VERBS

Only auxiliary verbs, not the verbs they "help," change form to indicate person, number, and tense.

Present: We <u>have</u> to eat.

Past: We <u>had</u> to eat. (*not* "We had to ate.")

<u>Modal auxiliaries</u> (such as *can* and *should*) do not change form to indicate tense, person, or number.

EXERCISE 49.1

A student wrote the following two paragraphs as part of a paper for his ESL composition class. He was asked to write about several interviews he conducted with people in his future profession, hotel management. The paragraphs contain errors in subject-verb agreement and verb tense, which the student's instructor underlined. Correct the underlined verbs by changing their form: begin by considering when the action took place, and then choose the simplest appropriate verb form to express that time. (Be sure to pay attention to the meaning and context of the sentences to determine which verb form is appropriate.)

In the past, when someone ►(1) <u>ask</u> me why I was interested in the hotel business, I always ►(2) <u>have</u> a hard time answering that question. I do not know exactly when and why I ►(3) <u>decide</u> to be a hotel manager. The only reason I can think of is my father. In his current job, he ►(4) <u>travel</u> a lot, and I have had a few chances to follow him and see other cities. Every time I went with him on a business trip, we ►(5) <u>spended</u> the night in a hotel, and I was surprised at how much hotels ►(6) <u>does</u> to satisfy their customers. All the employees are always friendly and polite. This gave me a positive image of hotels that made me ►(7) <u>decided</u> that the hotel business would be right for me.

For this paper, I (8) <u>spended</u> almost two weeks interviewing department heads at a local Hilton Hotel. Mr. Andrew Plain, the person who (9) <u>spend</u> the most time with me, (10) <u>share</u> an experience related to when he first got into the business. One of his first jobs was to plan a wedding, and he (11) <u>feel</u> a lot of responsibility because he (12) <u>believe</u> that a wedding is a one-time life experience for most people. So he wanted to take care of everything and make sure that everything was on track. To prepare for the wedding, he (13) <u>need</u> to work almost every Sunday, and one night he even (14) <u>have</u> to sleep in his office to attend the early wedding ceremony the next morning. From my experience with this interview, I realized that the people who are interested in the hotel business (15) <u>needs</u> great dedication to their career.

4 Negative Verbs

The meaning of a verb may be made negative in English in a variety of ways, chiefly by adding the words *not* or *does not* to the verb (is, is *not;* can ski, *can't* ski; drives a car, *does not* drive a car).

CLOSE-UP

CORRECTING DOUBLE NEGATIVES

A **double negative** occurs when the meaning of a verb is made negative not just once but twice in a single sentence.

Henry doesn't have ~~no~~ ^{any} friends. (*or* Henry ~~doesn't have~~ ^{has} no friends.)

I looked for articles in the library, but there weren~~'t~~ none. (*or* I looked for articles in the library, but there weren't ^{any} ~~none~~.)

Note: Some ESL writers whose first language is Spanish tend to use double negatives.

---

5 Phrasal Verbs

Many verbs in English are composed of two or more words that are combined to create a new idiomatic expression—for example, *check up on, run for, turn into,* and *wait on.* These verbs are called **phrasal verbs.** It is important to become familiar with phrasal verbs and their definitions so you will recognize these verbs as phrasal verbs (instead of as verbs that are followed by prepositions).

Separable Phrasal Verbs   Often, the words that make up a phrasal verb can be separated from each other by a direct object. In these **separable phrasal verbs,** the object can come either before or after the preposition. For example, "Ellen turned down the job offer" and "Ellen turned the job offer down" are both correct. However, when the object is a pronoun, the pronoun must come before the preposition. Therefore, "Ellen turned it down" is correct, but "Ellen turned down it" is incorrect.

CLOSE-UP

SEPARABLE PHRASAL VERBS

Verb	Definition
call off	cancel
carry on	continue
cheer up	make happy
clean out	clean the inside of

Verb	Definition
cut down	reduce
figure out	solve
fill in	substitute
find out	discover
give back	return something
give up	stop doing something or stop trying
leave out	omit
pass on	transmit
put away	place something in its proper place
put back	place something in its original place
put off	postpone
start over	start again
talk over	discuss
throw away/out	discard
touch up	repair

Inseparable Phrasal Verbs Some phrasal verbs—such as *look into, make up for,* and *break into*—consist of words that can never be separated. With these **inseparable phrasal verbs,** you do not have a choice about where to place the object; the object must always directly follow the preposition. For example, "<u>Anna</u> <u>cared for</u> her niece" is correct, but "<u>Anna</u> <u>cared</u> her niece <u>for</u>" is incorrect.

CLOSE-UP

INSEPARABLE PHRASAL VERBS

Verb	Definition
come down with	develop an illness
come up with	produce
do away with	abolish
fall behind in	lag
get along with	be congenial with
get away with	avoid punishment
keep up with	maintain the same achievement or speed
look up to	admire
make up for	compensate
put up with	tolerate
run into	meet by chance
see to	arrange
show up	arrive
stand by	wait or remain loyal to
stand up for	support
watch out for	beware of or protect

See
22d

6 Voice

Verbs may be in either active or passive <u>voice</u>. When the subject of a sentence performs the action of the verb, the verb is in **active voice.** When the action of the verb is performed on the subject, the verb is in **passive voice.**

<u>Karla and Miguel</u> <u>purchased</u> the tickets. (active voice)

<u>The tickets</u> <u>were purchased</u> by Karla and Miguel. (passive voice)

<u>The tickets</u> <u>were purchased</u>. (passive voice)

Because your writing will usually be clearer and more concise if you use the active voice, you should use the passive voice only when you have a good reason to do so.

When deciding whether to use the passive or active voice, you need to consider what you want to focus on. In the first example above, the focus is on Karla and Miguel. However, the second and third examples above, which use the passive voice, put the focus on the fact that the tickets were *purchased* rather than on *who* purchased them.

Note: ESL writers whose first language is Creole, Japanese, Korean, Russian, Thai, or Vietnamese may encounter challenges with voice when writing in English.

7 Transitive and Intransitive Verbs

Many nonnative English speakers find it difficult to decide whether or not a verb needs an object and in what order direct and indirect objects should appear in a sentence. Learning the difference between transitive verbs and intransitive verbs can help you with such problems.

A **transitive verb** is a verb that has a direct object: "<u>My father</u> <u>asked</u> a question" (subject + verb + direct object). In this example, *asked* is a transitive verb; it needs an object to complete its meaning.

An **intransitive verb** is a verb that does not take an object: "<u>The doctor</u> <u>smiled</u>" (subject + verb). In this example, *smiled* is an intransitive verb; it does not need an object to complete its meaning.

A transitive verb may be followed by a direct object or by both an indirect object and a direct object. (An indirect object answers the question "To whom?" or "For whom?") The indirect object may come before or after the direct object. If the indirect object follows the direct object, the preposition *to* or *for* must precede the indirect object.

s   v   do
<u>Keith</u> <u>wrote</u> a letter. (subject + verb + direct object)

s   v   io   do
<u>Keith</u> <u>wrote</u> his friend a letter. (subject + verb + indirect object + direct object)

```
 s      v      do        io
```
<u>Keith</u> <u>wrote</u> a letter to his friend. (subject + verb + direct object + *to/for* + indirect object)

Some verbs in English look similar and have similar meanings, except that one is transitive and the other is intransitive. For example, *lie* is intransitive, *lay* is transitive; *sit* is intransitive, *set* is transitive; *rise* is intransitive, *raise* is transitive. Knowing whether a verb is transitive or intransitive will help you with troublesome verb pairs like these and will help you place words in the correct order. (See the **Glossary of Usage** for more on these verb pairs.)

Note: It is also important to know whether a verb is transitive or intransitive because only transitive verbs can be used in the <u>passive voice</u>. To determine whether a verb is transitive or intransitive—that is, to determine whether or not it needs an object—consult the example phrases in a dictionary.

See 22d

8 Infinitives and Gerunds

In English, two verb forms may be used as nouns: **infinitives,** which always begin with *to* (as in *to work, to sleep, to eat*), and **gerunds,** which always end in *-ing,* (as in *working, sleeping, eating*).

<u>To bite into this steak</u> <u>requires</u> better teeth than mine. (infinitive used as a noun)

<u>Cooking</u> <u>is</u> one of my favorite hobbies. (gerund used as a noun)

Sometimes the gerund and the infinitive form of the same verb can be used interchangeably. For example, "He continued *to sleep*" and "He continued *sleeping*" convey the same meaning. However, this is not always the case. Saying, "Marco and Lisa stopped *to eat* at Julio's Café" is not the same as saying, "Marco and Lisa stopped *eating* at Julio's Café." In this example, the meaning of the sentence changes depending on whether a gerund or infinitive is used.

Note: ESL writers whose first language is Arabic, Chinese, Farsi, French, Greek, Korean, Portuguese, Spanish, or Vietnamese may have difficulty with gerunds.

9 Participles

In English, verb forms called **present participles** and **past participles** are frequently used as adjectives. Present participles usually end in *-ing,* as in *working, sleeping,* and *eating,* and past participles usually end in *-ed, -t,* or *-en,* as in *worked, slept,* and *eaten.*

According to the Bible, God spoke to Moses from a <u>burning</u> bush. (present participle used as an adjective)

Some people think raw fish is healthier than <u>cooked</u> fish. (past participle used as an adjective)

A **participial phrase** is a group of words consisting of the participle plus the noun phrase that functions as the object or complement of the action being expressed by the participle. To avoid confusion, the participial phrase must be placed as close as possible to the noun it modifies.

<u>Having visited San Francisco last week</u>, Jim and Lynn showed us pictures from their vacation. (The participial phrase is used as an adjective that modifies *Jim and Lynn*.)

Note: See 30d When a participial phrase falls at the beginning of a sentence, a <u>comma</u> is used to set it off. When a participial phrase is used in the middle of a sentence, commas should be used only if the phrase is not essential to the meaning of the sentence. No commas should be used if the participial phrase is essential to the meaning of the sentence.

10 Verbs Formed from Nouns

In English, nouns can sometimes be used as verbs, with no change in form (other than the addition of an *-s* for agreement with third-person singular subjects or the addition of past tense endings). For example, the nouns *chair, book, frame,* and *father* can all be used as verbs.

She <u>chairs</u> a committee on neighborhood safety.

We <u>booked</u> a flight to New York for next week.

I will <u>frame</u> my daughter's diploma after she graduates.

He <u>fathered</u> several children out of wedlock.

49b Using Nouns

See 21a <u>Nouns</u> name things: people, animals, objects, places, feelings, ideas. If a noun names one thing, it is singular; if a noun names more than one thing, it is plural.

1 Recognizing Noncount Nouns

Some English nouns do not have a plural form. They are called **noncount nouns** because what they name cannot be counted.

Note: ESL writers whose first language is Chinese or Japanese may have trouble with noncount nouns.

> **CLOSE-UP**
>
> **NONCOUNT NOUNS**
>
> The following commonly used nouns are noncount nouns. These words have no plural forms. Therefore, you should never add -s to them.
>
> | | | |
> |---|---|---|
> | advice | evidence | knowledge |
> | clothing | furniture | luggage |
> | education | homework | merchandise |
> | equipment | information | revenge |

EXERCISE 49.2

An ESL student wrote the following paragraph as part of a composition paper about her experiences learning English. Read the paragraph, and decide which of the underlined words need to be made plural and which should remain unchanged. If a word should be made plural, make the necessary correction. If a word is correct as is, mark it with a C. If you are not sure whether or not a noun is countable, look it up in a dictionary.

Visiting Ireland for three ▶(1) <u>month</u> expanded my ▶(2) <u>knowledge</u> of English. I took a part-time English ▶(3) <u>course</u>, which was the key to improving my writing. The ▶(4) <u>course</u> helped me understand the essential ▶(5) <u>rule</u> of English, and I learned a lot of new (6) <u>vocabulary</u> and expressions. In the first three (7) <u>lecture</u>, the teacher, Mr. Nelson, explained the fundamentals of writing in English. My (8) <u>enthusiasm</u> for the English language increased because I realized the importance of this (9) <u>language</u> for my (10) <u>future</u>. Mr. Nelson recommended that I read more English (11) <u>book</u>. I took his advice, and my English got better.

2 Using Articles with Nouns

English has two kinds of **articles,** indefinite and definite.

Use an **indefinite article** (*a* or *an*) with a noun when readers are not familiar with the noun you are naming—for example, when you are introducing a noun for the first time. To say, "Jim entered *a* building," signals to the audience that you are introducing the idea of the building for the first time. The building is indefinite, or not specific, until it has been identified.

The indefinite article *a* is used when the word following it (which may be a noun or an adjective) begins with a consonant or with a consonant sound: *a tree, a onetime offer*. The indefinite article *an* is used if the word following it begins with a vowel (*a, e, i, o,* or *u*) or with a vowel sound: *an apple, an honor*.

Use the **definite article** (*the*) when the noun you are naming has already been introduced, when the noun is already familiar to readers, or when the noun to which you refer is specific. To say, "Jim entered *the* building," signals to readers that you are referring to the same building you mentioned earlier. The building has now become specific and may be referred to by the definite article.

Note: ESL writers whose first language is Chinese, Farsi, Russian, or Swahili are likely to have difficulty with articles.

CLOSE-UP

USING ARTICLES WITH NOUNS

There are three main exceptions to the rules governing the use of articles with nouns:

1. **Plural nouns** do not require indefinite articles: "I love horses," not "I love *a* horses." (However, plural nouns do require definite articles if you have already introduced the noun to your readers or if you are referring to a specific plural noun: "I love *the* horses in the national park near my house.")

2. **Noncount nouns** may or may not require articles.

    "Love conquers all," not "*A* love conquers all" or "*The* love conquers all."

    "*A* good education is important," not "Good education is important."

    "*The* homework is difficult" or "Homework is difficult," not "*A* homework is difficult."

    To help determine whether or not a noncount noun requires an article, look up that noun in a dictionary and consult the sample sentences provided.

3. **A proper noun,** which names a particular person, place, or thing, sometimes takes an article and sometimes does not. When you use an article with a proper noun, do not capitalize the article unless the article is the first word of the sentence.

    "*The Mississippi River* is one of the longest rivers in the world," not "Mississippi River is one of the longest rivers in the world."

    "Teresa was born in *the* United States," not "Teresa was born in United States."

    "China is the most populous nation on earth," not "*The* China is the most populous nation on earth."

    To find out whether or not a proper noun requires an article, look up that noun in a dictionary, and consult the sample sentences provided.

EXERCISE 49.3

The following introductory paragraph of a paper about renewable energy power sources was written for an ESL composition course. Read the paragraph, and decide whether or not each of the underlined noun phrases requires an article. If a noun phrase is correct as is, mark it with a C. If a noun phrase needs an article, indicate whether that article should be *a, an,* or *the.*

▶(1) <u>Use of electrical power</u> has increased dramatically over ▶(2) <u>last thirty years</u> and continues to rise. ▶(3) <u>Most ordinary sources</u> of ▶(4) <u>electricity</u> require ▶(5) <u>oil</u>, ▶(6) <u>gas</u>, or ▶(7) <u>uranium</u>, which are not ▶(8) <u>renewable resources</u>. Living without ▶(9) <u>electrical power</u> is not feasible as long as everything in our lives depends on ▶(10) <u>electricity</u>, but (11) <u>entire world</u> will be in (12) <u>big crisis</u> if (13) <u>ignorance regarding renewable energy</u> continues. (14) <u>Renewable energy</u>, including (15) <u>solar energy</u>, (16) <u>wind energy</u>, (17) <u>hydro energy</u>, and (18) <u>biomass energy</u>, need (19) <u>more attention</u> from (20) <u>scientists</u>.

3 Using Other Determiners with Nouns

<u>Determiners</u> are words that function as <u>adjectives</u> to limit or qualify the meaning of nouns. In addition to articles, **demonstrative pronouns, possessive nouns and pronouns, numbers** (both **cardinal** and **ordinal**), and other words indicating number and order can function in this way.

See 20d2

CLOSE-UP

USING OTHER DETERMINERS WITH NOUNS

♦ **Demonstrative pronouns** (*this, that, these, those*) communicate the following:
1. the relative nearness or farness of the noun from the speaker's position (*this* and *these* for things that are *near, that* and *those* for things that are *far*): *this* book on my desk, *that* book on your desk; *these* shoes on my feet, *those* shoes in my closet.
2. the number of things indicated (*this* and *that* for *singular* nouns, *these* and *those* for *plural* nouns): *this* (or *that*) flower in the vase, *these* (or *those*) flowers in the garden.

♦ **Possessive nouns** and **possessive pronouns** (*Ashraf's, his, their*) show who or what the noun belongs to: *Maria's* courage, *everybody's* fears, the *country's* natural resources, *my* personality, *our* groceries.

♦ **Cardinal numbers** (*three, fifty, a thousand*) indicate how many of the noun you mean: *seven* continents. **Ordinal** numbers (*first, tenth, thirtieth*) indicate in what order the noun appears among other items: *third* planet.

♦ Words other than numbers may indicate **amount** (*many, few*) and **order** (*next, last*) and function in the same ways as cardinal and ordinal numbers: *few* opportunities, *last* chance.

49c Using Pronouns

Any English noun may be replaced by a <u>pronoun</u>. Pronouns enable you to avoid repeating a noun over and over. For example, *doctor* may be replaced by *he* or *she, books* by *them*, and *computer* by *it*.

See 20b, Ch. 21

See
21c

1 Pronoun Reference

Pronoun reference is very important in English sentences, where the noun the pronoun replaces (the **antecedent**) must be easily identified. In general, you should place the pronoun as close as possible to the noun it replaces so the noun to which the pronoun refers is clear. If this is impossible, use the noun itself instead of replacing it with a pronoun.

> **Unclear:** When Tara met Emily, she was nervous. (Does *she* refer to Tara or to Emily?)
>
> **Clear:** When Tara met Emily, <u>Tara</u> was nervous.
>
> **Unclear:** Stefano and Victor love his DVD collection. (Whose DVD collection—Stefano's, Victor's, or someone else's?)
>
> **Clear:** Stefano and Victor love <u>Emilio's</u> DVD collection.

Note: ESL writers whose first language is Spanish or Thai may have difficulty with pronoun reference.

2 Pronoun Placement

Never use a pronoun immediately after the noun it replaces. For example, do not say, "Most of my classmates they are smart"; instead, say, "Most of my classmates are smart."

The only exception to this rule occurs with an **intensive pronoun,** which ends in *-self* and emphasizes the preceding noun or pronoun: *Marta herself was eager to hear the results.*

3 Indefinite Pronouns

Unlike **personal pronouns** (*I, you, he, she, it, we, they, me, him, her, us, them,* and so on), **indefinite pronouns** do not refer to a particular person, place, or thing. Therefore, an indefinite pronoun does not require an antecedent. **Indefinite pronoun subjects** (*anybody, nobody, each, either, someone, something, all, some*), like personal pronouns, must <u>agree</u> in number with the sentence's verb.

See
26a4

> has
> Nobody have failed the exam. (*Nobody* is a singular subject and requires a singular verb.)

4 Appositives

Appositives are nouns or noun phrases that identify or rename an adjacent noun or pronoun. An appositive usually follows the noun it explains or modifies but can sometimes precede it.

> My parents, <u>Mary and John</u>, live in Louisiana. (*Mary and John* identifies *parents.*)

Note: The <u>case</u> of a pronoun in an appositive depends on the case of the word it identifies.

See 21b3

If an appositive is *not* essential to the meaning of the sentence, use commas to set off the appositive from the rest of the sentence. If an appositive *is* essential to the meaning of the sentence, do not use commas.

His aunt <u>Trang</u> is in the hospital. (*Trang* is necessary to the meaning of the sentence because it identifies which aunt is in the hospital.)

Akta's car, <u>a 1997 Jeep</u>, broke down last night, so she had to walk home. (*a 1997 Jeep* is not essential to the meaning of the sentence.)

5 Pronouns and Gender

A pronoun must agree in **gender** with the noun to which it refers.

My sister sold <u>her</u> old car.

Your uncle is walking <u>his</u> dog.

Keep in mind that in English, most nonhuman nouns are referred to as *it* because they do not have grammatical gender. However, exceptions are sometimes made for pets, ships, and countries. Pets are often referred to as *he* or *she,* depending on their sex, and ships and countries are sometimes referred to as *she.*

Note: ESL writers whose first language is Bengali, Farsi, Gujarati, or Thai may have problems with pronouns and gender.

EXERCISE 49.4

There are no pronouns in the following passage. The repetition of the nouns again and again would seem strange to a native English speaker. Rewrite the passage, replacing as many of the nouns as possible with appropriate pronouns. Be sure that the connection between the pronouns and the nouns they replace is clear.

▶The young couple seated across from Daniel at dinner the night before were newlyweds from Tokyo. ▶The young couple and Daniel ate together with other guests of the inn at long, low tables in a large dining room with straw mat flooring. ▶The man introduced himself immediately in English, shook Daniel's hand firmly, and, after learning that Daniel was not a tourist but a resident working in Osaka, gave Daniel a business card. ▶The man had just finished college and was working at the man's first real job, clerking in a bank. ▶Even in a sweatsuit, the man looked ready for the office: chin closely shaven, bristly hair neatly clipped, nails clean and buffed. After a while the man and Daniel exhausted the man's store of English and drifted into Japanese.

The man's wife, shy up until then, took over as the man fell silent. The woman and Daniel talked about the new popularity of hot springs spas in the countryside around the inn, the difficulty of finding good schools for the children the woman hoped to have soon, the differences between food in Tokyo and Osaka. The woman's husband ate busily. From time to time the woman refilled the man's beer glass or served the man radish pickles from a china bowl in the middle of the table, and then returned to the conversation.

49d Using Adjectives and Adverbs

See Ch. 23

Adjectives and adverbs are words that **modify** (describe, limit, or qualify) other words.

1 Position of Adjectives and Adverbs

Adjectives in English usually appear *before* the nouns they modify. A native speaker of English would not say, "*Cars red and black* are involved in more accidents than *cars blue or green*" but would say instead, "*Red and black* cars are involved in more accidents than *blue or green* cars."

However, adjectives may appear *after* linking verbs ("The name seemed *familiar*"), *after* direct objects ("The coach found them *tired* but *happy*"), and *after* indefinite pronouns ("Anything *sad* makes me cry").

Adverbs may appear before or after the verbs they describe, but they should be placed as close to the verb as possible: not "I told John that I couldn't meet him for lunch *politely*," but "I *politely* told John that I couldn't meet him for lunch" or "I *told* John *politely* that I couldn't meet him for lunch." When an adverb describes an adjective or another adverb, it usually comes *before* that adjective or adverb: "The essay has *basically* sound logic"; "You must express yourself *absolutely* clearly."

Never place an adverb between the verb and the direct object.

Incorrect: Rolf *drank quickly* the water.

Correct: Rolf *drank* the water *quickly* (or, Rolf *quickly* drank the water).

Incorrect: Suong *took quietly* the test.

Correct: Suong *quietly took* the test (or, Suong *took* the test *quietly*).

Note: ESL writers whose first language is Creole, French, or Haitian may have problems with adverbs.

2 Order of Adjectives

A single noun may be modified by more than one adjective, perhaps even by a whole list of adjectives. Given a list of three or four adjectives, most native speakers would arrange them in a sentence in the same order. If, for example, shoes are to be described as *green* and *big*, numbering *two*, and of the type worn for playing *tennis*, a native speaker would say "two big green tennis shoes." Generally, the adjectives that are most important in completing the meaning of the noun are placed closest to the noun.

CLOSE-UP

ORDER OF ADJECTIVES

1. Articles (*a, the*), demonstratives (*this, those*), and possessives (*his, our, Maria's, everybody's*)
2. Amounts (*one, five, many, few*), order (*first, next, last*)
3. Personal opinions (*nice, ugly, crowded, pitiful*)
4. Sizes and shapes (*small, tall, straight, crooked*)
5. Age (*young, old, modern, ancient*)
6. Colors (*black, white, red, blue, dark, light*)
7. Nouns functioning as adjectives to form a unit with the noun (*soccer ball, cardboard box, history class*)

EXERCISE 49.5

Write five original sentences in which two or three adjectives describe a noun. Be sure that the adjectives are in the correct order.

49e Using Prepositions

See 20f

In English, <u>prepositions</u> (such as *to, from, at, with, among, between*) give meaning to nouns by linking them with other words and other parts of the sentence. Prepositions convey several different kinds of information:

♦ Relations to **time** (*at* nine o'clock, *in* five minutes, *for* a month)
♦ Relations of **place** (*in* the classroom, *at* the library, *beside* the chair) and **direction** (*to* the market, *onto* the stage, *toward* the freeway)
♦ Relations of **association** (go *with* someone, the tip *of* the iceberg)
♦ Relations of **purpose** (working *for* money)

1 Commonly Used Prepositional Phrases

In English, the use of prepositions is often idiomatic rather than governed by grammatical rules. In many cases, therefore, learners of English as a second language need to memorize which prepositions are used in which phrases.

In English, some prepositions that relate to time have specific uses with certain nouns, such as days, months, and seasons:

♦ *On* is used with days and specific dates: *on* Monday, *on* September 13, 1977.
♦ *In* is used with months, seasons, and years: *in* November, *in* the spring, *in* 1999.

- *In* is also used when referring to some parts of the day: *in* the morning, *in* the afternoon, *in* the evening.
- *At* is used to refer to other parts of the day: *at* noon, *at* night, *at* seven o'clock.

CLOSE-UP

DIFFICULT PREPOSITIONAL PHRASES

The following phrases (accompanied by their correct prepositions) sometimes cause difficulties for ESL writers:

according *to*	*at* least	relevant *to*
apologize *to*	*at* most	similar *to*
appeal *to*	refer *to*	subscribe *to*
different *from*		

---

2 **Commonly Confused Prepositions**

The prepositions *to, in, on, into,* and *onto* are very similar to one another and are therefore easily confused.

CLOSE-UP

USING COMMON PREPOSITIONS

- *To* is the basic preposition of direction. It indicates movement toward a physical place: "She went *to* the restaurant"; "He went *to* the meeting." (*To* is also used to form the infinitive of a verb: "He wanted *to deposit* his paycheck before noon"; "Irene offered *to drive* Maria to the baseball game.")
- *In* indicates that something is within the boundaries of a particular space or period of time: "My son is *in* the garden"; "I like to ski *in* the winter"; "The map is *in* the car."
- *On* indicates position above or the state of being supported by something: "The toys are *on* the porch"; "The baby sat *on* my lap"; "The book is *on* top of the magazine."
- *Into* indicates movement to the inside or interior of something: "She walked *into* the room"; "I threw the stone *into* the lake"; "He put the photos *into* the box." Although *into* and *in* are sometimes interchangeable, note that usage depends on whether the subject is stationary or moving. *Into* usually indicates movement, as in "I jumped *into* the water." *In* usually indicates a stationary position relative to the object of the preposition, as in "Mary is swimming *in* the water."
- *Onto* indicates movement to a position on top of something: "The cat jumped *onto* the chair"; "Crumbs are falling *onto* the floor." Both *on* and *onto* can be used to indicate a position on top of something (and therefore they can sometimes be used interchangeably), but *onto* specifies that the subject is moving to a place from a different place or from an outside position.

CLOSE-UP

PREPOSITIONS IN IDIOMATIC EXPRESSIONS

Many nonnative speakers use incorrect prepositions in idiomatic expressions. Compare the incorrect expressions in the left-hand column below with the correct expressions in the right-hand column.

Incorrect	Correct
according *with*	according *to*
apologize *at*	apologize *to*
appeal *at*	appeal *to*
believe *at*	believe *in*
different *to*	different *from*
for least, *for* most	*at* least, *at* most
refer *at*	refer *to*
relevant *with*	relevant *to*
similar *with*	similar *to*
subscribe *with*	subscribe *to*

EXERCISE 49.6

An ESL student in a composition class wrote the following paragraphs as part of a paper about her experiences learning to write in English. In several cases, she chose the wrong prepositions. The student's instructor has underlined the misused prepositions. Your task is to replace each underlined preposition with a correct preposition. (In some cases, there may be more than one possible correct answer.) If you have trouble, consult a dictionary, and look up a noun or verb that is part of the phrase in question.

My first experience writing ►(1) of English took place ►(2) at my early youth. I don't remember what the experience was like, but I do know that I have improved my writing skills since then. The improvement stems from various reasons. One major impact ►(3) to my writing was the fact that I attended an American school ►(4) of my country. This helped a lot because the first language ►(5) to the school was English. Being surrounded (6) in English helped me improve both my verbal skills and my writing skills. Another major factor that helped me develop my English writing skills, especially my grammar and vocabulary, was reading novels.

(7) At the future, I plan to improve my writing skills in English by participating (8) to several activities. I plan to read more novels so I can further develop the grammar and vocabulary skills that will help me earn my degree. I also plan to communicate verbally with native speakers and to listen (9) at public speeches (such as the president's state of the union address), which usually contain rich vocabulary. But my main plan is to keep writing more papers and discussing my writing (10) to my instructor. The more I write, the more confident I will become and the more my writing will improve. And there is always room for improvement.

49f Understanding Word Order

In English, word order is extremely important, contributing a good deal to the meaning of a sentence.

1 Standard Word Order

Like Chinese, English is an SVO language, or one in which the most typical sentence pattern is "subject-verb-object." (Arabic, by contrast, is an example of a VSO language.)

2 Word Order in Questions

Word order in questions can be particularly troublesome for speakers of languages other than English, partly because there are so many different ways to form questions in English.

CLOSE-UP

WORD ORDER IN QUESTIONS

1. To create a **yes/no question** from a statement whose verb is a form of *be* (*am, is, are, was, were*), move the verb so it precedes the subject.

   Rasheem is in his laboratory.
   Is Rasheem in his laboratory?

   When the statement is *not* a form of *be*, change the verb to include a form of *do* as a helping verb, and then move that helping verb so it precedes the subject.

   Rasheem researched the depletion of the ozone level.
   Did Rasheem research the depletion of the ozone level?

2. To create a **yes/no question** from a statement that includes one or more helping verbs, move the first helping verb so it precedes the subject.

   Rasheem is researching the depletion of the ozone layer.
   Is Rasheem researching the depletion of the ozone layer?

3. To create a **question asking for information**, replace the information being asked for with an **interrogative** word (*who, what, where, why, when, how*) at the beginning of the question, and invert the order of the subject and verb as with a yes/no question.

   Rasheem is in his laboratory.
   Where is Rasheem?
   Rasheem is researching the depletion of the ozone layer.
   What is Rasheem researching?
   Rasheem researched the depletion of the ozone level.
   What did Rasheem research?

   If the interrogative word is the subject of the question, however, do *not* invert the subject and verb.

   Who is researching the depletion of the ozone level?

4. You can also form a question by adding a **tag question** (such as *won't he?* or *didn't I?*) to the end of a statement. If the verb of the main statement is *positive*, then the verb of the tag question is *negative*; if the verb of the main statement is *negative*, then the verb of the tag question is *positive*.

<u>Rasheem</u> <u>is</u> researching the depletion of the ozone layer, <u>isn't</u> <u>he</u>?

<u>Rasheem</u> <u>doesn't</u> intend to write his dissertation about the depletion of the ozone layer, <u>does</u> <u>he</u>?

---

3 Word Order in Imperative Sentences

Imperative sentences state commands. It is common for the subject of an imperative sentence to be left out because the word *you* is understood to be the subject: "Go to school"; "Eat your dinner." Therefore, the word order pattern in an imperative sentence is usually "verb-object," or VO.

49g Distinguishing Commonly Confused Words

A number of word pairs in English have similar meanings. These word pairs can be confusing to nonnative English speakers because the ways in which the expressions are used in sentences are different although their meanings may be similar.

NO AND NOT

No is an adjective; *not* is an adverb. Therefore, use *no* with nouns, and use *not* with verbs, adjectives, and other adverbs.

She has <u>no</u> desire to go to the football game.

Sergio's sisters are <u>not</u> friendly.

TOO AND VERY

Too is an intensifier. It is used to add emphasis in a sentence and to indicate excess.

It is <u>too</u> cold outside to go swimming.

Very is also an intensifier. It means greatly or intensely, but not to excess.

It was <u>very</u> cold outside, but not cold enough to keep us from playing in the backyard.

EVEN, EVEN IF, AND EVEN THOUGH

When used as an adverb, *even* is used to intensify or indicate surprise.

Greta felt <u>even</u> worse than she looked.

<u>Even</u> my little brother knows how to figure that out!

Even if is used in a sentence where there is a condition that may or may not occur.

<u>Even if</u> it rains tomorrow, I'm going to the park.

Even though is similar in meaning to *although*.

<u>Even though</u> Christopher is a very fast runner, he did not make the national track team.

A FEW/A LITTLE AND FEW/LITTLE

A few and *a little* mean not much, but some or enough. *A few* is used with count nouns. *A little* is used with noncount nouns.

We have <u>a few screws</u> remaining from the project.

There is <u>a little bit of paint</u> left in the can.

Few and *little* mean a small number—there are some, but perhaps not as much as one would like.

<u>Few singers</u> are as talented as Kelly.

I have <u>little hope</u> that this situation will change.

MUCH AND MANY

Both *much* and *many* mean "a great quantity" or "to a great degree." Use *much* to modify noncount nouns: "much experience"; "much money." Use *many* to modify count nouns: "many people"; "many incidents."

MOST OF, MOST, AND THE MOST

Most and *most of* have similar meanings. *Most of* means "nearly all of something." Use *most of* when the noun that follows is a specific plural noun. When you use *most of*, be sure to use the definite article the before *the* noun.

<u>Most of the children</u> had cookies for dessert.

Most is used for more general observations and means nearly all.

<u>Most houses</u> in the United States have electricity.

The most is used for comparing more than two of something.

Thomas has <u>the most jellybeans</u>.

Pedro is <u>the most experienced</u> of the engineers.

SOME AND ANY

Some denotes an unspecified amount or quantity that may be part of a larger amount. It can modify both count and noncount nouns: "some water"; "some melons." *Any* indicates an unspecified amount, which may be none, some, or all. It can modify both count and noncount nouns: "any person"; "any luggage."

Glossary of Usage

This glossary of usage lists words and phrases that writers often find troublesome and explains how they are used.

> ## ESL TIP
> For a list of commonly confused words that present particular challenges for ESL writers, **see 49g.**

a, an   Use *a* before words that begin with consonants and words with initial vowels that sound like consonants: *a* person, *a* historical document, *a* one-horse carriage, *a* uniform. Use *an* before words that begin with vowels and words that begin with a silent *h*: *an* artist, *an* honest person.

accept, except   *Accept* is a verb that means "to receive"; *except* as a preposition or conjunction means "other than" and as a verb means "to leave out": The auditors will *accept* all your claims *except* the last two. Some businesses are *excepted* from the regulation.

advice, advise   *Advice* is a noun meaning "opinion or information offered"; *advise* is a verb that means "to offer advice to": The broker *advised* her client to take his attorney's *advice*.

affect, effect   *Affect* is a verb meaning "to influence"; *effect* can be a verb or a noun—as a verb it means "to bring about," and as a noun it means "result": We know how the drug *affects* patients immediately, but little is known of its long-term *effects*. The arbitrator tried to *effect* a settlement between the parties.

all ready, already   *All ready* means "completely prepared"; *already* means "by or before this or that time": I was *all ready* to help, but it was *already* too late.

all right, alright   Although the use of *alright* is increasing, current usage calls for *all right*.

allusion, illusion   An *allusion* is a reference or hint; an *illusion* is something that is not what it seems: The poem makes an *allusion* to the Pandora myth. The shadow created an optical *illusion*.

a lot   *A lot* is always two words.

among, between   *Among* refers to groups of more than two things; *between* refers to just two things: The three parties agreed *among* themselves to settle the case. There will be a brief intermission *between* the two acts. (Note that *amongst* is British, not American, usage.)

amount, number   *Amount* refers to a quantity that cannot be counted; *number* refers to things that can be counted: Even a small *amount* of caffeine can be harmful. Seeing their commander fall, a large *number* of troops ran to his aid.

an, a   See **a, an.**

and/or   In business or technical writing, use *and/or* when either or both of the items it connects can apply. In college writing, however, avoid the use of *and/or.*

as . . . as . . .   In such constructions, *as* signals a comparison; therefore, you must always use the second *as:* John Steinbeck's *East of Eden* is *as* long *as* his *The Grapes of Wrath.*

as, like   *As* can be used as a conjunction (to introduce a complete clause) or as a preposition; *like* should be used as a preposition only: In *The Scarlet Letter,* Hawthorne uses imagery as (not *like*) he does in his other works. After classes, Fred works *as* a manager of a fast food restaurant. Writers *like* Carl Sandburg appear once in a generation.

at, to   Many people use the prepositions *at* and *to* after *where* in conversation: *Where* are you working *at*? *Where* are you going *to*? This usage is redundant and should not appear in college writing.

awhile, a while   *Awhile* is an adverb; *a while*, which consists of an article and a noun, is used as the object of a preposition: Before we continue, we will rest *awhile* (modifies the verb *rest*); Before we continue, we will rest for *a while* (object of the preposition *for*).

bad, badly   *Bad* is an adjective, and *badly* is an adverb: The school board decided that *Adventures of Huckleberry Finn* was a *bad* book. American automobile makers did not do *badly* this year. After verbs that refer to any of the senses or after any other linking verb, use the adjective form: He looked *bad*. He felt *bad*. It seemed *bad*.

being as, being that   These awkward phrases add unnecessary words, thereby weakening your writing. Use *because* instead.

beside, besides   *Beside* is a preposition meaning "next to"; *besides* can be either a preposition meaning "except" or "other than" or an adverb meaning "as well": *Beside* the tower was a wall that ran the length of the city. *Besides* its industrial uses, laser technology has many other applications. Edison invented not only the lightbulb but the phonograph *besides*.

between, among   See **among, between.**

bring, take   *Bring* means "to transport from a farther place to a nearer place"; *take* means "to carry or convey from a nearer place to a farther place": *Bring* me a souvenir from your trip. *Take* this message to the general, and wait for a reply.

can, may   *Can* denotes ability; *may* indicates permission: If you *can* play, you *may* use my piano.

capital, capitol   *Capital* refers to a city that is an official seat of government; *capitol* refers to a building in which a legislature meets: Washington, DC, is the *capital* of the United States. When we were there, we visited the *Capitol* building.

cite, site   *Cite* is a verb meaning "to quote as an authority or example"; *site* is a noun meaning "a place or setting"; it is also a shortened form of *Web site*: Jeff *cited* five sources in his research paper. The builder cleared the *site* for the new bank. Marisa uploaded her *site* to the Web.

climactic, climatic   *Climactic* means "of or related to a climax"; *climatic* means "of or related to climate": The *climactic* moment of the movie occurred unexpectedly. If scientists are correct, the *climatic* conditions of Earth are changing.

complement, compliment   *Complement* means "to complete or add to"; *compliment* means "to give praise": A double-blind study would *complement* their preliminary research. My instructor *complimented* me on my improvement.

conscious, conscience   *Conscious* is an adjective meaning "having one's mental faculties awake"; *conscience* is a noun that means the moral sense of right and wrong: The patient will remain *conscious* during the procedure. His *conscience* would not allow him to lie.

continual, continuous   *Continual* means "recurring at intervals"; *continuous* refers to an action that occurs without interruption: A pulsar is a star that emits a *continual* stream of electromagnetic radiation. (It emits radiation at regular intervals.) A small battery allows the watch to run *continuously* for five years. (It runs without stopping.)

could of, should of, would of   The contractions *could've, should've*, and *would've* are often misspelled as the nonstandard constructions *could of, should of*, and *would of*. Use *could have, should have*, and *would have* in college writing.

council, counsel   A *council* is "a body of people who serve in a legislative or advisory capacity"; *counsel* means "to offer advice or guidance": The city *council* argued about the proposed ban on smoking. The judge *counseled* the couple to settle their differences.

couple, couple of   *Couple* means "a pair," but *couple of* is often used colloquially to mean "several" or "a few." In your college writing, specify "four points" or "two examples" rather than using "a couple of."

criterion, criteria   *Criteria*, from the Greek, is the plural of *criterion*, meaning "standard for judgment": Of all the *criteria* for hiring graduating seniors, class rank is the most important *criterion*.

data   *Data* is the plural of the Latin *datum*, meaning "fact." In everyday speech and writing, *data* is often used as the singular as well as the plural form. In college writing, use *data* only for the plural: The *data* discussed in this section *are* summarized in Appendix A.

different from, different than   *Different than* is widely used in American speech. In college writing, use *different from*.

discreet, discrete   *Discreet* means "careful or prudent"; *discrete* means "separate or individually distinct": Because Madame Bovary was not *discreet*, her reputation suffered. Atoms can be broken into hundreds of *discrete* particles.

disinterested, uninterested   *Disinterested* means "objective" or "capable of making an impartial judgment"; *uninterested* means "indifferent or unconcerned": The American judicial system depends on *disinterested* jurors. Finding no treasure, Hernando de Soto was *uninterested* in going farther.

don't, doesn't   *Don't* is the contraction of *do not; doesn't* is the contraction of *does not.* Do not confuse the two: My dog *doesn't* (not *don't*) like to walk in the rain. (Note that contractions are generally not acceptable in college writing.)

effect, affect   See **affect, effect.**

e.g.   *E.g.* is an abbreviation for the Latin *exempli gratia,* meaning "for example" or "for instance." In college writing, do not use *e.g.* Instead, use "for example" or "for instance."

emigrate from, immigrate to   To *emigrate* is "to leave one's country and settle in another"; to *immigrate* is "to come to another country and reside there." The noun forms of these words are *emigrant* and *immigrant*: My great-grandfather *emigrated from* Warsaw along with many other *emigrants* from Poland. Many people *immigrate* to the United States for economic reasons, but such *immigrants* still face great challenges.

eminent, imminent   *Eminent* is an adjective meaning "standing above others" or "prominent"; *imminent* means "about to occur": Oliver Wendell Holmes Jr. was an *eminent* jurist. In ancient times, a comet signaled *imminent* disaster.

enthused   *Enthused,* a colloquial form of *enthusiastic,* should not be used in college writing.

etc.   *Etc.,* the abbreviation of *et cetera,* means "and the rest." Do not use it in your college writing. Instead, use "and so on"—or, better yet, specify exactly what *etc.* stands for.

everyday, every day   *Everyday* is an adjective that means "ordinary" or "commonplace"; *every day* means "occurring daily": In the Gettysburg Address, Lincoln used *everyday* language. She exercises almost *every day.*

everyone, every one   *Everyone* is an indefinite pronoun meaning "every person"; *every one* means "every individual or thing in a particular group": *Everyone* seems happier in the spring. *Every one* of the packages had been opened.

except, accept   See **accept, except.**

explicit, implicit   *Explicit* means "expressed or stated directly"; *implicit* means "implied" or "expressed or stated indirectly": The director *explicitly* warned the actors to be on time for rehearsals. Her *implicit* message was that lateness would not be tolerated.

farther, further   *Farther* designates distance; *further* designates degree: I have traveled *farther* from home than any of my relatives. Critics charge that welfare subsidies encourage *further* dependence.

fewer, less   Use *fewer* with nouns that can be counted: *fewer* books, *fewer* people, *fewer* dollars. Use *less* with quantities that cannot be counted: *less* pain, *less* power, *less* enthusiasm.

firstly (secondly, thirdly, . . .)   Archaic forms meaning "in the first . . . second . . . third place." Use *first, second, third* instead.

further, farther   See **farther, further.**

good, well   *Good* is an adjective, never an adverb: She is a *good* swimmer. *Well* can function as an adverb or as an adjective. As an adverb, it means "in a good manner": She swam *well* (not *good*) in the meet. *Well* is used as an adjective with verbs that denote a state of being or feeling. Here *well* can mean "in good health": I feel *well*.

got to   *Got to* is not acceptable in college writing. To indicate obligation, use *have to, has to,* or *must.*

hanged, hung   Both *hanged* and *hung* are past participles of *hang. Hanged* is used to refer to executions; *hung* is used to mean "suspended": Billy Budd was *hanged* for killing the master-at-arms. The stockings were *hung* by the chimney with care.

he, she   Traditionally *he* has been used in the generic sense to refer to both males and females. To acknowledge the equality of the sexes, however, avoid the generic *he.* Use plural pronouns whenever possible. **See 19e2.**

hopefully   The adverb *hopefully,* meaning "in a hopeful manner," should modify a verb, an adjective, or another adverb. Do not use *hopefully* as a sentence modifier meaning "it is hoped." Rather than "*Hopefully,* scientists will soon discover a cure for AIDS," write "*I hope* scientists will soon discover a cure for AIDS."

i.e.   *I.e.* is an abbreviation for the Latin *id est,* meaning "that is." In college writing, do not use *i.e.* Instead, use its English equivalent.

if, whether   When asking indirect questions or expressing doubt, use *whether*: He asked *whether* (not *if*) the flight would be delayed. The flight attendant was not sure *whether* (not *if*) it would be delayed.

illusion, allusion   See **allusion, illusion.**

immigrate to, emigrate from   See **emigrate from, immigrate to.**

implicit, explicit   See **explicit, implicit.**

imply, infer   *Imply* means "to hint" or "to suggest"; *infer* means "to conclude from": Mark Antony *implied* that the conspirators had murdered Caesar. The crowd *inferred* his meaning and called for justice.

infer, imply   See **imply, infer.**

inside of, outside of   *Of* is unnecessary when *inside* and *outside* are used as prepositions. *Inside of* is colloquial in references to time: He waited *inside* (not *inside of*) the coffee shop. He could run a mile in *under* (not *inside of*) eight minutes.

irregardless, regardless   *Irregardless* is a nonstandard version of *regardless.* Use *regardless* or *irrespective* instead.

is when, is where   These constructions are faulty when they appear in definitions: A playoff is (not *is when*) an additional game played to establish the winner of a tie.

its, it's   *Its* is a possessive pronoun; *it's* is a contraction of *it is: It's* no secret that the bank is out to protect *its* assets.

kind of, sort of   *Kind of* and *sort of* to mean "rather" or "somewhat" are colloquial and should not appear in college writing: It is well known that Napoleon was *rather* (not *kind of*) short.

lay, lie   See **lie, lay.**

leave, let   *Leave* means "to go away from" or "to *let* remain"; *let* means "to allow" or "to permit": *Let* (not *leave*) me give you a hand.

less, fewer   See **fewer, less.**

let, leave   See **leave, let.**

lie, lay   *Lie* is an intransitive verb (one that does not take an object) meaning "to recline." Its principal forms are *lie, lay, lain, lying:* Each afternoon she would *lie* in the sun and listen to the surf. *As I Lay Dying* is a novel by William Faulkner. By 1871, Troy had *lain* undisturbed for two thousand years. The painting shows a nude *lying* on a couch.

   Lay is a transitive verb (one that takes an object) meaning "to put" or "to place." Its principal forms are *lay, laid, laid, laying:* The Federalist Papers *lay* the foundation for American conservatism. In October 1781, the British *laid* down their arms and surrendered. He had *laid* his money on the counter before leaving. We watched the stonemasons *laying* a wall.

like, as   See **as, like.**

loose, lose   *Loose* is an adjective meaning "not rigidly fastened or securely attached"; *lose* is a verb meaning "to misplace": The marble facing of the building became *loose* and fell to the sidewalk. After only two drinks, most people *lose* their ability to judge distance.

lots, lots of, a lot of   These words are colloquial substitutes for *many, much,* or *a great deal of.* Avoid their use in college writing: The students had many (not *lots of* or *a lot of*) options for essay topics.

man   Like the generic pronoun *he, man* has been used in English to denote members of both sexes. This usage is being replaced by *human beings, people,* or similar terms that do not specify gender. **See 19e2.**

may, can   See **can, may.**

may be, maybe   *May be* is a verb phrase: *maybe* is an adverb meaning "perhaps": She *may be* the smartest student in the class. *Maybe* her experience has given her an advantage.

media, medium   *Medium*, meaning "a means of conveying or broadcasting something," is singular; *media* is the plural form and requires a plural verb: The *media* have distorted the issue.

might have, might of   *Might of* is a nonstandard spelling of the contraction of *might have* (*might've*). Use *might have* in college writing.

number, amount   See **amount, number.**

OK, O.K., okay   All three spellings are acceptable, but this term should be avoided in college writing. Replace it with a more specific word or words: The lecture was *adequate* (not *okay*), if uninspiring.

outside of, inside of   See **inside of, outside of.**

passed, past   *Passed* is the past tense of the verb *pass; past* means "belonging to a former time" or "no longer current": The car must have been going eighty miles per hour when it *passed* us. In the envelope was a bill marked *past* due.

percent, percentage   *Percent* indicates a part of a hundred when a specific number is referred to: "*10 percent* of his salary." *Percentage* is used when no specific number is referred to: "a *percentage* of next year's receipts." In technical and business writing, it is permissible to use the % sign after percentages you are comparing. Write out the word *percent* in college writing.

phenomenon, phenomena   A *phenomenon* is a single observable fact or event. It can also refer to a rare or significant occurrence. *Phenomena* is the plural form and requires a plural verb: Many supposedly paranormal *phenomena* are easily explained.

plus   As a preposition, *plus* means "in addition to." Avoid using *plus* as a substitute for *and:* Include the principal, *plus* the interest, in your calculations. Your quote was too high; moreover (not *plus*), it was inaccurate.

precede, proceed   *Precede* means "to go or come before"; *proceed* means "to go forward in an orderly way": Robert Frost's *North of Boston* was *preceded* by an earlier volume. In 1532, Francisco Pizarro landed at Tumbes and *proceeded* south.

principal, principle   As a noun, *principal* means "a sum of money (minus interest) invested or lent" or "a person in the leading position"; as an adjective, it means "most important"; a *principle* is a noun meaning a rule of conduct or a basic truth: He wanted to reduce the *principal* of the loan. The *principal* of the high school is a talented administrator. Women are the *principal* wage earners in many American households. The Constitution embodies certain fundamental *principles*.

quote, quotation   *Quote* is a verb. *Quotation* is a noun. In college writing, do not use *quote* as a shortened form of *quotation:* Scholars attribute these *quotations* (not *quotes*) to Shakespeare.

raise, rise   *Raise* is a transitive verb, and *rise* is an intransitive verb—that is, *raise* takes an object, and *rise* does not: My grandparents *raised* a large family. The sun will *rise* at 6:12 this morning.

real, really   *Real* means "genuine" or "authentic"; *really* means "actually." In your college writing, do not use *real* as an adjective meaning "very."

reason is that, reason is because   *Reason* should be used with *that* and not with *because*, which is redundant: The *reason* he left is *that* (not *because*) you insulted him.

regardless, irregardless   See **irregardless, regardless.**

respectably, respectfully, respectively   *Respectably* means "worthy of respect"; *respectfully* means "giving honor or deference"; *respectively* means "in the order given": He skated quite *respectably* at his first Olympics. The seminar taught us to treat others *respectfully*. The first- and second-place winners were Tai and Kim, *respectively*.

rise, raise   See **raise, rise.**

set, sit   *Set* means "to put down" or "to lay." Its principal forms are *set* and *setting*: After rocking the baby to sleep, he *set* her down carefully in her crib. After *setting* her down, he took a nap.

     Sit means "to assume a sitting position." Its principal forms are *sit, sat,* and *sitting*: Many children *sit* in front of the television five to six hours a day. The dog *sat* by the fire. We were *sitting* in the airport when the flight was canceled.

shall, will   *Will* has all but replaced *shall* to express all future action.

should of   See **could of, should of, would of.**

since   Do not use *since* for *because* if there is any chance of confusion. In the sentence "*Since* President Nixon traveled to China, trade between China and the United States has increased," *since* could mean either "from the time that" or "because." To be clear, use *because.*

sit, set   See **set, sit.**

so   Avoid using *so* as a vague intensifier meaning "very" or "extremely." Follow *so* with *that* and a clause that describes the result: She was *so* pleased with their work *that* she took them out to lunch.

sometime, sometimes, some time   *Sometime* means "at some time in the future"; *sometimes* means "now and then"; *some time* means "a period of time": The president will address Congress *sometime* next week. All automobiles, no matter how reliable, *sometimes* need repairs. It has been *some time* since I read that book.

sort of, kind of   See **kind of, sort of.**

stationary, stationery   *Stationary* means "staying in one place"; *stationery* means "materials for writing" or "letter paper": The communications satellite appears to be *stationary* in the sky. The secretaries supply departmental offices with *stationery.*

supposed to, used to   *Supposed to* and *used to* are often misspelled. Both verbs require the final *d* to indicate past tense.

take, bring   See **bring, take.**

than, then   *Than* is a conjunction used to indicate a comparison; *then* is an adverb indicating time: The new shopping center is bigger *than* the old one. He did his research; *then,* he wrote a report.

that, which, who   Use *that* or *which* when referring to a thing, use *who* when referring to a person: It was a speech *that* inspired many. The movie, *which* was a huge success, failed to impress her. Anyone *who* (not *that*) takes the course will benefit.

their, there, they're   *Their* is a possessive pronoun; *there* indicates place and is also used in the expressions *there is* and *there are*; *they're* is a contraction of *they are*: Watson and Crick did *their* DNA work at Cambridge University. I love Los Angeles, but I wouldn't want to live *there*. *There* is nothing we can do to resurrect an extinct species. When *they're* well treated, rabbits make excellent pets.

themselves, theirselves, theirself   *Theirselves* and *theirself* are nonstandard variants of *themselves*.

then, than   See **than, then.**

till, until, 'til   *Till* and *until* have the same meaning, and both are acceptable. *Until* is preferred in college writing. *'Til*, a contraction of *until*, should be avoided.

to, at   See **at, to.**

to, too, two   *To* is a preposition that indicates direction; *too* is an adverb that means "also" or "more than is needed"; *two* expresses the number 2: Last year we flew from New York *to* California. "Tippecanoe and Tyler, *too*" was William Henry Harrison's campaign slogan. The plot was *too* complicated for the average reader. Just north of *Two* Rivers, Wisconsin, is a petrified forest.

try to, try and   *Try and* is the colloquial equivalent of the more formal *try to:* He decided to *try to* (not *try and*) do better. In college writing, use *try to.*

-type   Deleting this empty suffix eliminates clutter and clarifies meaning. Found in the wreckage was an *incendiary* (not *incendiary-type*) device.

uninterested, disinterested   See **disinterested, uninterested.**

unique   Because *unique* means "the only one," not "remarkable" or "unusual," never use constructions like "the most unique" or "very unique."

until   See **till, until, 'til.**

used to   See **supposed to, used to.**

utilize   In most cases, replace *utilize* with *use* (*utilize* often sounds pretentious).

wait for, wait on   To *wait for* means "to defer action until something occurs." To *wait on* means "to act as a waiter": I am *waiting for* (not *on*) dinner.

weather, whether   *Weather* is a noun meaning "the state of the atmosphere"; *whether* is a conjunction used to introduce an alternative: The *weather* will improve this weekend. It is doubtful *whether* we will be able to ski tomorrow.

well, good   See **good, well.**

were, we're   *Were* is a verb; *we're* is the contraction of *we are:* The Trojans *were* asleep when the Greeks attacked. We must act now if *we're* going to succeed.

whether, if   See **if, whether.**

which, who, that   See **that, which, who.**

who, whom   When a pronoun serves as the subject of its clause, use *who* or *whoever*; when it functions in a clause as an object, use *whom* or *whomever*: Sarah, *who* is studying ancient civilizations, would like to visit Greece. Sarah, *whom* I met in France, wants me to travel to Greece with her. To determine which to use at the beginning of a question, use a personal pronoun to answer the question: *Who* tried to call me? *He* called. (subject); *Whom* do you want for the job? I want *her.* (object)

who's, whose   *Who's* means "who is" or "who has"; *whose* indicates possession: *Who's* going to take calculus? *Who's* already left for the concert? The
writer *whose* book was in the window was autographing copies.

will, shall   See **shall, will.**

would of   See **could of, should of, would of.**

your, you're   *Your* indicates possession; *you're* is the contraction of *you are*:
You can improve *your* stamina by jogging two miles a day. *You're* certain to
be the winner.

Answers to Selected Exercises

Answers are provided here for exercise items marked with a ► throughout the text.

Exercise 3.1 (p. 31)
1. An announcement, not a thesis.
2. A subject, not a thesis. Gives no indication of essay's focus or direction, let alone writer's position.
3. A subject, not a thesis. Why should it be avoided? What coast? What kind of development? What constitutes overdevelopment?
4. No position indicated. What aspects will be considered? What patterns of development might be used? What standards of judgment will be used?
5. A good start, but "but it has a number of disadvantages" is not specific enough.

Exercise 5.4 (p. 74)
1. **A.** Give specific examples; exemplification. The paragraph could be developed further by exemplification—that is, by giving examples of words that came into the English language from computer terminology, from popular music, from politics, and from films or TV. If enough examples are given, the paragraph can be expanded into an essay.

Exercise 6.1 (p. 80)
1. F
2. O
3. F
4. O
5. F

Exercise 6.4 (pp. 88–89)
Rewritten statements will vary. Here are the logical fallacies.
1. *Post hoc* fallacy
2. Argument to the person; sweeping generalization
3. Argument to the person
4. Equivocation
5. Begging the question

Exercise 14.1 (p. 157)
1. Isaac Asimov first saw science fiction stories (do) in the newsstand of his parent's Brooklyn candy store.
2. He pr acticed writing (do) by telling his schoolmates (io) stories (do).
3. Asimov published his first story (do) in *Astounding Science Fiction*.
4. The magazine's editor, John W. Campbell, encouraged Asimov (do) to continue writing.
5. The young writer researched scientific principles (do) to make his stories more accurate.

Exercise 14.2 (pp. 159–60)
1. IC
2. DC
3. P
4. IC
5. IC

Exercise 14.3 (pp. 161–62)
1. The average American consumes 128 pounds of sugar each year; therefore, most Americans eat much more sugar than any other food additive, including salt.
2. Many of us are determined to reduce our sugar intake; consequently, we have consciously eliminated sweets from our diets.
3. Unfortunately, sugar is found not only in sweets but also in many processed foods.
4. Processed foods like puddings and cake contain sugar, and foods like ketchup and spaghetti sauce do too.
5. We are trying to cut down on sugar, yet we find limiting sugar intake extremely difficult.

Exercise 14.4 (pp. 163–64)
1. Many high school graduates who are out of work need new skills for new careers.
2. Although talented high school students are usually encouraged to go to college, some high school graduates are now starting to see that a college education may not guarantee them a job.
3. Because a college education can cost a student more than $100,000, vocational education is becoming an increasingly attractive alternative.
4. Because vocational students complete their work in less than four years, they can enter the job market more quickly.
5. Nurses' aides, paralegals, travel agents, and computer technicians, who do not need college degrees, have little trouble finding work.

Exercise 15.1 (p. 166)
Answers will vary. Here is one revision.
The first modern miniature golf course, built in New York in 1925, was an indoor course with eighteen holes. As the game caught on, entrepreneurs Drake Delanoy and John Ledbetter built one hundred fifty more indoor and outdoor courses; Garnet Carter, who made miniature golf a worldwide fad with his elaborate miniature courses, later joined with Delanoy and Ledbetter to build more courses.

Exercise 15.2 (p. 167)
Answers will vary. Here is one revision.
In surveying two thousand Colorado schoolchildren, Dr. Alice I. Baumgartner and her colleagues at the Institute for Equality in Education found some star-

tling results. They asked, "If you woke up tomorrow morning and discovered that you were a (girl) (boy), how would your life be different?" The answers were sad and shocking.

Exercise 15.3 (pp. 168–69)
Answers will vary. Here are some possibilities.
1. When he was a very young child, Momaday was taken to Devil's Tower, the geological formation in Wyoming that is called Tsoai (Bear Tree) in Kiowa, and given the name Tsoai-talee (Bear Tree Boy). (adverb clause)
2. In the Kiowa myth of the origin of Tsoai, a boy playfully chases his seven sisters up a tree, which rises into the air as the boy is transformed into a bear. (prepositional phrase)

Exercise 16.1 (pp. 170–71)
Listening to diatribes by angry callers or ranting about today's news, the talk radio host <u>spreads ideas over the air waves</u>. (climactic order)
<u>Every day at the same time</u>, the political talk show host discusses national events and policies, the failures of the opposing view, and the foibles of the individuals who espouse those views. (beginning)
<u>Listening for hours a day</u>, some callers become recognizable contributors to many different talk radio programs. (beginning)
<u>Other listeners are less devoted</u>, tuning in only when they are in the car and never calling to voice their opinions. (beginning)

Exercise 16.2 (p. 171)
1. Because criminals are better armed than ever before, police want to upgrade their firepower.
2. A few years ago, felons used small-caliber, six-shot revolvers—so-called Saturday night specials.

Exercise 16.3 (pp. 172–73)
1. A. <u>However different in their educational opportunities</u>, [both Jefferson and Lincoln as young men became known to their contemporaries as "hard students."] (periodic)
   B. Both Lincoln and Jefferson as young men became known to their contemporaries as "hard students," however different their educational opportunities.

Exercise 16.4 (p. 174)
Answers will vary. Here is one revision.
Many readers distrust newspapers and magazines; they also distrust what they hear on radio and television. Of these media, newspapers have been the most responsive to audience criticism. Some newspapers even have ombudsmen, who listen to reader complaints and act on these grievances.

Exercise 16.5 (p. 175)
Answers will vary. Here is one revision.
Jack Dempsey, the heavyweight champion between 1919 and 1926, had an interesting but uneven career. Many considered him one of the greatest boxers of all time. Dempsey began fighting as "Kid Blackie," but his career did not take off until 1919, when Jack "Doc" Kearns became his manager. Dempsey won the championship when he defeated Jess Willard in Toledo, Ohio, in 1919. Dempsey immediately became a popular sports figure; President Franklin D. Roosevelt was one of his biggest fans.

Exercise 17.1 (p. 177)
Answers will vary. Here is one revision.
The shopping mall is no longer so important to American culture. In the 1980s, shopping malls became gathering places where teenagers met, walkers came to get in a few miles, and shoppers looking for selection (not value) went to shop. Several factors have undermined the mall's popularity. First, today's shopper is interested in value and is more likely to shop in discount stores or bulk-buying warehouse stores than in the small, expensive specialty shops in large shopping malls.

Exercise 17.2 (pp. 178–79)
For different reasons, people today are choosing a vegetarian diet. Strict vegetarians eat no animal foods; lactovegetarians eat dairy products but no meat, fish, poultry, or eggs; and ovolactovegetarians eat eggs and dairy products but no meat, fish, or poultry. Famous vegetarians include George Bernard Shaw, Leonardo da Vinci, Ralph Waldo Emerson, Henry David Thoreau, and Mahatma Gandhi. Like them, people today have become vegetarians for good reasons.

Exercise 17.3 (p. 180)
Some colleges that have supported fraternities for many years are reevaluating the fraternities' positions on campus. Opposing the fraternities are students, faculty, and administrators, who claim that fraternities are inherently sexist and, therefore, are unacceptable in coed institutions that offer equal opportunities. Many members of the college community see fraternities as elitist as well as sexist and favor their abolition.

Exercise 18.1 (p. 182)
1. After he completed his engineering degree, Manek returned to India [to visit his large extended family] and [to find a wife].
2. [Unfamiliar with marriage practices in India] and [accustomed to the American notion of marriage for love], Manek's American friends disapproved of his plans.

Exercise 18.2 (pp. 183–84)
1. The world is divided between those who wear galoshes and those who discover continents.
2. World leaders, members of Congress, and religious groups are all concerned about global warming.

Exercise 19.2 (p. 187)
Answers will vary. Here are some examples.
1. deceive, mislead, beguile
2. antiquated, old, antique
3. pushy, assertive, goal-oriented
4. pathetic, unfortunate, touching
5. cheap, inexpensive, economical

Exercise 19.3 (p. 188)
Answers will vary. Here is one revision.
Part-time jobs I have held include waiting tables, landscaping, and selling stereo equipment. Each of these jobs requires strong communications skills. In my most recent position, I sold automobile stereos.

Exercise 19.5 (p. 192)
Answers will vary. Here are some examples.
  forefathers, ancestors
  man-eating shark, carnivorous shark
  manpower, workforce
  workman's compensation, worker's compensation
  men at work, workers
  waitress, server
  first baseman, first base
  congressman, representative
  manhunt, search

Exercise 21.1 (p. 204)
1. he; it is the subject of the sentence
2. me; it is the direct object

Exercise 21.2 (pp. 205–06)
1. Herb Ritts, who got his start by taking photographs of Hollywood stars, has photographed world leaders, leading artistic figures in dance and drama, and a vanishing African tribe.
2. Tim Green, who once played for the Atlanta Hawks and has a law degree, has written several novels about a fictional football team.

Exercise 21.3 (p. 207)
1. the expedition
2. Lewis and Clark

Exercise 22.1 (p. 211)
sold, sneaked

Exercise 22.2 (p. 211)
1. set
2. laying

Exercise 22.3 (pp. 215–16)
1. give
2. have read
3. established
4. becoming
5. had made

Exercise 22.4 (p. 217)
performed, challenged, were, was

Exercise 22.5 (pp. 218–219)
The Chinese invented rockets about AD 1000. They packed gunpowder into bamboo tubes and ignited it by means of a fuse. Soldiers fired these rockets at enemy armies and usually caused panic. In the thirteenth century, England's Roger Bacon introduced an improved form of gunpowder. As a result, soldiers used rockets as a common—although unreliable—weapon in battle.

Exercise 22.6 (p. 219)
Answers will vary.
The Regent Diamond is one of the world's most famous and coveted jewels. The 410-carat diamond was discovered by a slave in 1701 in an Indian mine. [Emphasis is on the diamond rather than on who discovered it.] Over the years, it was stolen and sold several times. [Emphasis is on what happened rather than on people.]

Exercise 23.1 (p. 221)
A popular self-help trend in the United States today is downloadable motivational lectures. These lectures, with titles like *How to Attract Love, Freedom from Acne,* and *I Am a Genius,* are intended to solve every problem known to modern society—quickly and easily. The lectures are said to work because they contain "hidden messages" that bypass conscious defense mechanisms. The listener hears only music or relaxing sounds, like waves rolling slowly and steadily.

Exercise 23.2 (p. 221)
Answers will vary. Here are some possibilities.
1. David seemed tired.
Jerry was anxious.
Lienne appeared happy.
Maggie is depressed.
Chris remained confident.

Exercise 23.3 (p. 223)
1. difficult/more difficult/most difficult
2. eccentric/more eccentric/most eccentric
3. confusing/more confusing/most confusing
4. bad/worse/worst
5. mysterious/more mysterious/most mysterious

Exercise 24.1 (p. 225)
   1. F
   2. F
   3. CS
   4. F
   5. F

Exercise 24.2 (p. 227)
The drive-in movie came into being just after World War II, <u>when both movies and cars were central to the lives of many young Americans</u>. Drive-ins were especially popular with teenagers and young families during the 1950s, <u>when cars and gas were relatively inexpensive</u>. Theaters charged by the carload, <u>which meant that a group of teenagers or a family with several children could spend an evening at the movies for a few dollars</u>. In 1958, when the fad peaked, there were more than four thousand drive-ins in the United States, <u>while today there are fewer than three thousand</u>.

Exercise 24.3 (p. 228)
Most college athletes are caught in a conflict <u>between their athletic and academic careers</u>. Sometimes college athletes' responsibilities on the playing field make it difficult for them to be good students. Often, athletes must make a choice <u>between sports and a degree</u>. Some athletes would not be able to afford college <u>without athletic scholarships</u>. Ironically, however, their commitments to sports (training, exercise, practice, and travel to out-of-town games, for example) deprive athletes <u>of valuable classroom time</u>. The role of college athletes is constantly being questioned.

Exercise 24.4 (p. 229)
Answers will vary. Here is one revision.
Many food products have well-known trademarks, <u>identified by familiar faces on product labels</u>. Some of these symbols have remained the same, while others have changed considerably. Products like Sun-Maid Raisins, Betty Crocker potato mixes, Quaker Oats, and Uncle Ben's Rice use faces <u>to create a sense of quality and tradition and to encourage shopper recognition of the products</u>. Many of the portraits have been updated several times <u>to reflect changes in society</u>.

Exercise 24.5 (pp. 230–31)
Answers will vary. Here is one revision.
Until the early 1900s, communities in West Virginia, Tennessee, and Kentucky were isolated by the mountains that surrounded them, <u>the great chain of the Appalachian Mountains</u>. Set apart from the emerging culture of a growing America and American language, these communities retained a language rich with the dialect of Elizabethan English and with hints of a Scotch-Irish influence. In the 1910s and '20s, the communities in these mountains began to long for a better future for their children. The key to that future, as they saw it, was education.

Exercise 24.6 (pp. 231–32)
Answers will vary. Here is one revision.
As more and more Americans discover the pleasures of the wilderness, our national parks are feeling the stress. Wanting to get away for a weekend or a week, hikers and backpackers stream from the cities into nearby state and national parks. They bring with them a hunger for the wilderness <u>and very little knowledge about how to behave ethically in the wild</u>. They also do not know how to keep themselves safe. Some of them think of the national parks as inexpensive amusement parks. Without proper camping supplies and lacking enough food and water for their trip, they are putting at risk their lives and the lives of those who will be called on to save them. One family went for a hike up a desert canyon with an eight-month-old infant <u>and their seventy-eight-year-old grandmother</u>.

Exercise 25.1 (p. 235)
Answers will vary. To illustrate the various responses, each sentence below is followed with the four possible types of correction. You should balance the types of choices in a piece of writing rather than adhering to a single method of correction.
Entrepreneurship is the study of small businesses, college students are embracing it enthusiastically.
  1. businesses. College students
  2. businesses; college students
  3. businesses, and college students
  4. Entrepreneurship, the study of small businesses, is being embraced enthusiastically by college students.
Many schools offer one or more courses in entrepreneurship these courses teach the theory and practice of starting a small business.
  1. entrepreneurship. These courses
  2. entrepreneurship; these courses
  3. entrepreneurship, and these courses
  4. entrepreneurship, which teach the theory and practice of starting a small business.
Students are signing up for courses, moreover, they are starting their own businesses.
  1. courses. Moreover,
  2. courses; moreover,
  3. courses, and, moreover,
  4. Students who sign up for courses are even starting their own businesses.
One student started with a car-waxing business, now he sells condominiums.
  1. business. Now
  2. business; now
  3. business, and now
  4. One student, who started with a car-waxing business, now sells condominiums.

Exercise 25.2 (pp. 235–36)
  1. Several recent studies indicate that many American high school students have a poor sense of history; this is affecting our future as a democratic nation and as individuals.

2. Surveys show that nearly one-third of American seventeen-year-olds cannot identify the countries the United States fought against in World War II, and one-third think Columbus reached the New World after 1750.
3. Several reasons have been given for this decline in historical literacy, but the main reason is the way history is taught.
4. Although this problem is bad news, the good news is that there is increasing agreement among educators about what is wrong with current methods of teaching history.
5. History can be exciting and engaging, but too often it is presented in a boring manner.

Exercise 26.1 (pp. 240–41)
1. C
2. C
3. Neither Western novels nor science fiction appeals to me.
4. Stage presence and musical ability make a rock performer successful today.
5. C

Exercise 26.2 (p. 243)
1. The core of a computer is a collection of electronic circuits that is called the central processing unit.
2. Computers, because of advanced technology that allows the central processing unit to be placed on a chip, a thin square of semiconducting material about one-quarter of an inch on each side, have been greatly reduced in size.
3. No error
4. Pressing keys on keyboards resembling typewriter keyboards generates electronic signals that are input for the computer.
5. Computers have built-in memory storage, and equipment such as disks or tapes provides external memory.

Exercise 27.1 (p. 245)
1. He wore his almost new jeans. [He wore his nearly new jeans.]

   He almost wore his new jeans. [He decided at the last minute not to wear his new jeans.]

2. He had only three dollars in his pocket. [Besides the three dollars, he had nothing else in his pocket.]

   Only he had three dollars in his pocket. [He alone had this amount of money in his pocket.]

Exercise 27.2 (pp. 245–46)
1. The bridge across the river swayed in the wind.

2. The spectators on the shore were involved in the action.

3. Mesmerized by the spectacle, they watched the drama unfold.

4. The spectators were afraid of a disaster.

5. Within the hour, the state police arrived.

Exercise 27.3 (p. 246)

1. The lion, watching Jack, paced up and down in its cage, ignoring the crowd.

2. In terror, Jack stared back at the lion.

Exercise 27.4 (pp. 246–47)
1. She realized after the wedding that she had married the wrong man.
2. *The Prince and the Pauper,* by Mark Twain, is a novel about an exchange of identities.

Exercise 27.5 (pp. 247–48)
1. The people in the audience finally quieted down when they saw the play was about to begin and realized the orchestra had finished tuning up and had begun the overture.
2. Expecting to enjoy the first act very much, they settled into their seats.

Exercise 27.6 (p. 249)
1. Writing for eight hours a day, she publishes a lengthy book every year or so.
2. As an out-of-state student without a car, Joe had difficulty getting to off-campus cultural events.
3. To build a campfire, one needs kindling.
4. With every step we took upward, the trees became sparser.
5. Because I am an amateur tennis player, my backhand is weaker than my forehand.

Exercise 28.1 (pp. 251–52)
1. C
2. Women went to work in the textile mills of Lowell, Massachusetts, in the late 1800s; their efforts at reforming the workplace are seen by many as the beginning of the equal rights movement.
3. Farm girls from New Hampshire, Vermont, and western Massachusetts came to Lowell to make money and to experience life in the city.
4. The factories promised the girls decent wages and promised their parents that their daughters would live in a safe, wholesome environment.
5. Dormitories were built by the factories to ensure a safe environment for the girls.

Exercise 28.2 (p. 252)
Answers will vary. Here are some possibilities.

1. Implementing the "motor voter" bill has made it easier for people to register to vote.
2. They won the game because she sank the basket.

Exercise 28.3 (p. 254)
Answers will vary. Here are some possibilities.
1. Inflation is a decline in the purchasing power of currency.
2. Hypertension is elevated blood pressure.

Exercise 28.4 (p. 254)
1. Opportunities in technical writing are more promising than those in business writing. (illogical comparison)
2. Technical writing is more challenging than business writing. (incomplete comparison)

Exercise 29.1 (pp. 258–59)
1. Julius Caesar was killed in 44 BC.
2. Dr. McLaughlin worked hard to earn his PhD.

Exercise 29.2 (p. 260)
1. He wondered whether he should take a nine o'clock class.
2. The instructor asked, "Was the Spanish-American War a victory for America?"

Exercise 30.1 (p. 261)
1. The Pope did not hesitate to visit Cuba, nor did he hesitate to meet with President Fidel Castro.
2. Advertisers place brand-name products in prominent positions in films, and the products are seen and recognized by large audiences.

Exercise 30.2 (pp. 262–63)
1. Seals, whales, dogs, lions, and horses are all mammals.
2. C

Exercise 30.3 (p. 264)
While childhood is shrinking, adolescence is expanding. Whatever the reason, girls are maturing earlier. The average onset of puberty is now two years earlier than it was only forty years ago. What's more, both boys and girls are staying in the nest longer. At present, it is not unusual for children to stay in their parents' home until they are twenty or twenty-one, delaying adulthood and extending adolescence.

Exercise 30.4 (p. 266)
The Statue of Liberty, which was dedicated in 1886, has undergone extensive renovation. Its supporting structure, whose designer was the French engineer Alexandre Gustave Eiffel, is made of iron.

Exercise 30.5 (p. 267)

1. Kermit the Frog is a Muppet, a cross between a marionette and a puppet.
2. The common cold, a virus, is frequently spread by hand contact, not by mouth.
3. C
4. C
5. The submarine *Nautilus* was the first to cross under the North Pole, wasn't it?

Exercise 30.6 (p. 269)

1. India became independent on August 15, 1947.
2. The UAW has more than 1,500,000 dues-paying members.
3. Nikita Khrushchev, former Soviet premier, once said, "We will bury you!"
4. Mount St. Helens, northeast of Portland, Oregon, began erupting on March 27, 1980, and eventually killed at least thirty people.
5. Located at 1600 Pennsylvania Avenue, Washington, DC, the White House is a popular tourist attraction.

Exercise 30.7 (p. 270)

1. According to Bob, Frank's computer is obsolete.
2. Da Gama explored Florida; Pizarro, Peru.
3. By Monday, evening students must begin preregistration for fall classes.
   OR
   By Monday evening, students must begin preregistration for fall classes.
4. Whatever they built, they built with care.

Exercise 30.8 (p. 272)

1. A book is like a garden carried in the pocket.
2. Like the iodine content of kelp, air freight is something most Americans have never pondered.

Exercise 31.1 (p. 273)

During the 1950s movie attendance declined because of the increasing popularity of television. As a result, numerous gimmicks were introduced to draw audiences into theaters. One of the first of these was Cinerama; in this technique three pictures were shot side by side and projected on a curved screen. Next came 3-D, complete with special glasses; *Bwana Devil* and *The Creature from the Black Lagoon* were two early 3-D ventures. *The Robe* was the first picture filmed in Cinemascope; in this technique a shrunken image was projected on a screen twice as wide as it was tall.

Exercise 31.2 (p. 274)

Answers will vary. Here are some possibilities.

1. The Aleutians lie between the North Pacific Ocean and the Bering Sea, where the weather is harsh; for example, dense fog, 100-mile-per-hour winds, and even tidal waves and earthquakes are not uncommon.
2. These islands constitute North America's largest network of active volcanoes; still, the Aleutians boast some beautiful scenery, and they are relatively unexplored.

Exercise 31.3 (pp. 275–76)

1. The history of modern art seems at times to be a collection of "isms": Impressionism, a term that applies to painters who attempted to depict contemporary life by reproducing an "impression" of what the eye sees; Abstract Expressionism, which applies to artists who stress emotion and the unconscious in their nonrepresentational works; and, more recently, Minimalism, which applies to painters and sculptors whose work reasserts the physical reality of the object.

2. Although the term *Internet* is widely used to refer only to the World Wide Web and email, the Internet consists of a variety of discrete elements, including newsgroups, which allow users to post and receive messages on an unbelievably broad range of topics; interactive communication forums, such as blogs, discussion forums, and chat rooms; and FTP, which allows users to download material from remote computers.

Exercise 31.4 (p. 277)

Barnstormers were aviators who toured the country after World War I, giving people short airplane rides and exhibitions of stunt flying; in fact, the name *barnstormer* was derived from the use of barns as airplane hangars. Americans' interest in airplanes had all but disappeared after the war. The barnstormers helped popularize flying, especially in rural areas. Some were pilots who had flown in the war; others were just young men with a thirst for adventure.

Exercise 32.1 (p. 279)

1. Addams's
2. The popularity of *A Room of One's Own*

Exercise 32.2 (p. 280)

1. It's; you're
2. Who's
3. They're; their
4. Who's
5. its

Exercise 32.3 (p. 281)

1. *x*'s and *o*'s
2. *R*'s

Exercise 32.4 (p. 282)

1. Schaefers'; ours
2. colleges; outsiders
3. its
4. yours
5. favorites

Exercise 33.1 (p. 284)
1. Few people can explain what Descartes's words "I think, therefore I am" actually mean.
2. Gertrude Stein said, "You are all a lost generation."

Exercise 33.2 (p. 289)
1. "Kilroy was here" and "Women and children first" are two expressions *Bartlett's Familiar Quotations* attributes to Anon.
2. C; indirect quotation
3. "The answer, my friend," Bob Dylan sang, "is blowin' in the wind."
4. The novel was a real thriller, complete with spies and counterspies, mysterious women, and exotic international chases.
5. The sign said, "Road liable to subsidence"; it meant that we should look out for potholes.

Exercise 34.1 (pp. 291–92)
1. Books about the late John F. Kennedy include the following: *A Hero for Our Time; Johnny, We Hardly Knew Ye; One Brief Shining Moment;* and *JFK: Reckless Youth.*
2. Only one task remained: to tell his boss he was quitting.

Exercise 34.2 (p. 293)
1. Tulips, daffodils, hyacinths, lilies—all these flowers grow from bulbs.
2. St. Kitts and Nevis—two tiny island nations—are now independent after 360 years of British rule.

Exercise 34.3 (p. 294)
1. During the Great War (1914–1918), Britain censored letters written from the front lines.
2. Those who lived in towns on the southern coast (such as Dover) could often hear the mortar shells across the channel in France.

Exercise 34.4 (p. 297)
Answers will vary. Some possibilities follow.
1. "When I was eighteen . . . my mother told me that when out with a young man I should always leave a half-hour before I wanted to."
2. "When I was eighteen or thereabouts, . . . I recognized the advice as sound, and exactly the same rule applies to research."

Exercise 34.5 (pp. 297–98)
1. Mark Twain (Samuel L. Clemens) made the following statement: "I can live for two months on a good compliment."
2. Liza Minnelli, the actress/singer who starred in several films, is the daughter of legendary performer Judy Garland. [For emphasis, dashes may replace the commas.]
3. Saudi Arabia, Oman, Yemen, Qatar, and the United Arab Emirates—all these are located on the Arabian Peninsula.

4. John Adams (1735–1826) was the second president of the United States; John Quincy Adams (1767–1848) was the sixth.
5. The sign said, "No tresspassing [*sic*]."

Exercise 35.1 (p. 303)
1. rec ei pt
2. var ie ty
3. caff ei ne
4. ach ie ve
5. kal ei doscope

Exercise 35.2 (p. 304)
1. surprising
2. surely
3. forcible
4. manageable
5. duly

Exercise 35.3 (p. 305)
1. journeying
2. studied
3. carrying
4. shyly
5. studying

Exercise 36.1 (p. 312)
1. Two of the Brontë sisters wrote *Jane Eyre* and *Wuthering Heights*, nineteenth-century novels that are required reading in many English classes that study Victorian literature.
2. It was a beautiful day in the spring—it was April 15, to be exact—but all Ted could think about was the check he had to write to the Internal Revenue Service and the bills he had to pay by Friday.
3. Traveling north, they hiked through British Columbia, planning a leisurely return on the cruise ship *Canadian Princess*.
4. Alice liked her mom's apple pie better than Aunt Nellie's rhubarb pie, but she liked Grandpa's punch best of all.
5. A new elective, Political Science 30, covers the Vietnam War from the Gulf of Tonkin to the fall of Saigon, including the roles of Ho Chi Minh, the Viet Cong, and the Buddhist monks; the positions of Presidents Johnson and Nixon; and the influence of groups such as the Student Mobilization Committee and the Vietnam Veterans against the War.

Exercise 37.1 (p. 315)
1. I said <u>Carol</u>, not <u>Darryl</u>.
2. A *deus ex machina*, an improbable device used to resolve the plot of a fictional work, is used in Charles Dickens's novel <u>Oliver Twist</u>.
3. He dotted every <u>i</u> and crossed every <u>t</u>.

4. The Metropolitan Opera's production of <u>Carmen</u> was a <u>tour de force</u> for the principal performers.
5. C

Exercise 38.1 (p. 318)
1. One of the restaurant's blue-plate specials is chicken-fried steak.
2. Virginia and Texas are both right-to-work states.
3. He stood on tiptoe to see the near-perfect statue, which was well hidden by the security fence.
4. The five-and-ten-cent store had a self-service make-up counter and many up-to-the-minute gadgets.
5. The so-called Saturday night special is opposed by pro-gun-control groups.

Exercise 39.1 (pp. 321–22)
1. The committee meeting, attended by representatives from Action for Children's Television (ACT) and the National Organization for Women (NOW), Senator Putnam, and the president of ABC, convened at 8 a.m. on Monday, February 24, at the YWCA on Germantown Avenue.
2. An economics professor was suspended after he encouraged his students to speculate on securities issued by a corporation under investigation by the Securities and Exchange Commission (SEC).
3. Benjamin Spock, who wrote *Baby and Child Care*, was a respected doctor known throughout the United States.
4. C [if this sentence can be defined as "technical writing"]
5. The Reverend Dr. Martin Luther King Jr., leader of the Southern Christian Leadership Conference (SCLC), led the famous Selma, Alabama, march.

Exercise 40.1 (pp. 324–25)
1. C [*1984* is a book title.]
2. C
3. In a control group of 247 patients, almost 3 out of 4 suffered serious adverse reactions to the new drug.
4. Before the Thirteenth Amendment to the Constitution, slaves were counted as three-fifths of a person.
5. The intensive membership drive netted 2,608 new members and additional dues of over five thousand dollars.

Exercise 42.1 (pp. 359–60)
You are encouraged to try to find the information in more than one source. Here are some possibilities.
1. *EBSCOhost, LexisNexis, Expanded Academic ASAP.*
2. *Consumer Information Catalog* or *Monthly Catalog of U.S. Government Documents* will list available publications.
3. *Dictionary of American Biography, Encyclopedia Americana, Webster's Biographical Dictionary*
4. Catalog

5. *The Encyclopedia of Associations* lists organizations by subject; there are several with the word *wolves* in the title

Exercise 42.2 (pp. 361–62)
1. Old but classic source. Information may establish role of women before they were given the right to vote. Note importance of author in history of women's suffrage.
2. Note the author's feminist bias. Also note popular source may not be appropriate. Essay may also be dated.

Exercise 49.1 (p. 471)
1. asked
2. had
3. decided
4. travels
5. spent
6. do
7. decide

Exercise 49.2 (p. 477)
1. months
2. C
3. C
4. C
5. rules

Exercise 49.3 (pp. 478–79)
1. The
2. the
3. C
4. C
5. C
6. C
7. C
8. C
9. C
10. C

Exercise 49.4 (pp. 481–82)
The young couple seated across from Daniel at dinner the night before were newlyweds from Tokyo. The young couple and Daniel ate together with other guests of the inn at long, low tables in a large dining room with straw mat flooring. The man introduced himself immediately in English, shook Daniel's hand firmly, and, after learning that <u>he</u> was not a tourist but a resident working in Osaka, gave <u>him</u> a business card. The man had just finished college and was working at <u>his</u> first real job, clerking in a bank. Even in a sweatsuit, the man

looked ready for the office: chin closely shaven, bristly hair neatly clipped, nails clean and buffed.

Exercise 49.6 (p. 485)
1. delete *of*
2. in
3. on
4. in
5. in

Credits

This page constitutes an extension of the copyright page. We have made every effort to trace the ownership of all copyrighted material and to secure permission from copyright holders. In the event of any question arising as to the use of any material, we will be pleased to make the necessary corrections in future printings. Thanks are due to the following authors, publishers, and agents for permission to use the material indicated.

Text

p. 11: "Aria: Memoir of a Bilingual Childhood" by Richard Rodriguez. Copyright © 1980 by Richard Rodriguez. Originally appeared in *The American Scholar*. Reprinted by permission of Georges Borchardt, Inc. for the author.

p. 12: Statement on nuclear energy by Greenpeace Nuclear Campaigner Jim Ricco. http://www.greenpeace.org/usa/campaigns. Used by permission of Greenpeace.

p. 12: Review of *The Appeal* by John Grisham by Augustine J. Fredrich. Reprinted by permission of the author.

p. 13: "What Makes a Credit Score Rise or Fall?" by Jennifer Bayot from the *New York Times*, June 29, 2003. Copyright © 2003 The New York Times Co. Reprinted by permission.

p. 78: Reprinted by arrangement with The Heirs to the Estate of Martin Luther King Jr., c/o Writers House as agent for the proprietor New York, NY. Copyright 1963 Martin Luther King Jr.; copyright renewed 1991 Coretta Scott King.

p. 82: "Commentary: Children in the Family Madhouse" by Froma Harrop as appeared in the *Providence Journal*, June 27, 2001. Reprinted by permission of The Providence Journal Company.

p. 105: "The True-Blue American" by Delmore Schwartz, from *Selected Poems: Summer Knowledge*, copyright © 1959 by Delmore Schwartz. Reprinted by permission of New Directions Publishing Corp.

p. 116: Excerpt from "The Consumer: A Republic of Fat" from *The Omnivore's Dilemma* by Michael Pollan, copyright © 2006 by Michael Pollan. Used by permission of The Penguin Press, a division of Penguin Group (USA) Inc.

p. 373: "Freedom of Hate Speech?" by Phil Sudo from *Scholastic Update*, 1992. Copyright © 1992 by Scholastic Inc. Reprinted by permission of Scholastic Inc.

p. 402: "A Song in the Front Yard" by Gwendolyn Brooks. Reprinted by consent of Brooks Permissions.

p. 433: Andrea L. Foster, "Professor Predicts Bleak Future for the Internet," *Chronicle of Higher Education*, April 18, 2008: A29.

Photos and Illustrations

pp. 9, 11, 17, 27, 33, 61, 78, 89, 102: Viktor Pravdica/istockphoto

p. 41: From wadsworth.com.http://insite2.wadsworth.com, a part of Cengage Learning, Inc. Reproduced by Permission. www.cengage.com/permissions

p. 57: Wikipedia, Inc.

pp. 113, 115, 118, 125, 135, 145: Facsimile of Codex Atlanticus fol. 386r: Archimedes Screws and Water Wheels, 1478–1518 (pen and ink on paper), Leonardo da Vinci (1452–1519), Biblioteca Ambrosiana, Milan, Italy/The Bridgeman Art Library

p. 139: Cengage Learning

p. 140: Cengage Learning

p. 141 (top): Cengage Learning

p. 141 (bottom): Reprinted by permission of Lyric Opera of Waco

p. 142: Cengage Learning

p. 143: Cengage Learning

Index

Note: Page numbers in blue indicate definitions.

Mrs., Miss, Ms., 191
Much, many, 488
MUDs, 149
Multiple author(s)
  APA in-text citations, 442
  APA reference list, 448, 455
  MLA parenthetical references, 400
  MLA works-cited list, 408
Multivolume work(s)
  APA reference list, 448
  MLA parenthetical references, 400–01
  MLA works-cited list, 409–10
Music
  APA reference list, 450
  italicizing titles of, 313
  MLA works-cited list, 415
  quotation marks for titles, 286
Musical(s). *See* Dramatic work(s)

Name(s). *See* Author name(s); Place
  name(s); Proper noun(s); Pub-
  lisher's name
Namely, 291
Narration, as pattern of development, 30,
  69–70
Narrative paragraph(s), 69
Narrowing of focus, for essay topic, 21–26
Nationalities
  capitalizing names of, 309
  stereotypes, 190
n.d. (no date of publication), 416, 452
Negative verb(s), 472
Neither . . . nor, 238, 241
Neologisms, 189
Net meeting software, 18
Netiquette, 149
News service(s), MLA works-cited list,
  420
News wire, MLA works-cited list, 420
Newsgroup(s), 148
  APA reference list, 452
Newsletter article(s), MLA works-cited
  list, 418
Newspaper(s), italicizing titles of, 313
Newspaper article(s)
  APA reference list, 446, 453
  in library research, 356–57
  MLA parenthetical references,
    400–03
  MLA works-cited list, 405–06,
    418, 420
  in periodical indexes, 357
  previewing, 115

quotation marks for titles, 286
  in subscription databases, 356
  in working bibliography, 334
No., 320
No, not, 487
Non sequitur (does not follow), 87
Noncount noun(s)
  articles with, 478
  defined, 195, 476
  list of, 477
Nonessential material
  commas to set off, 264–67
  commas with, 267
  dashes to set off, 292
  nonrestrictive modifiers, 264–66
  parentheses to set off, 293
Nonexistent antecedent(s), 206–07
Nonrestrictive clause(s)
  nonrestrictive modifiers, 264–66
  who, which, that in, 207
Nonrestrictive modifier(s)
  commas to set off, 264–66
  defined, 264
  types of, 265
Nonstandard diction, 185
NOT, as Boolean operator, 352, 366–67
Note(s). *See* Content note(s); Endnote(s);
  Footnote(s); Note-taking
Note-taking, 372
  to avoid plagiarism, 21, 392
  computer printouts in, 340–41
  efficient, 372
  index cards in, 338, 339
  photocopies in, 340–41
  recording source information, 337–40
Noun(s). *See also specific types of noun*
  articles with, 477–78
  case, 203–05
  compound, 276, 306
  defined, 195, 476
  as determiners, 479
  ESL writers and, 476–79
  forming possessive case of, 277–79
  gerunds as, 475
  infinitives as, 475
  other determiners with, 479
  as part of speech, 195
  plural, 278, 306, 478
  possessive, 199, 479
  prepositions to introduce, 201
  subject-verb agreement, 236–40,
    469–70
  types of, 195

Refutation
in argumentative essay, 92, 94–95, 101
defined, 92
Regardless, irregardless, 493
Regionalisms, 185
Regular plural noun(s), forming possessive case of, 278
Regular verb(s)
defined, 208
principal parts of, 212–13
Relative clause(s). *See* Adjective (relative)
clause(s)
Relative pronoun(s)
at beginning of sentence, 224
in complex sentences, 162–63
defined, 196
in dependent clause fragments,
226–27
as determiners, 200
to introduce adjective (relative)
clauses, 158–59
to introduce noun clauses, 159
list of, 158, 163, 196, 200
in revising comma splices, 234
in revising fused sentences, 234
in revising run-on sentences, 234
subject-verb agreement with, 240
Relevance
defined, 81
of evidence, 81
Religion(s), capitalizing names of, 309
Religious work(s). *See* Sacred work(s)
Remote antecedent(s), 206
Repetition
conveying emphasis through, 173
eliminating unnecessary, 177–78
of key words and phrases, 66, 183
unnecessary, 173
Representativeness
defined, 81
of evidence, 81
Republished work(s), MLA works-cited
list, 409
Requirements, school and course, 3
Research, 351–92. *See also* Exploratory
research; Focused research; Internet
research; Library research
for argumentative essay, 92–94
defined, 329
field research, 362–63
Internet research, 363–72, 370–71
library research, 351–61
Research notebook, 331–32

Research paper(s), 329–51
APA-style, 455–65
assignment for, 329–30
checklists on, 330, 339–40, 341, 349–50
defined, 329
editing, 350–51
exploratory research, 332–33, 351–56
final draft, 350–51
focused research, 336–37
MLA-style, 424–38
note-taking, 337–40
organizing, 344–45
outlines, 342–44
plagiarism avoidance, 389–92
planning, 329–33
research notebook, 331–32
research question, 332, 351
revising, 347–50
rough draft, 344–45
search strategy, 332–33, 351–61
sources for, 333–35, 336–37, 345–46,
356–59
thesis statement, 335–36, 341
topic selection, 330–31
working bibliography, 333–35
Research question, 332, 351
Respectably, respectfully, respectively, 495
Restrictive clause(s)
restrictive modifiers, 265–66
types of, 265
Restrictive modifier(s)
defined, 264
using, 265–66, 271
Résumé(s), 128–32
chronological order, 128, 129, 131
components of, 129, 131
electronic, 130–32
print, 128–29
sample, 131, 132
scannable, 130–31
templates, 131
Web-based, 132
Review(s). *See also* Book review(s)
APA reference list, 446
MLA works-cited list, 406, 418
Revision. *See also* Editing
of agreement errors, 236–42
checklists for, 48–49, 349–50
of comma splices, 233–35
with Compare feature, 39, 150
computer software in, 39–41, 42–45,
347–49
of dangling modifiers, 248–49

BECOMING A SUCCESSFUL STUDENT

- ❑ Do you have a personal organizer? a calendar? Do you use them regularly?
- ❑ Have you set up a comfortable study space?
- ❑ Have you made a study schedule?
- ❑ Have you joined a study group?
- ❑ Have you read your course syllabi and orientation materials carefully?
- ❑ Are you attending classes regularly and keeping up with your assignments?
- ❑ Do you take advantage of your instructors' office hours?
- ❑ Do you participate in class?
- ❑ Do you participate in college life?
- ❑ Do you know how to use your college library? Do you use it?
- ❑ Are you satisfied with your level of technological expertise? Do you know where to get additional instruction?
- ❑ Are you trying to make contacts and find mentors?
- ❑ Do you see yourself as a lifelong learner?

Correction Symbols

abbr	Incorrect abbreviation: **39a–c**; *editing misuse*, **39d**	**p**	Punctuation error: **Pt. 5**
adj	Incorrect adjective: **20d; 23a–b;** *comparative/superlative forms*, **23d**	**par** *or* **¶**	New paragraph: **5a–e**
		no ¶	No paragraph: **5a–e**
		¶ coh	Paragraph not coherent: **5b**
adv	Incorrect adverb: **20e; 23a; 23c;** *comparative/superlative forms*, **23d**	**¶ dev**	Paragraph not developed: **5c**
		¶ un	Paragraph not unified: **5a**
		plan	Lack of planning: **2a–e; 7a; 10a; 45b**
agr	Faulty agreement: subject/verb, **26a;** *pronoun/antecedent*, **26b**	**purp**	Purpose not clear: *determining purpose*, **1a;** *purpose checklist*, **p. 13**
aud	Audience not clear: *identifying audience*, **1b**	**ref**	Incorrect pronoun reference: **21c**
awk	Awkward: **28a–d**	**rep**	Unnecessary repetition: *eliminating*, **17b**
ca	Incorrect case: **21a;** *case in special situations*, **21b**	**rev**	Revise: **4b–c; 7d; 10c; 41j**
cap	Incorrect capitalization: **36a–e;** *editing misuse*, **36f**	**run-on**	Run-on sentence: *correcting*, **25b–e**
		shift	Unwarranted shift: **28a**
coh	Lack of coherence: *paragraphs*, **5b**	**sl**	Inappropriate use of slang: *level of diction*, **19a2**
con	Be more concise: **17a–c**		
cs	Comma splice: *correcting*, **25b–e**	**sp**	Spelling error: **35b–c**
d	Inappropriate diction: *appropriate words*, **19a;** *inappropriate figures of speech*, **19c;** *inappropriate language*, **19d;** *offensive language*, **19e**	**sxt**	Sexist or biased language: **19e2**
		thesis	Unclear or unstated thesis: **3a–c; 41d; 41g**
		var	Lack of sentence variety: **15a–c**
		w	Wordiness: *eliminating*, **17a; 17c4–5**
dead	Deadwood: **17a1**	**ˇ**	Apostrophe: **32a–c;** *editing misuse*, **32d**
det	Use concrete details: **19b3–4**		
dev	Inadequate development: **5c**	**[ ]**	Brackets: **34d**
dm	Dangling modifier: **27c**	**:**	Colon: **34a1–3;** *editing misuse*, **34a4**
doc	Incorrect or inadequate documentation: *MLA*, **47a;** *APA*, **48a**	**‸**	Comma: **30a–f;** *editing misuse*, **30g**
emp	Inadequate or unclear emphasis: **16a–e**	**—**	Dash: **34b**
		. . .	Ellipsis: **34f**
exact	Use more exact word: **19b**	**!**	Exclamation point: **29c**
fig	Inappropriate figure of speech: **19c**	**//**	Faulty parallelism: *using parallelism*, **16c; 18a;** *revising*, **18b**
frag	Sentence fragment: *correcting*, **24b–d**		
fs	Fused sentence: *correcting*, **25b–e**	**-**	Hyphen: **38a–b**
ital	Use italics: **37a–c;** *for emphasis or clarity*, **37d**	**( )**	Parentheses: **34c**
		.	Period: **29a**
lc	Use lowercase: *editing misuse of capitals*, **36f**	**?**	Question mark: **29b1–2;** *editing misuse*, **29b3**
log	Incorrect or faulty logic: **6a–f; 28d**	**" "**	Quotation marks: **33a–d;** *with other punctuation*, **33e;** *editing misuse*, **33f**
mix	Mixed construction: **28b**		
mm	Misplaced modifier: **27a**	**;**	Semicolon: **31a–c;** *editing misuse*, **31d**
ms	Incorrect manuscript form: *MLA*, **47b;** *APA*, **48b**	**/**	Slash: **34e**
num	Incorrect use of numeral or spelled-out number: **32b2; 40a–b**		

Contents